WINNING BOOKS

WINNING BOOKS

To Mary Brigid (MBZ)
with love & all good
wishes.
Ruth.

BY
RUTH ALLEN

First published 2005 by:

Pied Piper Publishing Ltd.
80 Birmingham Road
Shenstone
Lichfield
Staffordshire
WS14 0JU

Cover illustration by Bob Graham
© 2004 Bob Graham/Blackbird
Design Pty Ltd
First featured in the Youth
Library Review
(Spring 2004 issue)

British Library Cataloguing in Publication
A catalogue record for this book is available from the British Library.

ISBN 0 9546384 5 X

Printed in Great Britain by Bookchase (UK) Limited, Suite 9, Grove House,
320 Kensal Road, London, W10 5BZ, UK

Dedication

For Rosanna, who knows what a good book is, and for Cherry-Cicely, Elspeth and Findlay, who are still in the process of finding out.

Acknowledgements

The following people and organisations have been kind enough to send me information or replies to questionnaires; or to talk to me about their view of the award scene, either in this edition, or the previous one. As explained in Chapter 15, which draws together the opinions of authors, illustrators and critics, most of the quotations therein are unattributed. The listing of a name here does not necessarily mean that the person has been directly quoted in one of those chapters, or indeed anywhere else in the book. It simply indicates that s/he has either written in reply to my letters faxes or emails, spoken to me on the telephone, discussed matters face to face or provided information in some other way. I would also like to thank Debbie Mynott for her faith in this book which has led to Pied Piper Publishing producing it in a new edition. Last, but not least, I want to mention Peter Hubbard, the fixed point in my firmament, with my love and gratitude for all the support that he has given to me over the past thirty years. To all these people and organisations, and any I may have inadvertently left out of the following alphabetical list, I am extremely grateful.

Brian Alderson
Louise Aldridge (Youth Library Review)
Rita Auerbach
Elizabeth Bewick
Theresa Breslin
Anthony Browne
The Canadian Children's Book Centre
Aidan Chambers
Children's Literature New England (CLNE)
Susan Cooper
Sharon Creech
Kevin Crossley-Holland
Robert Dunbar
John Dunne (HCL)
Sarah Ellis
Federation of Children's Book Groups
Anne Fine
Michael Foreman
Alan Garner
Barbara Greenwood
Hampshire County Libraries (HCL)
Pat Hancock
Erik Christian Haugaard
Elie Hayman (Walker Books Ltd.)
Kathleen T. Horning
Leslie Howarth
Shannon Howe
Diana Wynne Jones
Leslie Kaufman, Kaufman Communications
Ginny Moore Kruse
Madeleine L'Engle
Geraldine McCaughrean
Gregory Maguire
Margaret Mahy
Jan Mark
Anne Marley (HCL)
Kathleen Milne
Michael Morpurgo
Alison Morrison (Walker Books Ltd.)
Louisa Myatt (CILIP)
Finian O'Shea
Helen Oxenbury
Katherine Paterson
Philippa Pearce
Peters Library Service
Susan Price
Sheila & Colin Ray
Lance Salway
Hugh Scott
Peter Sheldon (Peters Bookselling Services)
Leslie Sim (YLG and HCL)
Louise Steyn (Tafelberg Publishers, South Africa)
John Rowe Townsend
Walker Books Limited
Jill Paton Walsh
Young Book Trust
Youth Libraries Group (YLG)

Contents

Preface

When I was a child, I used to take the backs off clocks, in order to see what made the tick, and the tock. Sometimes, I would take the works right out of the case, the better to understand how the hands moved. Occasionally I would take the mechanism apart, examine and clean the pieces, and reassemble them. Usually the clock would go again, but perhaps it would run too slow, or, more often, too fast. It did not work exactly as it did before. This was part of the "'satiable curtiosity" which I shared with Kipling's elephant's child[1]; which it is the right of every child to pursue.

A clock is a mechanical object, and if I had been fortunate enough to have a 'wise mentor' who knew about clocks, I might eventually have been able to reassemble one so that it went normally afterwards: I did not know enough about what I was doing. In these days of open heart surgery and organ transplant, of radio- and chemo-therapy, and the laser correction of short sight, we can see that it is becoming possible to open up living beings, and replace parts. Even so, they do not always work exactly as they did before.

How much more careful, then must we be when we try to dissect, with our clumsy, fumbling, post-literate adult perceptions, such elemental constructs as myths and children's stories. Do we know enough about what we are doing? We must try to ensure that, in our enthusiasm to give the children with whom we come into contact 'the best we know', we do not overburden what we give them with the adult baggage of our own lives, so that all children may experience the story 'shiny new' – as it will be to them – something which still and always will 'work exactly as it did before'.

What I have attempted in these pages is an overview of the books that have won awards, and a brief history both of the individual awards themselves, and of the concept of making awards for children's books. Inevitably there will be some who disagree with my opinions; that I would expect. I hope that despite this there will be sufficient within these covers to enable anyone to form their own opinions, regardless of mine, and to use the titles listed to enrich the lives of the children with whom they come into contact – and who knows, perhaps their own lives, too.

The hands of the clock have turned through many days since the first edition of this book, and our hearts have continued to pulse, missing a beat on September 11, 2001, but then steadily resuming, with renewed purpose in a world where some wonder if things will ever work 'the same as they did before'.

The books which have won awards in the last seven years are as controversial – and as safe – as many of those listed in the previous edition, but among them are new treasures to plunder and new worlds to explore.

Perhaps one day a clock *will* strike thirteen, as it did for Tom, allowing access to a long-ago garden; maybe there *is* a train waiting at Platform 9¾ to steam away to a magical destination. For a child, to whom all things are new and wonderful, it must seem that these things are – nearly – possible. For us as world-weary adults, who worry more because we know more, it is difficult to recapture that wonder, but – like Thomas Hardy on Christmas Eve[2] – surely most of us would '...go with him.../Hoping it might be so'.

1. Rudyard Kipling. 'The Elephant's Child', from *Just So Stories.* Macmillan & Co.
2.Thomas Hardy. 'The Oxen', from *Collected Poems.* Macmillan & Co.

Chapter 1: About this Book

The germ of this book was contained in the booklet *Winning Books*, published to accompany a collection of books exhibited for sale on the Bufo Books stand at the 'Childhood Re-Collected' Book Fair organised by the Provincial Booksellers Fairs Association (PBFA) in Oxford in 1994. In it were listed the winners of the Newbery, Caldecott, Carnegie, & Greenaway Medals, and the publishing details of those books which had won some of the other notable awards in the UK and US. In 1998 *Children's Book Prizes* was published by Ashgate, expanding that listing to cover nearly forty major awards for the English-speaking countries of the world, and adding a discussion of the aims, achievements and merits of those awards. This, a revised and renamed new edition, brings the total of awards to nearly seventy, and I have reverted to the earlier title as I believe it best describes the guiding principle behind the book. That idea is to discuss the books which have won awards, and the history behind the medals or prizes awarded for these books.

I have not attempted to deal with those awards which are made to authors in recognition of the body of their work. Thus the Hans Andersen Medal, the Eleanor Farjeon Award, and others of that nature, worthy though they be, have no place in this discussion. Those awards are intended as an acknowledgement of the contribution made to children's literature by an author, artist, or other worker in that field, and can be understood as a mark of appreciation made to someone by their colleagues or contemporaries. Awards given to specific titles, on the other hand, should not be subject to the considerations or influences of the author's or artist's previous work. It can nonetheless be shown that this has not always been the case, and that the motives of judges have not, consciously or otherwise, been as consistently pure as the criteria of their awards would imply. It is generally recognised, for instance, that at least two winners of the Carnegie Medal were given the award more in recognition of past achievement than for the outstanding quality of the book they happened to produce in that year.

This book will attempt to discover what the prizes are, and what they set out to do. It will compare awards across the English-speaking world, their history, and the effect they have on sales and readership of their authors. In addition, the desirability of books, from the point of view of a collector, is here briefly treated, alongside the aspects of interest to a critic or librarian, such as readability and quality of writing. However this is intended to be a book about books and reading. Thus it will aim to show how well the books that won have stood up to the changed world in which they are now read. Books which did not win are also discussed, particularly if they have proved to be of more lasting quality than those that did.

The different approaches of the countries which make these awards are inherent to the effects the awards may have. There is widespread agreement that the Newbery Medal is the giant among children's book awards. It is also the oldest, and celebrated its eightieth anniversary in 2002. One of the advantages of the Newbery is that it confers a practical immortality on a book winning it guarantees that a title is kept in print in perpetuity. This is also true of its younger sibling the Caldecott Medal, awarded for illustration. Consequently a book published in the 1920s which was thought to speak to American children in its day, is still available to today's young Americans. What do today's children make of these books? Are they, indeed, still held to be of value? All the other awards under discussion are in some degree either imitations of the Newbery, or reactions to it, but they do not share this particular feature. For example the UK awards which imitate and loosely match the Newbery and Caldecott Medals, the CILIP Carnegie Medal and Kate Greenaway Medal, do not give any guarantee that the winning title will stay in print. Some have remained available, not always continuously, though many have been regularly reprinted; others are almost impossible to find, even in the second-hand market. This tells us almost as much about the differing publishing milieus in America and England as it does about the books themselves.

The runners-up, usually called Commended or Honor Books, also have a great deal to say about the 'spirit of the time' in which they just missed the accolade. Some of these titles now seem more worthy of the medal than the titles that did win. Is there any pattern to this? Is the supposed timeless quality we recognise now in such a book as Alan Garner's *Elidor* (Carnegie Commended in 1965) the very reason that it seemed such an unusual book in its year, so that the award was given to the more immediately accessible, *Grange at High Force* by Philip Turner? Today it is all too easy to wonder at the choices our predecessors made. With more knowledge of the circumstances it may be possible to show why they chose the titles they did, and why a book which has survived as a 'children's modern classic' or collectible of today would not have been the best choice at the time. There are other occasions when it seems inconceivable, even under the prevailing standards of the day, that a particular title won, where another published in the same year was not even commended.

The people who were making the judgements at the time were constrained by their time. Indeed, the historian wielding hindsight, insight, and any other sight available (other than second sight), is similarly bound in his or her own time, and must recognise that his or her view, too, is partial. With this in mind, I will state here and now that the opinions in this book are my own, and whilst I have consulted many people who have, over the years, expressed strong opinions of their own about the question of awards, I have only quoted them directly if I could do so without distorting what they said or meant. For the first edition a questionnaire was sent to a number of authors and illustrators who, over the years, had won awards, or been runners-up. They, too, have been quoted only sparingly, but selections from their responses, together with opinions that have been expressed to me more recently, both in conversation and from the platform in the course of an author event or conference, have been used in Chapter 15. Those who responded, or to whom I have spoken in the course of my researches, are listed within the Acknowledgements.

No consensus has emerged from the authors consulted about their reactions to winning or being shortlisted for awards. In general they split along the line of the mid-Atlantic ridge. In the UK many authors felt that being shortlisted was the recognition of the quality of their work, and that whether or not it won after that was not of particular importance. This attitude stems in part from the lack of financial reward to accompany most awards. A big money prize would naturally be welcome, but in the light of the lack of it, then the publicity which nowadays accrues from being shortlisted (which was not always the case) is enough to affect the standing, status, reputation – the feeling of self-worth which all authors need. However, the opposing point of view was expressed by one author who felt that if a book was shortlisted and had then *not* won, someone must have disliked it very much! One advantage of winning an award agreed by most authors of English-language books in all the countries under discussion here, is in the field of translations and overseas editions. If editors from another country are looking to republish, whether in translation or not, they will be encouraged by the measure of supposed quality which winning an award confers.

In dealing with Children's Book Awards, an invention of the twentieth century, this book would seem to constrict itself and its discussions to the years since the First World War. This, still referred to as 'The Great War' in many circles, was a watershed of more aspects of western culture than just the world of children's literature. However, there will be a brief survey of the history and development of children's literature in Chapter 2. There will also be a brief look backwards at the question of 'prize books'. Did the choices made by teachers and ministers when awarding school and Sunday School prizes foreshadow the choices made by the early award judges, or was the idea of awarding a medal or prize to a specific title more in the way of a reaction to the industry which had built up around the provision of cheap 'prize books' for the many schools and churches in the English-speaking world?

It is worth noting that a large part of the thinking behind the establishment of children's book awards stems from a concern with standards of writing for children. A closer look at these standards and how they are defined reveals that they have a great deal to do with the perception on the part of the award's instigator that standards (of all sorts) have declined since the 'golden age' of his, or more rarely, her childhood.

Golden Ages merit a study of their own; every generation, every culture since at least the ancient Egyptians, the classical Greeks and the Old Testament Fathers has had one. There seems always to have been a legendary time or place, just out of memory or reach, from which we are supposed to have degenerated or been ejected. Each generation has something of this feeling for its own childhood. My generation found the 1950s a time of renewal and hope; for our elders it was a time of fear of 'The Bomb'. Their generation looked back to the carefree years of the 1930s and early 40s, which to their elders was full of the threat of war. The early 1920s, when so much hope was invested in the League of Nations and the new world of peace for which so many had died, was a golden age to the children of those for whom nothing could compare with the long Edwardian Summer – and so it goes on. At the beginning of the nineteenth century Charles Lamb could write to Coleridge complaining that current authors were pushing the old stories from the shelves. However far back we may look, the idea that 'once upon a time' there was a Golden Age seems to have been perpetually present.

We may come closer to understanding the origin and ubiquity of this notion by reflecting how, within our own lives, our perception of time changes. Most of us remember what Lewis Carroll called a 'golden afternoon' which seemed to last forever. The luckier among us may remember several of these idylls, or the seeming eternity of the six weeks of summer holiday which stretched before us in late July. And we all now remark how quickly the years go by as we grow older. But for an eight-year-old six weeks is nearly one and a half per cent of the total experience of her life; a year is twelve and a half per cent – one eighth. By the time she is twenty, that six weeks has shrunk to just over half a per cent of her life, and a year to five per cent; at the age of fifty, six weeks is less than a quarter per cent and a year only two per cent. Each successive day is a diminishing proportion of our lives as we experience them. No wonder childhood is so often remembered as a time of endless sunshine.

Concern for high standards in children's literature is nonetheless a larger issue than nostalgia. All of us who are engaged in the provision of books to children, be they our own children or grandchildren, the children whom we teach or those who come into our libraries and bookshops, are concerned to offer the best we know. To this extent prizes and awards for children's literature may provide some signposts along the path between the books we remember with affection from our own childhood reading, and the jewels among the recent – and not so recent – publishing output.

Most of the awards were set up with the stated aim of improving the quality of children's book publishing in their particular country. In the early years of the last century members of the new profession of children's librarianship were trying to carve out their own niche. It is hardly surprising that they should look closely at what was being published and, in their terms, find it wanting. Cheaply produced books had been flooding the market since the later years of the nineteenth century, aimed at the school prize market. They were printed on thick brittle paper, to bulk the book out and make it seem to contain more pages than was the case. Illustrations were often crude and sometimes bore little resemblance to the characters or events described in the text. Their subject matter ranged from the overtly pious and moralising tales which were thought particularly suitable for Sunday School prizes to the blood-and-thunder adventures not much superior to the 'penny dreadful' thrillers.

Those first awards were made in America, and named after the early publisher John Newbery, and the famous illustrator Randolph Caldecott. When the British introduced their similar awards, they honoured the great benefactor of libraries and the arts, Andrew Carnegie, and the Victorian illustrator Kate Greenaway. More recently introduced awards commemorate authors (Kathleen Fidler Award), journalists (Esther Glen), or publishers (Kurt Maschler). In addition several commercial concerns have inaugurated prizes which are fiercely contested each year. These include the UK brewery firm of Whitbread and the Canadian biscuit firm Christie Brown Nabisco, the South African broadcaster M-Net, the *Guardian* newspaper in the UK and the American periodical on children's literature the *Horn Book*, in conjunction with the *Boston Globe* newspaper. These awards include cash prizes, whereas, at least at first, those set up by librarians did not, hence the designation 'medal'. The early awards were solely concerned with the honour of winning, with no financial benefit to the author at all. In more recent years, awards for books aimed at teenage readers – sometimes designated 'Young Adults' have been instituted. It had been argued strongly in the past that these books should be eligible for the main prizes – or that the main awards should not exclude books aimed at this readership, but the Michael Printz and the Askew Torchlight awards have subtly altered the situation.

The original purpose of the awards considered in this book was to highlight individual outstanding titles each year, and in time other awards were established which allowed an author's or illustrator's body of work to be honoured. One of these is named for Eleanor Farjeon, though it is open not just to authors and illustrators, but for substantial contributions to children's literature by anyone working in that field. Another, the Hans Christian Andersen Medal, is awarded by the International Board on Books for Young People (IBBY), again for a body of achievement, and now made in two categories; for illustration as well as for writing. In the United States, the Phoenix Award is given in recognition of a book that is still held to have relevance 20 years after publication. These awards, together with the proliferation of other awards world-wide for individual books, have freed the major national awards for their original – some would say their real – purpose.

There is sometimes confusion over the year to which an award should belong. In most cases the award is judged and presented in the year after publication. Practice of terminology in different countries means that for instance the 2003 Carnegie and Greenaway Medals (UK) were awarded in mid-2004. However, the 2004 Newbery and Caldecott Medals (US) were awarded early in that year for books published in 2003. Where it has been possible to obtain the information I have indicated which practice is followed in the appropriate chapter.

For this edition a new chapter has been added to cover the development of a phenomenon that was just beginning at the time of the publication of *Children's Book Prizes*. The 'Harry Potter' books and the Philip Pullman 'His Dark Materials' trilogy have taken the world of children's literature by storm – and have made a strong mark on the adult literature world, too. The whole question of what are being termed 'crossover' books is covered in Chapter 14.

Book prizes are a source of endless disagreement. For every librarian who tries to promote 'good' reading to the children coming into the library there is a bookseller who thinks the whole concept of awards is simply a publicity stunt by the publisher. However, it has been said that, to adults at least, awards do sell books. How often children buy books for themselves, and what notice – if any – they may take of award stickers, is more difficult to determine. In the United States the inclusion of a book in even the Honor list makes an immense difference to the sales, as well as status, of that title. There, the publicity machine for the Newbery and Caldecott Medals is so effective that being 'the winner' is a significant achievement. In the years when only one or two Honor Books are chosen, inclusion in this list, too, will have a good effect on sales. The constituency of children's book buyers in the US is so much greater, and the propensity of American book-buyers to be more 'Award-led' means larger sales, and therefore larger print-runs, for winning authors in the US.

There has been considerable discussion as to the merit of prizes; whether in fact they have contributed in any way to the improvement in the range of books available to children; whether indeed the range of books available to children, though greater, has actually improved. Whilst this has largely to be a matter of opinion, it need not be uninformed opinion. This book sets out to find a way through the maze of children's literature. It does not purport to show the only path, but one which it is hoped will be enjoyable and rewarding.

Chapter 2: Books and Children

Bringing children and books together is a task shared by parents, teachers and librarians. In an ideal world the balance is about equal, though at different points in the child's life, one will have more input or influence than the others. Dorothy Butler, in *Babies Need Books* (1980), puts the strongest case for introducing children to books at an extremely early age. Stories are the way in which we make sense of our world; one is never too young to be given the first pieces in the jigsaw puzzle of life. Bruno Bettelheim's *Uses of Enchantment* (1975) makes a convincing case for the relevance of fairy stories in the world of today's child. Other books, in particular those of Mircea Eliade, and Joseph Campbell's *Hero with a Thousand Faces* (1949), trace the development of the hero figure in story, myth and legend. In the same way that it is known that music can be heard in the womb, and that talking to very young babies is vital for their mental development, there is overwhelming evidence that fiction, far from being mere escapism, or simply recreational reading, plays an important part in the healthy psychological growth of the child.

The association between children and stories is naturally far older than that between children and books. One can imagine children, perhaps half asleep, wrapped in furs, rugs, woven grass mats – long before there were duvets or sheets and blankets – listening to the stories their elders told round the fire. Perhaps they would be about the cunning of the animals hunted that day; the enemies defeated; the mountains climbed or the rivers forded; or about new food plants discovered. They might have been stories woven about the stars and planets; about the gods of earth, sky and sea; or about the ancestors of the people. They could have contained elements which would reach us as tales of the fairies or the little folk. These were stories for everybody: the concept of a separate literature for children would not develop for thousands of years. Some of these stories might have been sung rather than spoken. The repetition that we notice when – as readers of the written word – we consider a text on the page, is a mnemonic and reinforcing technique for tellers and hearers of the oral tradition. It was no accident that among the earliest English printed texts were the ballads of Guy of Warwick, Robin Hood and Bevis of Hampton. Such stories were known to have the necessary popular appeal to guarantee sales and, together with the Arthurian cycle, were thus natural choices. The early printers realised that it would be necessary for the fruits of this untried method of production to make some profit, and used texts that they knew would sell in large numbers. Here is not the place for a lengthy history of books and printing: those who would be interested to read a fuller treatment are referred to F J Harvey Darton's *Children's books in England*, which is still arguably the best history of children's books as literature, even though it was first published some seventy years ago. I merely wish to touch on a few of the landmarks within that development where improvements in techniques resulted in children and books coming closer together.

Ballads were certainly one early link between stories, books and children, but there are other points of contact. It should be noted that ballads and chapbooks, cheaply produced small booklets usually containing a woodcut illustration, continued to be available from at least the seventeenth until well into the nineteenth century, and whilst their quality, in terms of paper as well as textual content and illustration, was variable, they did serve to disseminate many of the rhymes and stories we now consider to be traditional. 'Ring a Ring o' Roses' is notorious for having arisen from a description of the symptoms of the Black Death. Many other nursery rhymes which are now considered an intrinsic part of children's literature had their origins in satirical verse and political commentary. These found their way even into remote country districts through pedlars and chapmen, or itinerant salesmen.

An important point of correspondence between children and books occurs when, in the eighteenth century, the publisher John Newbery was active in the field. He was not the first publisher, nor indeed author, of children's books, but may be said to have been one of the first to direct his sales pitch at those who might buy books for their children. Literacy among the middle and especially the growing professional classes of the eighteenth century was relatively high, and parents were concerned that their children should have at least the standard of education they had themselves received, and preferably a better. The methods by which that education was imparted was in a state of flux, however. New philosophies increasingly encouraged people to look at children as being different from adults, rather than as miniature versions of themselves. The emerging middle classes were the most likely people to follow such fashionable developments. This, then, was Newbery's market; his *Little Pretty Pocket Book* (c. 1744) was not a 'cheap' production. At a price of 'the Book alone, 6d., with a Ball or a Pincushion 8d.' – already the concept of turning an educational product into a toy was present in advertising children's wares – it was, however well within the reach of doting parents who wanted their child to have the latest thing from London. Newbery's advertising was pitched ostensibly at children, but in reality, as with present-day advertising, filtered through the children to their parents who, then as now, controlled the cash. His covers and titles or subtitles emphasised the educational value of the books for the benefit of the parents, but in fact their contents were almost entirely entertainment for the child. From Newbery's time onwards, books specifically aimed at children, with a more or less didactic element, would be published in increasing numbers on both sides of the Atlantic.

In addition, children have appropriated stories originally intended for adults, sometimes immediately, sometimes not until they have gone out of fashion with the older generation. Jonathan Swift's *Gulliver's Travels*, especially the first section dealing with the Lilliputians, was an obvious candidate, even if its satire was ignored or missed. That miniature people continue to hold a fascination for children is exemplified by the popularity of the more recent 'Borrowers' series by Mary Norton and Raymond Briggs's *The Man*. Stories such as Daniel Defoe's *Robinson Crusoe*, along with many of Sir Walter Scott's novels, were written for adults, but had a great appeal for adventurous young minds, and were taken up with enthusiasm by child readers. Often, and especially in the late nineteenth and early twentieth century, these titles would be bowdlerised or abridged into 'children's versions'. This was done with varying degrees of competence, and sometimes succeeded only in losing the very qualities which had appealed to young people in the first place.

Nonsense rhymes which might entertain anyone were also adopted with relish by children. Both strands together come to the fore in the third quarter of the nineteenth century, with the publication of the rhymes of Edward Lear and the 'Alice' books of Lewis Carroll, which were in the nonsense tradition, yet equally firmly aimed at and intended for children.

Technical improvements in illustration are our next point of contact. Colour in most early books was an optional extra, and made a difference to the price. It was probably never true that 'penny plain, twopence coloured' reflected the actual price of illustrated books; even in the early nineteenth century a nearer value would be the 'One Shilling Plain, Eighteen-pence Coloured' charged by John Harris, the successor to Newbery's family business. Harris was at this time targeting the middle and upper classes: the children described in the books he published are all well-to-do. Colouring, however applied, had to be paid for. Since labour was at the time cheaper than technology, hand-colouring was usually done by children who had been specially trained; children for whom picture books were a drudgery from which no pleasure was forthcoming. In the later years of the nineteenth century, when chromolithography began to be reasonably priced, books for all ages started to appear with shiny colour plates, some of the most garish in *The Prize* and other similar annual volumes. Eventually as techniques of printing in colour were refined, masters of wood engraving, such as Edmund Evans, were able to bring to the printed illustrations of Randolph Caldecott, Kate Greenaway and later Beatrix Potter, all the subtlety of their original watercolours.

It should be noted that what we perceive as stereotypes of brave knights and fair ladies were in some real sense a preparation for adult roles in a literate society. This holds true for the middle ages, when the knightly classes and clerics were the only people who could read. The virtues of manly strength, feminine chastity and marital constancy displayed within chivalric romances were certainly seen by at least one medieval matron as a good reason for encouraging her daughters to read them! We do not now consider that books should be such overt exemplars. The situation where literacy was limited to the upper classes and an increasing number of the growing middle class, as part of their desire for upward mobility, lasted at least until the middle of the nineteenth century. Commentators in earlier centuries thought that universal literacy would give the lower classes ideas above their station. Even as recently as the 1960s, at the *Lady Chatterley* trial, a witness was asked whether he would 'allow his wife or servants' to read it. Issues of race, class and gender, once deemed too dangerous and revolutionary to be put before even 'the eyes of women and the lower orders' are treated within today's children's books.

Nowadays it is a commonplace in the developed world that every child learns to read and write. It should be remembered that in England this 'tradition' is not yet a hundred and fifty years old: the Education Act which compelled education for all children up to the age of 13 was passed in 1870. Even so, fees in local authority elementary schools were not entirely abolished until 1918. Whilst the literary heritage of the English-speaking world is long and rich, it has not always been - and is not now - universally available. We speak glibly of universality and global communications today, but need to bear in mind that such communication and immediacy are available only within the developed world, and have emerged very recently.

Towards the end of the nineteenth century publishing firms such as the Society for the Promotion of Christian Knowledge (SPCK) began producing 'prize' volumes. These, which were soon imitated by series from other publishers, were cheaply produced titles on thick lightweight paper, which were bought in large quantities by schools, Sunday Schools, missions and other institutions to give away to children for 'Good Attendance' or 'Perseverance'. Because the standards of writing as well as the production of books in these 'prize' series were so poor, there was an inevitable reaction from teachers and more particularly librarians. In the early years of the twentieth century these groups headed a movement towards improving the standards of children's books and were concerned to raise the level of literature available to children, thereby justifying higher standards of binding and paper quality so that the physical form of the book would be as lasting, and as pleasing, as its intellectual content. One of the results of this concern was manifested in the foundation of the Newbery Medal and its successors and companion awards.

Over the last thirty years there has been a growing movement, perhaps more apparent in the US and Canada, but which is increasingly seen in the UK, to view modern children's literature as a valid academic subject, and to treat it as such. This has resulted in an increased number of courses in children's literature at universities and colleges. In the UK, the University of Surrey, Roehampton, the University of Newcastle and Reading University run undergraduate and Masters courses in children's literature, and offer research opportunities; Nottingham's children's literature course is aimed at teachers, and seems to focus on the history of children's literature rather than modern and contemporary titles. The first establishment on this side of the Atlantic to offer a Master's degree in children's literature was Trinity College, Dublin, while Simmons College in Boston, Mass. (US) has for a number of years been giving teachers, librarians and writers the opportunity of postgraduate study in this subject. These courses have quite different aims and content from the modules on children's books which form a part of teacher training courses and the even smaller, and discretionary, part of current librarianship courses. Following on from courses and institutes held in the 1970s at Loughborough College (UK), and at Simmons College, the organisation Children's Literature New England Inc. (CLNE) was set up, which has run a summer institute each year since 1987. At these institutes there are lectures by well-established and award-winning authors, serious critics of children's literature, and discussion groups with leaders who share a long experience in seeing into the heart of a children's text. At the institutes run by CLNE, some two hundred delegates, who work with children in the capacities of writer, librarian, teacher, storyteller or bookseller, come together for an intense week of learning and discussion. It is a renewal and a revelation to become part of such an enthusiastic group of people, all with a single aim – to give the best books they know to the children with whom they come into contact. The concept of this book has grown in depth and range as a result of the conversations I have had with other delegates and organisers at these institutes, and I must put on record my appreciation to them all.

The case is, therefore, already well proven by others that stories are important for children. This was one of the points made very strongly by Philip Pullman when his *Northern Lights* (published in US and Canada as *The Golden Compass*) won the Carnegie Medal for 1995. It remains to consider which books we should give them. Some people argue very strongly that quality is all-important, that children must only be given the very best. Others say that what matters is that they read something, whatever the supposed quality. I incline to the latter view, with the proviso that if we ensure that children see, and thus have the opportunity to read, 'the very best' then they will have been exposed to quality, and can be trusted to find the level of reading at which they are most comfortable. Some adults are not particularly interested in reading. Those of us who live our lives with a book in one hand whatever else we are doing – cooking, eating, travelling – may believe that the bookless are missing out on a great deal, but we should not be patronising or elitist about it. All we can do is show children what depths of enjoyment and interest, knowledge and amusement, may be found in books; to be enthusiastic about books we have enjoyed.

It is a great mistake to force children to give too much feedback from what they are reading. If we turn every book into a 'school exercise' then the pure enjoyment, the ability to lose oneself in a world of one's own (albeit one created in part by the author), is itself lost. All too many children and teenagers have been turned away from Shakespeare in school by teachers of English who reduce his plays merely to 'character' and 'plot'. Shakespeare's plays were originally seen and enjoyed by all levels of society, people with varying standards of education; they were not intended as comprehension exercises and passages for précis. Very seldom are children given the chance of experiencing the dramatic quality of theatre – the concept of the play as a whole, the excitement of staging; of being part of a cast, or even an audience, for a live performance. There are some teachers, however, who can open the door into new worlds by their own enthusiasm for a book or author, be it Shakespeare's plays, Susan Cooper's 'Dark is Rising' sequence, Byron's poetry, Virginia Hamilton's *M. C. Higgins the Great*, or any one of a number of powerful and exhilarating reading experiences. It is those inspirational teachers whom we should try to emulate.

What signposts are there to direct us through the forest of children's publications so that we can at least be sure, not only of getting to

Grandmother's house before the wolf, but of visiting the seven dwarfs and the three bears, as well as the gingerbread cottage, on the way? I could have used other examples from the world of fairy tale, and I have deliberately chosen fairytale locations because of their archetypal importance. Literary theory states that there are only two fundamental shapes for a story: 'the journey' and 'the stranger comes to town', and four – or some say ten or twelve – basic plots. Such reductionism is useful from the critic's vantage point, less so in evaluating the quality of children's books. Nonetheless it shows the integral relationship between all forms of story, and the danger of dismissing out of hand the deceptively simple elements of the fairy or folk tale. I could equally have used the metaphor of the maze, as I did at the end of Chapter 1, for its resonances of myth and legend. The point is to demonstrate how such frames of reference are built up in the mind through years of reading, from earliest childhood. They are not solely gained from so-called serious adult reading, but acquired through every book ever encountered, from the very first rag-book or ABC. In today's culture there are many more story media available: films and television naturally contribute to the whole of life experience, and increasingly the Internet will play its part. These other media must be recognised as producing shared references: *Sesame Street*, the *Magic Roundabout*, the Disney film versions of fairy tales, which are no less valid than books. Indeed books themselves may become – may already have become – a minority interest. They may be superseded by electronic means; this has already begun, with the Internet as the most usual source of information – be it for homework or train timetables – and the debate on the (in)accuracy of that information has no place here. It is at the moment hard to imagine that the book, with its convenient capacity to be carried in a pocket or taken to bed, for pages to be reread or skipped, could be entirely replaced by any electronic device. The book format serves many purposes; this is no less true of books for children than it is of books for adults. With a novel or a storybook the writer, together with the illustrator if it is a picture book, and the reader collude to produce a unique experience. No two readers will ever get exactly the same out of a book, however short or apparently simple.

Books are part of the armoury with which we prepare children for the world. A strong imagination and the chance to explore a range of emotions and experiences vicariously can empower a child to cope with modern living. This does not mean that so-called 'problem' novels, written to a formula, are desirable. If an author is intrigued by a situation, and writes a book showing how her characters deal with it, that is one thing, a book written to order, because a particular 'situation' is fashionable, is quite another, and is almost certainly doomed to fail in its purpose.

Our progress through children's literature should not be signposted solely along well-trodden paths. However, if someone has been there before us, and can tell us the way they went through the forest, through the maze, into that new world, then it is worth listening to what they have to say. We may decide on a slightly different route – miss out on the three bears and go to see the three little pigs instead; take in Jack's Beanstalk or Cinderella's kitchen – but if someone says, 'You really mustn't miss the view from Rapunzel's tower' or,

'I found Bluebeard's Castle really scary', it makes you want to look for yourself. So it is with award-winning books. Someone has thought these were 'the best'; 'the most outstanding'; 'the most distinguished' of their year: they have to be worth a look. You may not agree; you may see why the book was adjudged to be top of its class, or you may not. It might leave you completely cold but your child or your parent or your brother or sister or your best friend might choose that book above all other to take to their desert island. It is a very personal choice, and everyone should be free to make it.

As well as celebrating the strength of stories, awards have the important task of spotlighting the power of pictures. Not every picture is worth the proverbial thousand words; certainly not without the provision, through education or experience, of a mental key to unlock its meaning. But the right picture can enhance and transform a story; it provides the images on which a child can draw in adult life; it can form forever the way in which a particular character is remembered.

The purpose of this book, therefore, is not to prescribe the books that every child should read, or even to set out the best books written for children in the twentieth and early twenty-first century – though it is true that the lists included in it contain some of the most enjoyable as well as the better-written children's books of the last hundred years. What it does attempt is to bring into focus the titles that have been examined and have been found good; most of which are true to the truth that is in them. They are books which have been read and reread with pleasure and occasionally pain. At the very least, these titles and authors are worthy of investigation.

In the central section of this book, which deals with the awards themselves, each chapter includes something of the history of the award or awards under discussion, and the main ideas and ideals behind them. In addition I have tried to give a flavour of a few of the books that have won or been commended for each award, as well as a little information about some of their authors or artists. The rest is up to you.

Chapter 3: The Newbery Medal (USA)

The Newbery Medal is the major American award, given for 'the most distinguished contribution to American Literature for children' published during the preceding year. Instituted in 1922, it is named after the London publisher and bookseller, John Newbery (1713-1767). It may be awarded for fiction, non-fiction, drama or poetry. Each year the acceptance speeches for the Medal and biographical sketches of the winning authors are printed in the *Horn Book Magazine*. The *Horn Book* has published a series of books which bring together these acceptance speeches, biographical pieces and a commentary on the winning titles. The first of these dealt solely with Newbery winners, and a corresponding volume was devoted to the early Caldecott Medallists. Later books in the series include both Medals and deal with blocks of some ten or twenty years. More recently the Association for Library Service to Children (ALSC) have published annual paperback volumes which list all the winners and Honor Books for both Newbery and Caldecott Medals from their inception, in which a profile of each award's current Medallist is always included. Naturally I have no wish to duplicate such rich resources which are readily available in the US, though less easily obtainable in the UK, but I have selected for particular comment some of the winning titles and Honor Books over the years. I also endeavour to show the ways in which the emphasis may have shifted over the years in terms of the type of book chosen, and to provide an overview of the titles which have won. In accordance with the current practice of the ALSC, the term 'Honor Book' is here used throughout the Newbery and Caldecott Medal listings, as this term was made retrospective when it was introduced in 1971, although such titles were originally designated 'Runners-Up'.

The origins of the Newbery Medal are worth looking at in some detail, since it was the earliest award for Children's books to come into being. In 1918 Frederic Melcher, the founder who endowed both the Newbery and Caldecott Medals, was working in a Boston bookstore. He was given the task of organizing the first National Children's Book Week. As he said in 1949:

> The Book Week program came fortunately at a time when there was a rising tide of interest in children's books, their writing, illustrating, and publishing, and this seemed to start fresh interest in the history of books for children and the systematic collecting of the best books of the past and the classics of the future. It occurred to me then that honor paid to the best children's books of current production would be a deserved recognition of their importance and would encourage others to write and publish ... children's librarians would be the most competent judges of merit, for they see all types of books in the hands of all kinds of readers, and I proposed an award of merit to the Children's Library Section of the American Library Association meeting . . . in 1922. On the impulse of the moment I suggested that the award . . . should be called the John Newbery Medal in honor of the publisher who first, in the mid-eighteenth century, saw the need of providing for children their own special books. The use of his name was a happy plan for it took us back over two centuries of book-making for children and increased the study and appreciation of the books of the past while encouraging by intelligent attention the writers of the present.
> [Frederic G. Melcher, from his foreword to Irvin Kerlan, (1949) *Newbery and*

Caldecott Awards: a bibliography of first editions, Minneapolis: University of Minnesota.]

Melcher's 'happy plan' has influenced children's book collectors and award organisers ever since. Newbery's *Little Pretty Pocket Book* (1744) and facsimiles of other early children's titles have been reprinted; and the interest in collecting original editions, as well as reprinted or facsimile editions, was a growing market for most of the twentieth century. As we have now passed the eightieth anniversary of the institution of the Newbery Medal, it is instructive to note the changes in book production, in the world-wide marketing of titles, and in the expectation parents and children have of their books, since the 1920s. Melcher was also responsible for the establishment of the Randolph Caldecott Medal, first awarded in 1938.

Winning the Newbery Medal is one of the highest accolades to which American children's authors can aspire. It brings not only great prestige within the children's book world, but also a measure of fame nationally. As already mentioned, it promises immortality for the winning title, since all Newbery winners are kept in print, as are most of the Newbery Honor Books. What is more, there is so much for parents to chose from among the welter of titles published annually that winning the Newbery Medal ensures that every middle-class American child of the appropriate age is likely to receive it for Christmas. This is an immense contrast to the situation in the UK, where the Carnegie Medal is almost unknown outside a small circle of children's librarians and interested teachers. This cannot be solely because of the difference in the size of the market in the US, although naturally print runs can be larger there as the market is potentially greater. It seems to me to have more to do with the American psyche – or perhaps I had better say the difference between the 'English' and the 'American' outlooks, for it is the English who seem to be different from most of the other countries whose awards are under discussion in this book.

Whilst conscious of my own Englishness, I believe the reasons for these differences are both historical and geographical. England is a small, overcrowded and overpopulated country. It has been so for a number of years; this was one of the reasons behind its colonial expansion, or rather, behind its government's readiness to finance and support such ventures. This is not the place to discuss the merits and, indeed, demerits of British imperialism, but to see its results, even in the seemingly enclosed world of children's books. The people who left Europe to found the countries of the new world, whether by choice or coercion, were faced with what seemed to them empty lands. By today's standards their treatment of such native peoples as they were displacing are questionable, and in many cases deplorable. Even so, the space that the fortunate among the settlers moved into was far greater than had been possible for anywhere in Europe to provide. Whilst it may no longer be the case that their nearest neighbour is several miles away, the mental outlook and attitude that this situation produces still prevails among many Americans and Antipodeans. If they see a stranger, they approach and greet him; if they arrive at a beach and another family is there, they sit by them. The English are the exact opposite: they will sit as far away on the beach as possible.

Hence there is a paradox: in the US, which was founded on the ideal of freedom, there is an immense pressure to conform; in England, which is seen as a hide-bound and class-ridden society, it is more acceptable to be 'different'. Consequently the English will, from this natural perversity, shy away not only from other people, but also from their opinions. If the critics slate a play on Broadway, no New Yorker will wish to go to it, if the same thing happens in the West End of London, there will be some number who set out to prove the critics wrong. There is a wealth of material published on both sides of the Atlantic which gives advice to parents on all aspects of child care. Until recently the British were reluctant to heed them. Now that the 'transatlantic generation' has reached adulthood there is a convergence in some respects, but in the matter of children's reading, many parents in the UK will rely on their own memories of what they enjoyed when young; in the US, most parents' first thought is to look and see what has recently won an award.

There is also a difference in education. Most schools in the US have a librarian, or a teacher/librarian, who regularly gives book talks. Teachers 'teach books' – they use them in class and read them to and with the children. This does not happen to the same extent in England, where many modern children's books are just not known by teachers – the third Children's Laureate Michael Morpurgo (himself an ex-teacher) recently deplored the situation in English schools, where:

> Time and time again, there are instances of a writer going into a school and the teacher doesn't even come, leaving it instead to a teaching assistant. This shouldn't happen even once. There are far too many teachers teaching our young children who don't love books.
> [Michael Morpurgo, interviewed by *The Times* after his 2004 Children's Book Award win]

Despite the fact that a single person was concerned in the inception of the award, the styles of the authors who have won the medal have been, from the earliest years, greatly varied. One man's inspiration has not, thankfully, meant one man's taste. The Newbery and Caldecott Medals and Honor Books are each awarded by a committee of children's librarians. This has always been the case, and the latest regulations make it clear that to serve on these committees, which comprise fifteen persons, it is necessary to be a member of the ALSC. The chair is elected by the ALSC membership, as are seven members who are chosen from a larger number listed by the nominating committee. The remaining seven members of each committee are appointed by the ALSC president-elect. Every committee member reads as many of the eligible books as possible during the year. Some of these will be titles recommended or suggested by other committee members, or other ALSC members. There are two preliminary ballots during the autumn, nominating titles in an attempt to focus discussion in the committee selection meetings. These preliminary ballots do not remove titles from the possibility of winning, however. All the titles which have been suggested, as well as those nominated by the ballots, are discussed by the committee before the balloting begins. In the final ballot, each committee member chooses three books, allocating four points to the first choice, three to the second, and two to the third. A winning title must be placed first on the lists of at least eight committee members, and must in addition be eight or more points clear of any other title. After the medallist is established, the committee considers Honor Books; it is up to them how many, if any, to designate.

It has been suggested that the American writers are better at fantasy writing than the English. This is supposed to be because they have a shorter written history in their country, and so instead they invent imaginary worlds. Whether or not this is so, the writers of American children's books have been able to create, from the history they do possess, a feeling of the heritage of the American past for European immigrants, African-American forced settlers and Native Americans. The Latino and Asian sections within the US are also represented in the Newbery lists with increasing frequency. With the advent of the Américas Award in 1993 the Latin American literature has come into prominence, and the Coretta Scott King Award has since 1970 given due attention to African-American writers. These awards, as will be seen in Chapter 9, show that the literatures have come of age. Their winners are not ghettoised within the confines of their own culture however, but are equally eligible with other American authors for the Newbery Medal. Thus they bring positive rôle models for minority peoples before all American children, both in terms of the characters portrayed within them, and by the increased standing of the authors who write them. American writers of every race and creed have an equal opportunity to win the Newbery Medal. The experience of childhood has some common ground in all cultures, and it is recognised that all children should be aware that all families and all cultures are not alike. Equality is one thing, assimilation (and blinkered vision) is quite another.

The books which have won the Newbery, or been shortlisted for it, show a splendid variety. Many of the earlier titles in the list are period pieces, not much read today; others are perhaps more popular now than at the time they were published. For 1923, 1924 and 1927 there is no record of any runners-up to the Newbery Medal, so Hugh Lofting's *The Voyages of Dr Dolittle*, Charles B. Hawes's *The Dark Frigate* and Will James's *Smoky* all stand alone to represent their years. In addition, these were the only appearances for two of these authors in the lists although Charles Hawes had been a runner-up in 1922.

The first winner, Hendrik van Loon's *The Story of Mankind*, was a non-fiction book, and over the years a sprinkling of non-fiction has appeared among the winners and Honor Books. A dozen or so of these have been biographies of past presidents and early heroes of American history. More recently the true stories of slaves coming to freedom, and tales drawing on the experience of the Native American peoples, have come to prominence. Even among the fiction there has been an emphasis on the pioneering years of American history, though more recently the experiences of the Great Depression, or the 1940s, have provided rich source material.

Lofting's 'Dr Dolittle' series, despite some of the concerns – more recently expressed – about his lack of 'political correctness', is still read and collected today. His books are trapped in the attitudes of his time, and their treatment of African and Polynesian peoples is execrable by today's standards. It is also incongruous to our eyes that Dr Dolittle, who is portrayed as such an ardent animal rights campaigner, and who actually talks to animals, including pigs, in their own languages, is described as eating liver and bacon, or sausages! However, the idea of being able to communicate with animals, and moreover for them to talk back, is fascinating to children, and this feature alone is almost certainly responsible for the lasting popularity of the series.

During the 1920s and early 1930s Cornelia Meigs (1934 Medallist; Honor Books in 1922, 1929, 1933) was prominent in the lists; as was Padraic Colum (Honor Books in 1922, 1926, 1934, but never a medallist). Meigs is probably better-known today for the biography of Louisa M. Alcott with which she won the medal, and for her literary criticism in volumes such as *A Critical History of Children's Literature*, which she edited with Anne Thaxter Eaton, Elizabeth Nesbitt and Ruth Hill Viguers, than she is for her works of fiction. Rachel Field, the 1930 medallist, made her only other appearance in the Honor Books list of 1932. Of the medallists for the first twenty years, only six appear as runners-up in other years, the other two being Kate Seredy, 1938 medallist, and Elizabeth Enright, the 1939 medallist, whose second appearance would not be until 1958, despite the appearance in those intervening years of books about her much-loved Melendy family. From 1942 until 1961, twelve medallists were listed as runner-up in other years, and two won again: Joseph Krumgold within the same twenty-year period, his only two appearances in the list being as medallist in 1954 and 1960, and Elizabeth George Speare, medallist in 1959 and 1962, who was on the Honor list again in 1984 with her first publication after a gap of nearly twenty years.

Other names which seemed to predominate in the 1940s and 1950s were Lois Lenski, Eleanor Estes and Marguerite Henry, whose books about horses were a far cry from the 'pony books' of the UK, though appealing to something of the same readership. Robert Lawson has the distinction of having won both the Newbery (1946) and the Caldecott (1941) Medals. Laura Ingalls Wilder, whose name has been given to an award for authors and illustrators whose work has made a lasting contribution to US children's literature, had several titles listed as Honor Books (1938, 1940, 1941, 1942 and 1944) but never won the medal. Her work has itself made a lasting contribution to American literature and heritage. E. B. White is another surprising non-medallist; his *Charlotte's Web*, an Honor Book in 1953, has become a classic, while the book which won the medal ahead of it, Ann Nolan Clark's *Secret of the Andes*, together with the rest of the Honor list that year, is far less often read today. Meindert DeJong, the 1955 Medallist, who had two titles listed as Honor Books in 1954, and one each in 1957 and 1959, has a less obvious appeal to today's children, but his beautifully-written stories of children in Europe and Asia contain struggles and emotions which are real, and will still speak to the contemplative child. Maurice Sendak's illustrations splendidly enhance DeJong's books, and are the main reason for their present-day collectability.

Scott O'Dell's 1961 medal-winning *Island of the Blue Dolphins*, whilst drawing inevitable comparisons with the theme of Robinson Crusoe, breaks new ground in so far as Karana, the heroine, is not just a Native American coping with hardship and surviving, but is a female 'castaway survivor'. This book has tinges of the 'Noble Savage' ideology, but the demonstration that women can cope is sufficient compensation. O'Dell produced another tale of Native Americans in the 1971 Honor Book, *Sing Down the Moon*. Many of the winners in the 1960s were historical in subject or flavour; a trend which was also prominent in the UK during this decade.

The late 1960s and early 1970s also saw high fantasy from the pens of Lloyd Alexander and Susan Cooper. Alexander appeared twice on the Newbery list; his *The Black Cauldron*, the second book in a series of five, was an Honor Book in 1966, and the final book of the series, *The High King*, won the medal in 1969. A similar feat was achieved by Susan Cooper, whose *The Dark is Rising*, the second in her 'Dark is Rising' sequence of five books, was the only Honor Book in 1974. Two years later she won the medal itself with the fourth in that sequence, *The Grey King*.

In the 1970s African-American literature began to come into its own. Julius Lester presented some true stories of the experience of black slavery in the 1969 Honor Book, *To Be a Slave*. Virginia Hamilton's *M. C. Higgins the Great* won the 1975 medal and Mildred Taylor's *Roll of Thunder, Hear My Cry* won in 1977. In 1972 Virginia Hamilton's *The Planet of Junior Brown* was an Honor Book, and she continued to appear in the Honor Book lists throughout the 1980s and 1990s. Walter Dean Myers showed Harlem teenage gangs in the 1989 Honor Book *Scorpions*. Other cultures, too, began to be treated from the inside: Laurence Yep's 1976 Honor Book *Dragonwings* and 1994 Honor Book *Dragon's Gate* depict Chinese culture surviving within the American way of life in the early years of the twentieth century. There are, in addition, many true-life tales of immigrants to the US from various European countries, sometimes depicting their struggles in the new environment, sometimes remembering life in the old, or as in the 1998 Honor Book, *Lily's Crossing*, showing how their story touches an 'ordinary' American child.

In the late 1970s and early 1980s the realistic modern-day stories of Katherine Paterson gained her the medal on two occasions, with *Bridge to Terabithia* (1978) and *Jacob Have I Loved* (1981), and an appearance on the Honor List in 1979 with *The Great Gilly Hopkins*. Fantasy returned to the fore with the 1985 winner, *The Hero and the Crown* by Robin McKinley, whose *The Blue Sword* was a 1983 Honor Book.

The 1986 medal went to a gentle but realistic story from Patricia MacLachlan's own family history, *Sarah, Plain and Tall*. Non-Fiction, especially biographical and autobiographical narrative, has shown up more frequently in the last twenty years than in the early years of the medal. Poetry, represented by Paul Fleischman's *Joyful Noise* (1989 Medallist) and Nancy Willard's *A Visit to William Blake's Inn* (1982 Medallist), is a welcome addition. Gary Paulsen's tales of fighting the elements have brought him three Honor listings, in 1986, 1988 and 1990. Lois Lowry, the 1990 winner with *Number the Stars*, a book about the Danish Jews during the Nazi regime, repeated her achievement in 1994 with *The Giver*, set in a putative future where apparent similarities to present-day life give place to some disturbing results of decisions which had originally been made with the best of intentions.

The 1995 winner, Sharon Creech, in *Walk Two Moons*, tells a story which is both universal and tied specifically to the American landscape: a part-Native American girl's search for her mother. This is a beautifully written and crafted piece, with the shape of 'the journey', and rich with the patterning of bird and flower names, imbued with nature and yet with a thoroughly present-day setting. The heroine, during a car trip with her grandparents which follows the route of the bus journey her mother had taken the previous year, finds out the truth about her mother, a truth which she may already know intellectually, but needs to accept emotionally. *Walk Two Moons* was preceded in the UK by *Absolutely Normal Chaos*, which is set in the same place some months earlier and with which it has several characters in common. In the US, the publication of *Chaos* followed the success of *Walk*. A third title, *Chasing Redbird* draws on several the same characters and has the same location. Sharon Creech is the only person to have won both the Newbery and Carnegie (UK) Medals, the latter being awarded to her *Ruby Holler* for 2002. The nearest anyone else has so far come to this achievement is Susan Cooper, English-born but now living in the US, who won the Newbery in 1976 and has appeared in the Carnegie Commended lists on several occasions, but has never actually won the Medal. The uniqueness of this distinction may not last for much longer, as the 2003 Carnegie winner is an American writer.

The 1996 winner, *The Midwife's Apprentice* by Karen Cushman, is set in Medieval times. Realistic and humorous, it builds on the success of the author's earlier *Catherine, called Birdy*, an Honor Book in 1995. The 1997 winner, *The View from Saturday*, is by E. L. Konigsburg, who had last won the Newbery some thirty years previously in 1968. Also in that year another of her titles appeared as an Honor Book, yet she had not been included in the listings in any of the intervening years, mainly because her output during these years had chiefly been either adult titles or picture books. 1998 saw Karen Hesse's *Out of the Dust* win the medal, this like the 2000 winner, Christopher Curtis's *Bud, Not Buddy*, is set during the Great Depression – another rich literary vein in America's past. Patricia Reilly Giff's *Lily's Crossing*, a 1998 Honor Book, also set in a specific time and place of America's heritage, this time in the mid-1940s. The only Honor Book in 1999, Richard Peck's *A Long Way from Chicago* is also set in the 1940s, and might have won in another year – Peck's sequel, *A Year Down Yonder* was the 2001 medallist. Louis Sachar's *Holes* – a remarkable book, since filmed, that is part humour, part adventure, part fantasy, and wholly delightful, is a nonetheless worthy winner.

In Linda Sue Park's *A Single Shard*, the 2002 winner, the judges choice fell on an historical theme – this time medieval Korea, and the 2003 winner *Crispin: The Cross of Lead* set in Medieval England, similarly shows the value placed on traditions from countries whose populations have contributed to modern-day US culture. Kate Di Camillo's 2004 winner, *The Tale of Despereaux*, is a new take on an old fairytale – another rich source of inspiration. The Honor Books in recent years include biography, memoir, modern-day and futuristic stories – there is no overall pattern; that itself is a cause for celebration.

It was Frederic Melcher's wish that the medal should never be withheld. He felt that the judges should always show the best of the year in which they were considering titles. This means that there can be no absolute standard which must be reached for a book to be considered; nevertheless the quality of the lists taken as a whole have been remarkably consistent. The main changes of emphasis which can be discerned have been reflections of the interests pursued by children, and to some degree the fashions in writing for children generally. In general, librarians, and the medals they award, have maintained standards in children's books which are still valid after more than three-quarters of a century. The Newbery Medal may have been the first award, but it has produced many healthy offspring, as the following chapters will show.

The Newbery Medal: complete list of winners and honor books

1922 Hendrik Willem Van LOON. *The Story of Mankind.* Boni and Liveright.

Honor Books
William BOWEN. *The Old Tobacco Shop: A True Account of What Befell a Little Boy in Search of Adventure*, ills Reginald BIRCH. Macmillan.

Padraic COLUM. *The Golden Fleece and the Heroes Who Lived before Achilles*, ills Willy POGANY. Macmillan.

Charles HAWES. *The Great Quest*, ills George VARIAN. Little, Brown.

Bernard MARSHALL. *Cedric the Forester.* Appleton-Century.

Cornelia MEIGS. *Windy Hill.* Macmillan.

1923 Hugh LOFTING. *The Voyages of Doctor Dolittle.* Frederick A. Stokes.

Honor Books
No record

1924 Charles Boardman HAWES. *The Dark Frigate*, ills Anton Otto FISCHER. The Atlantic Monthly Press/Little, Brown.

Honor Books
No Record

1925 Charles J. FINGER. *Tales from Silver Lands*, ills Charles HONORE. Doubleday, Page & Co.

Honor Books
Anne Carroll MOORE. *Nicholas: A Manhattan Christmas Story*, ills Jay Van EVEREN. Putnam.

Anne PARRISH. *The Dream Coach.* Macmillan.

1926 Arthur Bowie CHRISMAN. *Shen of the Sea*, ills Else HASSELRIIS. E. P. Dutton & Co.

Honor Book
Padraic COLUM. *The Voyagers: Being Legends and Romances of Atlantic Discovery*, ills Wildred JONES. Macmillan.

1927 Will JAMES. *Smoky, the Cowhorse.* Scribner.

Honor Books
No Record

1928 Dhan Gopal MUKERJI. *Gay-neck, the Story of a Pigeon.* E. P. Dutton & Co.

Honor Books
Caroline SNEDEKER. *Downright Dencey*, ills Maginel Wright BARNEY. Doubleday.

Ella YOUNG. *The Wonder-Smith and His Son*, ills Boris ARTZYBASHEFF. Longmans.

1929 Eric P. KELLY. *The Trumpeter of Krakow,* ills Angela PRUSZYNSKA. Macmillan.

Honor Books
John BENNETT. *The Pigtail of Ah Lee Ben Loo.* Longmans.

Wanda GÁG. *Millions of Cats.* Coward-McCann.

Grace HALLOCK. *The Boy Who Was*, ills Harrie WOOD. Dutton.

Cornelia MEIGS. *Clearing Weather*, ills Frank DOBIAS. Little, Brown.

Grace MOON. *Runaway Papoose*, ills Carl MOON. Doubleday.

Elinor WHITNEY. *Tod of the Fens*, ills Warwick GOBLE. Macmillan.

1930 Rachel FIELD. *Hitty, Her First Hundred Years*, ills Dorothy P. LATHROP. Macmillan.

Honor Books
Julia Davis ADAMS. *Vaino*, ills Lempi OSTMAN. Dutton.

Jeanette EATON. *A Daughter of the Seine: the Life of Madame Roland.* Harper.

Marian Hurd McNEELY. *The Jumping-Off Place*, ills William SIEGEL. Longmans.

Elizabeth MILLER. *Pran of Albania*, ills Maud & Miska PETERSHAM. Doubleday.

Hildegarde SWIFT. *Little Blacknose*, ills Lynd WARD. Harcourt.

Ella YOUNG. *The Tangle-Coated Horse and Other Tales*, ills Vera BOCK. Longmans.

1931 Elizabeth COATSWORTH. *The Cat who went to Heaven*, ills Lynd WARD. Macmillan.

Honor Books
Julia Davis ADAMS. *Mountains Are Free*, ills Theodore NADEJEN. Dutton.

Herbert BEST. *Garram the Hunter: A Boy of the Hill Tribes*, ills Erick BERRY, *pseud.* (Allena BEST). Doubleday.

Elizabeth Janet GRAY. *Meggy MacIntosh*, ills Marguerite de ANGELI. Doubleday.

Agnes HEWES. *Spice and the Devil's Cave*, ills Lynd WARD. Knopf.

Ralph HUBBARD. *Queer Person*, ills Harold von SCHMIDT. Doubleday.

Alice LIDE & Margaret JOHANSEN. *Ood-le-uk the Wanderer*, ills Raymond LUFKIN. Little, Brown.

Alida MALKUS. *The Dark Star of Itza: The Story of a Pagan Princess*, ills Lowell HOUSER. Harcourt.

Anne PARRISH. *Floating Island.* Harper.

1932 Laura Adams ARMER. *Waterless Mountain*, ills Sidney & Laura ARMER. Longmans.

Honor Books

Marjorie ALLEE. *Jane's Island*, ills Maitland de GORGOZA. Houghton Mifflin.

Mary Gould DAVIS. *Truce of the Wolf and Other Tales of Old Italy*, ills Jay Van EVEREN. Harcourt.

Rachel FIELD. *Calico Bush*, ills Allen LEWIS. Macmillan.

Dorothy P. LATHROP. *The Fairy Circus.* Macmillan.

Eloise LOWNSBERY. *Out of the Flame*, ills Elizabeth Tyler WOLCOTT. Longmans.

Eunice TIETJENS. *Boy of the South Seas*, ills Myrtle SHELDON. Coward-McCann.

1933 Elizabeth Foreman LEWIS. *Young Fu of the Upper Yangtze*, ills Kurt WIESE. Winston.

Honor Books

Nora BURGLON. *Children of the Soil: A Story of Scandinavia*, ills Edgar Parin d'AULAIRE. Doubleday.

Cornelia MEIGS. *Swift Rivers*, ills Forrest W. ORR. Little, Brown.

Hildegarde SWIFT. *The Railroad to Freedom: A Story of the Civil War*, ills James DAUGHERTY. Harcourt.

1934 Cornelia MEIGS. *Invincible Louisa: The Story of the Author of Little Women.* Little, Brown.

Honor Books

Erick BERRY *pseud.* (Allena BEST). *Winged Girl of Knossos.* Appleton-Century.

Padraic COLUM. *The Big Tree of Bunlahy: Stories of My Own Countryside*, ills Jack YEATS. Macmillan.

Wanda GÁG. *The ABC Bunny.* Coward-McCann.

Agnes HEWES. *Glory of the Seas*, ills N. C. WYETH. Knopf.

Anne KYLE. *The Apprentice of Florence*, ills Erick BERRY *pseud.* (Allena BEST). Houghton Mifflin.

Sarah SCHMIDT. *New Land*, ills Frank DOBIAS. McBride.

Elsie SINGMASTER. *Swords of Steel*, ills David HENDRICKSON. Houghton.

Caroline SNEDEKER. *The Forgotten Daughter*, ills Dorothy P. LATHROP. Doubleday.

1935 Monica SHANNON. *Dobry*, ills Atanas KATCHAMAKOFF. Viking.

Honor Books
Constance ROURKE. *Davy Crockett*, ills James MacDONALD. Harcourt.

Elizabeth SEEGER. *Pageant of Chinese History*, ills Bernard WATKINS. Longmans.

Hilda Van STOCKUM. *A Day on Skates: The Story of a Dutch Picnic.* Harper.

1936 Carol Ryrie BRINK. *Caddie Woodlawn.* Macmillan.

Honor Books
Elizabeth Janet GRAY. *Young Walter Scott.* Viking.

Kate SEREDY. *The Good Master.* Viking.

Armstrong SPERRY. *All Sail Set: the Romance of the 'Flying Cloud'.* Winston.

Phil STONG. *Honk, the Moose*, ills Kurt WIESE. Dodd, Mead.

1937 Ruth SAWYER. *Roller Skates*, ills Valenti ANGELO. Viking.

Honor Books
Ludwig BEMELMANS. *The Golden Basket.* Viking.

Margery BIANCO. *Winterbound.* Viking.

Agnes HEWES. *The Codfish Musket*, ills Armstrong SPERRY. Doubleday.

Idwal JONES. *Whistler's Van*, ills Zhena GAY. Viking.

Lois LENSKI. *Phebe Fairchild: Her Book.* Stokes.

Constance ROURKE. *Audubon*, ills James MacDONALD. Harcourt.

1938 Kate SEREDY. *The White Stag*. Viking.

Honor Books
James Cloyd BOWMAN. *Pecos Bill*, ills Laura BANNON. Little, Brown.

Mabel ROBINSON. *Bright Island*, ills Lynd WARD. Random House.

Laura Ingalls WILDER. *On the Banks of Plum Creek*, ills Helen SEWELL & Mildred BOYLE. Harper.

1939 Elizabeth ENRIGHT. *Thimble Summer*. Farrar & Rinehart.

Honor Books
Valenti ANGELO. *Nino*. Viking.

Richard & Florence ATWATER. *Mr. Popper's Penguins*, ills Robert LAWSON. Little, Brown.

Phyllis CRAWFORD. *"Hello the Boat!"*, ills Edward LANNING. Holt.

Jeanette EATON. *Leader by Destiny: George Washington, Man and Patriot*, ills Jack Manley ROSE. Harcourt.

Elizabeth Janet GRAY. *Penn*, ills George Gillett WHITNEY. Viking.

1940 James DAUGHERTY. *Daniel Boone*. Viking.

Honor Books
Stephen W. MEADER. *Boy with a Pack*, ills Edward SHENTON. Harcourt.

Mabel ROBINSON. *Runner of the Mountain Tops: The Life of Louis Agassiz*, ills Lynd WARD. Random House.

Kate SEREDY. *The Singing Tree*. Viking.

Laura Ingalls WILDER. *By the Shores of Silver Lake*, ills Helen SEWELL & Mildred BOYLE. Harper.

1941 Armstrong SPERRY. *Call it Courage*. Macmillan. (Published in UK as *The Boy who was afraid*)

Honor Books
Mary Jane CARR. *Young Mac of Fort Vancouver*, ills Richard HOLBERG. Crowell.

Doris GATES. *Blue Willow*, ills Paul LANTZ. Viking.

Anna Gertrude HALL. *Nansen*, ills Boris ARTZYBASHEFF. Viking.

Laura Ingalls WILDER. *The Long Winter*, ills Helen SEWELL & Mildred BOYLE. Harper.

1942 Walter D. EDMONDS. *The Matchlock Gun*, ills Paul LANTZ. Dodd, Mead.

Honor Books

Genevieve FOSTER. *George Washington's World*. Scribner.

Eva Roe GAGGIN. *Down Ryton Water*, ills Elmer HADER. Viking.

Lois LENSKI. *Indian Captive: The Story of Mary Jemison*. Lippincott.

Laura Ingalls WILDER. *Little Town on the Prairie*, ills Helen SEWELL & Mildred BOYLE. Harper.

1943 Elizabeth Janet GRAY. *Adam of the Road*, ills Robert LAWSON. Viking.

Honor Books

Eleanor ESTES. *The Middle Moffat*, ills Louis SLOBODKIN. Harcourt.

Mabel Leigh HUNT. *'Have You Seen Tom Thumb?'*, ills Fritz EICHENBERG. Lippincott.

1944 Esther FORBES. *Johnny Tremain: A Novel for Old and Young*, ills Lynd WARD. Houghton Mifflin.

Honor Books

Eleanor ESTES. *Rufus M.*, ills Louis SLOBODKIN. Harcourt.

Julia SAUER. *Fog Magic*, ills Lynd WARD. Viking.

Laura Ingalls WILDER. *These Happy Golden Years*, ills Helen SEWELL & Mildred BOYLE. Harper.

Elizabeth YATES. *Mountain Born*, ills Nora S. UNWIN. Coward-McCann.

1945 Robert LAWSON. *Rabbit Hill*. Viking.

Honor Books

Alice DALGLIESH. *The Silver Pencil*, ills Katherine MILHOUS. Scribner.

Jeanette EATON. *Long Journey: The Life of Roger Williams*, ills Woodi ISHMAEL. Harcourt.

Eleanor ESTES. *The Hundred Dresses*, ills Louis SLOBODKIN. Harcourt.

Genevieve FOSTER. *Abraham Lincoln's World*. Scribner.

1946 Lois LENSKI. *Strawberry Girl*. Lippincott.

Honor Books
Marguerite HENRY. *Justin Morgan Had a Horse*, ills Wesley DENNIS. Rand McNally.

Florence Crannell MEANS. *The Moved-Outers*, ills Helen BLAIR. Houghton Mifflin.

Katherine SHIPPEN. *New Found World*, ills C. B. FALLS. Viking.

Christine WESTON. *Bhimsa, the Dancing Bear*, ills Roger DUVOISIN. Scribner.

1947 Carolyn Sherwin BAILEY. *Miss Hickory*, ills Ruth Chrisman GANNETT. Viking.

Honor Books
Nancy BARNES. *Wonderful Year*, ills Kate SEREDY. Messner.

Mary and Conrad BUFF. *Big Tree*. Viking.

Cyrus FISHER *pseud.* (Darwin L. TEILHET). *The Avion My Uncle Flew*, ills Richard FLOETHE. Appleton.

Eleanore JEWETT. *The Hidden Treasures of Glaston*, ills Frederick T. CHAPMAN. Viking.

William MAXWELL. *The Heavenly Tenants*, ills Ilonka KARASZ. Harper.

1948 William PÈNE DU BOIS. *The Twenty One Balloons*. The Viking Press.

Honor Books
Catherine BESTERMAN. *The Quaint and Curious Quest of Johnny Longfoot*, ills Warren CHAPPELL. Bobbs-Merrill.

Claire Huchet BISHOP. *Pancakes-Paris*, ills Georges SCHREIBER. Viking.

Harold COURLANDER. *The Cow-tail Switch, and Other West African Stories*, ills Madye Lee CHASTAIN. Holt.

Marguerite HENRY. *Misty of Chincoteague*, ills Wesley DENNIS. Rand McNally.

Carolyn TREFFINGER. *Li Lun, Lad of Courage*, ills Kurt WIESE. Abingdon.

1949 Marguerite HENRY. *King of the Wind*, ills Wesley DENNIS. Rand McNally.

Honor Books
Arna BONTEMPS. *Story of the Negro*, ills Raymond LUFKIN. Knopf.

Ruth S. GANNETT. *My Father's Dragon*, ills Ruth Chrisman GANNETT. Random House.

Holling C. HOLLING. *Seabird.* Houghton Mifflin.

Louise RANKIN. *Daughter of the Mountain*, ills Kurt WIESE. Viking.

1950 Marguerite de ANGELI. *The Door in the Wall.* Doubleday.

Honor Books
Rebecca CAUDILL. *Tree of Freedom*, ills Dorothy B. MORSE. Viking.

Catherine COBLENTZ. *The Blue Cat of Castle Town*, ills Janice HOLLAND. Longmans.

Genevieve FOSTER. *George Washington.* Scribner.

Walter and Marion HAVIGHURST. *Song of the Pines: A Story of Norwegian Lumbering in Wisconsin*, ills Richard FLOETHE. Winston.

Rutherford MONTGOMERY. *Kildee House*, ills Barbara COONEY. Doubleday.

1951 Elizabeth YATES. *Amos Fortune, Free Man*, ills Nora S. UNWIN. Dutton.

Honor Books
Jeanette EATON. *Gandhi, Fighter Without a Sword*, ills Ralph RAY. Morrow.

Mabel Leigh HUNT. *Better Known as Johnny Appleseed*, ills James DAUGHERTY. Lippincott.

Clara Ingram JUDSON. *Abraham Lincoln, Friend of the People*, ills with drawings by Robert FRANKENBERG & Kodachromes of the Chicago Historical Society Lincoln Dioramas. Wilcox & Follett.

Anne PARRISH. *The Story of Appleby Capple.* Harper.

1952 Eleanor ESTES. *Ginger Pye.* Harcourt.

Honor Books
Elizabeth BAITY. *Americans Before Columbus*, ills C. B. FALLS. Viking.

Mary and Conrad BUFF. *The Apple and the Arrow.* Houghton Mifflin.

Holling C. HOLLING. *Minn of the Mississippi.* Houghton Mifflin.

Nicholas KALASHNIKOFF. *The Defender*, ills Claire & George LOUDEN. Scribner.

Julia SAUER. *The Light at Tern Rock*, ills Georges SCHREIBER. Viking.

1953 Ann Nolan CLARK. *Secret of the Andes*, ills Jean CHARLOT. Viking.

Honor Books
Alice DALGLIESH. *The Bears on Hemlock Mountain*, ills Helen SEWELL. Scribner.

Genevieve FOSTER. *Birthdays of Freedom, Vol. I.* Scribner.

Eloise Jarvis McGRAW. *Moccasin Trail*, ills Paul GALDONE. Coward-McCann.

Ann WEIL. *Red Sails to Capri*, ills C. B. FALLS. Viking.

E. B. WHITE. *Charlotte's Web*, ills Garth WILLIAMS. Harper.

1954 Joseph KRUMGOLD. *...And Now Miguel*, ills Jean CHARLOT. Crowell.

Honor Books
Claire Huchet BISHOP. *All Alone*, ills Feodor ROJANKOVSKY. Viking.

Mary and Conrad BUFF. *Magic Maize*, ills authors. Houghton Mifflin.

Meindert DEJONG. *Hurry Home, Candy*, ills Maurice SENDAK. Harper.

Meindert DEJONG. *Shadrach*, ills Maurice SENDAK. Harper.

Clara Ingram JUDSON. *Theodore Roosevelt, Fighting Patriot*, ills Lorence F. BJORKLUND. Follett.

1955 Meindert DEJONG. *The Wheel on the School*, ills Maurice SENDAK. Harper & Row.

Honor Books
Alice DALGLIESH. *Courage of Sarah Noble*, ills Leonard WEISGARD. Scribner.

James ULLMAN. *Banner in the Sky.* Lippincott.

1956 Jean Lee LATHAM. *Carry on Mr. Bowditch*, ills John O'Hara COSGROVE. Houghton Mifflin.

Honor Books
Jennie LINDQUIST. *The Golden Name Day*, ills Garth WILLIAMS. Harper.

Marjorie Kinnan RAWLINGS. *The Secret River*, ills Leonard WEISGARD. Scribner.

Katherine SHIPPEN. *Men, Microscopes, and Living Things*, ills Anthony RAVIELLI. Viking.

1957 Virginia SORENSEN. *Miracles on Maple Hill*, ills Beth & Joe KRUSH. Harcourt.

Honor Books
Marguerite de ANGELI. *Black Fox of Lorne*. Doubleday.

Meindert DEJONG. *The House of Sixty Fathers*, ills Maurice SENDAK. Harper.

Fred GIPSON. *Old Yeller*, ills Carl BURGER. Harper.

Clara Ingram JUDSON. *Mr. Justice Holmes*, ills Robert TODD. Follett.

Dorothy RHOADS. *The Corn Grows Ripe*, ills Jean CHARLOT. Viking.

1958 Harold KEITH. *Rifles for Watie*. Crowell.

Honor Books
Elizabeth ENRIGHT. *Gone-Away Lake*, ills Beth & Joe KRUSH. Harcourt.

Leo GURKO. *Tom Paine, Freedom's Apostle*, ills Fritz KREDEL. Crowell.

Robert LAWSON. *The Great Wheel*. Viking.

Mari SANDOZ. *The Horsecatcher*. Westminster.

1959 Elizabeth George SPEARE. *The Witch of Blackbird Pond*. Houghton Mifflin.

Honor Books
Natalie S. CARLSON. *The Family Under the Bridge*, ills Garth WILLIAMS. Harper.

Meindert DEJONG. *Along Came a Dog*, ills Maurice SENDAK. Harper.

Francis KALNAY. *Chucaro: Wild Pony of the Pampa*, ills Julian de MISKEY. Harcourt.

William O. STEELE. *The Perilous Road*, ills Paul GALDONE. Harcourt.

1960 Joseph KRUMGOLD. *Onion John*, ills Symeon SHIMIN. Crowell.

Honor Books
Jean GEORGE. *My Side of the Mountain*. Dutton.

Gerald W. JOHNSON. *America is Born: A History for Peter*, ills Leonard Everett FISHER. Morrow.

Carol KENDALL. *The Gammage Cup*, ills Erik BLEGVAD. Harcourt.

1961 Scott O'DELL. *Island of the Blue Dolphins*. Houghton Mifflin.

Honor Books
Gerald W. JOHNSON. *America Moves Forward: A History for Peter*. Morrow.

Jack SCHAEFER. *Old Ramon*, ills Harold WEST. Houghton Mifflin.

George SELDON, *pseud.* (George THOMPSON). *The Cricket in Times Square*, ills Garth WILLIAMS. Farrar, Straus.

1962 Elizabeth George SPEARE. *The Bronze Bow.* Houghton Mifflin.

Honor Books
Eloise Jarvis McGRAW. *The Golden Goblet.* Coward-McCann.

Mary STOLTZ. *Belling the Tiger*, ills Beni MONTRESOR. Harper.

Edwin TUNIS. *Frontier Living.* World.

1963 Madeleine L'ENGLE. *A Wrinkle in Time.* Farrar, Straus & Giroux.

Honor Books
Olivia COOLIDGE. *Men of Athens*, ills Milton JOHNSON. Houghton Mifflin.

Sorche Nic LEODHAS, *pseud.* (Leclaire ALGER). *Thistle and Thyme: Tales and Legends from Scotland*, ills Eveline NESS. Holt.

1964 Emily NEVILLE. *It's Like this, Cat*, ills Emil WEISS. Harper & Row.

Honor Books
Sterling NORTH. *Rascal: A Memoir of a Better Era*, ills John SCHOENHERR. Dutton.

Ester WIER. *The Loner*, ills Christine PRICE. McKay.

1965 Maia WOJCIECHOWSKA. *Shadow of a Bull*, ills Alvin SMITH. Atheneum.

Honor Book
Irene HUNT. *Across Five Aprils.* Follett.

1966 Elizabeth Borton de TREVINO. *I, Juan de Pareja.* Farrar, Straus & Giroux.

Honor Books
Lloyd ALEXANDER. *The Black Cauldron.* Holt

Randall JARRELL. *The Animal Family*, ills Maurice SENDAK. Pantheon.

Mary STOLTZ. *The Noonday Friends*, ills Louis GLANZMAN. Harper

1967 Irene HUNT. *Up a Road Slowly.* Follett.

Honor Books
Scott O'DELL. *The King's Fifth*, ills Samuel BRYANT. Houghton.

Isaac Bashevis SINGER. *Zlateh the Goat and Other Stories*, ills Maurice SENDAK. Harper.

Mary Hays WEIK. *The Jazz Man*, ills Ann GRIFALCONI. Atheneum.

1968 Elaine L. KONIGSBURG. *From the Mixed-Up Files of Mrs. Basil E. Frankweiler.* Atheneum.

Honor Books
Elaine L. KONIGSBURG. *Jennifer, Hecate, Macbeth, William McKinley, and Me, Elizabeth.* Atheneum.

Scott O'DELL. *The Black Pearl*, ills Milton JOHNSON. Houghton

Isaac Bashevis SINGER. *The Fearsome Inn*, ills Nonny HOGROGIAN. Scribner.

Zilpha Keatley SNYDER. *The Egypt Game*, ills Alton RAIBLE. Atheneum

1969 Lloyd ALEXANDER. *The High King: The Chronicles of Prydain, Part Five.* Holt, Rinehart & Winston.

Honor Books
Julius LESTER. *To Be A Slave*, ills Tom FEELINGS. Dial.

Isaac Bashevis SINGER. *When Schlemiel Went to Warsaw and Other Stories*, ills Margot ZEMACH. Farrar.

1970 William H. ARMSTRONG. *Sounder*, ills James BARKLEY. Harper & Row.

Honor Books
Sulamith ISH-KISHOR. *Our Eddie.* Pantheon

Janet Gaylord MOORE. *The Many Ways of Seeing: An Introduction to the Pleasures of Art*, ills with black-and-white and color reproductions and photographs. World.

Mary Q. STEELE. *Journey Outside*, ills Rocco NEGRI. Viking.

1971 Betsy BYARS. *Summer of the Swans*, ills Ted CoCONIS. Viking.

Honor Books
Natalie BABBITT. *Knee Knock Rise.* Farrar.

Sylvia Louise ENGDAHL. *Enchantress from the Stars*, ills Rodney SHACKELL. Atheneum.

Scott O'DELL. *Sing Down the Moon.* Houghton.

1972 Robert O'BRIEN. *Mrs. Frisby and the Rats of NIMH*, ills Zena BERNSTEIN. Atheneum.

Honor Books
Allan W. ECKERT. *Incident at Hawk's Hill*, ills John SCHOENHERR. Little, Brown.

Virginia HAMILTON. *The Planet of Junior Brown.* Macmillan.

Ursula LE GUIN. *The Tombs of Atuan*, ills Gail GARRATY. Atheneum.

Miska MILES. *Annie and the Old One*, ills Peter PARNALL. Atlantic Little.

Zilpha Keatley SNYDER. *The Headless Cupid*, ills Alton RAIBLE. Atheneum.

1973 Jean Craighead GEORGE. *Julie of the Wolves*, ills John SCHOENHERR. Harper & Row.

Honor Books
Arnold LOBEL. *Frog and Toad Together.* Harper.

Johanna REISS. *The Upstairs Room.* Crowell.

Zilpha Keatley SNYDER. *The Witches of Worm*, ills Alton RAIBLE. Atheneum.

1974 Paula FOX. *The Slave Dancer*, ills Eros KEITH. Bradbury.

Honor Book
Susan COOPER. *The Dark is Rising*, ills Alan COBER. McElderry/Atheneum.

1975 Virginia HAMILTON. *M. C. Higgins, the Great.* Macmillan.

Honor Books
James Lincoln COLLIER & Christopher COLLIER. *My Brother Sam is Dead.* Four Winds.

Bette GREENE. *Philip Hall Likes Me, I Reckon Maybe*, ills Charles LILLY. Dial.

Elizabeth Marie POPE. *The Perilous Gard*, ills Richard CUFFARI. Houghton.

Ellen RASKIN. *Figgs and Phantoms.* Dutton.

1976 Susan COOPER. *The Grey King*, ills Michael HESLOP. McElderry/ Atheneum.

Honor Books
Sharon Bell MATHIS. *The Hundred Penny Box*, ills Leo & Diane DILLON. Viking.

Laurence YEP. *Dragonwings.* Harper.

1977 Mildred D. TAYLOR. *Roll of Thunder, Hear My Cry.* Dial.

Honor Books
Nancy BOND. *A String in the Harp.* Atheneum.

William STEIG. *Abel's Island.* Farrar.

1978 Katherine PATERSON. *Bridge to Terabithia*, ills Donna DIAMOND. Crowell.

Honor Books
Beverly CLEARY. *Ramona and her Father*, ills Alan TIEGREEN. Morrow.

Jamake HIGHWATER. *Anpao: An American Indian Odyssey*, ills Fritz SCHOLDER. Lippincott.

1979 Ellen RASKIN. *The Westing Game.* Dutton.

Honor Book
Katherine PATERSON. *The Great Gilly Hopkins.* Crowell.

1980 Joan W. BLOS. *A Gathering of Days: A New England Girl's Journal, 1830-1832.* Scribner.

Honor Book
David KHERDIAN. *The Road from Home: The Story of an Armenian Girl.* Greenwillow.

1981 Katherine PATERSON. *Jacob Have I Loved.* Crowell.

Honor Books
Jane LANGTON. *The Fledgling*, ills Erik BLEGVAD. Harper.

Madeleine L'ENGLE. *A Ring of Endless Light.* Farrar.

1982 Nancy WILLARD (ed.). *A Visit to William Blake's Inn: Poems for Innocent and Experienced Travelers*, ills Alice & Martin PROVENSEN. Harcourt Brace Jovanovich.

Honor Books
Beverly CLEARY. *Ramona Quimby, Age 8*, ills Alan TIEGREEN. Morrow.

Aranka SIEGAL. *Upon the Head of the Goat: A Childhood in Hungary 1939-44.* Farrar.

1983 Cynthia VOIGT. *Dicey's Song.* Atheneum.

Honor Books
Paul FLEISCHMAN. *Graven Images*, ills Andrew GLASS. Harper.

Jean FRITZ. *Homesick: My Own Story*, ills Margot TOMES. Putnam

Virginia HAMILTON. *Sweet Whispers, Brother Rush.* Philomel.

Robin McKINLEY. *The Blue Sword.* Greenwillow.

William STEIG. *Doctor De Soto.* Farrar.

1984 Beverly CLEARY. *Dear Mr. Henshaw*, ills Paul O. ZELINSKY. Morrow.

Honor Books
Bill BRITTAIN. *The Wish Giver: Three Tales of Coven Tree*, ills Andrew GLASS. Harper.

Kathryn LASKY. *Sugaring Time*, photographs by Christopher G. KNIGHT. Macmillan.

Elizabeth George SPEARE. *The Sign of the Beaver.* Houghton.

Cynthia VOIGT. *A Solitary Blue.* Atheneum.

1985 Robin McKINLEY. *The Hero and the Crown.* Greenwillow.

Honor Books
Bruce BROOKS. *The Moves Make the Man.* Harper.

Paula FOX. *One-Eyed Cat.* Bradbury.

Mavis JUKES. *Like Jake and Me*, ills Lloyd BLOOM. Knopf.

1986 Patricia MacLACHLAN. *Sarah, Plain and Tall.* Zolotow/Harper.

Honor Books
Rhoda BLUMBERG. *Commodore Perry in the Land of the Shogun.* Lothrop.

Gary PAULSEN. *Dogsong.* Bradbury.

1987 Sid FLEISCHMAN. *The Whipping Boy*, ills Peter SÍS. Greenwillow.

Honor Books
Marion D. BAUER. *On My Honor.* Clarion.

Patricia LAUBER. *Volcano: The Eruption and Healing of Mount St. Helens.* Bradbury.

Cynthia RYLANT. *A Fine White Dust.* Bradbury.

1988 Russell FREEDMAN. *Lincoln: a Photobiography.* Clarion/Houghton.

Honor Books
Norma Fox MAZER. *After the Rain.* Morrow.

Gary PAULSEN. *Hatchet.* Bradbury.

1989 Paul FLEISCHMAN. *Joyful Noise: Poems for Two Voices*, ills Eric BEDDOWS. Zolotow/Harper.

Honor Books
Virginia HAMILTON. *In the Beginning: Creation Stories from Around the World*, ills Barry MOSER. Harcourt.

Walter Dean MYERS. *Scorpions.* Harper.

1990 Lois LOWRY. *Number the Stars.* Houghton Mifflin.

Honor Books
Janet Taylor LISLE. *Afternoon of the Elves.* Jackson/Orchard.

Gary PAULSEN. *The Winter Room.* Jackson/Orchard.

Suzanne Fisher STAPLES. *Shabanu, Daughter of the Wind.* Knopf.

1991 Jerry SPINELLI. *Maniac Magee.* Little, Brown.

Honor Book
AVI. *The True Confessions of Charlotte Doyle.* Jackson/Orchard.

1992 Phyllis Reynolds NAYLOR. *Shiloh.* Atheneum.

Honor Books
AVI. *Nothing But the Truth: A Documentary Novel.* Jackson/Orchard.

Russell FREEDMAN. *The Wright Brothers: How They Invented the Airplane.* Holiday House.

1993 Cynthia RYLANT. *Missing May.* Jackson/Orchard.

Honor Books
Bruce BROOKS. *What Hearts.* Laura Geringer/HarperCollins.

Patricia C. McKISSACK. *The Dark-thirty: Southern Tales of the Supernatural.* Knopf.

Walter Dean MYERS. *Somewhere in the Darkness.* Scholastic.

1994 Lois LOWRY. *The Giver.* Houghton.

Honor Books
Jane Leslie CONLY. *Crazy Lady.* HarperCollins.

Russell FREEDMAN. *Eleanor Roosevelt: A Life of Discovery.* Clarion.

Laurence YEP. *Dragon's Gate.* HarperCollins.

1995 Sharon CREECH. *Walk Two Moons.* HarperCollins.

Honor Books
Karen CUSHMAN. *Catherine, Called Birdy.* Clarion.

Nancy FARMER. *The Ear, the Eye and the Arm.* Orchard.

1996 Karen CUSHMAN. *The Midwife's Apprentice.* Clarion.

Honor Books
Carolyn COMAN. *What Jamie Saw.* Front Street Press.

Christopher Paul CURTIS. *The Watsons Go to Birmingham – 1963.* Delacotte.

Carol FENNER. *Yolonda's Genius.* McElderry.

Jim MURPHY. *The Great Fire.* Scholastic.

1997 E. L. KONIGSBURG. *The View from Saturday.* Atheneum.

Honor Books
Nancy FARMER. *A Girl Named Disaster.* Richard Jackson/Orchard.

Eloise McGRAW. *The Moorchild.* McElderry.

Megan Whalen TURNER. *The Thief.* Greenwillow.

Ruth WHITE. *Belle Prater's Boy.* Farrar Straus Giroux.

1998 Karen HESSE. *Out of the Dust.* Scholastic.

Honor Books
Patricia Reilly GIFF. *Lily's Crossing.* Delacorte.

Gail Carson LEVINE. *Ella Enchanted.* HarperCollins.

Jerry SPINELLI. *Wringer.* HarperCollins.

1999 Louis SACHAR. *Holes.* Frances Foster.

Honor Book
Richard PECK. *A Long Way from Chicago.* Dial.

2000 Christopher Paul CURTIS. *Bud, Not Buddy.* Delacorte.

Honor Books
Audrey COULOUMBIS. *Getting Near to Baby.* Putnam.

Jennifer L. HOLM. *Our Only May Amelia.* HarperCollins.

Tomie DEPAOLA. *26 Fairmount Avenue.* Putnam.

2001 Richard PECK. *A Year Down Yonder.* Dial.

Honor Books
Joan BAUER. *Hope Was Here.* G.P. Putnam's Sons.

Sharon CREECH. *The Wanderer.* Joanna Cotler Books/HarperCollins.

Kate DI CAMILLO. *Because of Winn-Dixie.* Candlewick Press.

Jack GANTOS. *Joey Pigza Loses Control.* Farrar, Straus & Giroux.

2002 Linda Sue PARK. *A Single Shard.* Clarion Books/Houghton Mifflin.

Honor Books
Polly HORVATH. *Everything on a Waffle.* Farrar Straus Giroux.

Marilyn NELSON. *Carver: A Life In Poems.* Front Street.

2003 AVI. *Crispin: The Cross of Lead.* Hyperion Books for Children.

Honor Books
Nancy FARMER. *The House of the Scorpion.* Atheneum.

Patricia Reilly GIFF. *Pictures of Hollis Woods.* Random House/Wendy Lamb Books.

Carl HIAASEN. *Hoot.* Knopf.

Ann M. MARTIN. *A Corner of The Universe.* Scholastic.

Stephanie S. TOLAN. *Surviving the Applewhites.* HarperCollins.

2004 Kate DI CAMILLO. *The Tale of Despereaux: Being the Story of a Mouse, a Princess, Some Soup, and a Spool of Thread*, ills by Timothy Basil ERING. Candlewick Press.

Honor Books
Kevin HENKES. *Olive's Ocean.* Greenwillow Books.

Jim MURPHY. *An American Plague: The True and Terrifying Story of the Yellow Fever Epidemic of 1793.* Clarion Books.

2005 Cynthia KADOHATA. *Kira-Kira.* Atheneum.

Honor Books

Gennifer CHOLDENKO. *Al Capone Does my Shirts.* G. P. Putnam's Sons.

Russell FREEDMAN. *The Voice that Challenged a Nation: Marian Anderson and the Struggle for Equal Rights.* Clarion.

Gary D. SCHMIDT. *Lizzie Bright and the Buckminster Boy.* Clarion.

Chapter 4: The CILIP Carnegie Medal (UK)

The Carnegie Medal has been awarded since 1936 for 'an outstanding book for children and young people' published in the previous year. The original stipulation 'the best book of the year' was changed during the 1940s, and the wording 'and young people' was added in 2001. It is administered by the Youth Libraries Group (YLG) of the Chartered Institute of Library and Information Professionals (CILIP). The Library Association (LA) amalgamated with the Institute of Information Scientists in 2002 to become CILIP, and the Medal is now officially the CILIP Carnegie Medal. A list of winners from 1936 to 1984 compiled by Derek Lomas, with annotations, which included commended titles was published in 1986 by the YLG to mark the Golden Jubilee of the Award. In the same year the late and much missed Keith Barker produced a booklet *In the Realms of Gold* for the YLG giving a brief history and overview of the award over its first fifty years. Whilst not wishing to duplicate information available from these sources, I shall nevertheless give an overview of the award and its winners here.

Andrew Carnegie (1835-1918), for whom the medal is named, was a Victorian philanthropist whose most famous memorial is probably Carnegie Hall in New York. Scottish-born, he provided the cash for over six hundred libraries in the UK, and some three thousand world-wide. In 1935, the Library Association decided that an appropriate gesture to commemorate the centenary of his birth would be a medal for Children's books. In this they were following the lead of the American Library Association (ALA), whose Newbery Medal was by then twenty-three years old. In more recent years the ALA has instituted a Carnegie award of its own, the Andrew Carnegie Medal for Excellence in Children's Video.

The first Carnegie Medal was awarded in 1936, to Arthur Ransome for *Pigeon Post*. This was seen by many as an opportunity to recognise a long-term achievement, rather than the book itself being 'the best' of the year. Ransome is himself on record as saying that this title was not as good as the others, and it is generally recognised as the weakest in the 'Swallows and Amazons' series. The quality of writing in this series as a whole, which broke new ground in that it showed boys and girls having holiday adventures on almost equal terms, ensured that Ransome's contribution to children's literature would be recognised. The stated aim of the Carnegie Medal was, after all, to improve the standard of publishing output for children in the UK. There would be six further books following *Pigeon Post* in the 'Swallows and Amazons' series, so it was not the last chance to honour Ransome, though it proved to be his only appearance in the lists.

It seems that many of the awards made by the Carnegie Medal judges in the early years were deliberate opportunities to recognise the 'quality' authors of the day before they stopped writing. This idea persisted to some degree into the 1950s, when the last, and normally accounted least successful, of C. S. Lewis's 'Narnia' series, *The Last Battle*, was awarded the 1956 medal. This, from its title, would obviously be Lewis's final opportunity for a medal. Walter

De la Mare's *Collected Stories for Children* and Eleanor Farjeon's *The Little Bookroom*, both collections of stories all of which had been published previously elsewhere, again must surely have been seen as the only opportunities to recognise established quality authors whose best work had appeared in earlier years.

There is a point of view from which it may have been somewhat less defensible to have awarded the first Carnegie Medal to *Pigeon Post*. Although considerably better written than many of the so-called 'adventure' stories available at the time, it was not all that dissimilar to the kind of book the medal had been set up to counterbalance. We should nonetheless be charitable; the choice of a first winner will always be difficult. What standard should the judges set? If it is too high, nothing will meet the criteria; if too low, there is no point having the award. The Carnegie judges decided on three occasions to withhold the award. The decisions for 1943 and 1945, as war years, may be more easily understood than that of 1966 when a Highly Commended and three Commended titles were listed. Was this a question of disagreement among the judges, or one of perfect accord that although these four titles were good, nothing could really be called 'outstanding'?

Keith Barker, in his short book *In the Realms of Gold*, and in his more recent essays about awards (for example 'Prize Fighting' in *Children's Book Publishing Since 1945*, edited by Kimberley Reynolds and Nicholas Tucker. Aldershot: Scolar Press, 1998) charted the changes which took place between 1936 and 2000 – both in terms of personnel on the judging panel and criteria used in the judging. Barker noted that a major early problem was that there were very few practising specialist children's librarians in the 1930s. When they did begin to try to make their voices heard, they had difficulty in getting their body recognised by the Library Association. What began as the entirely separate Circle of Library Workers with Children, became first The Association of Children's Librarians, then an affiliated body, in 1947 a 'Section' and eventually a 'Group' of the Library Association (itself now CILIP) currently known as the Youth Libraries Group (YLG). This was not their only difficulty, however, as even when children's librarians were more commonly found, and they were permitted to produce the shortlist of titles, their recommendations were not necessarily followed. Thus in a year that the panel of children's librarians recommended that no award be made, the medal was given to *The Radium Woman*, and in a year when, so we are told, a title was suggested that the chief librarians did not like much, no award was given.

It was probably inevitable that in an era without sponsorship or any other extra funding, the early winners were not particularly well publicised. Publicity was not an issue at the time. The enclosed world of libraries and education contained their secret – these were the books one could safely offer to the children who were in one's class at school, or who came into one's library. In fact, even the Library Association's own journal, the Library Association Record, after noting the first year's winner, did not publish news of the winning titles for the next two. No wonder then that Lucy Boston had such an awful experience in 1962, when her *Stranger at Green Knowe* was awarded the

1961 medal. The chapter 'A Snub of Success' in Mrs. Boston's *Memory in a House*, is worth mentioning here, for the points she makes are of considerable concern, and although some have been addressed – in large part because of her account of the event – some still have not been resolved. In that chapter Mrs Boston talks about the background to writing *Stranger*: it had been inspired by a picture in *The Times* of Guy the Gorilla in the London Zoo. Mrs Boston was not particularly thrilled at the news the book had won:

> . . . because it seemed to me unlikely that a really wonderful book for children would be written every year, and as the same writer could then never receive it twice, that left one as the best in a period of twelve months after all the notable writers have already been excluded. It did not strike me as a dizzy peak. However my publishers wrote ardent congratulations, and letters from the awarding body of librarians wrote awesomely of the 'supreme award'. I was gradually coaxed away by such professional shibboleths from my common sense. I began to feel perhaps I had done something good, and that it was arrogant to deprecate an award. And not only one's vanity but one's proper pride as an artist longs to believe in recognition. . . . .

Mrs Boston had mixed feelings, too, about attending the Library Association Conference, and having, she was told, to make an official acceptance speech before this large gathering. Indeed she went to the trouble of taking lessons in public speaking, and learnt her speech by heart in order not to have the distraction of reading from notes. She suffered real agonies at the very idea of appearing on a platform, and considered it far more difficult than writing a book. The journey to Aberystwyth was tedious, and she was made to feel an intruder on the special train which was laid on for the occasion. The room where she stayed the night before the conference was small and dirty, on the ground floor and with no curtains. The final blow was when the people who were particularly assigned to take care of her told her that no speech was required, that in fact there was no time allocated for it:

> . . . 'I myself am only allotted five minutes for introducing you,' said my sponsor. 'So how could you have twenty minutes?' All the effort and strain of the last weeks had keyed my self-control up to go through my performance, but not to be so meanly punctured. I lost my temper and hit the table till the cups danced. I poured out my rage at the wasted time and nervous exhaustion, the nights of fear. With rage came adrenalin and I knew I could address thousands without turning a hair, that I was in fact all agog to do it and mad at being defrauded . . .

A visiting children's librarian from the US – where, it must be remembered, they had a longer tradition of children's book awards and were accustomed to award presentations with acceptance speeches which were later published – argued Mrs Boston's case, but a simple 'thank you' was all that would be allowed. The next day she met that year's Greenaway winner, Antony Maitland, who had also been made to feel unwelcome and unimportant. The conference session was long and dull. The mayoral welcome was obviously an all-purpose one trotted out for whatever conference happened to be taking place. No press or photographers were in evidence. Eventually the time came for the Carnegie and Greenaway Medals to be awarded:

> ... and then our two sponsors said their pieces. I was assured that my book was really quite up to the required standard. We received our medals like school children and said our brief thanks, and all was over for us. While other business continued we compared our medals with incredulity. Mine was almost exactly like one I got for swimming the mile when I was eleven. His was not even as adult as that. Of course the medals were only symbols, but of what? Later I sat beside the President for the official luncheon. It was clear that children's books were so far below his interest that he had neglected to inform himself about this last unnecessary addition to them. Beyond saying he believed I had written a book he risked no conversation at all to my side, having some easier neighbour on his left. It was an excellent meal and I gave it my attention ... [from L. Boston, (1973) *Memory in a House*, London: The Bodley Head]

The impression left on Mrs Boston was that of being ignored and made to feel unworthy to be there by the very people she thought had invited her to the occasion. The major problem, as she indeed recognised, was that the majority of those attending the Library Association conference were adult lending and reference librarians, who, particularly at that time, had little interest in children or their literature. Later, Eileen Colwell arranged for the speech into which Mrs Boston had put so much effort to be given in London before a meeting of children's librarians, where it received due acclaim. Mrs Boston's experience, and her vivid account of it, has gone down in the annals of children's librarians ever since. Indeed her vehemence, together with the 'good fight' hard-won by Eileen Colwell began to work towards a more author-friendly system of awarding the Carnegie and Greenaway medals. Two years later, the Children's Group of the Publishers Association organised a dinner at which the official announcement was made that Hester Burton's *Time of Trial* had won the 1963 Medal – largely, it seems, to prompt or goad the Library Association into making more of the occasion, but the lethargy of the LA as a whole took a considerable time to produce any noticeable improvement.

Since the 1960s there have been several important changes to the administration and thinking behind the Carnegie award process. The criteria were changed in 1969 so that it was no longer limited to books by English writers first published in England, but open to any book written in English as long as it received its first publication in the UK, or co-publication elsewhere within three months. This has recently led to the awarding of the Medal to US authors in consecutive years, for 2002 and 2003. Additionally, it is no longer 'understood' that an author may win only once: six authors have been selected twice: Robert Westall in 1975 and 1981; Jan Mark in 1976 and 1983; Peter Dickinson in consecutive years (1979 and 1980); Margaret Mahy, a New Zealander, in 1982 and 1984; Berlie Doherty in 1986 and 1991 and Anne Fine in 1989 and 1992.

Other major changes have been the emergence of the Youth Libraries Group at the forefront of the selection and final choice of the medal-winning titles and the sponsorship of the Carnegie and Greenaway Medals from 1991 until 1997 by the Library Supply firm, Peters. It is now acknowledged by Chief Librarians that children's librarians are dynamic, and that their role is prestigious and important – since they nurture future readers. Peters, by retaining a publicity consultant, and by enabling the YLG to produce high quality publicity material such as posters, bookmarks and flyers, by publicising the shortlist, so that appearance on it has become an achievement in its own right, and providing books to the value of £1000 to the winners for a library of their choosing, contributed greatly to the award scene within the library world. How much of this, even now, impinges on even literary circles in the UK, let alone the consciousness of the general public, is questionable.

Controversy surrounding the winners is seen by many as healthy publicity – presumably on the assumption that any publicity is better than none. Much of the concern seems to lie in the accepted view of what is a children's book. One famous dictum is attributed to C S Lewis: that a children's book is a book for adults that can be enjoyed by children. Other opinions turn this about and say that a good children's book is one which adults can enjoy. Enjoyment, of course, has no part in 'literary merit'. The story is told of a former Principal of my old college who, on being told by an enthusiastic young lecturer in the English Department that the first-year students 'seemed to be enjoying their course', was unimpressed. Leaning forward in his seat, he fixed her with a dour glare and said 'My dear Miss --, they are not here to *enjoy* anything.' More recently course enjoyment as well as non-academic pleasures have come to be rather more generally accepted as a vital part of the experience of being at university.

Things have been far from tranquil over the last decade and the 1995 winner Philip Pullman, at the announcement ceremony in July 1996, made several forceful remarks about the world of children's writing in general, and prizes in particular. He argued strongly for the importance of story in the world, not only of the child, but of adults, and criticised some recent prize-winning adult novels for its lack. This was reported widely, and may have helped raise the profile of the award a little. The whole question of 'Crossover books' and the popularity with adults, as well as children, of some recent series such as the inescapable 'Harry Potter', will be discussed in Chapter 14.

There have been moves to introduce an award for so-called 'teenage' books, since many of the past Carnegie winners have been in this category. Other countries, as will be seen in Chapter 12, have made such moves; and there is now the BookTrust Teenage Prize in the UK, which is covered in Chapter 9. The thinking in the UK, as given in Youth Library Review 18, Autumn 1994, was that a teenage award would both devalue past winners, and perhaps dilute the 'honour' in future years. This does not seem to have happened in the US with the Michael Printz award, and indeed Printz winners also regularly appear as Newbery Medallists and Honor Books. The 1993 Carnegie winner, *Stone Cold* was particularly castigated in the press for dealing with 'concepts outside childhood's experience', and the 1996 winner, *Junk* similarly produced inches of column space – in this instance on the unsuitability of the drug scene as a subject for children's reading. The facts are that children today are growing up in a world which is far from the cosy 1950s idyll pictured in the sub-Blytonesque memories of some commentators;

equally, any child of today who is a keen reader will, almost by definition, be likely to possess a more 'adult' mind than non-bookish children of a similar age – these are realities which fail to impinge on many *soi-disant* critics.

The Carnegie Medal, like its US counterpart and predecessor, the Newbery Medal, is judged and awarded by librarians. Publishers are not directly involved in any stage of the process. Any member of CILIP, individual or corporate, may nominate two titles for the Carnegie Medal for consideration by the judging panel (as well as two nominations for the Greenaway Medal, which is judged by the same panel). Each nomination, to be valid, must be accompanied by a 'supporting statement' of some thirty to fifty words. Several library authorities have set up discussion days, which may involve local teachers as well as librarians who work with children. During these days they discuss six or seven titles for each of the Carnegie and Greenaway, which they have all read beforehand, ending with a vote which will determine the library authority's two nominations as a corporate member. Hampshire County Library, for instance, has for a number of years arranged such days, which include talks by authors or children's literature experts, as well as small discussion groups where a different person 'leads' on each of the books under consideration.

These 'corporate nominations' carry no greater weight in the first instance than nominations by individuals. And of course individual members who have attended such a discussion day are not precluded from making their own nominations, if the books they thought the most outstanding did not accrue sufficient votes to become the corporate entry, or were not up for discussion on the day. As long as the nomination meets the conditions: that it is sent in by the end of February, nominated by a member of the CILIP, and accompanied by a supporting statement, it will be noted by the Carnegie/Greenaway co-ordinator. Books intended for all age-groups may be included. Poetry and information books are also eligible. The co-ordinator has to check that the titles are eligible in terms of the publication criteria: that it has received first publication in the UK during the preceding year, or co-publication elsewhere within a three-month time lapse.

At the beginning of March, the co-ordinator will send a list of titles, each annotated with its supporting statement (or statements), to each member of the judging panel. The judging panel of thirteen is composed of a representative from each of the YLG branches, the Carnegie and Greenaway co-ordinator, the Chair of the YLG (who Chairs the Panel) and the Vice-Chair of the YLG as an observer, since s/he will need to be aware of procedures on becoming Chair the following year. Each of these will already have been sent the full criteria and guidelines for judging. There are seven weeks during which the members of the judging panel must read through the nominated titles – sometimes as many as 120 books. It will be apparent from the number of supporting statements how many nominations an individual title has received, but this adds no weight to the nomination *per se*; the panel gives thorough consideration to every book that has been properly nominated.

The panel then meets, late in April. This meeting will continue over two days should the nomination list be sufficiently long to warrant it. By the end of the meeting, the judges will have produced a shortlist for each award. There is no specification laid down for the length of these shortlists, but each normally contains six to eight titles. These days the shortlist is given considerable publicity. The publishers are immediately notified by phone and later a shortlist party is held. This is an area which responded well to the sponsorship made available by Peters Library Service, then Royal Mail, and now CILIP itself.

Meanwhile, in the four weeks between the shortlist decision in April and their final meeting in May, the members of the judging panel are re-reading the shortlisted titles and preparing their cases so that each will be prepared to support the book s/he feels most deserving of the award. The May meeting considers the Carnegie in the morning and the Greenaway in the afternoon. It is naturally more focused than the April meeting – fewer titles are under consideration, so each has more detailed discussion. Each one will have been re-read at least once by everyone on the panel.

At the end of the day, the decisions have been made, and the winning publisher for each award is telephoned. The decision is under strict embargo for another two months; this is very difficult to achieve, but has been successfully managed so far. Only the winners are contacted, and that is done solely to ensure that the winning author will be present at the award announcement ceremony. The authors and publishers of any Commended or Highly Commended titles are not informed ahead of the ceremony. This secrecy leading to a surprise winner naturally adds to the publicity value of the eventual announcement, and allows CILIP's own publications, which have long lead times between their copy and publication dates, to list the winners and commended titles in the issues which come out in the week that the official announcement is made. All the extra publicity which is gained from the announcement of a shortlist, and the 'surprise' of the final announcement is part of the phenomenal changes which occured to the public face of the awards during the sponsorship of Peters which ran from 1991 until 1997. In this period, six planning meetings each year were held between Peters, CILIP and the YLG.

The announcement ceremony takes place in July, at a venue in London, with a celebrity to make the presentation. In September there is an award dinner during the YLG annual conference, at which the Carnegie and Greenaway winners are invited to make speeches after the dinner. The full texts of these speeches are nowadays published either in *CILIP Update* or *Youth Library Review*. This smoothly-run operation has come a very long way from the sorry tale told in Lucy Boston's autobiography.

The sequence of winning titles reflects the development of children's literature over the last sixty years. They show, too, how the perceptions of the various judging panels have changed during this time. Arthur Ransome, Eve Garnett and Noel Streatfeild, winners of the first three medals, wrote about families or groups of children whose adventures did not stray far from the experience of the prospective child readers.

The 1940 and 1941 winners dealt with wartime situations, evacuees and the occupation of the Channel Islands, but the other two wartime winners were an escape into faerie and fantasy. BB's *The Little Grey Men* described the adventures of elves in the Forest, and was followed by two sequels, *Down the Bright Stream*, and *The Forest of Boland Light Railway.* Eric Linklater's *The Wind on the Moon* is a story nearer in spirit to Carroll's *Alice* or even the ideas of Franz Kafka: the two child heroines are metamorphosed into kangaroos while they have their adventures.

Some early winners were information books: the biography of Marie Curie told in 1939 winner, Eleanor Doorly's *Radium Woman*; the history of houses depicted in 1949 winner, Agnes Allen's *The Story of Your Home;* landscape history shown in 1953 winner, Edward Osmond's *A Valley Grows Up;* finally, anthropology and the history of mankind related in Ian Cornwall's 1960 winner, *The Making of Man.* The other more recent non-fiction winners, *The God Beneath the Sea* by Leon Garfield and Edward Blishen (Medallist 1970), and *City of Gold* by Peter Dickinson (Medallist 1980) are retellings of Greek myths and Old Testament stories respectively which, although technically non-fiction, are not in quite the same mode as the earlier medallists. Indeed non-fiction has not featured strongly even among the Commended titles, and has not been included at all since the 1980 appearance of *City of Gold.*

During the 1950s and 1960s there was a preponderance of historical fiction. These were the years when Rosemary Sutcliff was at her peak. Ronald Welch (Medallist 1954) and Hester Burton (Medallist 1963) also contributed to the genre. Fantasy of a more integrated kind – the world that might be just out of sight, was being included in Mary Norton's *Borrowers* series, Philippa Pearce's *Tom's Midnight Garden* and Pauline Clarke's *The Twelve and the Genii.* This too was the period of the Oxford University Press's dominance of the medals; they published the medal-winning titles in 1950, 1953-1959, 1963-1965 and 1969. From 1954 until 1965 Oxford also featured strongly in the commended lists, publishing twenty-six of the Highly Commended and Commended titles over this period. Since then, their proportion has fallen to what may be considered a more equitable share of the winners and Commended appearances. The late 1960s, 1970s and 1980s show a broad cross-section of children's writing. High fantasy is represented by Alan Garner (Medallist 1967; Commended 1965), Susan Cooper (Commended 1973 and 1975) and Peter Dickinson (Medallist 1979 and 1980; Commended 1970, 1976, 1988 and 1992), though his work is not always in this vein, even among the titles included in the award lists. Ghosts, or the possibility of ghostly deeds, are treated by Penelope Lively (Medallist 1973) and Margaret Mahy (Medallist 1982 and 1984). World War Two still produced powerful echoes in Robert Westall's *Machine-Gunners* (Medallist 1975), David Rees's *Exeter Blitz* (Medallist 1978) and Michelle Magorian's *Goodnight Mr. Tom* (Commended 1981). Jan Mark (Medallist 1976 and 1983), Michelle Magorian (Commended 1981), Berlie Doherty (Medallist 1986 and 1991), Anne Fine

(Medallist 1989 and 1992), Tim Bowler's *River Boy* (Medallist 1997), David Almond (Medallist 1998 and Highly Commended 1999) and Sharon Creech (Commended 2001 and Medallist 2002), show children coming to terms with who they are and with their place in their family, school and the wider society.

The 1990s produced more in the way of social realism. Teenage pregnancy is treated in Berlie Doherty's 1991 winner, *Dear Nobody*, homelessness is shown in Robert Westall's 1993 winner *Stone Cold*, dyslexia and its attendant problems in Theresa Breslin's 1994 winner *Whispers in the Graveyard*. These are not 'problem novels', they are novels which arise from the authors' consideration of young people in the modern word, and the way in which they deal with life. Philip Pullman's 1995 winner *Northern Lights* (published as *Golden Compass* in the US) may mark another change. This is strong on both narrative thrust and imagination, and draws on Milton's Paradise Lost for some of its themes.

In 1996 there was publicity of a different kind about the winner. Melvin Burgess's *Junk*, also the Guardian Award-winner for 1997, is not for small children; its two main characters, aged about fourteen, become involved in drugs. It is intended for readers of about fourteen or fifteen years old. But people of this age are still legally children, books must be provided for them, and it is right that authors are writing specifically for the age-group. Critics should realise that by their mid-teens young people will not be reading *Peter Pan*; they will more likely be enjoying a Point Horror title, or something by Stephen King or Dean Koontz, intended for adults. This is not to say that reading adult books is wrong at this age; Charles Dickens and Jane Austen should also have been sampled by then. Well-written, strong stories intended for teenagers are necessary to supplement and complement the classics. Anne Fine's *The Tulip Touch*, which was Highly Commended, is another novel which treats the so-called darker side of life, and the dangers of being dazzled by a new friend. It was also the Whitbread Children's Book of the Year for 1996.

The 1997 winner, Tim Bowler's *River Boy*, coping with the death of Jess's grandfather and the challenge of swimming a river from source to sea, makes a sharp contrast to Henrietta Branford's *Fire, Bed and Bone*, set in medieval times and told from the point of view of a dog, which was the only Highly Commended title of the year. Branford's tragic death not long afterwards has prompted a new award, for a first book for children, which will be discussed in Chapter 9. The beginning of the Harry Potter phenomenon was marked by the choice of *Harry Potter and the Philosopher's Stone* as that year's single Commendation.

David Almond made his first appearance in the Carnegie list as a winner with *Skellig*, the 1998 winner and was Highly Commended the following year with *Kit's Wilderness*, and was on the shortlist for 2003 with *Fire Eaters*. Aidan Chambers's *Postcards From No Man's Land* marks a return to the theme of war as the 1999 winner, and Beverley Naidoo's *The Other Side of Truth*, the 2000 medallist, deals with illegal immigration from the point of view of children who have seen their mother killed and their father arrested. Pullman's last volume in the 'His Dark Materials' sequence, *The Amber Spyglass*, was Highly Commended, marking his achievement in completing such an immense imaginative task.

Terry Pratchett, long a successful adult author, whose earlier children's books included *Johnny & the Bomb* (Highly Commended 1996), was the 2001 medallist with *The Amazing Maurice and his Educated Rodents*, a new take on the story behind *The Pied Piper of Hamelin.* Highly Commended for 2001 was Geraldine McCaughrean's *Stop the Train*, one of the few titles listed in recent years aimed at younger children, and Sharon Creech's *Love That Dog* was Commended. Sharon Creech would make Award history in 2003, becoming the 2002 Carnegie medallist with *Ruby Holler*, having previously won a Newbery Medal in 1995; the only person to have the distinction of winning both medals. Another American author was awarded the 2003 medal: Jennifer Donnelly, for *A Gathering Light* (published in US as *A Northern Light*). Set in rural New York State this combines stories from Jennifer Donnelly's own family past and the notorious murder case that also inspired Theodore Dreiser's novel *An American Tragedy.* It was chosen ahead of the winners of the Whitbread Book of the Year, Mark Haddon's *The Curious Incident of the Dog in the Night Time* and the Whitbread Children's Book of the Year, David Almond's *The Fire Eaters* which had both been on the shortlist. No commendations were made as the panel felt that the rest of the shortlist were on equal par.

These winners reflect the changing literary scene as well as the changes in social conditions and social awareness of children. Many of the earlier winners are interesting as period pieces but are not read with any degree of enjoyment by today's children. Others, such as Ransome's 'Swallows and Amazons' series, C. S. Lewis's 'Narnia' series and the books of William Mayne, Philippa Pearce and Alan Garner still offer as much to children as they always have.

The Carnegie Medal: complete list of winners & commended titles

1936 Arthur RANSOME. *Pigeon Post.* Jonathan Cape.

Commended
'Second' - Howard SPRING. *Sampson's Circus.* Faber.

'Third' - Noel STREATFEILD. *Ballet Shoes.* Dent.

1937 Eve GARNETT. *The Family from One End Street.* Muller.

1938 Noel STREATFEILD. *The Circus is Coming.* Dent.

1939 Eleanor DOORLY. *Radium Woman.* Heinemann.

1940 Kitty BARNE. *Visitors from London.* Dent.

1941 Mary TREADGOLD. *We Couldn't Leave Dinah.* Cape.

1942 'BB' (D. J. WATKINS-PITCHFORD). *The Little Grey Men; A story for the Young in Heart.* Eyre & Spottiswoode.

1943 Award withheld as no book considered suitable.

1944 Eric LINKLATER. *The Wind on the Moon; A Story for Children*, ills Nicolas BENTLEY. Macmillan & Co. Ltd.

1945 Award withheld as no book considered suitable.

1946 Elizabeth GOUDGE, ills C. Walter HODGES. *The Little White Horse.* University of London Press.

1947 Walter DE LA MARE. *Collected Stories for Children.* Faber.

1948 Richard ARMSTRONG. *Sea Change.* Dent.

1949 Agnes ALLEN. *The Story of Your Home.* Faber.

1950 Elfrida VIPONT. *The Lark on the Wing.* Oxford U. P.

1951 Cynthia HARNETT. *The Wool-pack.* Methuen.

1952 Mary NORTON. *The Borrowers.* Dent.

1953 Edward OSMOND. *A Valley Grows Up.* Oxford U. P.

1954 Ronald WELCH. *Knight Crusader.* Oxford U. P.

Special Commendation
Harold JONES (ills), ed. Kathleen LINES. *Lavender's Blue; a Book of Nursery Rhymes.* Oxford U. P.

Commended
Lucy M. BOSTON. *The Children of Green Knowe.* Faber.

Nicholas Stuart GRAY. *Over the Hills to Fabylon.* Oxford U. P.

C. S. LEWIS. *The Horse and His Boy.* Macmillan.

Barbara Leonie PICARD. *Lady of the Linden Tree.* Oxford U. P.

James REEVES. *English Fables and Fairy Stories.* Oxford U. P.

Rosemary SUTCLIFF. *The Eagle of the Ninth.* Oxford U. P.

1955 Eleanor FARJEON. *The Little Bookroom.* Oxford U. P.

Commended
Lancelot HOGBEN. *Man Must Measure: The Wonderful World of Mathematics.* Rathbone.

Margaret JOWETT. *Candidate for Fame.* Oxford U. P.

Jo MANTON. *The Story of Albert Schweitzer.* Methuen.

William MAYNE. *A Swarm in May.* Oxford U. P.

A. Philippa PEARCE. *Minnow on the Say.* Oxford U. P.

1956 C. S. LEWIS. *The Last Battle: A Story for Children.* Oxford U. P.

Commended
Rumer GODDEN. *The Fairy Doll.* Macmillan.

William MAYNE. *Choristers' Cake.* Oxford U. P.

William MAYNE. *The Member for the Marsh.* Oxford U. P.

Barbara Leonie PICARD. *Ransom for a Knight.* Oxford U. P.

Ian SERRAILLIER. *The Silver Sword.* Cape.

Rosemary SUTCLIFF. *The Shield Ring.* Oxford U. P.

1957 William MAYNE. *A Grass Rope*. Oxford U. P.

Commended
Gillian AVERY. *The Warden's Niece*. Collins.

Anne BARRETT. *Songberd's Grove*. Collins.

Antonia FOREST. *Falconer's Lure*. Faber.

William MAYNE. *The Blue Boat*. Oxford U. P.

Katharine SAVAGE. *Story of the Second World War*. Oxford U. P.

Rosemary SUTCLIFF. *The Silver Branch*. Oxford U. P.

1958 A. Philippa PEARCE. *Tom's Midnight Garden*. Oxford U. P.

Commended
Lucy M. BOSTON. *The Chimneys of Green Knowe*. Faber.

Rosemary SUTCLIFF. *Warrior Scarlet*. Oxford U. P.

1959 Rosemary SUTCLIFF. *The Lantern Bearers*. Oxford U. P.

Commended
Cynthia HARNETT. *The Load of Unicorn*. Methuen.

Mary NORTON. *The Borrowers Afloat*. Dent.

Margery SHARP. *The Rescuers*. Collins.

John VERNEY. *Friday's Tunnel*. Collins.

Andrew YOUNG. *Quiet as Moss: 36 poems*, chosen by Leonard CLARK. Hart-Davis.

1960 Ian Wolfram CORNWALL. *The Making of Man*. Phoenix House.

Commended
Hester BURTON. *The Great Gale*. Oxford U. P.

Robert GRAVES. *The Penny Fiddle*. Cassell.

Frederic GRICE. *The Bonny Pit Laddie*. Oxford U. P.

Mary K. HARRIS. *Seraphina*. Faber.

Ian SERRAILLIER. *The Ivory Horn*. Oxford U. P.

1961 Lucy M. BOSTON. *A Stranger at Green Knowe*. Faber.

Commended
Antonia FOREST. *Peter's Room.* Faber.

Rumer GODDEN. *Miss Happiness & Miss Flower.* Macmillan.

James REEVES. *Ragged Robin.* Heinemann.

John VERNEY. *February's Road.* Collins.

1962 Pauline CLARKE. *The Twelve and the Genii.* Faber.

Commended
Gillian AVERY. *The Greatest Gresham.* Collins.

Hester BURTON. *Castors Away.* Oxford U. P.

Samuel E. ELLACOTT. *Armour and Blade.* Abelard-Schuman.

Penelope FARMER. *The Summer Birds.* Harcourt.

Jo MANTON. *The Story of John Keats.* Methuen.

K. M. PEYTON. *Windfall.* Oxford U. P.

1963 Hester BURTON. *Time of Trial.* Oxford U. P.

Commended
Eric ALLEN. *The Latchkey Children.* Oxford U. P.

Ralph ARNOLD. *Kings, Bishops, Knights, and Pawns: Life in a Feudal Society.* Constable.

Margaret J. BAKER. *Castaway Christmas.* Methuen.

Antonia FOREST. *The Thursday Kidnapping.* Faber.

John Rowe TOWNSEND. *Hell's Edge.* Hutchinson.

1964 Sheena PORTER. *Nordy Bank.* Oxford U. P.

Commended
Eric S. de MARE. *London's River.* Bodley Head.

Jenny Grace FYSON. *The Three Brothers of Ur.* Oxford U. P.

C. Walter HODGES. *The Namesake.* Bell.

K. M. PEYTON. *The Maplin Bird.* Oxford U. P.

1965 Philip TURNER. *The Grange at High Force.* Oxford U. P.

Commended
Alan GARNER. *Elidor.* Collins.

Jenny GRACE. *The Journey of the Eldest Son.* Oxford U. P.

Mary K. HARRIS. *The Bus Girls.* Faber.

C. HEADINGTON. *The Orchestra and its Instruments.* Bodley Head.

K. M. PEYTON. *The Plan for Birdmarsh.* Oxford U. P.

Barbara Leonie PICARD. *One is One.* Oxford U. P.

1966 Award withheld as no book considered suitable.

Highly Commended
Norman DENNY & Josephine FILMER-SANKEY. *The Bayeux Tapestry: The Story of the Norman Conquest 1066.* Collins.

Commended
Helen GRIFFITHS. *The Wild Horse of Santander.* Hutchinson.

K. M. PEYTON. *Thunder in the Sky.* Oxford U. P.

Morna STUART. *Marassa and Midnight.* Heinemann.

1967 Alan GARNER. *The Owl Service.* Collins.

Highly Commended
Henry TREECE. *The Dream Time.* Brockhampton.

Commended
Helen CRESSWELL. *The Piemakers.* Faber.

Leon GARFIELD. *Smith.* Constable.

K. M. PEYTON. *Flambards.* Oxford U. P.

1968 Rosemary HARRIS. *The Moon in the Cloud.* Faber.

Commended
Joan AIKEN. *The Whispering Mountain.* Cape.

Margaret BALDERSON. *When Jays Fly to Barbmo.* Oxford U. P.

Leon GARFIELD. *Black Jack.* Longman.

1969 K. M. PEYTON. *The Edge of the Cloud.* Oxford U. P.

Commended
Helen CRESSWELL. *The Nightwatchmen.* Faber.

K. M. PEYTON. *Flambards in Summer.* Oxford U. P.

John Rowe TOWNSEND. *The Intruder.* Oxford U. P.

1970 Leon GARFIELD & Edward BLISHEN. *The God Beneath the Sea.* Longman.

Commended
Peter DICKINSON. *The Devil's Children.* Gollancz.

Leon GARFIELD. *The Drummer Boy.* Longman.

William MAYNE. *Ravensgill.* Hamish Hamilton.

1971 Ivan SOUTHALL. *Josh.* Angus & Robertson.

Commended
Gillian AVERY. *A Likely Lad.* Collins.

Helen CRESSWELL. *Up the Pier.* Faber.

Rosemary SUTCLIFF. *Tristan and Iseult.* Bodley Head.

1972 Richard ADAMS. *Watership Down.* Rex Collings.

Commended
Peter DICKINSON. *The Dancing Bear.* Gollancz.

Emma SMITH. *No Way of Telling.* Bodley Head.

1973 Penelope LIVELY. *The Ghost of Thomas Kempe.* Heinemann.

Commended
Nina BAWDEN. *Carrie's War.* Gollancz.

Susan COOPER. *The Dark is Rising.* Chatto & Windus.

Helen CRESSWELL. *The Bongleweed.* Faber.

1974 Mollie HUNTER. *The Stronghold.* Hamish Hamilton.

Highly Commended
Ian RIBBONS. *Battle of Gettysburg, 1-3 July 1863.* Oxford U. P.

Commended
Winifred CAWLEY. *Gran at Coalgate.* Oxford U. P.

Jill Paton WALSH. *The Emperor's Winding Sheet.* Macmillan.

1975 Robert WESTALL. *The Machine-Gunners.* Macmillan.

Commended
Susan COOPER. *The Grey King*. Chatto & Windus.

Diana Wynne JONES. *Dogsbody*. Macmillan.

1976 Jan MARK. *Thunder and Lightnings*. Kestrel.

Commended
Peter DICKINSON. *The Blue Hawk*. Gollancz.

1977 Gene KEMP. *The Turbulent Term of Tyke Tyler*. Faber.

Commended
Peter CARTER. *Under Goliath*. Oxford U. P.

Diana Wynne JONES. *A Charmed Life*. Macmillan.

Philippa PEARCE. *The Shadow-Cage and Other Tales of the Supernatural*. Kestrel.

1978 David REES. *The Exeter Blitz*. Hamish Hamilton.

Commended
Bernard ASHLEY. *A Kind of Wild Justice*. Oxford U. P.

Philippa PEARCE. *The Battle of Bubble and Squeak*. Deutsch.

Robert WESTALL. *Devil on the Road*. Macmillan.

1979 Peter DICKINSON. *Tulku*. Gollancz.

Highly Commended
Sheila SANCHA. *The Castle Story*. Kestrel.

Commended
Eva IBBOTSON. *Which Witch?* Macmillan.

Ann SCHLEE. *The Vandal*. Macmillan.

1980 Peter DICKINSON. *City of Gold, and Other Stories from the Old Testament*. Gollancz.

Highly Commended
Jan MARK. *Nothing to be Afraid of*. Kestrel.

Commended
John BRANFIELD. *The Fox in Winter*. Gollancz.

Jan NEEDLE. *A Sense of Shame, and Other Stories*. Deutsch.

1981 Robert WESTALL. *The Scarecrows.* Chatto & Windus.

Highly Commended
Jane GARDAM. *The Hollow Land.* Julia MacRae.

Commended
Jane GARDAM. *Bridget and William.* Julia MacRae.

Michelle MAGORIAN. *Goodnight Mr Tom.* Kestrel.

1982 Margaret MAHY. *The Haunting.* Dent.

Highly Commended
Gillian CROSS. *The Dark Behind the Curtain.* Oxford U. P.

Commended
Tim KENNEMORE. *Wall of Words.* Faber.

1983 Jan MARK. *Handles.* Kestrel.

Highly Commended
James WATSON. *Talking in Whispers.* Gollancz.

Commended
Philippa PEARCE. *The Way to Sattin Shore.* Kestrel.

Patricia WRIGHTSON. *A Little Fear.* Hutchinson.

1984 Margaret MAHY. *The Changeover.* Dent.

Highly Commended
Robert SWINDELLS. *Brother in the Land.* Oxford U. P.

1985 Kevin CROSSLEY-HOLLAND. *Storm.* Heinemann.

Highly Commended
Janni HOWKER. *The Nature of the Beast.* Julia MacRae.

1986 Berlie DOHERTY. *Granny was a Buffer Girl.* Methuen.

Highly Commended
Janni HOWKER. *Isaac Campion.* Julia MacRae.

Commended
Bernard ASHLEY. *Running Scared.* Julia MacRae.

Gillian CROSS. *Chartbreak.* Oxford U. P.

Andrew TAYLOR. *The Coal House.* Collins.

1987 Susan PRICE. *The Ghost Drum.* Faber.

Highly Commended
Margaret MAHY. *Memory.* Dent.

Commended
Eileen DUNLOP. *The House on the Hill.* Oxford U. P.

Monica FURLONG. *Wise Child.* Gollancz.

Michael MORPURGO. *King of the Cloud Forests.* Heinemann.

1988 Geraldine McCAUGHREAN. *A Pack of Lies.* Oxford U. P.

Highly Commended
Gillian CROSS. *A Map of Nowhere.* Oxford U. P.

Peter DICKINSON. *Eva.* Gollancz.

Elizabeth LAIRD. *Red Sky in the Morning.* Heinemann.

Commended
Vivian ALCOCK. *The Monster Garden.* Methuen.

Judy ALLEN. *Awaiting Developments.* Julia MacRae.

Diana Wynne JONES. *The Lives of Christopher Chant.* Methuen.

1989 Anne FINE. *Goggle-Eyes.* Hamish Hamilton.

Highly Commended
Anne FINE. *Bill's New Frock.* Methuen.

Carole LLOYD. *The Charlie Barber Treatment.* Walker Books.

Commended
Vivian ALCOCK. *The Trial of Anna Cotman.* Methuen.

1990 Gillian CROSS. *Wolf.* Oxford U. P.

Highly Commended
Melvin BURGESS. *Cry of the Wolf.* Andersen Press.

Robert WESTALL. *The Kingdom by the Sea.* Methuen.

Commended
Theresa TOMLINSON. *Riding the Waves.* Julia MacRae.

1991 Berlie DOHERTY. *Dear Nobody.* Hamish Hamilton.

Highly Commended
Jacqueline WILSON. *The Story of Tracy Beaker.* Doubleday.

Commended
Annie DALTON. *The Real Tilly Beany.* Methuen.

Garry KILWORTH. *The Drowners.* Methuen.

1992 Anne FINE. *Flour Babies.* Hamish Hamilton.

Highly Commended
Robert WESTALL. *Gulf.* Methuen.

Commended
Gillian CROSS. *The Great Elephant Chase.* Oxford U. P.

Peter DICKINSON. *A Bone from a Dry Sea.* Gollancz.

1993 Robert SWINDELLS. *Stone Cold.* Hamish Hamilton.

Highly Commended
Melvin BURGESS. *The Baby and Fly Pie.* Andersen Press.

Jenny NIMMO. *The Stone Mouse.* Walker Books.

Commended
Anne MERRICK. *Someone Came Knocking.* Spindlewood.

1994 Theresa BRESLIN. *Whispers in the Graveyard.* Methuen.

Highly Commended
Berlie DOHERTY. *Willa and Old Miss Annie.* Walker Books.

Lesley HOWARTH. *Maphead.* Walker Books.

1995 Philip PULLMAN. *Northern Lights. His Dark Materials: Book 1.* [published in US as *The Golden Compass*]. Scholastic.

Highly Commended
Jacqueline WILSON. *Double Act.* Doubleday.

Commended
Susan GATES. *Raider.* Oxford U. P.

1996 Melvin BURGESS. *Junk.* Andersen Press

Highly Commended
Anne FINE. *The Tulip Touch.* Hamish Hamilton.

Terry PRATCHETT. *Johnny & the Bomb.* Doubleday.

1997 Tim BOWLER. *River Boy*. Oxford University Press.

Highly Commended
Henrietta BRANFORD, *Fire, Bed and Bone*. Walker Books.

Commended
J. K. ROWLING, *Harry Potter and the Philosopher's Stone*. Bloomsbury.

1998 David ALMOND. *Skellig*. Hodder Children's Books.

Commended
Chris D'LACEY. *Fly, Cherokee, Fly*. Doubleday.

1999 Aidan CHAMBERS, *Postcards From No Man's Land*. Bodley Head.

Highly Commended
David ALMOND. *Kit's Wilderness*. Hodder Children's Books.

Jacqueline WILSON. *The Illustrated Mum*. Doubleday.

Commended
Jenny NIMMO. *The Rinaldi Ring*. Mammoth.

2000 Beverley NAIDOO, *The Other Side of Truth*. Puffin.

Highly Commended
Adele GERAS. *Troy*. David Fickling Books/Scholastic.

Philip PULLMAN. *The Amber Spyglass*. David Fickling Books/Scholastic.

Commended
Melvin BURGESS. *The Ghost Behind the Wall*. Andersen Press.

2001 Terry PRATCHETT, *The Amazing Maurice and his Educated Rodents*. Doubleday.

Highly Commended
Geraldine McCAUGHREAN. *Stop the Train*. Oxford U.P.

Commended
Sharon CREECH, *Love That Dog*. Bloomsbury Children's Books.

2002 Sharon CREECH, *Ruby Holler*. Bloomsbury Children's Books.

Highly Commended
Anne FINE. *Up on Cloud Nine*. Doubleday.

2003 Jennifer DONNELLY. *A Gathering Light*. Bloomsbury Children's Books.

No Commendations.

2004 Frank Cottrell BOYCE. *Millions.* Macmillan.

No Commendations.

Chapter 5: The Caldecott Medal (USA)

Awarded each year since 1938 by the American Library Association for 'the most distinguished American Picture Book for Children' published during the preceding year, the Caldecott Medal is named after the English artist and illustrator, Randolph Caldecott (1846-86). Caldecott is still held to be one of the liveliest illustrators of children's books. In terms of technique and talent he was a much better artist than his near contemporary, Kate Greenaway. Despite his short life – he died in Florida a few weeks before his fortieth birthday – Caldecott had gained a reputation as 'Lord of the Nursery' for his sixteen picture books. These were engraved by Edmund Evans, and first published by Routledge in card wrappers, two titles being produced each year from 1878 to 1885, with numerous reprints, both singly and in collections, since. Although he also illustrated stories by other authors, it is by virtue of these small square booklets of poems and nursery rhymes that he can be said to have invented the genre of picture book. As Maurice Sendak puts it in his essay 'Randolph Caldecott' (in *Caldecott & Co.* Farrar, Straus & Giroux. 1988), 'Words are left out – but the picture says it. Pictures are left out – but the word says it.' In this essay Sendak acknowledges the influence which Caldecott's ideas have had on his own work.

The Caldecott Medal was instituted fifteen years after the Newbery, by the same man, Frederic G. Melcher, who had the original inspiration and set up the trust which funds both medals. The specification 'picture book' as opposed to 'illustration' is the main difference between the terms of the Caldecott Medal and its British near-equivalent, the Kate Greenaway Medal. Certainly the description 'picture book' does not entirely preclude non-fiction texts, indeed three of the first four winning titles could be considered 'non-fiction', but it does mean that an information book, or the illustrations for a story for older children, would be less likely to be accepted as meeting the Caldecott criteria. The point is that a picture book is, or should be, a concept complete in itself. This means that anything considered for the Caldecott Medal must have been conceived as an entirety, and have been successful in the attempt to produce something in which text and illustration combine to produce a whole of which either part would be incomplete without the other. In this respect, the Kurt Maschler 'Emil' is closer in concept as a British counterpart to the Caldecott than is the Greenaway. In more recent years awards have been established in the US to recognise new illustrators (the Ezra Jack Keats Award), and picture-book text (the Charlotte Zolotow Award), as discussed in Chapter Eight.

The policy which had begun with the Newbery Medal, of keeping the winning titles in print, was also perpetuated in the setting up of the Caldecott. This means that the books which have won either of these medals have the opportunity to form part of the childhood experience of those unborn at the time of original publication. In a very real sense, the judges of these two awards are responsible for creating children's classics. Some two hundred and fifty titles are listed as winners or honor books for the Caldecott Medal: it would be difficult for many children of the appropriate age to have read, let alone possess, even the sixty or so winning titles. But this is to miss the point. The range of titles kept in print ensures that a book which speaks to a particular child will be available, and not every child would, or should, be moved by the same thing.

Considering the cost of colour printing at the time, a surprising number of the early winners contained coloured illustrations. Of the first five winners, four were black (or brown) and white, but the next five winning titles were all in colour. The year that Robert McCloskey's *Make way for Ducklings* won (1942), its lively and expressive brown and white line drawings beat into the Honor list the colour work of Holling C. Holling's *Paddle to the Sea.* Both books in their different ways celebrated the American way of life, and in another year, *Paddle to the Sea*, with the breadth of vision shown by its journey against all odds, might have won. However the idea of the Boston policemen stopping the traffic for a duck and her brood obviously produced such echoes of not letting sparrows fall that it was an inevitable winner. These two books have kept their magic and their appeal to children for over fifty years.

The 1940s lists included prayers, songbooks and biographies, as well as the original stories and retellings of folk tales and bible stories, which might be the more expected fare. By the 1950s, the cartoon-like pictures of 'Dr Seuss' (Theodore Seuss Geisel) were being recognised by their regular inclusion in Honors lists (1948 for *McElligot's Pool*; 1950 for *Bartholomew and the Oobleck*; 1951 for *If I ran the Zoo*). Geisel never won the Caldecott; it looks as if he 'fell out of favour'. Perhaps he became too predictable in his zaniness, but many American children, and not a few English ones, learned to read with his *Cat in the Hat* and others in the 'Beginning Readers' series. Geisel's work cannot aspire to be beautiful, but has tremendous appeal by virtue of its very ugliness Children laugh when they see his creatures, both at their names and their appearance. They quite enjoy the fact that the adult reading to or with them has no more idea than they do what an Oobleck, or a Grinch, or a Lox, might be. Seuss/Giesel has pictured it for them – a strange creature, probably standing on two legs, with animal-like feet and human-like hands. Its face will be a cross between a baby animal and a cartoon child, and it will be grinning directly out of the page. This immediate inclusion of the reader into the book must be what has gained the Dr Seuss books such a following. This is not to say that beauty is always present in the Caldecott winners, nor indeed that it is an overriding criterion. Some of the winning illustrators have produced work which can only be described in that way; others display a more earthy charm.

In the 1950s and early 1960s the emphasis was still on the safety of home and family. The families were not necessarily typically 'American'. As well as prairie and small-town families, many were reminiscences of the author's or artist's European or Mexican childhood, or drawing on the myriad traditions brought from the countries whose emigrants make up the American people.

Maurice Sendak's portrayal of Else Minarik's *Little Bear* continued the home and family trend. The book which eventually won Sendak the Caldecott in

1964, however, was his own story *Where the Wild Things Are.* This book occasioned puzzled reviews in the UK, indeed it was considered far too frightening for children, and many of the UK reviewers could not understand why it had won an award in the US. But by 1964 it was beginning to be recognised, at least in the US, that children must confront their monsters, and master them, and then they can more confidently return to 'where someone loved [them] best of all'. Sendak's story acknowledges above all that parents do not stop loving you when you become 'a wild thing', even though your behaviour might annoy and upset them, and that when you return to being human again, supper will be waiting, and 'still hot'. The rich subtle colours of the artwork, particularly the three wordless double spreads of the 'wild rumpus', bring out the theme. The 'wild things' themselves are prefigured by a drawing 'by MAX' shown on the wall of his house in the second picture. This confirms that they are creatures of Max's own imagination, and thus that he will be able to be their 'king'.

Also during the 1960s came recognition for realistic representations of black life in the city. Ezra Jack Keats shows real children, not anthropomorphised animals, and city streets rather than fields and woods. His name has now been given to an award for new picture book illustrators, discussed in Chapter 8. Keats's *The Snowy Day* (1963 medallist) along with others in the series (*Goggles* was a Honor Book in 1970), use bright blocks of colour to convey buildings and sidewalks, with minimal line to allow facial expressions and clothing details. By the early 1970s the influences from the African American heritage were being recognised as important contributions to the childhood reading of all American children, not only those from whose cultural background they were drawn. These included Anansi stories and other folk tales such as Gerald McDermott's *Anansi the Spider*, (Honor Book 1973), Gail E Haley's *A Story, A Story* (1975 medallist) and Leo and Diane Dillon's *Why Mosquitoes Buzz in People's Ears* (1976 medal-winners). There were also Swahili alphabet and counting books from Tom and Muriel Feelings: *Moja Means One* (Honor Book 1972) and *Jambo Means Hello* (the only Honor Book in 1975).

Arnold Lobel (1972 Honor Book), Tomie dePaola (1976 Honor Book) and Uri Shulevitz (1969 medallist & 1980 Honor Book) also represented the European heritage during these years. Nor were the Native American or the Jewish heritages ignored. The 1975 winner was a 'Pueblo Indian Tale', Gerald McDermott's *Arrow to the Sun.* The 1977 Honor Books included Beverly McDermott's *The Golem*, and Peter Parnall and Byrd Baylor's *Hawk, I'm Your Brother.* Alongside these were the usual retellings of Perrault and Grimm, and a wealth of original stories. There was non-fiction, too. David Macaulay's *Cathedral* (Honor Book 1974), and *Castle* (Honor Book 1978) were finely detailed expositions of these buildings, with interiors, exteriors, cutaway drawings and clear explanations and diagrams of construction methods. By the 1980s Alice and Martin Provensen's illustrations ensured the Newbery-winning *A Visit to William Blake's Inn* a place in the Caldecott Honor list for 1982, and *The Glorious Flight*, telling how Louis Blériot flew across the English Channel, won them the medal in 1984.

The late 1980s and early 1990s saw new names as well as old favourites. Chris van Allsburg, whose first picture book was a 1980 Honor Book, won the 1986 medal with *Polar Express.* David Macaulay, with a change of style from his non-fiction Honor Books, won the 1991 medal with *Black and White*. In 1993, the humorous *The Stinky Cheese Man*, by Lane Smith, a picture book for children old enough to appreciate parody, shared the Honor listing with the 1990 medallist, Ed Young's *Seven Blind Mice* and a non-fiction title *Working Cotton*, by Carole Byard. The 1994 awards again gave prominence to non-fiction with the winning title *Grandfather's Journey* illustrated by Allen Say, and to folklore with the Honor Book *Raven*, illustrated by Gerald McDermott, along with the more traditional picture books for younger children. The 1995 list included a tall tale from pioneer days (Paul Zelinsky's *Swamp Angel*), another tall tale retold (Jerry Pinkney's *John Henry*), and *Time Flies*, all supporting David Diaz's winning *Smoky Night.*

In 1996 one of the Honor Books, Brian Pinkney's *The Faithful Friend* was also on the Honor list for the Coretta Scott King Illustrator Award, underlining the way that an outstanding book may make an impression on more than one award jury. The winning title in 1996, Peggy Rathmann's *Officer Buckle and Gloria* is a children's picture story book in the more conventional sense.

The 1997 winner, David Wisniewski's *Golem* takes a sixteenth-century tale of a golem, the creature of clay from Jewish folklore, and illustrates it with sharp-edged paper collage. Among the Honor Books, Peter Sís's *Starry Messenger* uses script and paintings to show not only events from Galileo's life, but a continuing sense of wonder at the night sky. David Pelletier's *Graphic Alphabet* uses the letters as starting-off points for ideas, and with its computer-generated images is of interest as much to students of graphic design as it is to children. When Honor lists include books such as this, in which there is more to see than the immediately obvious, the richness of the variety available to children is clearly indicated. This inclusion recognises the fact that 'picture books' are not just for the very young.

Paul O. Zelinsky won the medal in 1998 with *Rapunzel*, another folk retelling, and the Honor Books included *Harlem*, by the father-and-son team of Christopher (illustrator) and Walter Dean (writer) Myers, and the first appearance in the list of Simms Taback, who would go on to win the medal in 2000.

The 1999 winner, Mary Azarian, brought wonder to the biography of a scientist, *Snowflake Bentley*, with text by Jacqueline Briggs Martin, and Honor Books included another biography, Brian Pinkney's *Duke Ellington: The Piano Prince and the Orchestra*, as well as another of Peter Sís's beautifully realised creations, *Tibet Through the Red Box*. Peter Sís brings a thoughtfulness and depth to picture books, emphasising the trend towards picture books being not only for small children or beginning readers, but works that an older child or adult can find meaning, information or beauty within their pages.

Apart from the award-winner, relative newcomer Simms Taback, who was himself on the Honor list in 1998, the 2000 list contained names who had all appeared in previous years; Pinkney and Hyman three times each, Wiesner (who would go on to win in 2002 with *The Three Pigs*) and Bang twice each. In 2001 David Small's *So You Want to Be President?* took the medal, with Doreen Cronin's hilarious tale of farm animals going on strike, *Click, Clack, Moo: Cows that Type*, a worthy Honor Book. Marc Simont, who appeared twice in the 1950s, once as an Honor, once as Medallist, returned with *The Stray Dog* in the Honor Books of 2002. Jerry Pinkney was again among the Honors in 2003, the Medal going to Eric Rohmann's *My Friend Rabbit*, a winner aimed at younger children.

In 2004 Mordicai Gerstein's *The Man Who Walked Between the Towers* commemorates the thirtieth anniversary of the tightrope walk (in 1974) by Philippe Petit between the twin towers of the World Trade Center, as well as being a tribute to the memory of the towers themselves and the people who lost their lives on 9/11. A real feeling of the height – and the potential drop! – of those towers is conveyed here. Mo Willems's persistent pigeon (*Don't Let the Pigeon Drive the Bus*), Margaret Chodos-Irvine's *Ella Sarah Gets Dressed* and Steve Jenkins and Robin Page's *What Do You Do with a Tail Like This?* complete the Honor list.

As it approaches its 70th year, the Caldecott continues to celebrate the range of titles produced in picture-book form, for small children and older readers alike.

Caldecott Medal: complete list of winners and honor books

1938 Dorothy P. LATHROP. *Animals of the Bible*, text selected from the King James Bible by Helen Dean FISH. Stokes.

Honor Books
Boris ARTZYBASHEFF. *Seven Simeons: a Russian Tale*. Viking.

Robert LAWSON. *Four and Twenty Blackbirds*, compiled by Helen Dean FISH. Stokes.

1939 Thomas HANDFORTH. *Mei Li*. Doubleday.

Honor Books
Laura Adams ARMER. *The Forest Pool*. Longmans.

James DAUGHERTY. *Andy and the Lion*. Viking.

Wanda GÁG. *Snow White and the Seven Dwarfs*. Coward-McCann.

Robert LAWSON. *Wee Gillis*, text by Munro LEAF. Viking.

Clare Turlay NEWBERRY. *Barkis*. Harper.

1940 Ingri & Edgar d'AULAIRE. *Abraham Lincoln*. Doubleday, Doran & Company, Inc.

Honor Books
Ludwig BEMELMANS. *Madeline*. Viking.

Lauren FORD. *The Ageless Story*. Dodd Mead.

Berta & Elmer HADER. *Cock-a-doodle Doo*. Macmillan.

1941 Robert LAWSON. *They Were Strong and Good*. The Viking Press.

Honor Book
Clare Turlay NEWBERRY. *April's Kittens*. Harper.

1942 Robert McCLOSKEY. *Make Way for Ducklings*. The Viking Press.

Honor Books
Wanda GÁG. *Nothing at All*. Coward-McCann.

Velino HERRERA. *In My Mother's House*, text by Ann Nolan CLARK. Viking.

Holling C. HOLLING. *Paddle-to-the-Sea*. Houghton Mifflin.

Maud & Miska PETERSHAM. *An American ABC*. Macmillan.

1943 Virginia Lee BURTON. *The Little House*. Houghton Mifflin.

Honor Books
Mary & Conrad BUFF. *Dash and Dart*. Viking.

Clare Turlay NEWBERRY. *Marshmallow*. Harper.

1944 Louis SLOBODKIN. *Many Moons*, text by James THURBER. Harcourt.

Honor Books
Arnold E. BARE. *Pierre Pigeon*, text by Lee KINGMAN. Houghton Mifflin.

Plato CHAN. *Good-Luck Horse*, text by Chih-Yi CHAN. Whittlesey.

Jean CHARLOT. *A Child's Good Night Book*, text by Margaret Wise BROWN. W. R. Scott.

Berta & Elmer HADER. *The Mighty Hunter*. Macmillan.

Elizabeth Orton JONES. *Small Rain: Verses from the Bible*, text selected by Jessie Orton JONES. Viking.

1945 Elizabeth Orton JONES. *Prayer for a Child*, text by Rachel FIELD. Macmillan.

Honor Books
Marguerite de ANGELI. *Yonie Wondernose*. Doubleday.

Marie Hall ETS. *In the Forest*. Viking.

Kate SEREDY. *The Christmas Anna Angel*, text by Ruth SAWYER. Viking.

Tasha TUDOR. *Mother Goose*. Walck.

1946 Maud & Miska PETERSHAM. *The Rooster Crows*. Macmillan.

Honor Books
Ruth Chrisman GANNETT. *My Mother Is the Most Beautiful Woman in the World*, text by Becky REYHER. Lothrop.

Marjorie TORREY. *Sing Mother Goose*, music by Opal WHEELER. Dutton.

Leonard WEISGARD. *Little Lost Lamb*, text by Golden MacDONALD, *pseud.* (Margaret Wise BROWN). Doubleday.

Kurt WIESE. *You Can Write Chinese*. Viking.

1947 Leonard WEISGARD. *The Little Island*, text by Golden MacDONALD, *pseud.* (Margaret Wise BROWN). Doubleday.

Honor Books
Jay Hyde BARNUM. *Boats on the River*, text by Marjorie FLACK. Viking.

Tony PALAZZO. *Timothy Turtle*, text by Al GRAHAM. Robert Welch.

Leo POLITI. *Pedro, the Angel of Olvera Street.* Scribner.

Marjorie TORREY. *Sing in Praise: A Collection of the Best Loved Hymns*, stories of hymns and musical arrangements by Opal WHEELER. Dutton.

Leonard WEISGARD. *Rain Drop Splash*, text by Alvin TRESSELT. Lothrop.

1948 Roger DUVOISIN. *White Snow, Bright Snow*, text by Alwin TRESSELT. Lothrop.

Honor Books
Marcia BROWN. *Stone Soup.* Scribner.

Virginia Lee BURTON. *Song of Robin Hood*, text by Anne MALCOLMSON. Houghton Mifflin.

Georges SCHREIBER. *Bambino the Clown.* Viking.

Dr. SEUSS, *pseud.* (Theodore Seuss GEISEL). *McElligot's Pool.* Random House.

Hildegard WOODWARD. *Roger and the Fox*, text by Lavinia R. DAVIS. Doubleday.

1949 Berta & Elmer HADER. *The Big Snow.* Macmillan.

Honor Books
Robert McCLOSKEY. *Blueberries for Sal.* Viking.

Leo POLITI. *Juanita.* Scribner.

Helen STONE. *All Around the Town*, text by Phyllis McGINLEY. Lippincott.

Kurt WIESE. *Fish in the Air.* Viking.

1950 Leo POLITI. *Song of the Swallows.* Scribner.

Honor Books
Marcia BROWN. *Henry Fisherman.* Scribner.

Dr. SEUSS, *pseud.* (Theodore Seuss GEISEL). *Bartholomew and the Oobleck.* Random House.

Marc SIMONT. *The Happy Day*, text by Ruth KRAUSS. Harper.

Lynd WARD. *America's Ethan Allen*, text by Stewart HOLBROOK. Houghton Mifflin.

Hildegard WOODWARD. *The Wild Birthday Cake*, text by Lavinia R. DAVIS. Doubleday.

1951 Katherine MILHOUS. *The Egg Tree.* Scribner.

Honor Books
Marcia BROWN. *Dick Whittington and His Cat.* Scribner.

Claire Turlay NEWBERRY. *T-Bone, the Baby Sitter.* Harper.

NICOLAS, *pseud.* (Nicolas MORDVINOFF). *The Two Reds*, text by WILL, *pseud.* (Will LIPKIND). Harcourt Brace.

Dr. SEUSS, *pseud.* (Theodore Seuss GEISEL). *If I Ran the Zoo.* Random House.

Helen STONE. *The Most Wonderful Doll in the World*, text by Phyllis McGINLEY. Lippincott.

1952 NICOLAS, *pseud.* (Nicolas MORDVINOFF). *Finders Keepers*, text by WILL, *pseud.* (Will LIPKIND). Harcourt Brace.

Honor Books
Marcia BROWN. *Skipper John's Cook.* Scribner.

Marie Hall ETS. *Mr. T. W. Anthony Woo.* Viking.

Margaret Bloy GRAHAM. *All Falling Down*, text by Gene ZION. Harper.

Elizabeth OLDS. *Feather Mountain.* Houghton Mifflin.

William PÈNE DU BOIS. *Bear Party.* Viking.

1953 Lynd WARD. *The Biggest Bear.* Houghton Mifflin.

Honor Books
Marcia BROWN. *Puss in Boots*, text by Charles PERRAULT. Scribner.

Fritz EICHENBERG. *Ape in a Cape: An Alphabet of Odd Animals.* Harcourt.

Margaret Bloy GRAHAM. *The Storm Book*, text by Charlotte ZOLOTOW. Harper.

Juliet KEPES. *Five Little Monkeys.* Houghton Mifflin.

Robert McCLOSKEY. *One Morning in Maine.* Viking.

1954 Ludwig BEMELMANS. *Madeline' s Rescue.* Viking.

Honor Books
A. BIRNBAUM. *Green Eyes.* Capitol.

Marcia BROWN. *The Steadfast Tin Soldier*, text by Hans ANDERSEN. Scribner.

Jean CHARLOT. *When Will the World Be Mine?*, text by Miriam SCHLEIN. W. R. Scott.

Robert McCLOSKEY. *Journey Cake, Ho!*, text by Ruth SAWYER. Viking.

Maurice SENDAK. *A Very Special House*, text by Ruth KRAUSS. Harper.

1955 Marcia BROWN. *Cinderella, or the Little Glass Slipper*, text by Charles PERRAULT. Scribner.

Honor Books
Marguerite de ANGELI. *Book of Nursery and Mother Goose Rhymes.* Doubleday.

Tibor GERGELY. *Wheel on the Chimney*, text by Margaret Wise BROWN. Lippincott.

Helen SEWELL. *The Thanksgiving Story*, text by Alice DALGLIESH. Scribner.

1956 Feodor ROJANKOVSKY. *Frog Went A-Courtin'*, text by John LANGSTAFF. Harcourt Brace.

Honor Books
Marie Hall ETS. *Play With Me.* Viking.

Taro YASHIMA. *Crow Boy.* Viking.

1957 Marc SIMONT. *A Tree is Nice*, text by Janice May UDRY. Harper.

Honor Books
James DAUGHERTY. *Gillespie and the Guards*, text by Benjamin ELKIN. Viking.

Marie Hall ETS. *Mr. Penny's Race Horse.* Viking.

Paul GALDONE. *Anatole*, text by Eve TITUS. McGraw-Hill.

William PÈNE DU BOIS. *Lion.* Viking.

Tasha TUDOR. *1 is One.* Walck.

1958 Robert McCLOSKEY. *Time of Wonder.* Viking.

Honor Books
Don FREEMAN. *Fly High, Fly Low.* Viking.

Paul GALDONE. *Anatole and the Cat*, text by Eve TITUS. McGraw-Hill.

1959 Barbara COONEY. *Chanticleer and the Fox.* Crowell.

Honor Books
Antonio FRASCONI. *The House that Jack Built: La Maison Que Jacques a Batie.* Harcourt.

Maurice SENDAK. *What Do You Say, Dear?*, text by Sesyle JOSLIN. W. R. Scott.

Taro YASHIMA. *Umbrella.* Viking.

1960 Marie Hall ETS. *Nine Days to Christmas*, text by Marie Hall ETS & Aurora LABASTIDA. Viking.

Honor Books
Adrienne ADAMS. *Houses from the Sea*, text by Alice E. GOUDEY. Scribner.

Maurice SENDAK. *The Moon Jumpers*, text by Janice May UDRY. Harper.

1961 Nicolas SIDJAKOV. *Baboushka and the Three Kings*, text by Ruth ROBBINS. Parnassus.

Honor Book
Leo LIONNI. *Inch by Inch.* Obolensky.

1962 Marcia BROWN. *Once a Mouse.* Scribner.

Honor Books
Adrienne ADAMS. *The Day We Saw the Sun Come Up*, text by Alice E. GOUDEY. Scribner.

Maurice SENDAK. *Little Bear's Visit*, text by Else H. MINARIK. Harper.

Peter SPIER. *The Fox Went Out on a Chilly Nigh:; An Old Song.* Doubleday.

1963 Ezra Jack KEATS. *The Snowy Day.* Viking.

Honor Books
Bernard BRYSIN. *The Sun is a Golden Earring*, text by Natalia M. BELTING. Holt.

Maurice SENDAK. *Mr. Rabbit and the Lovely Present*, text by Charlotte ZOLOTOW. Harper.

1964 Maurice SENDAK. *Where the Wild Things Are.* Harper & Row.

Honor Books
Leo LIONNI. *Swimmy.* Pantheon.

Evaline NESS. *All in the Morning Early*, text by Sorche Nic LEODHAS, *pseud.* (Leclaire ALGER). Holt.

Philip REED. *Mother Goose and Nursery Rhymes.* Atheneum.

1965 Beni MONTRESOR. *May I Bring a Friend?* text by Beatrice Schenk de REGNIERS. Atheneum.

Honor Books
Marvin BILECK. *Rain Makes Applesauce*, text by Julian SCHEER. Holiday House.

Blair LENT. *The Wave*, text by Margaret HODGES. Houghton Mifflin.

Evaline NESS. *A Pocketful of Cricket*, text by Rebecca CAUDILL. Holt.

1966 Nonny HOGROGIAN. *Always Room for One More*, text by Sorche Nic LEODHAS, *pseud.* (Leclaire ALGER). Holt.

Honor Books
Roger DUVOISIN. *Hide and Seek Fog*, text by Alvin TRESSELT. Lothrop.

Marie Hall ETS. *Just Me.* Viking.

Evaline NESS. *Tom Tit Tot.* Scribner.

1967 Evaline NESS. *Sam, Bangs and Moonshine.* Holt.

Honor Book
Ed EMBERLEY. *One Wide River to Cross*, text by Barbara EMBERLEY. Prentice-Hall.

1968 Ed EMBERLEY. *Drummer Hoff*, text by Barbara EMBERLEY. Prentice-Hall.

Honor Books
Leo LIONNI. *Frederick.* Pantheon.

Taro YASHIMA. *Seashore Story.* Viking.

Ed YOUNG. *The Emperor and the Kite*, text by Jane YOLEN.

1969 Uri SHULEVITZ. *The Fool of the World and the Flying Ship*, text by Arthur RANSOME. Farrar.

Honor Book
Blair LENT. *Why the Sun and the Moon Live in the Sky*, text by Elphinstone DAYRELL. Houghton.

1970 William STEIG. *Sylvester and the Magic Pebble.* Windmill.

Honor Books
Ezra Jack KEATS. *Goggles!* Macmillan.

Leo LIONNI. *Alexander and the Wind-Up Mouse.* Pantheon.

Robert Andrew PARKER. *Pop Corn and Ma Goodness*, text by Edna Mitchell PRESTON. Viking.

Brinton TURKLE. *Thy Friend, Obadiah.* Viking.

Margot ZEMACH. *The Judge: An Untrue Tale*, text by Harve ZEMACH. Farrar.

1971 Gail E. HALEY. *A Story – a Story: An African Tale.* Atheneum.

Honor Books
Blair LENT. *The Angry Moon*, text by William SLEATOR. Atlantic.

Arnold LOBEL. *Frog and Toad Are Friends.* Harper.

Maurice SENDAK. *In the Night Kitchen.* Harper.

1972 Nonny HOGROGIAN. *One Fine Day.* Macmillan.

Honor Books
Janina DOMANSKA. *If All the Seas Were One Sea.* Macmillan.

Tom FEELINGS. *Moja Means One: A Swahili Counting Book*, text by Muriel FEELINGS. Dial.

Arnold LOBEL. *Hildilid's Night*, text by Cheli Duran RYAN. Macmillan.

1973 Blair LENT. *The Funny Little Woman*, text by Arlene MOSEL. Dutton.

Honor Books
Tom BAHTI. *When Clay Sings*, text by Byrd BAYLOR. Scribner.

Leonard BASKIN. *Hosie's Alphabet*, text by Hosea, Tobias and Lisa BASKIN. Viking.

Nancy Eckholm BURKERT. *Snow White and the Seven Dwarfs*, text translated from GRIMM by Randall JARRELL. Farrar.

Gerald McDERMOTT. *Anansi the Spider: A Tale from the Ashanti.* Holt.

1974 Margot ZEMACH. *Duffy and the Devil*, text by Harve ZEMACH. Farrar.

Honor Books
Susan JEFFERS. *Three Jovial Huntsmen.* Bradbury.

David MACAULAY. *Cathedral.* Houghton.

1975 Gerald McDERMOTT. *Arrow to the Sun: A Pueblo Indian Tale.* Viking.

Honor Book
Tom FEELINGS. *Jambo Means Hello; a Swahili Alphabet*, text by Muriel FEELINGS. Dial.

1976 Leo & Diane DILLON. *Why Mosquitoes Buzz in People's Ears: a West African Tale*, text by Verna AARDEMA. Dial.

Honor Books
Tomie DE PAOLA. *Strega Nona*. Prentice-Hall.

Peter PARNALL. *The Desert is Theirs*, text by Byrd BAYLOR. Scribner.

1977 Leo & Diane DILLON. *Ashanti to Zulu: African Traditions*, text by Margaret MUSGROVE. Dial.

Honor Books
M. B. GOFFSTEIN. *Fish for Supper*. Dial.

Nonny HOGROGIAN. *The Contest*. Greenwillow.

Beverly Brodsky McDERMOTT. *The Golem; a Jewish Legend*. Lippincott.

Peter PARNALL. *Hawk, I'm Your Brother*, text by Byrd BAYLOR. Scribner.

William STEIG. *The Amazing Bone*. Farrar.

1978 Peter SPIER. *Noah's Ark*. Doubleday.

Honor Books
David MACAULAY. *Castle*. Houghton.

Margot ZEMACH. *It Could Always Be Worse*. Farrar.

1979 Paul GOBLE. *The Girl Who Loved Wild Horses*. Bradbury.

Honor Books
Donald CREWS. *Freight Train*. Greenwillow.

Peter PARNALL. *The Way to Start a Day*, text by Byrd BAYLOR. Scribner.

1980 Barbara COONEY. *Ox Cart Man*, text by Donald HALL. Viking.

Honor Books
Chris van ALLSBURG. *The Garden of Abdul Gasazi*. Houghton.

Rachel ISADORA. *Ben's Trumpet*. Greenwillow.

Uri SHULEVITZ. *The Treasure*. Farrar.

1981 Arnold LOBEL. *Fables*. Harper & Row.

Honor Books
Molly BANG. *The Grey Lady and the Strawberry Snatcher*. Four Winds.

Donald CREWS. *Truck*. Greenwillow.

Joseph LOW. *Mice Twice.* Atheneum/McElderry.

Ilse PLUME. *The Bremen-Town Musicians.* Doubleday.

1982 Chris van ALLSBURG. *Jumanji.* Houghton Mifflin.

Honor Books
Stephen GAMMELL. *Where the Buffaloes Begin*, text by Olaf BAKER. Warne.

Anita LOBEL. *On Market Street*, text by Arnold LOBEL. Greenwillow.

Alice & Martin PROVENSEN. *A Visit to William Blake's Inn: Poems for Innocent and Experienced Travelers*, text by Nancy WILLARD. Harcourt.

Maurice SENDAK. *Outside Over There.* Harper.

1983 Marcia BROWN. *Shadow*, text by Blaise CENDRARS. Scribner.

Honor Books
Diane GOODE. *When I Was Young in the Mountains*, text by Cynthia RYLANT. Dutton.

Vera B. WILLIAMS. *A Chair for My Mother.* Greenwillow.

1984 Alice & Martin PROVENSEN. *The Glorious Flight: Across the Channel with Louis Blériot.* Viking.

Honor Books
Molly BANG. *Ten, Nine, Eight.* Greenwillow.

Trina Schart HYMAN. *Little Red Riding Hood.* Holiday.

1985 Trina Schart HYMAN. *Saint George and the Dragon*, text by Margaret HODGES. Little, Brown.

Honor Books
John STEPTOE. *The Story of Jumping Mouse.* Lothrop.

Nancy TAFURI. *Have You Seen My Duckling?* Greenwillow.

Paul O. ZELINSKY. *Hansel and Gretel*, text by Rika LESSER. Dodd.

1986 Chris van ALLSBURG. *Polar Express.* Houghton Mifflin.

Honor Books
Stephen GAMMELL. *The Relatives Came*, text by Cynthia RYLANT. Bradbury.

Don WOOD. *King Bidgood's in the Bathtub*, text by Audrey WOOD. Harcourt.

1987 Richard EGIELSKI. *Hey, Al!*, text by Arthur YORINKS. Farrar, Straus & Giroux.

Honor Books
Ann GRIFALCONI. *The Village of Round and Square Houses.* Little.

Suse MacDONALD. *Alphabatics.* Bradbury.

Paul O. ZELINSKY. *Rumpelstiltskin.* Dutton.

1988 John SCHOENHERR. *Owl Moon*, text by Jane YOLEN. Philomel.

Honor Book
John STEPTOE. *Mufaro's Beautiful Daughters: An African Tale.* Lothrop.

1989 Stephen GAMMELL. *Song and Dance Man*, text by Karen ACKERMAN. Knopf.

Honor Books
James MARSHALL. *Goldilocks.* Dial.

Jerry PINKNEY. *Mirandy and Brother Wind*, text by Patricia McKISSACK. Knopf.

Allan SAY. *The Boy of the Three-Year Nap*, text by Dianne SNYDER. Houghton.

David WIESNER. *Free Fall.* Lothrop.

1990 Ed YOUNG. *Lon Po Po: A Red Riding Hood Story from China.* Philomel.

Honor Books
Lois EHLERT. *Color Zoo.* Lippincott.

Trina Schart HYMAN. *Hershel and the Hanukkah Goblins*, text by Eric KIMMEL. Holiday House.

Bill PEET. *Bill Peet: An Autobiography.* Houghton.

Jerry PINKNEY. *The Talking Eggs*, text by Robert D. SAN SOUCI. Dial

1991 David MACAULAY. *Black and White.* Houghton Mifflin.

Honor Books
Fred MARCELLINO. *Puss in Boots.* Farrar/Michael di Capua.

Vera B. WILLIAMS. *'More, More, More', Said the Baby: 3 Love Stories.* Greenwillow.

1992 David WIESNER. *Tuesday.* Clarion Books.

Honor Book
Faith RINGGOLD. *Tar Beach.* Crown/Random House.

1993 Emily Arnold McCULLY. *Mirette on the High Wire.* Putnam.

Honor Books
Carole BYARD. *Working Cotton*, text by Sherley Anne WILLIAMS. Harcourt.

Lane SMITH. *The Stinky Cheese Man, and Other Fairly Stupid Tales*, text by Jon SCIESZKA. Viking.

Ed YOUNG. *Seven Blind Mice.* Philomel.

1994 Allen SAY. *Grandfather's Journey*, text edited by Walter LORRAINE. Houghton Mifflin.

Honor Books
Denise FLEMING. *In the Small, Small Pond.* Holt.

Kevin HENKES. *Owen*, text edited by Susan HIRSCHMAN. Greenwillow.

Ted LEWIN. *Peppe the Lamplighter*, text by Elisa BARTONE. Lothrop.

Gerald McDERMOTT. *Raven, a Trickster Tale from the Pacific Northwest.* Harcourt.

Chris RASCHKA. *Yo! Yes?*, text edited by Richard JACKSON. Orchard.

1995 David DIAZ. *Smoky Night*, text by Eve BUNTING. Harcourt.

Honor Books
Jerry PINKNEY. *John Henry*, text by Julius LESSER. Dial.

Eric ROHMANN. *Time Flies.* Crown.

Paul O. ZELINSKY. *Swamp Angel*, text by Anne ISAACS. Dutton.

1996 Peggy RATHMANN. *Officer Buckle and Gloria.* Putnam.

Honor Books
Stephen T. JOHNSON. *Alphabet City.* Viking.

Brian PINKNEY. *The Faithful Friend*, text by Robert D. SAN SOUCI.

Marjorie PRICEMAN. *Zin! Zin! Zin! A Violin*, text by Lloyd MOSS.

Janet STEVENS. *Tops & Bottoms.* Harcourt Brace.

1997 David WISNIEWSKI. *Golem.* Clarion Books.

Honor Books
Holly MEADE. *Hush! A Thai Lullaby*, text by Minfong HO. Kroupa/Orchard.

David PELLETIER. *The Graphic Alphabet*, text edited by Neal PORTER. Orchard.

Dav PILKEY. *The Paperboy*. Jackson/Orchard.

Peter SÍS. *Starry Messenger; Galileo Galilei*. Frances Foster/Farrar Straus Giroux.

1998 Paul O. ZELINSKY. *Rapunzel*. Dutton

Honor Books
Christopher MYERS. *Harlem*, text by Walter Dean MYERS. Scholastic.

David SMALL. *The Gardener*, text by Sarah STEWART. Farrar.

Simms TABACK. *There Was an Old Lady Who Swallowed a Fly*. Viking.

1999 Mary AZARIAN. *Snowflake Bentley*, text by Jacqueline Briggs MARTIN. Houghton.

Honor Books
Brian PINKNEY. *Duke Ellington: The Piano Prince and the Orchestra*, text by Andrea Davis PINKNEY. Hyperion.

David SHANNON. *No, David!* Scholastic.

Uri SHULEVITZ. *Snow*. Farrar.

Peter SÍS. *Tibet Through the Red Box*. Frances Foster.

2000 Simms TABACK. *Joseph Had a Little Overcoat*. Viking.

Honor Books
Molly BANG. *When Sophie Gets Angry – Really, Really Angry*. Scholastic.

Trina Schart HYMAN. *A Child's Calendar*, text by John Updike. Holiday House.

David WIESNER. *Sector 7*. Clarion Books.

Jerry PINKNEY. *The Ugly Duckling*, text by Hans Christian ANDERSEN, adapted by Jerry PINKNEY. Morrow.

2001 David SMALL. *So You Want to Be President?* text by Judith St. GEORGE. Philomel.

Honor Books
Christopher BING. *Casey at the Bat*, text by Ernest THAYER. Handprint.

Ian FALCONER. *Olivia*. Atheneum.

Betsy LEWIN. *Click, Clack, Moo: Cows that Type*, text by Doreen CRONIN. Simon & Schuster.

2002 David WIESNER. *The Three Pigs*. Clarion/Houghton Mifflin.

Honor Books
Bryan COLLIER. *Martin's Big Words: the Life of Dr. Martin Luther King, Jr.*, text by Doreen RAPPAPORT. Jump at the Sun/Hyperion.

Brian SELZNICK. *The Dinosaurs of Waterhouse Hawkins*, text by Barbara KERLEY. Scholastic.

Marc SIMONT. *The Stray Dog*. HarperCollins.

2003 Eric ROHMANN. *My Friend Rabbit*. Roaring Brook Press/Millbrook Press.

Honor Books
Tony DiTERLIZZI. *The Spider and the Fly*, text by Mary HOWITT. Simon & Schuster Books for Young Readers.

Peter McCARTY. *Hondo & Fabian*. Henry Holt & Co.

Jerry PINKNEY. *Noah's Ark*. SeaStar Books, a division of North-South Books Inc.

2004 Mordicai GERSTEIN. *The Man Who Walked Between the Towers*. Roaring Brook Press/Millbrook Press.

Honor Books
Margaret CHODOS-IRVINE. *Ella Sarah Gets Dressed*. Harcourt, Inc.

Steve JENKINS & Robin PAGE. *What Do You Do with a Tail Like This?* Houghton Mifflin.

Mo WILLEMS. *Don't Let the Pigeon Drive the Bus*. Hyperion.

2005 Kevin HENKES. *Kitten's First Full Moon*. Greenwillow.

Honor Books
Barbara LEHMAN. *The Red Book*. Houghton Mifflin.

E. B. LEWIS. *Coming on Home Soon*, text by Jacqueline WOODSON. Putnam.

Mo WILLEMS. *Knuffle Bunny: A Cautionary Tale*. Hyperion.

Chapter 6: The CILIP Kate Greenaway Medal (UK)

Established by the Library Association (now CILIP) in 1955, the Kate Greenaway Medal is awarded to the artist producing 'the most distinguished work in the illustration of children's books' for a book published in the UK in the preceding year. Peters Library Service were sponsors for it, as well as the Carnegie Medal, from 1990 until 1997 and both are administered by the Youth Libraries Group of CILIP. The mechanics of choosing the Greenaway are identical to those for the Carnegie Medal, and are described in Chapter 4.

Kate Greenaway (1846-1901) was an English artist, illustrator and writer of children's verse. Her fame has perhaps lasted the longest of those nineteenth-century people whose names are honoured by children's book awards. The children she drew, clothed in what was even at the time fancy dress, now romp gently in their petticoats and pantaloons across greetings cards and calendars, tea-towels and gift-wrapping paper and the pages of numerous reprints of her picture books.

Other artists and authors may have been more widely-known, both in their lifetimes and in the intervening years; yet others may be more highly regarded in terms of technique, particularly among the current crop of book illustrators, but the quintessentially 'olde English' character of Greenaway's figures, reflecting the Arts and Crafts Movement of the time, and the quality of the printer Edmund Evans, by whom the bulk of her work was reproduced, has ensured her a lasting place in the hearts of the English public. Only Beatrix Potter seems to rival her in reputation. When the Library Association was considering a name for the illustration award which they decided to institute in 1955, therefore, the name of Kate Greenaway must have seemed obvious.

Illustration awards have the potential for as much controversy as those for text. But the press and public seem somehow to be more timid when it comes to criticising the panels' choices for the Greenaway and other awards for illustration. This is perhaps because 'ordinary people' do not pretend to understand art in the same way as they reckon to know about writing. In this field, writing for children, they consider themselves experts since (hard though it may sometimes be to believe) they were all once children themselves. Sometimes there are murmurs when an illustration award goes to a book which is clearly meant for older children, however good the artwork is acknowledged to be, but on the whole, less notice is taken of the choices made. This is usually because the concept of 'picture book' in the public perception is linked with 'little children'. Thus a work such as Libby Hathorn's *Way Home*, illustrated by Gregory Rogers (1994 medal-winner) or even Rosemary Sutcliff's *Black Ships Before Troy*, illustrated by Alan Lee (1993 winner), which are capable of being 'read' at more than one level, evoke a certain puzzled response. Greenaway announcements seldom attract the outright criticism reserved for some of the Carnegie winners, such as *Stone Cold* (Carnegie 1993) or the two Robert Westall winners (Carnegie 1975 & 1981) which are deemed to include matters 'too adult' for the putative child reader – though in the past it has been rare that the Greenaway attract any mainstream publicity at all. In 2000 a bequest from Colin Mears, who had been a keen collector of children's books and toys, provided for a cash prize of £5,000 each year to the Kate Greenaway Medal-winner. As is perhaps inevitable, the introduction of money into the equation brings a measure of press interest, so that there is nowadays more coverage of the Greenaway than heretofore, though still less than that given to the Carnegie.

The major difference between the Greenaway Medal and its American counterpart, the Caldecott Medal, is that the latter specifies 'a picture book' and the Greenaway is for 'illustration'. This is not merely a question of interchangeable terminology. The Greenaway specification allows for the illustration of a work which could not in any way be considered a 'picture book', even for older readers, to win the Medal. Because of this, a book may appear on the lists for both the Carnegie and the Greenaway. A notable example is the 1970 Carnegie winner, *The God beneath the Sea*, by Leon Garfield and Edward Blishen, which was also included in the list of Greenaway Commended titles for Charles Keeping's illustrations. Similarly, Peter Dickinson's *City of Gold*, the 1980 Carnegie winner, was Highly Commended for the Greenaway because of its illustrations by Michael Foreman, and artwork by Victor Ambrus adorns winning and commended titles for both awards. This would not be as likely under US criteria, although the 1982 Newbery winner was also a Caldecott Honor Book. There are disadvantages as well as the obvious advantages to the distinction. Some have said that judging it would be easier if the award were for 'a picture book' – as indeed it might be – but others have appreciated that the illustrations are an integral part of many children's books, whether or not they are conceived as 'picture books' and that this design and illustrative element should be as eligible to receive an award as a picture book *per se*.

The Kate Greenaway Medal was instituted after a special commendation for illustration had been made by the Carnegie judges to Harold Jones in 1954, for *Lavender's Blue*. The list of winners and commended titles has, like the Carnegie list, its share of surprises and predictable choices. Perhaps the first surprise is that in the first year, no award was made. The listings just state 'No Award', or 'Award Withheld', which normally means that no book was considered to be of sufficiently high quality. Was 1955 such a poor year for book illustration in the UK, or were there internal politics at issue? It seems strange to have set up an award because of an especially good piece of illustrative material one year, and then find nothing worthy of receiving it the next. 1958 seems to have had a similar dearth – but were they really such dreadful years? Ernest Shepard, one of the greatest illustrators of the century, had illustrated Eleanor Farjeon's *The Glass Slipper*, which was published by Oxford University Press in 1955. This would surely have been a chance, perhaps the last, to honour Shepard, who never won the Greenaway. Also in 1955 came Oxford's *Welsh Legends and Folk-Tales*, part of a series they published during the 1950s (published by Walck in the US). These were all by different authors and all illustrated by Joan Kiddell-Monroe. Kiddell-Monroe's work is at least as good as that of V. H. Drummond or Gerald Rose, but for some reason she was passed over. In 1958, Margery Gill, another excellent artist, illustrated Esmé Hamilton's *The Heavenly Carthorse*, published by The Bodley Head. Also in 1958 appeared Farjeon's *Then There Were Three*, published by Michael Joseph and illustrated by John and Isobel Morton Sale, whose whimsical line drawings seem to catch the transience of childhood. Admittedly the last-mentioned is a collection of poetry combining three books previously published separately in the 1940s. That had not, however, deterred the judges from giving the 1955 Carnegie medal to Farjeon herself for *The Little Bookroom*, a collection of previously published stories. None of these titles was issued by a minor publisher, so they should have been easily available to the judges during these years. All are excellent books, so what was the problem? It may be that the judges were looking for coloured illustration, and indeed all the early winners were working in colour, whereas the Shepard, Gill and Morton Sales titles quoted were all examples of line illustration. Restrictions can nevertheless produce work which transcends the limitations of printing techniques, as the list of Caldecott winners had shown; Kiddell-Monroe's two-colour work is a particularly good example of this effect. Withholding the award must have been a difficult decision to take. Perhaps it arose from a concern that, particularly in its first year, the award should be seen to set a sufficiently high standard for the years to follow.

These omissions aside, the roll-call of 1950s and 1960s winners of the Kate Greenaway Medal is impressive. Edward Ardizzone, the first to receive a Greenaway Medal for his 1956 *Tim All Alone*, was inevitably destined to be an early winner. His reputation was, and continues to be, of the highest, and he appears again in the 1959 Commended list. Tim, with Ardizzone's other small child heroes and heroines, experiences mildly exciting adventures, but always comes home safely. V. H. Drummond, the 1957 medallist, has a zany style of drawing which to some degree anticipates that of Quentin Blake. Her gentle stories are well complemented by the brightly coloured illustrations, and the 'tall tale' element is intriguing for small children without descending into violence. These early winners reflect the ideal of a safe ordered world which adults in the post-war era tried to make for their children. William Stobbs uses a more immediate and exciting technique. His coloured shapes juxtapose with their backgrounds or are superimposed over other images with no intervening line. These are not drawings but paintings, though elsewhere he uses line, nor are they quite so 'safe'. Stobbs whirls us into the world of legend and folk tale, where everything is larger and more brightly coloured than life.

The 1960s mark something of a return to images of security. Gerald Rose, the 1960 winner, had been on the Commended list in 1959, and his line-and-wash technique shows some similarity to the illustrations of Ardizzone and Drummond. Victor Ambrus's sturdy realistic watercolours were also in the forefront in these years. His enormous output gained him places on the Commended list in 1963 and 1971. His 'work in general' was commended in 1964, as was that of William Papas. Papas also appeared several times on Commended lists during the 1960s, but never managed the medal, whereas Ambrus won it in 1965 and again ten years later. The 'look' of books in the 1950s and early 1960s was epitomised by the work Papas and Ambrus produced for Oxford University Press. This was true not just of picture books:

their illustrative work for children's novels appeared on the Greenaway lists, and may in addition have played some part in the number of Oxford titles which won, or were commended for, the Carnegie Medal. Raymond Briggs' *Mother Goose Treasury*, jolly and robust as it is, shows little of the subversion with which his illustrations for the 1973 winner *Father Christmas*, which he wrote himself, would delight and slightly shock young and old alike. I am not sure whether *Father Christmas* is the first children's book to show an old man sitting on the lavatory, but it certainly caused comment at the time. To show Father Christmas – until then romantically portrayed as genial, gentle and rather fey – as a grumpy old man who hated Christmas was a stroke of imaginative genius. The two *Father Christmas* books, along with *Gentleman Jim*, *When the Wind Blows* and the *Fungus the Bogeyman* books, are of course meant for older children, and are also intended to provoke adults to think. *The Snowman*, Highly Commended in 1978, shows Briggs in gentler mode.

The winners of the late 1960s and 1970s reflect the technical improvements, especially to colour printing, which were increasingly available at reasonable costs. Jan Pienkowski's 1971 winner, *The Kingdom Under the Sea* by Joan Aiken, delighted adults with its detailed silhouettes set against marbled backgrounds of bright and subtle colours. Pienkowski's 1979 winner, *Haunted House*, uses a style nearer to his *Meg and Mog* books, and as a 'moveable', has far more immediate appeal to children. *Haunted House* has the dubious distinction of being the only pop-up or moveable – or 'toy-book' to give it the dismissive epithet which many librarians would use – to win the Greenaway. Up to that time, pop-ups were not considered library fare, perhaps because of their inherent fragility. Even the *Spot* lift the flap books were viewed with considerable doubt. *Haunted House* was produced in a fairly strong paper with sturdy outer boards. This may have brought it before a larger number of librarians, thus enabling its undoubted charm and humour to become apparent to them. Despite its uniqueness as a winner, in terms of its format *Haunted House* was one among many. There was a growing number of moveable and pop-up books coming on to the market in the late 1970s, reflecting the growth of what has become known as paper engineering during that time. More recently the awards to Janet and Allan Ahlberg for *The Jolly Postman* (Commended 1986) and *The Jolly Christmas Postman* (Medallist 1991), with their integral 'envelopes' containing letters from fairy-tale characters, have recognised the fascination that opening flaps holds for small children. The first of these was viewed by some librarians with suspicion, as the 'letters', being separate pieces of card, were susceptible to loss in a library environment.

The incidence of non-fiction among Greenaway winning titles is surprisingly low. Non-fiction is an area for which illustration can make the difference between an intelligible exposition and a confusing mass of information. The criteria allow for its inclusion, whereas Caldecott criteria, with some honourable exceptions, have tended to its exclusion. But of the one hundred and forty or so books which won, or were Commended or Highly Commended for, the Greenaway, only about a dozen titles are non-fiction, that is a 'strike rate' of under ten per cent. C. Walter Hodges (1909-2004), an artist who had been working for many years in children's books, including illustrations for his own historical children's novels, received the Greenaway for *Shakespeare's Theatre* in 1964, the same year that his *The Namesake* was on the Commended list for the Carnegie. Hodges, had a long career, and designed a series of postage stamps for Royal Mail as recently as the 1990s. Pauline Baynes, whose illustrations defined C. S. Lewis's Narnia characters in the 1950s, did not win the Greenaway Medal until 1968, with a non-fiction book, Grant Uden's *A Dictionary of Chivalry*. The layout of *A Dictionary of Chivalry*, with its narrow columns of text, reminiscent of an adult encyclopaedia or dictionary, and wide balancing borders of clear colour or decisive line illustrations, is exemplary. Another non-fiction winner was *Horses in Battle*, one of the two titles with which Victor Ambrus won the 1975 medal, and the most recent was Michael Foreman's autobiographical *War Boy* in 1989 (the sequel, *War Game*, was Commended in 1993). A special commendation was given in 1988 for the team which put together one of Dorling Kindersley's 'Eyewitness' information books, *Bird*, because of the excellence of the integration of text and different types of illustration, including photography.

Most winners and commendations fall within the genre of the picture book as generally understood. Several are alphabets and counting books; there are many retellings of legends and folk tales, including clever reversals of old favourites, such as Helen Oxenbury's *Three Little Wolves and the Big Bad Pig* (story by Eugene Trivizas, Highly Commended for 1993), or Babette Cole's *Prince Cinders*, Commended in 1987. Others show the traditional underdogs fighting back, such as Mary Rayner's *Garth Pig and the Ice Cream Lady* (Commended 1977), one of a series about a family of pigs and their dealings with 'Mrs Wolf', or Helen Oxenbury's *Farmer Duck* (story by Martin Waddell, Highly Commended 1991). Some show subversion in other ways. Anthony Browne's surrealism was worrying to many when his books first began to appear. There was concern that the strange features which were contained in *A Walk in the Park* (1977), including a foot instead of a stone ball on top of a gatepost, would confuse children. But children are more intelligent than they are usually given credit for, and they saw the joke. Browne's books, like those of several Carnegie winners, are not appreciated by every child, but there is a richness of allusion within them. In his *Zoo* (Medallist 1992), it becomes apparent that we are given the viewpoint of the animals watching the humans who are looking at them. This is a conceit which small children love, and it makes their elders stop and think.

Charles Keeping (Medallist 1967, 1981; Highly Commended 1974; Commended 1969, 1970) and Errol Le Cain (Medallist 1984; Commended 1969, 1975, 1978, 1987) are also worthy of particular mention. Both these illustrators died in mid-career: Keeping in 1988 and Le Cain in 1989. They were honoured more than once by the Greenaway judges, their names appearing regularly in the Commended lists as well as their winning years, but one regrets their premature loss to the children's book world. A surprising omission from the list of winners in more recent years, though she has been commended on two occasions, in 1981 and 1990, is Nicola Bayley. Her exquisitely detailed drawings have been matched with top-flight authors such as William Mayne, Russell Hoban, Jan Mark, Antonia Barber and Richard Adams. The titles commended were those written by Mayne and Barber.

The 1980s and especially the 1990s saw a wider range of books being listed for the Greenaway. One of the more notable was the 1994 winner, *Way Home*, about a homeless boy and the cat he finds. Gregory Rogers shows both the stark and the warm elements of Libby Hathorn's story, and uses hands – those of the boy, and the Dürer engraving which the boy has pinned up in his 'home' – to convey a haunting and powerful message. The 1995 winner, P. J. Lynch's *The Christmas Miracle of Jonathan Toomey*, story by Susan Wojciechowski, may be seen by some as a return to honouring a detailed realist style of illustration, but the story is strong, and not an easy subject for a picture book, so is by no means a timid reaction to the controversy of the previous year's choice. Patrick Benson's *The Little Boat*, story by Kathy Henderson, which was Highly Commended, and Quentin Blake's zany and wordless *Clown*, the only Commended title, might both have been winners in another year. Blake is a previous winner, but Benson, a past Mother Goose winner (see Chapter 8), has yet to achieve the Greenaway.

The 1996 winner, Helen Cooper's *The Baby Who Wouldn't Go to Bed*, is for quite small children, probably three-year-olds. Not since 1991 had the winner been aimed at quite such young children, but this is a delightful book. It is reasonable, given that the age range that the Greenaway can cover, according to its criteria, is birth to sixteen, that a small children's book should take its place among the medallists every so often, and the choices for 1998 (Helen Cooper again), 2000 (Lauren Child's *I Will Not Ever Never Eat a Tomato*) and the 2001 Highly Commended title, Jez Alborough's *Fix-it Duck* have kept this flame alive.

P. J. Lynch won again in 1997, with *When Jessie Came Across the Sea*. The story by Amy Hest is a bittersweet tale of European immigration to the USA. Highly commended was Charlotte Voake's *Ginger*, dealing with the death of a loved pet, and Bob Graham, who would win the medal for 2002, for *Queenie the Bantam*.

In 1998 Shirley Hughes returned to the lists, with *The Lion & the Unicorn*, one of two Highly Commended titles; she would win the Medal itself for a second time in 2003 with *Ella's Big Chance*. Helen Cooper won for the second time in 1998 with *Pumpkin Soup*, and the other Highly Commended illustrator was Jane Simmons for *Come On Daisy!*.

1999 saw Helen Oxenbury's sixth appearance in the Greenaway listings and second Medal for her version of *Alice's Adventures in Wonderland*. Here Alice appears as a contemporary child, with untidy fair hair not constrained by the eponymous band, wearing a sleeveless blue sundress, and characters such as the playing-card gardeners have a more robust quality than was allowed them in the Tenniel drawings remembered by many adults. Highly Commended was Lauren Child for *Clarice Bean, That's Me!*. Child would win the medal itself in 2000 with *I Will Not Ever Never Eat a Tomato*. Chris Riddell's second appearance in these lists was in 1999 with his Highly Commended *Castle Diary*. He would be the 2001 medallist for *Pirate Diary*, and had been Commended in the 1994 list for *Something Else*. Commended in 1999 was Kevin Hawkes's *Weslandia*, illustrating a highly imaginative text by Paul Fleischman.

2000 marked Anthony Browne's fourth appearance for the Highly Commended *Willy's Pictures* and Ted Dewan's *Crispin: the Pig Who Had It All* was Commended. The 2001 list was strong on humour, with Riddell's *Pirate Diary* taking the Medal and Alborough's *Fix-it Duck* and Charles Fuge's *Sometimes I Like to Curl Up in a Ball*, with text by Vicki Churchill, the two Highly Commended titles.

Only two titles were listed for 2002; the Medallist Bob Graham with *Jethro Byrde – Fairy Child*, his second appearance in the list, and a single commendation for Lauren Child's *That Pesky Rat*, Child's third listing. 2003 saw *Ella's Big Chance* bring Shirley Hughes a second Greenaway Medal (the first being for *Dogger* in 1977) and her fifth listing. There were no Commendations, as the judges felt the other titles on the shortlist had been of equal quality.

The sponsorship of Peters Booksellers, as seen in the case of the Carnegie Medal, raised public awareness to some small degree, though the announcement is sometimes ignored or minimised, even in the broadsheet newspapers who publicise the Carnegie result. The Colin Mears bequest has helped raise the profile a little, too. The time and thought given to Greenaway Medal decisions are as detailed and thorough as for the Carnegie, as would be expected since they are considered by the same panel of librarians, and the attention now being paid to both Medals by CILIP promises well for the future.

The Kate Greenaway Medal: complete list of winners and commended titles

1955 No Award

1956 Edward ARDIZZONE. *Tim All Alone.* Oxford U. P.

1957 V. H. DRUMMOND. *Mrs. Easter and the Storks.* Faber.

1958 No Award

1959 William STOBBS. *Kashtanka* and *A Bundle of Ballads.* Oxford U. P.

Commended
Edward ARDIZZONE. *Titus in Trouble.* Bodley Head.

Gerald ROSE. *Wuffles goes to Town*, text by Elizabeth ROSE. Faber.

1960 Gerald ROSE. *Old Winkle and the Seagulls*, text by Elizabeth ROSE. Faber.

1961 Antony MAITLAND. *Mrs. Cockle's Cat*, text by Philippa PEARCE. Constable.

1962 Brian WILDSMITH. *A. B. C.* Oxford U. P.

Commended
Carol BARKER. *Achilles the Donkey*, text by H. E. BATES. Dobson.

1963 John BURNINGHAM. *Borka, the Adventures of a Goose with no Feathers.* Cape.

Commended
Victor AMBRUS. *Royal Navy*, text by Peter DAWLISH. Oxford U. P.

Victor AMBRUS. *Time of Trial*, text by Hester BURTON. Oxford U. P.

Brian WILDSMITH. *Lion and the Rat,* a fable of LA FONTAINE. Oxford U. P.

Brian WILDSMITH. *The Oxford Book of Poetry for Children*, compiled by Edward BLISHEN. Oxford U. P.

1964 C. Walter HODGES. *Shakespeare's Theatre.* Oxford U. P.

Commended
Victor AMBRUS & William PAPAS – for work in general

Raymond BRIGGS. *Fe Fi Fo Fum.* Hamish Hamilton.

1965 Victor AMBRUS. *The Three Poor Tailors.* Oxford U. P.

1966 Raymond BRIGGS. *Mother Goose Treasury.* Hamish Hamilton.

Commended
Doreen ROBERTS. *The Story of Saul*, abridged by Elaine MOSS (from Helen WADDELL. *Stories from the Holy Land*). Constable.

1967 Charles KEEPING. *Charley, Charlotte and the Golden Canary.* Oxford U. P.

Commended
William PAPAS. *The Church*, text by Geoffrey MOORHOUSE. Oxford U. P.

William PAPAS. *No Mules.* Oxford U. P.

Brian WILDSMITH. *Birds.* Oxford U. P.

1968 Pauline BAYNES. *Dictionary of Chivalry*, text by Grant UDEN. Longman.

Commended
Gaynor CHAPMAN. *The Luck Child*, based on a story by The Brothers GRIMM. Hamish Hamilton.

Shirley HUGHES. *Flutes and Cymbals: Poetry for the Young*, by Leonard CLARK. Bodley Head.

William PAPAS. *A Letter from India.* Oxford U. P.

William PAPAS. *A Letter from Israel.* Oxford U. P.

William PAPAS. *Taresh the Tea Planter.* Oxford U. P.

1969 Helen OXENBURY. *The Quangle Wangle's Hat*, text by Edward LEAR and *The Dragon of an Ordinary Family*, text by Margaret MAHY. Heinemann.

Commended
Charles KEEPING. *Joseph's Yard.* Oxford U. P.

Errol LE CAIN. *The Cabbage Princess.* Faber.

1970 John BURNINGHAM. *Mr. Gumpy's Outing.* Cape.

Commended
Charles KEEPING. *The God Beneath the Sea*, text by Leon GARFIELD & Edward BLISHEN. Longman.

Jan PIENKOWSKI. *The Golden Bird*, text by Edith BRILL. Dent.

Krystyna TURSKA. *Pegasus.* Hamish Hamilton.

1971 Jan PIENKOWSKI. *The Kingdom Under the Sea, and Other Stories*, text by Joan AIKEN. Jonathan Cape.

Commended
Victor AMBRUS. *The Sultan's Bath*. Oxford U. P.

Brian WILDSMITH. *The Owl and the Woodpecker*. Oxford U. P.

1972 Krystyna TURSKA. *The Woodcutter's Duck*. Hamish Hamilton.

Commended
Carol BARKER. *King Midas and the Golden Touch*. F. Watts.

Pauline BAYNES. *Snail and Caterpillar*. Longman.

Anthony MAITLAND. *The Ghost Downstairs*, text by Leon GARFIELD. Longman.

1973 Raymond BRIGGS. *Father Christmas*. Hamish Hamilton.

Commended
Fiona FRENCH. *King Tree*. Oxford U. P.

Errol LLOYD. *My Brother Sean*, text by Petronilla BREINBERG. Bodley Head.

1974 Pat HUTCHINS. *The Wind Blew*. Bodley Head.

Highly Commended
Charles KEEPING. *Railway Passage*. Oxford U. P.

Commended
Mitsumasa ANNO. *Anno's Alphabet*. Bodley Head

1975 Victor AMBRUS. *Horses in Battle* and *Mishka*. Oxford U. P.

Commended
Shirley HUGHES. *Helpers*. Bodley Head.

Errol LE CAIN. *Thorn Rose*. Faber.

1976 Gail HALEY. *The Post Office Cat*. Bodley Head.

Highly Commended
Graham OAKLEY. *The Church Mice Adrift*. Macmillan.

Maureen ROFFEY. *Tinker, Taylor, Soldier, Sailor*, verse by Bernard LODGE. Bodley Head.

Joanna TROUGHTON. *How the Birds changed their Feathers*. Blackie.

1977 Shirley HUGHES. *Dogger*. Bodley Head.

Commended
Janet AHLBERG. *Burglar Bill*, text by Janet & Allan AHLBERG. Heinemann.

Mary RAYNER. *Garth Pig and the Ice Cream Lady*. Macmillan.

1978 Janet AHLBERG. *Each Peach Pear Plum*, text by Allan AHLBERG. Kestrel.

Highly Commended
Raymond BRIGGS. *The Snowman*. Hamish Hamilton.

Commended
Michael FOREMAN. *Popular Folk Tales from The Brothers Grimm*, newly translated by Brian ALDERSON. Gollancz.

Errol LE CAIN. *Twelve Dancing Princesses*. Faber.

1979 Jan PIENKOWSKI. *Haunted House*. Heinemann.

Highly Commended
Quentin BLAKE. *The Wild Washerwomen*, text by John YEOMAN. Hamish Hamilton.

Commended
Pat HUTCHINS. *One Eyed Jake*. Bodley Head.

1980 Quentin BLAKE. *Mr. Magnolia*. Cape.

Highly Commended
Michael FOREMAN. *City of Gold*, text by Peter DICKINSON. Gollancz.

Commended
Beryl COOK. *Seven Years and a Day*, text by Colette O'HARE. Collins.

Jill MURPHY. *Peace at Last*. Macmillan.

1981 Charles KEEPING. *The Highwayman*. Oxford U. P.

Highly Commended
Jan ORMEROD. *Sunshine*. Viking Kestrel.

Commended
Nicola BAYLEY. *The Patchwork Cat*, text by William MAYNE. Cape.

1982 Michael FOREMAN. *Long Neck and Thunderfoot*. Kestrel. and *Sleeping Beauty and Other Favourite Fairy Tales*, text by Angela CARTER. Gollancz.

Highly Commended
Graham OAKLEY. *The Church Mice in Action*. Macmillan.

Commended
Janet AHLBERG. *The Baby's Catalogue*, text by Allan AHLBERG. Kestrel.

1983 Anthony BROWNE. *Gorilla*. Julia MacRae.

Commended
Molly BANG. *Ten, Nine, Eight*. Julia MacRae.

Michael FOREMAN. *The Saga of Erik the Viking*, text by Terry JONES. Pavilion.

Ron MARIS. *My Book*. Julia MacRae.

1984 Errol LE CAIN. *Hiawatha's Childhood.* Faber.

1985 Juan WIJNGAARD. *Sir Gawain and the Loathly Lady*, retold by Selina HASTINGS. Walker Books.

Commended
Michael FOREMAN. *Seasons of Splendour*, text by Madhur JAFFREY. Pavilion.

Gillian McCLURE. *Tog the Ribber or Granny's Tale*, text by Paul COLTMAN. André Deutsch.

1986 Fiona FRENCH. *Snow White in New York*. Oxford U. P.

Highly Commended
Jan ORMEROD. *Happy Christmas Gemma*. Walker Books.

Commended
Janet AHLBERG. *The Jolly Postman*, text by Allan AHLBERG. Heinemann.

Paddy BOUMA. *Are We Nearly There*? text by Louis BAUM. Bodley Head.

Babette COLE. *Princess Smartypants*. Hamilton.

Fiona PRAGOFF. *How Many? From 0 to 20*. Gollancz.

Tony ROSS. *I Want My Potty*. Andersen Press.

1987 Adrienne KENNAWAY. *Crafty Chameleon*. Hodder.

Commended
Babette COLE. *Prince Cinders*. Hamish Hamilton.

Errol LE CAIN. *The Enchanter's Daughter*, text by Antonia BARBER. Cape.

Jill MURPHY. *All in One Piece*. Walker Books.

1988 Barbara FIRTH. *Can't You Sleep, Little Bear?* text by Martin WADDELL. Walker Books.

Highly Commended
Anthony BROWNE. *Alice's Adventures in Wonderland*, text by Lewis CARROLL. Julia MacRae.

Roberto INNOCENTI. *The Adventures of Pinocchio*, text by Carlo COLLODI. Cape.

Alan LEE. *Merlin Dreams*, text by Peter DICKINSON. Gollancz.

Commended
Ruth BROWN. *Ladybird, Ladybird.* Andersen Press.

Penny DALE. *Wake Up Mr B.* Walker Books.

Special Commendation
To the team of designers, photographers and illustrators responsible for *Bird*, written by David BURNIE, a Dorling Kindersley Eyewitness Guide.

1989 Michael FOREMAN. *War Boy.* Pavilion.

Highly Commended
Helen OXENBURY. *We're Going on a Bear Hunt*, text by Michael ROSEN. Walker Books.

1990 Gary BLYTHE. *The Whale's Song.* Hutchinson.

Highly Commended
Tony ROSS. *Dr. Xargle's Book of Earth Tiggers*, translated into human by Jeanne WILLIS. Andersen Press.

Commended
Nicola BAYLEY. *The Mousehole Cat*, text by Antonia BARBER. Walker Books.

Roberto INNOCENTI. *A Christmas Carol*, text by Charles DICKENS. Cape.

1991 Janet AHLBERG. *The Jolly Christmas Postman*, text by Allan AHLBERG. Heinemann.

Highly Commended
Helen OXENBURY. *Farmer Duck*, text by Martin WADDELL. Walker Books.

Commended
Caroline BINCH. *Amazing Grace*, text by Mary HOFFMAN. Frances Lincoln.

1992 Anthony BROWNE. *Zoo.* Julia MacRae.

Highly Commended
Jill BARTON. *Pig in the Pond*, text by Martin WADDELL. Walker Books.

Caroline BINCH. *Hue Boy*, text by Rita P. MITCHELL. Gollancz.

1993 Alan LEE (ills), *Black Ships Before Troy*, text by Rosemary SUTCLIFF. Frances Lincoln.

Highly Commended
Helen OXENBURY (ills), *The Three Little Wolves and the Big Bad Pig*, text by Eugene TRIVIZAS. Heinemann.

Commended
Michael FOREMAN. *War Game.* Pavilion.

1994 Gregory ROGERS. *Way Home*, text by Libby HATHORN. Andersen Press.

Highly Commended
Helen OXENBURY. *So Much,* text by Trish COOKE. Walker Books.

Commended
Chris RIDDELL. *Something Else*, text by Kathryn CAVE. Viking.

1995 P. J. LYNCH. *The Christmas Miracle of Jonathan Toomey*, text by Susan WOJCIECHOWSKI. Walker Books.

Highly Commended
Patrick BENSON. *The Little Boat*, text by Kathy HENDERSON. Walker Books.

Commended
Quentin BLAKE. *Clown.* Cape.

1996 Helen COOPER. *The Baby Who Wouldn't go to Bed.* Doubleday.

Highly Commended
Caroline BINCH. *Down by the River*, text by Grace HALLWORTH. Heinemann.

Commended
Christina BALIT. *Ishtar and Tammuz: A Babylonian Myth of the Seasons*, text by Christopher J. MOORE. Frances Lincoln.

1997 P. J. LYNCH, *When Jessie Came Across the Sea*, text by Amy HEST. Walker Books.

Highly commended
Bob GRAHAM. *Queenie the Bantam.* Walker Books.

Charlotte VOAKE. *Ginger.* Walker Books.

1998 Helen COOPER. *Pumpkin Soup.* Doubleday.

Highly Commended
Shirley HUGHES. *The Lion & the Unicorn.* The Bodley Head.

Jane SIMMONS. *Come On Daisy!* Orchard Books.

1999 Helen OXENBURY. *Alice's Adventures in Wonderland.* Walker Books.

Highly Commended
Lauren CHILD. *Clarice Bean, That's Me!* Orchard Books.

Chris RIDDELL. *Castle Diary*, text by Richard PLATT. Walker Books.

Commended
Kevin HAWKES. *Weslandia*, text by Paul FLEISCHMAN. Walker Books.

2000 Lauren CHILD. *I Will Not Ever Never Eat a Tomato.* Orchard Books.

Highly Commended
Anthony BROWNE. *Willy's Pictures.* Walker Books.

Commended
Ted DEWAN. *Crispin: The Pig Who Had It All.* Doubleday.

2001 Chris RIDDELL. *Pirate Diary*, text by Richard PLATT. Walker Books.

Highly Commended
Jez ALBOROUGH. *Fix-it Duck.* Collins.

Charles FUGE. *Sometimes I Like to Curl Up in a Ball*, text by Vicki CHURCHILL. Gullane Publishing.

2002 Bob GRAHAM. *Jethro Byrde – Fairy Child.* Walker Books.

Commended
Lauren CHILD. *That Pesky Rat.* Orchard Books

2003 Shirley HUGHES. *Ella's Big Chance.* Bodley Head.

No Commendations.

2004 RIDDELL, Chris. *Jonathan Swift's 'Gulliver'*, ed. Martin JENKINS. Walker.

No Commendations.

Chapter 7: Choosing the Best in the Field – The Boston Globe-Horn Book Awards

Those awards which include several categories may be considered more difficult to evaluate than the ones that consider a single type of book. Certainly it requires of the commentator as well as the judges the ability to look with a critical eye at all aspects of children's publishing output, not just one.

The Horn Book Magazine has been committed to promoting high standards in children's books since the 1920s. The Boston Globe-Horn Book Awards were set up to 'Honor Excellence in Literature for Children and Young Adults' and *The Horn Book* can be argued to have more right than perhaps anyone else so to do. The awards, instituted in 1967, and made by *The Horn Book* in conjunction with the newspaper *The Boston Globe*, have consistently highlighted books of quality and distinction. For the first nine years these were presented each year for Fiction and Illustration, but in 1976 a third category, Nonfiction, was added. In 1988 the 'Illustration' category was redesignated 'Picture Book'. Within the list at the end of this chapter, the first-named person in the Illustration/Picture Book entry is always the artist. If the text is by someone else, the author's name follows the title. In the other categories, the author's name heads the entry, and any illustrator is noted after the title.

The judging panel for the Boston Globe-Horn Book Award comprises 'three professionals involved in the field of children's literature' who evaluate submissions from US publishers. Several thousand titles are submitted each year for the three categories. As well as a winner in each category, there may be one or more Honor books. In addition, a special citation is sometimes made for an unusual book of particular quality. To be eligible, books must be published in the US, but may have been written or illustrated by citizens of any country.

Thus the most obvious difference to strike an observer about the Boston Globe-Horn Book awards in contrast with the Newbery and Caldecott Medals is that the Boston Globe-Horn Book Award has no nationalistic straitjacket. Its awards are made for books which are published in the US, certainly, but not necessarily to those first published there. Hence books which were originally published elsewhere, such as John Rowe Townsend's *The Intruder* (BGH Fiction winner 1970; previously published in the UK), Tim Wynne-Jones' *Some of the Kinder Planets*, (BGH Fiction winner 1995; first published in Canada), or Ruth Park's *Playing Beatie Bow* (BGH Fiction winner 1982; first published in Australia), to give just a few examples are included among the winners alongside, for instance, Jerry Spinelli's *Maniac Magee* (BGH Fiction winner 1990 and the 1990 Newbery Medallist).

There has now been nearly forty years overlap between the Boston Globe-Horn Book Award and the Newbery and Caldecott Medals. During this period, the Boston Globe-Horn Book Fiction winner has been the Newbery medallist on five occasions: *M. C. Higgins, the Great* (BGH Fiction winner 1974, Newbery 1975); *The Westing Game* (BGH Fiction winner 1978, Newbery

1979); *Maniac Magee* (BGH Fiction winner 1990, Newbery 1991), *Missing May* (BGH Fiction winner 1992, Newbery 1993) and Louis Sachar's *Holes* in 1999. BGH Fiction winners have appeared on the Honor list for the Newbery on four occasions: *The Dark is Rising* (BGH Fiction winner 1973, Newbery Honor 1974), *Sweet Whispers, Brother Rush* in 1983, *The Moves Make the Man* in 1985 and Marilyn Nelson's *Carver: A Life in Poems* (BGH Fiction/Poetry winner 2001, Newbery Honor 2002). In addition there are several occasions when books have appeared in the Honor Lists for both the Newbery and the Boston Globe Fiction/Poetry section, most recently Polly Horvath's *Everything on a Waffle*, BGH Honor 2001 and Newbery Honor 2002.

The Illustration/Picture Book winner has been the Caldecott medallist on only three occasions: *Lon Po Po* in 1990, *Grandfather's Journey* in 1994, and – perhaps inevitably – *The Man Who Walked between the Towers* in 2004. The winner has been included in the Caldecott Honor list seven times, most recently *Seven Blind Mice* (BGH Picture Book winner 1992, Newbery Honor 1993). Again, titles have appeared on both Honor lists in several years; most recently Marc Simont's *The Stray Dog*, 2001 BGH Picture Book Honor, 2002 Caldecott Honor. Additionally, Peter Sís's *Tibet: Through the Red Box* was a Caldecott Honor in 1999 and received a special citation from the BGH judges in the same year.

The Nonfiction winner has never been the Newbery medallist, although Boston Globe-Horn Book Nonfiction winners have featured in the Newbery Honor lists three times, the most recent example being Jim Murphy's *An American Plague* 2004. In addition, the 1982 Boston Globe-Horn Book winner for illustration, *A Visit to William Blake's Inn*, was a Caldecott Honor Book in 1982, and was also the Newbery Medallist for that year.

There is of course the filter of publishers' choice: if a title is not published in the US, however excellent it may be, it will not be eligible for consideration for the Boston Globe-Horn Book Award. However, anything which has won an award in its own country is by virtue of that very fact more likely to be given an edition elsewhere in the world. This was a feature of winning an award mentioned by several of the authors contacted. Consequently, it is true that the best of the English-language children's books are normally published in the US – often with some alterations to suit the American taste. The problems that such alterations bring are a subject worthy of discussion, as may be seen from the two articles written for *The Horn Book* itself by Jane Whitehead, and published in its issues for November/December 1996 (p. 687) and January/February 1997 (p. 27).

What, then, of Boston Globe-Horn Book Award-winners from outside the US? John Rowe Townsend's *The Intruder* (BGH Fiction winner 1970) was Commended for the 1969 Carnegie; similarly Rosemary Sutcliff's *Tristan and Iseult* (BGH Fiction winner 1972) was on the 1971 Carnegie Commended list, and Susan Cooper's *The Dark is Rising* (BGH Fiction winner 1973) was on the Carnegie 1973 Commended list as well as being the only Honor Book for the 1974 Newbery. More recently, Davis Almond's *The Fire-Eaters* (BGH Fiction & Poetry winner 2004) appeared on the Carnegie and Whitbread shortlists for 2003, and was the Smarties Gold Book Award-winner for 2003. The fact that a different year is shown is a result of the differing procedures adopted by the various award committees. The 1974 Newbery Medal lists would have been announced early in that year; the 1973 Carnegie lists would have been announced in the middle of 1974. In both cases the books being considered would have been published in 1973. As the Boston Globe-Horn Book Award is announced in the autumn, sometimes a book from the end of the previous year will be included, making the BGH date for a winning or Honor title the same as the Newbery date, on most occasions the book would be from the year in question, making the date usually agree with the Carnegie date. However, as with Anne Fine's *Flour Babies*, which won the 1992 Carnegie Medal, and was an Honor Book for the 1994 BGH Fiction Award, there may be delays before publication in a different country.

Among the CILIP Kate Greenaway laureates, only John Burningham's *Mr Gumpy's Outing*, (BGH Illustration Award 1972, Greenaway 1970) has actually won both awards. Mitsumaso Anno's *Anno's Alphabet* (BGH Illustration Award 1975) had been on the Greenaway Commended list in 1974 and Raymond Briggs's *The Snowman* (BGH Illustration Award 1979) had been Highly Commended by the Greenaway judges in 1978. Molly Bang appears in both lists, but for different titles, and Bob Graham, whose *Let's get a Pup! said Kate* was the BGH Picture book winner for 2002, won the Greenaway Medal for 2002 with *Jethro Byrde – Fairy Child*, having been Highly Commended for *Queenie the Bantam* in the 1997 Greenaway list.

Turning to Canada, Tim Wynne-Jones's *Some of the Kinder Planets* (BGH Fiction winner 1995) had won the Governor-General's Literary Award for English Text in 1993. As already mentioned, Ruth Park's *Playing Beatie Bow* (BGH Fiction winner 1982; ACO 1981) is an Australian example of the international influence of this award.

The Boston Globe-Horn Book Award titles are being judged, not only against the rest of the massive US publishing output, but against the children's books of the whole English-speaking world. It could thus be argued that a title chosen for any of the Boston Globe-Horn Book categories potentially carries more prestige than any other award under discussion in this book.

Boston Globe-Horn Book Awards (USA): complete list of winners and honor books

1967 **Fiction**

Erik Christian HAUGAARD. *The Little Fishes.* Houghton Mifflin.

Honor Books

None Awarded

Illustration

Peter SPIER. *London Bridge is Falling Down.* Doubleday.

Honor Books

None Awarded

1968 **Fiction**

John LAWSON. *The Spring Rider.* Crowell.

Honor Books

E. M. ALMEDINGEN. *Young Mark.* Farrar.

Audrey White BEYER. *Dark Ventures.* Knopf.

Leon GARFIELD. *Smith.* Pantheon.

Esther HAUTZIG. *The Endless Steppe.* Crowell.

Illustration

Blair LENT. *Tikki Tikki Tembo*, by Arlene MOSEL. Holt Rinehart.

Honor Books

Adrienne ADAMS. *Jorinda and Joringel*, text by the Brothers GRIMM. Scribner.

Bernarda BRYSON. *Gilgamesh: Man's First Story.* Holt.

Pat HUTCHINS. *Rosie's Walk.* Macmillan.

Trina Schart HYMAN. *All in Free but Janey*, text by Elizabeth JOHNSON. Little, Brown.

1969 **Fiction**

Ursula LE GUIN. *The Wizard of Earthsea.* Parnassus.

Honor Books

Elizabeth Borton DE TREVIÑO. *Turi's Poppa.* Farrar.

K. M. PEYTON. *Flambards.* World.

Paul ZINDEL. *The Pigman.* Harper.

Illustration
John S. GOODALL. *The Adventures of Paddy Pork.* Harcourt.

Honor Books
Ann ATWOOD. *New Moon Cove.* Scribner.

Clement HURD. *Monkey in the Jungle*, text by Edna Mitchell PRESTON. Viking.

Brinton TURKLE. *Thy Friend, Obadiah.* Viking.

1970 **Fiction**
John Rowe TOWNSEND. *The Intruder.* Lippincott.

Honor Book
Vera & Bill CLEAVER. *Where the Lilies Bloom.* Lippincott.

Illustration
Ezra Jack KEATS. *Hi, Cat!* Macmillan.

Honor Book
Gail E. HALEY. *A Story, a Story: An African Tale.* Atheneum.

1971 **Fiction**
Eleanor CAMERON. *A Room Made of Windows.* Atlantic Little Brown.

Honor Books
Hester BURTON. *Beyond the Weir Bridge.* Crowell. (Published in UK as *Thomas*).

Olivia COOLIDGE. *Come Here.* Houghton Mifflin.

Robert C. O'BRIEN. *Mrs. Frisby and the Rats of NIMH.* Atheneum.

Illustration
Kazue MIZUMURA. *If I Built a Village.* Crowell.

Honor Books
Janina DOMANSKA. *If All the Seas Were One Sea.* Macmillan.

Blair LENT. *The Angry Moon*, text by William SLEATOR. Little.

Bernard WABER. *A Firefly Named Torchy.* Houghton.

1972 **Fiction**
Rosemary SUTCLIFF. *Tristan and Iseult.* Dutton.

Honor Books
None Awarded

Illustration
John BURNINGHAM. *Mr. Gumpy's Outing*. Holt.

Honor Books
None Awarded

1973

Fiction
Susan COOPER. *The Dark is Rising*. Atheneum.

Honor Books
Lloyd ALEXANDER. *The Cat Who Wished to Be a Man*. Dutton.

Mabel Esther ALLAN. *An Island in the Green Sea*. Atheneum.

Emma SMITH. *No Way of Telling*. Atheneum.

Illustration
Trina Schart HYMAN. *King Stork*, by Howard PYLE. Little.

Honor Books
Gerald McDERMOTT. *The Magic Tree*. Holt, Rinehart & Winston.

Ellen RASKIN. *Who, Said Sue, Said Whoo?* Atheneum.

Lynd WARD. *The Silver Pony*. Houghton Mifflin.

1974

Fiction
Virginia HAMILTON. *M. C. Higgins, the Great*. Macmillan.

Honor Books
Jean FRITZ. *And Then What Happened, Paul Revere?* Coward.

Jane GARDAM. *The Summer After the Funeral*. Macmillan.

Doris Buchanan SMITH. *Tough Chauncy*. Morrow.

Illustration
Tom FEELINGS. *Jambo Means Hello: A Swahili Alphabet Book*, by Muriel FEELINGS. Dial.

Honor Books
Jose ARUEGO & Ariane DEWEY. *Herman the Helper*, text by Robert KRAUS. Windmill.

Marcia BROWN. *All Butterflies*. Scribner.

William KURELEK. *A Prairie Boy's Winter*. Houghton Mifflin.

1975

Fiction
T. DEGENS. *Transport 7-41-R*. Viking.

Honor Book
Sharon Bell MATHIS. *The Hundred Penny Box*, ills Leo & Diane DILLON. Viking.

Illustration
Mitsumasa ANNO. *Anno's Alphabet.* Crowell.

Honor Books
Nola LANGER. *Scram, Kid!* text by Ann McGOVERN. Viking.

David McPHAIL. *The Bear's Bicycle*, text by Emilie Warren McLEOD. Atlantic-Little.

John STEPTOE. *She Come Bringing Me That Little Baby Girl*, text by Eloise GREENFIELD. Lippincott.

1976 **Fiction**
Jill Paton WALSH. *Unleaving.* Farrar, Straus & Giroux.

Honor Books
Nancy BOND. *A String in the Harp.* Atheneum/McElderry.

Mollie HUNTER. *A Stranger Came Ashore.* Harper.

Laurence YEP. *Dragonwings.* Harper.

Nonfiction
Alfred TAMARIN & Shirley GLUBOK. *Voyaging to Cathay: Americans in the China Trade.* Viking.

Honor Books
Jean FRITZ. *Will You Sign Here, John Hancock?* Coward.

David MACAULAY. *Pyramid.* Houghton

Milton MELTZER. *Never to Forget: The Jews of the Holocaust.* Harper.

Illustration
Remy CHARLIP & Jerry JOYNER. *Thirteen.* Four Winds/Parents.

Honor Books
Chris CONOVER. *Six Little Ducks.* Crowell

Leo & Diane DILLON. *Song of the Boat*, text by Lorenz GRAHAM. Crowell.

Peter PARNALL. *The Desert is Theirs*, text by Byrd BAYLOR. Scribner

1977 **Fiction**
Lawrence YEP. *Child of the Owl.* Harper & Row.

Honor Books
Rosemary SUTCLIFF. *Blood Feud.* Dutton.

Mildred TAYLOR. *Roll of Thunder, Hear My Cry.* Dial.

Robert WESTALL. *The Machine Gunners.* Greenwillow.

Nonfiction

Peter DICKINSON. *Chance, Luck and Destiny.* Atlantic Little.

Betty Ann KEVLES. *Watching the Wild Apes.* Dutton.

Lucille Recht PENNER. *The Colonial Cookbook.* Hastings

Lucille Schulberg WARNER. *From Slave to Abolitionist.* Dial.

Special Honorable Mention for Nonbook Illustration
Jörg MULLER. *The Changing City and The Changing Countryside.* Atheneum/McElderry.

Illustration

Wallace TRIPP. *Grandfa' Grig Had a Pig and Other Rhymes Without Reason from Mother Goose.* Little.

Honor Books
Mitsumasa ANNO. *Anno's Counting Book.* Crowell.

Leo & Diane DILLON. *Ashanti to Zulu: African Traditions*, text by Margaret MUSGROVE. Dial.

William STEIG. *The Amazing Bone.* Farrar.

1978 Fiction

Ellen RASKIN. *The Westing Game.* Dutton.

Honor Books
Beverly CLEARY. *Ramona and Her Father.* Morrow.

Jamake HIGHWATER. *Anpao: An American Odyssey.* Lippincott.

Myron LEVOY. *Alan and Naomi.* Harper.

Nonfiction

Ilse KOEHN. *Mischling: Second Degree.* Bantam.

Honor Books
Betty BAKER. *Settlers and Strangers: Native Americans of the Desert Southwest and History as They Saw It.* Macmillan.

David MACAULAY. *Castle.* Houghton.

Illustration
Mitsumasa ANNO. *Anno's Journey*. Philomel.

Honor Books
Philippe DUMAS. *The Story of Edward.* Parents.

Trina Schart HYMAN. *On To Widecombe Fair*, text by Patricia Lee GAUCH. Putnam.

Jenny RODWELL. *What Do You Feed Your Donkey On? Rhymes from a Belfast Childhood*, text by Collette O'HARE. Collins-World.

1979

Fiction
Sid FLEISCHMAN. *Humbug Mountain.* Atlantic Little.

Honor Books
Cecil BØDKER. *Silas and Ben-Godik.* Delacorte.

Sue Ellen BRIDGERS. *All Together Now.* Knopf.

Nonfiction
David KHERDIAN. *The Road from Home: the Story of an Armenian Girl.* Greenwillow.

Honor Books
Martin SANDLER. *The Story of American Photography: An Illustrated History for Young People.* Little.

Richard SNOW. *The Iron Road: A Portrait of American Railroading*, ills with photos by David PLOWDEN. Four Winds.

Margot ZEMACH. *Self-Portrait: Margot Zemach.* Addison.

Illustration
Raymond BRIGGS. *The Snowman.* Random House.

Honor Books
Erick INGRAHAM. *Cross-Country Cat*, text by Mary CALHOUN. Morrow.

Rachel ISADORA. *Ben's Trumpet.* Greenwillow.

1980

Fiction
Andrew DAVIES. *Conrad's War.* Crown.

Honor Books
Betsy BYARS. *The Night Swimmers*, ills Troy HOWELL. Delacorte.

Clive KING. *Me and My Million.* Crowell.

Jan SLEPIAN. *The Alfred Summer.* Macmillan.

Nonfiction
Mario SALVADORI. *Building: The Fight against Gravity*, ills Saralinda HOOKER & Christopher RAGUS. Atheneum/McElderry.

Honor Books
Jean FRITZ. *Stonewall*, ills Stephen GAMMELL. Putnam.

Eloise GREENFIELD. *Childtimes: A Three-Generation Memoir*, ills with drawings by Jerry PINKNEY, and photos. Crowell.

William JASPERSOHN. *How the Forest Grew*, ills Chuck ECKART. Greenwillow.

Illustration
Chris van ALLSBURG. *The Garden of Abdul Gasazi.* Houghton Mifflin.

Honor Books
Molly BANG. *The Grey Lady and the Strawberry Snatcher.* Four Winds.

Marc BROWN. *Why the Tides Ebb and Flow*, text by Joan Chase BOWDEN. Houghton.

Special Citation for Illustration
Graham OAKLEY. *Magical Changes.* Atheneum.

1981 **Fiction**
Lynn HALL. *The Leaving.* Scribners.

Honor Books
Robert BURCH. *Ida Early Comes Over the Mountain.* Viking.

Julia CUNNINGHAM. *The Flight of the Sparrow.* Pantheon.

Leon GARFIELD. *Footsteps.* Delacorte.

Nonfiction
Kathryn LASKY. *The Weaver's Gift*, illustrated with photographs by Christopher G. KNIGHT. Warne.

Honor Books
Betty Lou ENGLISH. *You Can't Be Timid with a Trumpet: Notes from the Orchestra.* Lothrop.

James HOWE. *The Hospital Book*, ills with photos by Mal WARSHAW. Crown.

Lila PERL. *Junk Food, Fast Food, Health Food: What America Eats and Why.* Clarion.

Illustration
Maurice SENDAK. *Outside Over There.* Harper.

Honor Books
Chris van ALLSBURG. *Jumanji.* Houghton.

Stephen GAMMELL. *Where the Buffaloes Begin*, text by Olaf BAKER. Warne.

Anita LOBEL. *On Market Street*, text by Arnold LOBEL. Greenwillow.

1982 Fiction
Ruth PARK. *Playing Beatie Bow.* Atheneum.

Honor Books
Nancy BOND. *The Voyage Begun.* Atheneum.

Ann SCHLEE. *Ask Me No Questions.* Holt.

Robert WESTALL. *The Scarecrows.* Greenwillow.

Nonfiction
Aranka SIEGAL. *Upon the Head of the Goat: A Childhood in Hungary 1939-1944.* Farrar.

Honor Books
John NANCE. *Lobo of the Tasaday.* Pantheon.

Helen Roney SADLER. *Dinosaurs of North America*, ills Anthony RAO. Lothrop.

Illustration
Alice & Martin PROVENSEN. *A Visit to William Blake's Inn: Poems for Innocent and Experienced Travelers*, text by Nancy WILLARD. Harcourt.

Honor Book
Tomie de PAOLA. *The Friendly Beasts: An Old English Christmas Carol.* Putnam.

1983 Fiction
Virginia HAMILTON. *Sweet Whispers, Brother Rush.* Philomel.

Honor Books
Jean FRITZ. *Homesick: My Own Story*, ills Margot TOMES. Putnam.

Rosemary SUTCLIFF. *The Road to Camlann.* Dutton.

Cynthia VOIGT. *Dicey's Song.* Atheneum.

Nonfiction
Daniel S. DAVIS. *Behind Barbed Wire: The Imprisonment of Japanese Americans During World War II.* Dutton.

Honor Books
Toshi MARUKI. *Hiroshima No Pika.* Lothrop.

Milton MELTZER. *The Jewish Americans: A History in Their Own Words, 1650-1950.* Crowell.

Illustration
Vera B. WILLIAMS. *A Chair for my Mother.* Greenwillow.

Honor Books
Helme HEINE. *Friends.* Atheneum/McElderry.

William STEIG. *Doctor De Soto.* Farrar.

Ed YOUNG. *Yeh Shen: A Cinderella Story from China*, text by Ai-Ling LOUIE. Philomel.

1984 Fiction
Patricia WRIGHTSON. *A Little Fear.* Atheneum/McElderry.

Honor Books
Diana Wynne JONES. *Archer's Goon.* Greenwillow.

Patricia MacLACHLAN. *Unclaimed Treasures.* Harper.

Cynthia VOIGT. *A Solitary Blue.* Atheneum.

Nonfiction
Jean FRITZ. *The Double Life of Pocohontas*, ills Ed YOUNG. Putnam.

Honor Books
Polly Schoyer BROOKS. *Queen Eleanor: Independent Spirit of the Medieval World.* Lippincott.

Russell FREEDMAN. *Children of the Wild West.* Clarion.

David & Charlotte YUE. *The Tipi: A Center of Native American Life.* Knopf.

Illustration
Warwick HUTTON. *Jonah and the Great Fish.* Atheneum/McElderry.

Honor Books
Molly BANG. *Dawn.* Morrow.

Kate DUKE. *The Guinea Pig ABC.* Dutton.

Anita LOBEL. *The Rose in My Garden*, by Arnold LOBEL. Greenwillow.

1985 Fiction
Bruce BROOKS. *The Moves Make the Man.* Harper & Row.

Honor Books
Dick KING-SMITH. *Babe: The Gallant Pig*, ills Mary RAYNER. Crown. (published in UK as *The Sheep-Pig.*)

Margaret MAHY. *The Changeover: A Supernatural Romance*. Atheneum/ McElderry.

Nonfiction
Rhoda BLUMBERG. *Commodore Perry in the Land of the Shogun.* Lothrop, Lee & Shephard.

Honor Books
Roald DAHL. *Boy*. Farrar.

Albert MARRIN. *1812: The War Nobody Won.* Atheneum.

Special Award
Tana HOBAN. *1, 2, 3*, illustrated with photographs. Greenwillow.

Illustration
Thacher HURD. *Mama Don't Allow.* Harper & Row.

Honor Books
Chris van ALLSBURG. *The Mysteries of Harris Burdick.* Houghton.

Lloyd BLOOM. *Like Jake and Me*, text by Mavis JUKES. Knopf.

Steven KELLOGG. *How Much Is a Million?* text by David SCHWARTZ. Lothrop.

1986

Fiction
Zibby ONEAL. *In Summer Light.* Viking.

Honor Books
Pam CONRAD. *Prairie Songs.* Harper.

Diana Wynne JONES. *Howl's Moving Castle.* Greenwillow.

Nonfiction
Peggy THOMSON. *Auks, Rocks and the Odd Dinosaur: Inside Stories from the Smithsonian's Museum of Natural History.* Crowell.

Honor Books
Brent ASHABRANNER. *Dark Harvest: Migrant Farmworkers in America.* Dodd.

James Cross GIBLIN. *The Truth About Santa Claus.* Crowell.

Illustration
Molly BANG. *The Paper Crane.* Greenwillow.

Honor Books
Chris van ALLSBURG. *The Polar Express.* Houghton.

Anthony BROWNE. *Gorilla.* Knopf.

Ann JONAS. *The Trek.* Greenwillow.

1987 **Fiction**
Lois LOWRY. *Rabble Starkey.* Houghton Mifflin.

Honor Books
Helen V. GRIFFITH. *Georgia Music*, ills James STEVENSON. Greenwillow.

Janni HOWKER. *Isaac Campion.* Greenwillow.

Nonfiction
Marcia SEWELL. *The Pilgrims of Plimoth.* Atheneum.

Honor Books
Joanna COLE. *The Magic School Bus at the Waterworks*, ills Bruce DEGEN. Scholastic.

John HARTFORD. *Steamboat in a Cornfield.* Crown.

Sheila KITZINGER. *Being Born*, ills with photos by Lennart NILSSON. Grosset.

Illustration
John STEPTOE. *Mufaro's Beautiful Daughters.* Lothrop, Lee and Shephard.

Honor Books
Thomas B. ALLEN. *In Coal Country*, text by Judith HENDERSHOT. Knopf.

Stephen GAMMELL. *Old Henry*, text by Joan W. BLOS. Morrow.

Vera B. WILLIAMS. *Cherries and Cherry Pits.* Greenwillow.

1988 **Fiction**
Mildred D. TAYLOR. *The Friendship*, ills Max GINSBURG. Dial.

Honor Books
Berlie DOHERTY. *Granny Was a Buffer Girl.* Orchard.

Paul FLEISCHMAN. *Joyful Noise: Poems for Two Voices*, ills Eric BEDDOWS. Harper.

Nonfiction
Virginia HAMILTON. *Anthony Burns; The Defeat and Triumph of a Fugitive Slave.* Knopf.

Honor Books
John CHIASSON. *African Journey*, ills author. Bradbury.

Jean LITTLE. *Little by Little: A Writer's Education*. Viking Kestrel.

Picture Book
Allen SAY. *The Boy of the Three-Year Nap*, text by Dianne SNYDER. Houghton Mifflin.

Honor Books
Jeannie BAKER. *Where the Forest Meets the Sea*. Greenwillow.

Jennifer & Vera B. WILLIAMS. *Stringbean's Trip to the Shining Sea*, by Vera B. WILLIAMS. Greenwillow.

1989

Fiction
Paula FOX. *The Village by the Sea*. Orchard Books.

Honor Books
Peter DICKINSON. *Eva*. Delacorte.

William MAYNE. *Gideon Ahoy!* Delacorte.

Nonfiction
David MACAULAY. *The Way Things Work*. Houghton Mifflin.

Honor Books
Philip M. ISAACSON. *Round Buildings, Square Buildings, & Buildings That Wiggle Like a Fish*. Knopf.

Laurence YEP. *The Rainbow People*. Harper.

Picture Book
Rosemary WELLS. *Shy Charles*. Dial.

Honor Books
Barbara COONEY. *Island Boy*. Viking Kestrel.

Julie VIVAS. *The Nativity*. Gulliver/Harcourt.

1990

Fiction
Jerry SPINELLI. *Maniac Magee*. Little, Brown.

Honor Books
Pam CONRAD. *Stonewords*. Harper.

Paul FLEISCHMAN. *Saturnalia*. Harper/Zolotow.

Nonfiction
Jean FRITZ. *The Great Little Madison*. Putnam.

Honor Books
Ron & Nancy GOOR. *Insect Metamorphosis*, ills with photos by Ron GOOR. Atheneum.

Tana HOBAN. *Shadows and Reflections*, ills with photos by author. Greenwillow.

Special Award for Excellence in Book Making
Nancy Ekholm BURKERT. *Valentine and Orson*, ills author. Farrar.

Picture Book
Ed YOUNG. *Lon Po Po: A Red Riding-Hood Story from China*. Philomel.

Honor Books
Lois EHLERT. *Chicka Chicka Boom Boom*, by Bill MARTIN Jr. & John ARCHAMBAULT. Simon.

Helen OXENBURY. *We're Going on a Bear Hunt*, retold by Michael ROSEN. McElderry.

1991

Fiction
AVI. *The True Confessions of Charlotte Doyle*. Orchard Books.

Honor Books
Martha BROOKS. *Paradise Café and Other Stories*. Joy Street.

Brenda SEABROOKE. *Judy Scuppernong*. Cobblehill.

Nonfiction
Cynthia RYLANT. *Appalachia: The Voices of Sleeping Birds*, ills Barry MOSER. Harcourt.

Honor Books
Russell FREEDMAN. *The Wright Brothers: How They Invented the Airplane*. Holiday.

Diane STANLEY & Peter VENNEMA. *Good Queen Bess: The Story of Queen Elizabeth I of England*, ills Diane STANLEY. Four Winds.

Picture Book
Leo & Diane DILLON. *The Tale of the Mandarin Ducks*, retold by Katherine PATERSON. Lodestar.

Honor Books
Ann JONAS. *Aardvarks, Disembark!* Greenwillow.

Petra MATHERS. *Sophie and Lou*. HarperCollins.

1992

Fiction
Cynthia RYLANT. *Missing May*. Jackson/Orchard.

Honor Books
AVI. *Nothing but the Truth*. Orchard.

Walter Dean MYERS. *Somewhere in the Darkness*. Scholastic.

Nonfiction
Pat CUMMINGS (ed). *Talking With Artists*. Bradbury Press.

Honor Books
Lois EHLERT. *Red Leaf, Yellow Leaf*. Harcourt.

Laura RANKIN. *The Handmade Alphabet*. Dial

Picture Book
Ed YOUNG. *Seven Blind Mice*. Philomel.

Honor Book
Denise FLEMING. *In the Tall, Tall Grass*. Holt.

1993 **Fiction**
James BERRY. *Ajeemah and His Son*. Perlman/HarperCollins.

Honor Book
Lois LOWRY. *The Giver*. Houghton.

Nonfiction
Patricia C. & Frederick McKISSACK. *Sojourner Truth: Ain't I a Woman?* Scholastic.

Honor Book
Kathleen KRULL. *Lives of the Musicians: Good Times, Bad Times (And What the Neighbours Thought)*, ills Kathryn HEWITT. Harcourt.

Picture Book
Trina Schart HYMAN. *The Fortune-tellers*, by Lloyd ALEXANDER. Dutton.

Honor Books
Gerald McDERMOTT. *Raven: A Trickster Tale from the Pacific Northwest*. Harcourt.

Peter SÍS. *Komodo!* Greenwillow.

1994 **Fiction**
Vera WILLIAMS. *Scooter*. Greenwillow.

Honor Books
Anne FINE. *Flour Babies*. Little.

Paula FOX. *Western Wind*. Orchard.

Nonfiction
Russell FREEDMAN. *Eleanor Roosevelt: a Life of Discovery.* Clarion.

Honor Books
Constance LEVY. *A Tree Place and Other Poems*, ills Robert SABUDA. McElderry.

Albert MARRIN. *Unconditional Surrender: U. S. Grant and the Civil War.* Atheneum.

Picture Book
Allen SAY. *Grandfather's Journey.* Houghton.

Honor Books
Kevin HENKES. *Owen.* Greenwillow.

Peter SÍS. *A Small Tale from the Far Far North.* Knopf.

1995

Fiction
Tim WYNNE-JONES. *Some of the Kinder Planets.* Kroupa/Orchard.

Honor Books
Janet HICKMAN. *Jericho.* Greenwillow.

Theresa NELSON. *Earthshine.* Jackson/Orchard.

Nonfiction
Natalie S. BOBER. *Abigail Adams: Witness to a Revolution.* Atheneum

Honor books
Robie H. HARRIS. *It's Perfectly Normal: A Book about Changing Bodies, Growing Up, Sex, and Sexual Health*, ills Michael EMBERLEY. Candlewick.

Jim MURPHY. *The Great Fire.* Scholastic.

Picture Book
Jerry PINKNEY. *John Henry*, by Julius LESTER. Dial.

Honor Book
Paul O. ZELINSKY. *Swamp Angel*, text by Anne ISAACS. Dutton.

1996

Fiction
AVI. *Poppy*, ills Brian FLOCA. Jackson/Orchard.

Honor Books
Eloise McGRAW. *The Moorchild.* McElderry.

Ruth WHITE. *Belle Prater's Boy.* Farrar.

Nonfiction
Andrea WARREN. *Orphan Train Rider: One Boy's True Story*. Houghton.

Honor Books
Joseph BRUCHAC. *The Boy Who Lived with the Bears: And Other Iroquois Stories*, ills Murv JACOB. Harper.

Bonnie & Arthur GEISERT. *Haystack*, ills Arthur GEISERT. Houghton.

1996 **Picture Book**
Jill BARTON. *In the Rain with Baby Duck*, text by Amy HEST. Candlewick.

Honor Books
Mark BUEHNER. *Fanny's Dream*, text by Caralyn BUEHNER. Dial.

Lynne Rae PERKINS. *Home Lovely*. Greenwillow.

1997 **Fiction and Poetry**
Kazumi YUMOTO, translated by Cathy HIRANO. *The Friends*. Farrar.

Honor Books
Patricia Reilly GIFF. *Lily's Crossing*. Delacourt.

Walter Dean MYERS. *Harlem*, ills Christopher MYERS. Scholastic Press.

Nonfiction
Walter WICK. *A Drop of Water: A Book of Science and Wonder*, ills with photographs by the author. Scholastic.

Honor Books
David A. ADLER. *Lou Gehrig: The Luckiest Man*, ills by Terry WIDENER. Gulliver/Harcourt.

Diane STANLEY. *Leonardo da Vinci*, ills by the author. Morrow.

Picture Book
Brian PINKNEY. *The Adventures of Sparrowboy*. Simon.

Honor Books
Lisa Campbell ERNST. *Potato: A Tale from the Great Depression*, text by Kate LIED. National Geographic.

G. Brian KARAS. *Home on the Bayou: A Coyboy's Story*. Simon.

1998 **Fiction and Poetry**
Francisco JIMÉNEZ. *The Circuit: Stories from the Life of a Migrant Child*. University of New Mexico Press.

Honor Books
Jane Leslie CONLY. *While No One Was Watching*. Holt.

Kimberly Willis HOLT. *My Louisiana Sky*. Holt.

Nonfiction
Leon Walter TILLAGE. *Leon's Story*, ills with collage art by Susan L. ROTH. Farrar.

Honor Books
Russell FREEDMAN. *Martha Graham: A Dancer's Life*. Clarion.

Jan GREENBERG & Sandra JORDAN. *Chuck Close Up Close*. DK Ink.

Picture Book
Georg HALLENSLEBEN. *And If the Moon Could Talk*, text by Kate BANKS. Foster/Farrar.

Honor Books
Bethanne ANDERSEN. *Seven Brave Women*, text by Betsy HEARNE. Greenwillow.

James STEVENSON. *Popcorn: Poems*. Greenwillow.

1999

Fiction
Louis SACHAR. *Holes*. Foster/Farrar.

Honor Books
Polly HORVATH. *The Trolls*. Farrar.

Walter Dean MYERS. *Monster*, ills by Christopher MYERS. HarperCollins.

Nonfiction
Steve JENKINS. *The Top of the World: Climbing Mount Everest*. Houghton.

Honor Books
ALIKI. *William Shakespeare & the Globe*. HarperCollins.

Jennifer ARMSTRONG. *Shipwreck at the Bottom of the World: The Extraordinary True Story of Shackleton and the Endurance*. Crown.

Picture Book
Nic BISHOP. *Red-Eyed Tree Frog*, ills with photographs, text by Joy COWLEY. Scholastic Press.

Honor Books
Susan KUKLIN. *Dance*, ills with photographs, text by Bill T. JONES & Susan KUKLIN. Hyperion.

James MARSHALL. *The Owl and the Pussycat*, text by Edward LEAR. di Capua/HarperCollins.

Special Citation
Peter SÍS. *Tibet: Through the Red Box*. Foster/Farrar.

2000

Fiction
Franny BILLINGSLEY. *The Folk Keeper.* Atheneum.

Honor Books
Susan COOPER. *King of Shadows.* McElderry.

Walter Dean MYERS. *145th Street: Short Stories.* Delacorte.

Nonfiction
Marc ARONSON. *Sir Walter Ralegh and the Quest for El Dorado.* Clarion.

Honor Books
Alan GOVENAR (collected & edited by). *Osceola: Memories of a Sharecropper's Daughter*, ills by Shane W. EVANS. Jump at the Sun/Hyperion.

Albert MARRIN. *Sitting Bull and His World.* Dutton.

Picture Book
D. B. JOHNSON. *Henry Hikes to Fitchburg.* Houghton.

Honor Books
Brock COLE. *Buttons.* Farrar.

Gabrielle VINCENT. *A day, a dog.* Front Street.

2001

Fiction and Poetry
Marilyn NELSON. *Carver: A Life in Poems.* Front Street.

Honor Books
Adèle GERAS. *Troy.* Harcourt.

Polly HORVATH. *Everything on a Waffle.* Farrar.

Nonfiction
Joan DASH. *The Longitude Prize*, ills Dušan PETRIČIĆ. Foster/Farrar.

Honor Books
Don BROWN. *Uncommon Traveler: Mary Kingsley in Africa.* Houghton.

Carol Otis HURST. *Rocks in His Head*, ills James STEVENSON. Greenwillow.

Picture Book
Robert Andrew PARKER. *Cold Feet*, by Cynthia DeFELICE. DK Ink.

Honor Books
Tomek BOGACKI. *Five Creatures*, text by Emily JENKINS. Foster/Farrar.

Marc SIMONT. *The Stray Dog.* HarperCollins.

2002

Fiction and Poetry
Graham SALISBURY. *Lord of the Deep*. Delacorte.

Honor Books
Hilary McKAY. *Saffy's Angel*. McElderry.

Vera B. WILLIAMS. *Amber Was Brave, Essie Was Smart*. Greenwillow.

Nonfiction
Elizabeth PARTRIDGE. *This Land was Made for You and Me: The Life and Songs of Woody Guthrie*. Viking.

Honor Book
M. T. ANDERSON. *Handel, Who Knew What He Liked*, ills Kevin HAWKES. Candlewick.

Picture Book
Bob GRAHAM. *Let's Get a Pup! Said Kate*. Candlewick.

Honor Books
Molly BANG. *Little Rat Sets Sail*, text by Monika BANG-CAMPBELL. Harcourt.

Bonnie CHRISTENSEN. *Woody Guthrie: Poet of the People*. Knopf.

Jim McMULLAN. *I Stink!* text by Kate McMULLAN. Cotler/Harper.

2003

Fiction and Poetry
Anne FINE. *The Jamie and Angus Stories*, ills Penny DALE. Candlewick.

Honor Books
M. T. ANDERSON. *Feed*. Candlewick.

Jacqueline WOODSON. *Locomotion*. Putnam.

Nonfiction
Maira KALMAN. *Fireboat: The Heroic Adventures of the John J. Harvey*. Putnam.

Honor Books
Wendie C. OLD. *To Fly: The Story of the Wright Brothers*, ills Robert Andrew PARKER. Clarion.

Nathaniel PHILBRICK. *Revenge of the Whale: The True Story of the Whaleship Essex*. Putnam.

Picture Book
Helen OXENBURY. *Big Momma Makes the World*, text by Phyllis ROOT. Candlewick.

Honor Books
Barbara McCLINTOCK. *Dahlia*. Foster/Farrar.

Walter Dean MYERS. *blues journey*, ills Christopher MYERS. Holiday.

2004 **Fiction and Poetry**
David ALMOND. *The Fire-Eaters*. Delacorte.

Honor Books
Cynthia RYLANT. *God Went to Beauty School*. HarperTempest.

Jonathan STROUD. *The Amulet of Samarkand: The Bartimaeus Trilogy, Book One*. Hyperion.

Nonfiction
Jim MURPHY. *An American Plague: The True and Terrifying Story of the Yellow Fever Epidemic of 1793*. Clarion.

Honor Books
Nicola DAVIES. *Surprising Sharks*, ills James CROFT. Candlewick.

Bea Uusma SCHYFFERT. *The Man Who Went to the Far Side of the Moon: The Story of Apollo 11 Astronaut Michael Collins*. Chronicle.

Picture Book
Mordicai GERSTEIN. *The Man Who Walked between the Towers*. Roaring Brook.

Honor Books
Anthony BROWNE. *The Shape Game*. Farrar.

Lynne Rae PERKINS. *Snow Music*. Greenwillow.

2005 **Fiction and Poetry**
Neal SHUSTERMAN. *The Schwa Was Here*. Dutton.

Honor Books
Judith CLARKE. *Kalpana's Dream*. Front Street.

Miriam NELSON. *A Wreath for Emmett Till*. ills Philippe LARDY. Houghton.

Nonfiction
Phillip HOOSE. *The Race to Save the Lord God Bird*. Kroupa/Farrar.

Honor Books
James Cross GIBLIN. *Good Brother, Bad Brother: The Story of Edwin Booth and John Wilkes Booth*. Clarion.

Michael ROSEN. *Michael Rosen's Sad Book*, ills Quentin BLAKE. Candlewick.

Picture Book
Mini GREY. *Traction Man Is Here!* Knopf.

Honor Books
Pierre PRATT. *That New Animal*, text by Emily JENKINS. Foster/Farrar.

Chris RASCHKA. *The Hello, Goodbye Window*, text by Norton JUSTER. Di Capua/Hyperion.

Chapter 8: Not Just Pretty Pictures – awards for picture book illustration & text

This chapter considers two UK awards, the Kurt Maschler 'Emil' & the Mother Goose Award both now discontinued; and three US awards, the Ezra Jack Keats Award, the Giverny Award and the Charlotte Zolotow Award. All are specifically concerned with picture books, the 'Emil' for picture books as an integral whole, the Mother Goose for new illustrators, the Ezra Jack Keats for new writers and illustrators, the Giverny for science picture books, and the Zolotow for outstanding writing in a picture book. Other major awards for illustration are the Caldecott Medal (US), discussed in Chapter 5 and the CILIP Kate Greenaway Medal (UK), treated in Chapter 6. The Boston Globe-Horn Book Award, which includes a Picture Book category among its three awards, is to be found in Chapter 7. There are illustration categories within the Awards with Special Intentions, Chapter 9, and illustration awards which have commercial sponsors are in Chapter 11. In addition, most other countries have illustration categories within their national awards, or have separate multi-category awards, and these are treated among the awards for that country within Chapter 12.

This chapter's five awards emerged many years later than the Caldecott and Greenaway Medals and were each created to fill a perceived gap in the range of awards. It is nonetheless noticeable that many names from them appear among the winners and honours of the two original awards. This demonstrates that for all the differences in aim of the newer awards, these people are quality artists and writers, who come to the fore in many different lists.

The Mother Goose Award was presented annually by Books for Your Children Book Club to the 'most exciting newcomer to children's book illustration' and only just manages to come within the definitions I have set out for this book, since its stated aim is to honour 'newcomers'. Since the award was made for a first illustrated *book*, however I have felt able to include discussion of it here. Similarly, the Ezra Jack Keats Award is for new writers and illustrators, though its rules are not quite so stringent on the definition of 'newness' as the Mother Goose, and again it is awarded for a particular title rather than for a body of work. The 'Emil', established in 1982 for 'a work of imagination in the children's field, in which the text and illustrations are balanced and enhance each other', was nearer in concept to the Caldecott than the Greenaway, which is in part why it was set up. It was for a book which is integrally a picture book, not merely 'for illustration'. Tom Maschler, the publisher, inaugurated it in 1982 in memory of his father Kurt Maschler, whose firm, William Verlag, was the original publisher of *Emil and the Detectives*, hence the name of the award. A bronze figure of Emil was given to the winning author and illustrator. Towards the end of its time the award seemed to be calling itself simply the Kurt Maschler Award, and dropping the 'Emil' from its title, but I have adhered to the original terminology throughout this chapter. It and the Mother Goose Award were discontinued in 2000, so that the last dated entry in the list for each is for 1999. The Giverny is a little different in that it is for illustration in a Science book, and the Charlotte Zolotow Award was set up to ensure that text – such an important and integral part of many picture books – should have its own award for excellence.

The idea of an exciting or promising newcomer to children's book illustration is an interesting concept, but there is always a likelihood that the person winning such an award may fall by the wayside. Some illustrators win, or are commended for, the Greenaway or Caldecott Medal with their first book, sometimes an artist who received the Mother Goose went on to win the Greenaway at a later point in their careers. Juan Wijngaard, for instance, who won the Mother Goose in 1981, was awarded the Greenaway in 1985. Patrick Lynch, the 1987 Mother Goose recipient, won the Greenaway Medal in 1995 and 1997. Patrick Benson, the 1984 recipient, has yet to win the Greenaway, although he was Highly Commended in the 1995 awards.

In 1982 and 1983, the first two years of the Maschler 'Emil', the winning titles were also the Greenaway medallists for those years. Whilst this might seem to invalidate the idea of the original setting up of the award, it did at least show that for these years the Greenaway was being awarded to books which were integrally picture books, with text and illustrations well balanced. More recent winning names included illustrators who won the Greenaway in other years; Michael Foreman and Anthony Browne, Raymond Briggs, John Burningham, Charles Keeping and Quentin Blake, as well as the team efforts from Allan and Janet Ahlberg, and Barbara Firth and Martin Waddell. Colin McNaughton, the 1991 'Emil' winner, was shortlisted for the 1995 Greenaway. Patrick Benson is the only Mother Goose winner (1984) to have also won an 'Emil' (1995).

The Ezra Jack Keats Award was set up in 1986 and was originally a new writer award for picture books, but now has separate illustrator and writer awards. At first the Award was made in alternate years and considered books published during the previous two years; since 1999 it is awarded each year. Faith Ringgold's *Tar Beach* was the only Caldecott Honor for 1992 and won the 1993 Ezra Jack Keats Writer Award. Bryan Collier, EJK Illustrator winner for 2001 with *Uptown*, received a Caldecott Honor in 2002 for *Martin's Big Words*. The 2001 EJK writer award winner, *Henry Hikes to Fitchburg* was also that year's Giverny winner.

The Giverny Award is made for 'the best children's science book'. Its first winner was the well-established illustrator Molly Bang, three times on the Honor list for the Caldecott Medal. None of the other winners have appeared in the Caldecott lists. Don Brown, whose *Rare Treasure* was the 2002 Giverny winner, was on the 2001 Boston Globe/Horn Book Honor list for Non-Fiction with his *Uncommon Traveler: Mary Kingsley in Africa*. None of the other Giverny winners has so far appeared in the BGH list for any category.

The Charlotte Zolotow Award was instituted in 1998. Books published in one year are eligible for the prize awarded in the following year, so that the 2005 award will be for books published during 2004. In this list, the text author's name is shown first, as having won the actual award, with the illustrator's name following the title unless the author is also the illustrator, when just the publisher will be shown after the title. Several names, such as Rosemary Wells, Molly Bang, Uri Shulevitz, Christopher Myers, Kevin Henkes, Kate Banks and Vera B Williams, are recognisable from their regular appearances in the Newbery, Caldecott and Boston Globe/Horn Book lists.

Taken together, this all suggests that in both the UK and the US there is a broad consensus of opinion regarding quality in illustration for both story and non-fiction. The importance of clarity in understanding science has been reinforced by the Giverny. In addition, the existence of awards which support new artists may encourage publishers on both sides of the Atlantic to use newcomers.

The breadth and variety of styles within the choices made by the sets of judges for these illustration awards demonstrates the vitality of the children's book illustration world. The Charlotte Zolotow Award holds aloft the banner for the words that go with the pictures – to ensure that the art is not let down by a trite text. One can see that quality is recognisable in types of illustration across the different styles of art, and that if words accompany that illustration, these too will be of high quality. The placing of text and choice of typeface or hand lettering should be part of the essential picture book design, but the literary quality of the words as well as their appearance, is important too. Whatever one's taste, and at whatever stage or age one's child has reached, there will be something that will not only appeal, but will put artwork of undeniable quality and words of power in front of his or her eyes.

Kurt Maschler 'Emil' Award (UK): complete list of winners

1982 Michael FOREMAN. *The Sleeping Beauty and Other Favourite Fairy Tales*, by Angela CARTER. Gollancz.

1983 Anthony BROWNE. *Gorilla*. Julia MacRae.

1984 John BURNINGHAM. *Granpa*. Cape.

1985 Ted HUGHES. *The Iron Man*, ills Andrew DAVIDSON. Faber.

1986 Janet & Allan AHLBERG. *The Jolly Postman*. Heinemann.

1987 Charles CAUSLEY. *Jack the Treacle Eater*, ills Charles KEEPING. Macmillan Children's Books.

1988 Anthony BROWNE. *Alice's Adventures in Wonderland*. Julia MacRae.

1989 Martin WADDELL (text) & Barbara FIRTH (ills). *The Park in the Dark*. Walker Books.

1990 Quentin BLAKE. *All Join In*. Cape.

1991 Colin McNAUGHTON. *Have You Seen Who's Just Moved In Next Door to Us?* Walker Books.

1992 Raymond BRIGGS. *The Man*. Julia MacRae.

1993 Karen WALLACE. *Think of an Eel*. Walker Books.

1994 Trish COOKE (text) & Helen OXENBURY (ills). *So Much*. Walker Books.

1995 Kathy HENDERSON (text) & Patrick BENSON (ills). *The Little Boat*. Walker Books.

1996 Babette COLE. *Drop Dead*. Cape.

1997 William MAYNE (text) & Jonathan HEALE (ills). *Lady Muck*. Heinemann.

1998 Anthony BROWNE. *Voices in the Park*. Doubleday.

Winning Books

1999 Helen OXENBURY (ills). *Alice's Adventures in Wonderland.* Walker Books.

2000 No Award Given, Kurt Maschler Award discontinued

Mother Goose Award (UK): complete list of winners

1979 Michelle CARTLIDGE. *Pippin and Pod.* Heinemann.

1980 Reg CARTWRIGHT. *Mr. Potter's Pigeon.* Hutchinson Young Books.

1981 Juan WIJNGAARD. *Green Finger House*, text by Rosemary HARRIS. Eel Pie.

1982 Jan ORMEROD. *Sunshine.* Viking.

1983 Satoshi KITAMURA. *Angry Arthur.* Andersen Press.

1984 Patrick BENSON. *The Red Book of Hob Stories*; *The Green Book of Hob Stories*, text by William MAYNE. Walker Books.

1985 Sue VARLEY. *Badger's Parting Gifts.* Andersen.

1986 No Award

1987 Patrick LYNCH. *A Bag of Moonshine*, text by Alan GARNER. Collins.

1988 Emma Chichester CLARK. *Listen to This.* Bodley Head.

1989 Charles FUGE. *Bush Vark's First Day Out.* Macmillan.

1990 David HUGHES. *Strat and Chatto.* Walker Books.

1991 Amanda HARVEY. *A Close Call.* Macmillan.

1992 Ted DEWAN. *Inside the Whale and Other Animals*, text by Steve PARKER. Dorling Kindersley.

1993 Claire FLETCHER. *The Seashell Song.* Bodley Head.

1994 Lisa FLATHER. *Where the Great Bear Watches.* ABC.

1995 Flora McDONNELL. *I Love Animals.* Walker Books.

1996 Bruce INGMAN. *When Martha's Away.* Methuen.

Winning Books

1997 Clare JARRETT. *Catherine and the Lion.* HarperCollins.

1998 Mary FEDDEN. *Motley the Cat.* Viking.

1999 Niamh SHARKEY. *The Gigantic Turnip and Tales of Wisdom and Wonder.* Barefoot Books.

2000 Award discontinued

The Ezra Jack Keats New Writer and New Illustrator Awards: complete list of winners

1986 **Writer Award**
Valerie FLOURNOY. *The Patchwork Quilt.* Dial Books.

1987 **Writer Award**
Juanita HAVILL. *Jamaica's Find.* Houghton Mifflin.

1989 **Writer Award**
Yoriko TSUTSUI. *Anna's Special Present.* Viking Kestrel.

1991 **Writer Award**
Angela JOHNSON. *Tell Me a Story, Mama.* Orchard.

1993 **Writer Award**
Faith RINGGOLD. *Tar Beach.* Crown Publishers.

1995 **Writer Award**
Cari BEST. *Taxi! Taxi!* Little Brown & Co..

1997 **Writer Award**
Juan Felipe HERRERA. *Calling the Doves.* Children's Book Press.

1999 **Writer Award**
Stephanie STUVE-BODEEN. *Elizabeti's Doll,* ills Christy HALE. Lee and Low Books.

2000 **Writer Award**
Soyung PAK. *Dear Juno.* Viking Children's Books.

2001 **Writer Award**
D. B. JOHNSON. *Henry Hikes to Fitchburg.* Houghton Mifflin Publishers.

Illustrator Award
Bryan COLLIER. *Uptown.* Henry Holt & Co.

2002 **Writer Award and Illustrator Award**
Deborah WILES. *Freedom Summer,* ills James LAGARRIGUE. Simon and Schuster.

2003 **Writer Award and Illustrator Award**
Shirin Yim BRIDGES. *Ruby's Wish,* ills Sophie BLACKALL. Chronicle.

2004 **Writer Award**
Jeron Ashford FRAME. *Yesterday I Had the Blues.* Ten Speed Press.

Illustrator Award
Gabi SWIATKOWSKA. *My Name is Yoon.* Frances Foster Books.

2005 **Writer Award**
Janice N. HARRINGTON. *Going North*, ills Jerome LAGARRIGUE. Melanie Kroupa Books.

Illustrator Award
Ana JUAN. *The Night Eater.* Scholastic.

Giverny Award for Best Children's Science Picture Book: complete list of winners

1998 Molly BANG. *Common Ground: The Water, Earth, and Air We Share*. Blue Sky Press/Scholastic.

1999 Axel SCHEFFLER. *Sam Plants a Sunflower*, text by Kate PETTY. Macmillan.

2000 Robin BRICKMAN. *A Log's Life*, text by Wendy PFEFFER. Simon & Schuster.

2001 D. B. JOHNSON. *Henry Hikes to Fitchburg*. Houghton Mifflin.

2002 Don BROWN. *Rare Treasure: Mary Anning and Her Remarkable Discoveries*. Houghton Mifflin.

2003 Jeannie BAKER. *The Hidden Forest*. Greenwillow Books.

2004 Jean CASSELS. *Lonesome George the Giant Tortoise*, text by Francine JACOBS. Walker.

Charlotte Zolotow Award: complete list of winners and honor books

1998 Vera B. WILLIAMS. *Lucky Song*. Greenwillow.

Honor Book
Keiko KASZA. *Don't Laugh, Joe!* Putnam.

Highly Commended
Marion Dane BAUER. *If You Were Born a Kitten*, ills JoEllen McAllister STAMMEN. Simon & Schuster.

Elisha COOPER. *Country Fair*. Greenwillow.

Denise FLEMING. *Time to Sleep*. Henry Holt.

Patricia C. McKISSACK. *Ma Dear's Aprons*, ills Floyd COOPER. Anne Schwartz/Atheneum.

Bernard WABER. *Bearsie Bear and the Surprise Sleepover Party*. Houghton Mifflin.

Rosemary WELLS. *Bunny Cakes*. Dial.

1999 Uri SHULEVITZ. *Snow*. Farrar Straus Giroux.

Honor Books
Holly MEADE. *John Willy and Freddy McGee*. Marshall Cavendish.

William STEIG. *Pete's a Pizza*. Michael di Capua/HarperCollins.

Highly Commended
Denise FLEMING. *Mama Cat Has Three Kittens*. Henry Holt.

Kevin HENKES. *Circle Dogs*, ills Dan YACCARINO. Greenwillow.

Bill T. JONES & Susan KUKLIN. *Dance*, photographs by Susan KUKLIN. Hyperion.

Lynn REISER. *Little Clam*. Greenwillow.

Stephanie STUVE-BODEEN. *Elizabeti's Doll*, ills Christy HALE. Lee & Low.

2000 Molly BANG. *When Sophie Gets Angry – Really, Really Angry...* Blue Sky/Scholastic.

Honor Books
Cari BEST. *Three Cheers for Catherine the Great!* ills Giselle POTTER. Melanie Kroupa/DK Ink.

Jules FEIFFER. *Bark, George*. Michael di Capua/HarperCollins.

Highly Commended
Baba Wagué DIAKITÉ. *The Hatseller and the Monkeys*. Scholastic.

Kristine O'Connell GEORGE. *Little Dog Poems*, ills June OTANI. Clarion.

Joan Bransfield GRAHAM. *Flicker Flash*, ills Nancy DAVIS. Houghton Mifflin.

Elizabeth Fitzgerald HOWARD. *When Will Sarah Come?*, ills Nina CREWS. Greenwillow.

Amy SCHWARTZ. *How to Catch an Elephant*. DK Ink.

Joyce Carol THOMAS. *You Are My Perfect Baby*, ills Nneka BENNETT. Harper Growing Tree / HarperCollins.

Andrea ZIMMERMAN & David CLEMESHA. *Trashy Town*. HarperCollins.

2001 Kate BANKS. *The Night Worker*, ills Georg HALLENSLEBEN. Frances Foster/Farrar Straus Giroux.

Honor Books
Christopher MYERS. *Wings*. Scholastic Press.

Highly Commended
Peggy CHRISTIAN. *If You Find a Rock*, ills Barbara Hirsch LEMBER. Harcourt.

Doreen CRONIN. *Click Clack Moo: Cows that Type*, ills Betsy LEWIN. Simon & Schuster.

Joy HARJO. *The Good Luck Cat*, ills Paul LEE. Harcourt.

Kimiko KAJIKAWA. *Yoshi's Feast*, ills Yumi HEO. Melanie Kroupa/DK Ink.

Sandra L. PINKNEY. *Shades of Black: A Celebration of Our Children*, photographs by Myles C. PINKNEY. Scholastic.

Nancy Van LAAN. *When Winter Comes*, ills Susan GABER. Anne Schwartz/Atheneum.

2002 Margaret WILLEY. *Clever Beatrice*, ills Heather SOLOMON. Atheneum, 2001.

Honor Books
Emily JENKINS. *Five Creatures*. Frances Foster/Farrar Straus Giroux.

Highly Commended
Lenore LOOK. *Henry's First Moon Birthday*, ills Yumi HEO. Anne Schwartz/Atheneum.

Margaret Read MacDONALD. *Mabela the Clever*, ills Tim COFFEY. Albert Whitman.

Marisabina RUSSO. *Come Back, Hannah.* Greenwillow/HarperCollins.

Catherine STOCK. *Gugu's House.* Clarion.

Janet S. WONG. *Grump*, ills John WALLACE. Margaret K. McElderry.

2003 Holly KELLER. *Farfallina & Marcel*, edited by Virginia DUNCAN. Greenwillow Books/HarperCollins Children's Books.

Honor Books
Susan Marie SWANSON. *The First Thing My Mama Told Me*, ills Christine DAVENIER, edited by Jeannette LARSON. Harcourt.

Highly Commended
Nancy ANDREWS-GOEBEL. *The Pot That Juan Built*, ills David DIAZ. Lee & Low.

Kate BANKS. *Close Your Eyes*, ills Georg HALLENSLEBEN. Frances Foster Books/Farrar, Straus & Giroux.

Kevin HENKES. *Owen's Marshmallow Chick.* Greenwillow Books/HarperCollins.

Juan Felipe HERRERA. *Grandma and Me at the Flea*, ills Anita de LUCIO-BROCK. Children's Book Press.

Kate & Jim McMULLAN. *I Stink!* Joanna Cotler Books/HarperCollins.

Jean Davies OKIMOTO & Elaine M. AOKI. *The White Swan Express: A Story about Adoption*, ills Meilo SO. Clarion.

Alice SCHERTLE. *All You Need for a Snowman*, ills Barbara LAVALLEE. Silver Whistle/Harcourt.

David SHANNON. *Duck on a Bike.* Blue Sky Press/Scholastic.

Karma WILSON. *Bear Snores On*, ills Jane CHAPMAN. McElderry.

Janet S. WONG. *Apple Pie 4th of July*, ills Margaret CHODOS-IRVINE. Harcourt.

2004 Amy SCHWARTZ. *What James Likes Best.* A Richard Jackson Book/Atheneum.

Honor Books
John COY. *Two Old Potatoes and Me*, ills Carolyn FISHER. Alfred A. Knopf.

Rebecca O'CONNELL. *The Baby Goes Beep*, ills Ken WILSON-MAX. A Deborah Brodie Book/Roaring Brook Press.

Won-Ldy PAYE & Margaret H. LIPPERT. *Mrs. Chicken and the Hungry Crocodile*, ills Julie PASCHKIS. Henry Holt.

James RUMFORD. *Calabash Cat and His Amazing Journey.* Houghton Mifflin.

George SHANNON. *Tippy-Toe Chick, Go!*, ills Laura DRONZEK. Greenwillow Books/HarperCollins.

Highly Commended
Kate BANKS. *Mama's Coming Home*, ills Tomek BOGACKI. Frances Foster Books/Farrar, Straus and Giroux.

Deborah CHANDRA & Madeleine COMORA. *George Washington's Teeth*, ills Brock COLE. Farrar, Straus and Giroux.

Denise FLEMING. *Buster.* Henry Holt.

Jeron Ashford FRAME. *Yesterday I Had the Blues*, ills R. Gregory CHRISTIE. Tricycle Press.

Steve JENKINS and Robin PAGE. *What Do You Do With a Tail Like This?* Houghton Mifflin.

Naomi Shihab NYE. *Baby Radar*, ills Nancy CARLSON. Greenwillow Books/HarperCollins.

Lynne Rae PERKINS. *Snow Music.* Greenwillow Books/HarperCollins.

Andrea U'REN. *Mary Smith.* Farrar, Straus and Giroux.

Mo WILLEMS. *Don't Let the Pigeon Drive the Bus.* Hyperion.

Chapter 9: Coming from another Angle – awards set up to complement or correct the mainstream award scene

This chapter covers the Guardian Award (UK); the Other Award (UK); the Red House Children's Book Award (UK); the Kathleen Fidler Award (UK); the Branford Boase Award (UK); the NASEN Award (UK); the Marsh Award (UK); the Mildred L. Batchelder Award (US); the Coretta Scott King Award (US); the Américas Award (US), the Pura Belpré Award (US); the Jane Addams Award (US); the Michael L. Printz Award (US); the Booktrust Teenage Prize (UK); the Booktrust Early Years Award & the Phoenix Award (US).

During the 1960s and 1970s there was disquiet among some critics and librarians in the UK that awards such as the Carnegie Medal were being given for 'safe' books. This was partly because they were judged by criteria which had to do with quality as seen by librarians. The choices seemed far removed from the modern world, and were considered remote from the experiences, likes and dislikes of children themselves. It is also true to say that the frequent appearance of winners published by Oxford University Press – no accident, since Mabel George, its Children's Editor for many years, was a person of considerable discernment whose influence was felt across the children's book world in the 1950s and 1960s – had given rise to concern that Oxford were monopolising the lists. Several attempts were made at solving the problem that was thus perceived.

The earliest of these was the Guardian Award, which produced winners of considerable literary merit, not quite such 'safe' choices – a deliberate policy – and invited the winning author to be a judge the following year. Rather than looking for a popular winner, the judges wished to choose a winner of literary quality, and try to make it popular. The Guardian Award has been given annually since 1967 for 'an outstanding work of fiction for children' by a British or Commonwealth author, which was first published in the UK in the preceding year. Even so, the Guardian Award-winner in only its second year was the Carnegie-winning *The Owl Service* by Alan Garner (Carnegie 1967; Guardian 1968). Certainly this is an outstanding book by any standards, so perhaps it is not fair to single it out as an example of convergence between the judges of the two awards.

Other instances of agreement in the judges' choices have been Richard Adams's *Watership Down* (Carnegie 1972; Guardian 1973), Robert Westall's *The Scarecrows* (winner for 1981 of both awards), Geraldine McCaughrean's *A Pack of Lies* (Carnegie 1988; Guardian 1989), Anne Fine's *Goggle-Eyes* (Carnegie 1989; Guardian 1990), and Philip Pullman's *Northern Lights* (Carnegie 1995; Guardian joint winner 1996). The date discrepancy for some titles is caused by the difference in the timing of the judging, and by the Carnegie terminology of using the date of the publication year for all the books which are considered for the award which is made in the summer of the following year. In addition, several of the Guardian Award-winners are on the Carnegie Commended lists for the appropriate year. The 1997 Guardian winner, Melvin Burgess's *Junk*, is a strong story which tackles the difficult subject of drugs, depicting children who become junkies. It also won the 1996 Carnegie Medal, and two of Burgess's earlier titles, *Cry of the Wolf* (1990) and *The Baby and Fly Pie* (1993), were Highly Commended by the Carnegie judges. More recently, Terry Pratchett's *Amazing Maurice and his Educated Rodents* (Carnegie 2001) was on the 2002 Guardian Shortlist and David Almond's *Kit's Wilderness* was on the 2000 Guardian shortlist and Highly Commended by the 1999 Carnegie judges. Several *Harry Potter* titles, perhaps inevitably, have appeared in both lists, and the late Henrietta Branford, whose name is given to the Branford Boase Award, discussed later in this chapter, was the 1998 Guardian winner with *Fire, Bed and Bone*, which was commended by the Carnegie judges for 1997.

The Other Award was an even more definite attempt to get away from the perceived cosiness of the Carnegie, and its judges set out to find books which were politically correct and reflected the world as it really was, whilst maintaining a high literary standard. The Other Award took the form of an annual commendation to a number of children's books published during the preceding year and was not accompanied by a prize or money. Established by the Children's Rights Workshop in 1975 as a counter-award to those which already existed, it aimed to draw attention both to important new work and to neglected work of a progressive nature from children's writers and illustrators. In 1976, the second year of this award, Shirley Hughes's *Helpers* was listed. This was a Greenaway Commended title for 1975. In 1977, its third year, one title listed, Gene Kemp's *The Turbulent Term of Tyke Tyler*, was also the Carnegie Medal-winner. James Watson's *Talking in Whispers* was a 1983 Other Award listing and was Highly Commended for the Carnegie. In 1984, Robert Swindells's *Brother in the Land*, was not only on the Other Award list, but won the Children's Book Award for that year, and was also Highly Commended by the Carnegie panel. In 1988 the Other Award was discontinued, partly through funding – the administrators chose not to seek sponsorship – but largely because it was felt to have served its purpose. In addition, they no longer considered an award an appropriate way to promote 'other' concerns. Certainly it can be maintained that if a book which is listed for the Other Award is also a Carnegie medallist or commendation, then either the Carnegie judges are, after all, recognising the modern world, or the Other Award judges may have played safe. In such cases the Award could be seen as becoming redundant. For the last three years of its life, however, there was no overlap with the Carnegie Award in terms of the titles listed. Virginia Hamilton's *The People Could Fly*, listed for the Other Award in 1986, was also recognised by the judging panel of the Coretta Scott King Award in that year.

The Red House Children's Book Award comes from yet another direction: it uses the votes of children as its judging process. The award is sponsored by Red House, the on-line children's bookshop, and organised by the Federation of Children's Book Groups. It has been awarded annually since 1980 for 'the best book of the year'. This award is unique in that it is the children themselves who make the decision. Members of the Children's Book Groups, which are based in schools and libraries throughout England and Scotland, read and test the books themselves. Publishers are invited to submit children's fiction published in the UK, including titles previously published elsewhere. Ideally these are sent as the books are published so that the books can be tested throughout the calendar year. There are twelve testing regions, and they send results and comments to the award co-ordinator to tabulate as the year progresses. These twelve regions are not permanent, but the turnover is not high, since it takes time to develop the testing network in an area. A title which is proving particularly popular will have further copies bought, or its publisher will be asked for more supplies. Each year a list of fifty 'best' books is assembled, usually by 1 March, from which a 'pick of the year' annotated reading list is produced. Within these fifty are a 'top ten' shortlist, and another vote is taken to choose, by the beginning of May, the winner in each of the three categories: longer novel, shorter novel and picture book. Then a portfolio is put together for each shortlisted book containing the comments and views of the children, including both written and illustrative work. These are presented to the shortlisted authors at the annual award ceremony, when the winner in each category is announced, and which some of the participating children attend. These arrangements manage to avoid a completely populist approach, whilst giving children a strong voice in the decision. There is also the possibility of better sales to children, or at least higher readership by some children, if something is approved by their peers, rather than being seen as 'good for them'. It is interesting that even so several of the choices have coincided with commended titles in the lists of awards chosen by adults. Indeed the very first Children's Book Award, in 1980, was made to Quentin Blake's *Mr. Magnolia* which also won the Greenaway Medal that year, and in 1983 their choice, Terry Jones's *The Saga of Erik the Viking*, illustrated by Michael Foreman, was a Greenaway Commended title. In 1995 their longer novel winner, Sharon Creech's *Walk Two Moons*, was also the Newbery Medallist. Similarly in 1996, the overall and longer novel winner, Jacqueline Wilson's *Double Act*, was Highly Commended by the Carnegie judges. In contrast, Michael Morpurgo, Children's Laureate until 2005, is represented several times in this award, whereas he has not yet got beyond a Commended (*King of the Cloud Forests* 1987) in the Carnegie listings, despite being shortlisted on a number of occasions since, most recently with *Private Peaceful*, the 2004 Red House overall winner.

The Kathleen Fidler Award was set up because of a perceived dearth of books written by Scottish authors for the age group 8 to 12 years. It was inaugurated in 1981 to encourage new and established authors to write for children in that range of ages. Sponsored by Blackie, who published the winning book each year, and administered by Book Trust Scotland. It was open to Scottish writers who had not before written for this age group. Kathleen Fidler, whom this award commemorates, wrote a number of children's books, several set in Scotland, and Blackie were her main publishers. The first winning title was published in 1983 and the award was discontinued in 2002 by Hodder, who had taken over Blackie.

The Branford Boase Award is also for new writers; awarded to: 'the most promising book for seven year-olds and upwards by a first-time novelist' and the author and the editor who brings the book to press are both cited. It is named in memory of two outstanding women in British publishing. The first is Henrietta Branford, whose *Fire, Bed and Bone* (1998 Guardian; 1997 Carnegie Commended) seemed to promise so much, only for those hopes to be dashed at her early death from cancer in 1999. Wendy Boase was Henrietta's editor at Walker Books, and had suggested writing from an animal's viewpoint – the point of difference that made *Fire, Bed and Bone* stand out from its peers. Wendy, too, contracted cancer and died just a month before Henrietta. The award was set up by Julia Eccleshare, Children's Book Editor of the Guardian newspaper, Ann Marley, Principal Librarian for Hampshire Children's and Schools' Library Service, and the publishers Walker Books. Still a young award, with only six winners so far, the Branford Boase Award has filled some of the vacuum left by the discontinuation of the Fidler Award, and brings a new element in its recognition of the importance of the editor, especially for a new writer.

The National Association for Special Educational Needs (NASEN) set up a children's book award which was given for the first time in 1994. It is awarded for 'a book written for children under 16 years of age which does most to put forward a positive image of children with special educational needs'. Berlie Doherty and Anne Fine, who won the NASEN Award in 1995 and 1996 respectively, are established writers who have won other major prizes, including, twice each, the Carnegie Medal, and Jack Gantos, author of *Joey Pigza Swallowed the Key*, the 2001 winner, is well-known in the US, where this title was first published.

Two awards, the Marsh Award in the UK and the Mildred Batchelder Award in the US, were set up to acknowledge and encourage the reading, by children whose only language is English, of books which were first published in other languages. Many of these are now recognised children's classics, including Eric Kästner's 'Emil' books. Kästner himself was the author of the first winner of the Batchelder Award. Antoine de Saint-Exupéry's *Petit Prince*, André Maurois' *Fattypuffs and Thinifers*, and Heinrich Hoffmann's *Struwwelpeter* (whatever one thinks of its depiction of morals) are earlier examples of the genre. The illustrative work of Hergé, in his *Tintin* stories; Laurent and Jean de Brunhoff for *Babar*; Albert Uderzo and René Goscinny's *Asterix the Gaul* series; as well as the Père Castor books for younger children would none of them be part of an English-speaking childhood had their texts not been translated, in the case of *Asterix*, by Anthea Bell, herself winner, more than once, of the Marsh Award. More recently several Japanese illustrators have also been made available in English-language editions, in particular the work of Mitsumasa Anno. His wordless 'Journeys' to various countries, which draw on the traditions of the countries themselves, are perhaps not relevant to the language debate, but his counting book, his alphabet and his books of mathematical puzzles are gems which one would like every child to have seen. Indeed, the fairy tales of Charles Perrault, Hans Andersen and the Brothers Grimm, which could be deemed necessary reading in childhood, are of course only accessible to the English-speaking child through translations. More recently, the German author Cornelia Funke has become popular in the

UK through the translation of her works into English; one of these was a winner of the Askews Torchlight Award for 2003.

The Marsh Award for Children's Literature in Translation is awarded biennially, but the period from which the first winning title was chosen ran from 1990 until 1996. It is open to British translators of books for 4-16 year olds, published in the UK by a British publisher. The Marsh Award has some similarities in concept to the Mildred L. Batchelder Award (US), except that it is given to the translator rather than to the publisher. The first – and the most recent – winner, Anthea Bell, is also the translator for four of the books in the Batchelder Award list.

The Association for Library Service to Children (ALSC), a division of the American Library Association (ALA), has presented the Mildred L. Batchelder Award since 1968. It was inaugurated in 1966, and is an annual award. Mildred L. Batchelder was a children's librarian and former Executive Director of the ALSC, whose work over three decades had an international influence. The ALSC gives the award to American publishers to encourage them to seek out superior children's books abroad and to promote communication between the peoples of the world. This is its main difference from the Marsh Award, which is made to the translator. The award is made annually unless the award committee is of the opinion that no book of the year in question is worthy of the award. Until 1979, the award had been given to a book published two years previously, but since then it has been given to a publisher for a book published in the preceding year. From the 1991 award onwards, the selection committee may also designate Honor Book publishers. Announced during ALA's annual Midwinter Conference, a citation is awarded to an American publisher for a children's book (any trade book for children from pre-nursery through ninth grade) considered to be the most outstanding of those books originally published in a foreign language in a foreign country, and subsequently translated into English and published in the United States. This award has brought into greater prominence throughout the US books which would not be available to English-speaking children, had they not been translated through the auspices of those publishers who have produced them in English-language editions.

In the US, librarians and commentators have long been concerned that literatures from what had previously been considered minority groups would have the chance to be judged within their own terms of reference, as well as against the rest of US publishing output. This has resulted in the Coretta Scott King Award for African American literature, the Américas Award, the Pura Belpré Award for Latino literature and the Jane Addams Award.

The Coretta Scott King Award (CSK) was established by the American Library Association (ALA) Social Responsibilities Round Table in 1969. It was felt to be an appropriate tribute to the memory of Martin Luther King, and to the continuing work undertaken in the field of civil rights by his widow, Coretta Scott King, that an award named for her should be instituted. It was even more apt that the first winning title, in 1970, should be a biography of Martin

Luther King himself. The award was specifically intended 'to commemorate and foster the life, work and dreams of Dr Martin Luther King, Jr., and to honor his wife Coretta Scott King for her courage and determination in continuing to work for peace and world brotherhood'. The original condition was that it be given to 'a black author, whose books, published in the preceding year, are outstanding, inspirational and educational contributions to literature for children and young people'. In 1979 an illustration category was added, so that awards are now made annually both to a black author and a black illustrator. The 1983 CSK Text Award winner, Virginia Hamilton's *Sweet Whispers, Brother Rush*, was the Fiction Boston Globe-Horn Book Award-winner that year as well as being a Newbery Honor Book, and the 1988 CSK Text Award-winner, Mildred D. Taylor's *The Friendship*, also won the 1988 Fiction Boston Globe-Horn Book Award. Both these authors have also been Newbery Medallists, Taylor in 1977 and Hamilton in 1975, and have been in the Honor lists on several other occasions. The 1993 CSK Text Award winner, Patricia McKissack's *The Dark-Thirty* was also a Newbery Honor Book in that year. In terms of illustration, Jerry Pinkney, the CSK Illustration Award winner for 1997, has appeared in the Caldecott Honor lists, the most relevant being for *Mirandy and Brother Wind*, the CSK Illustration Award winner for 1989. Faith Ringgold's *Tar Beach*, the CSK Illustration Award winner for 1992 was a Caldecott Honor Book the same year, and Tom Feelings, the CSK Illustration Award winner in 1979, had books in the Caldecott Honor lists for 1972 and 1975. John Steptoe, twice a CSK Illustration Award winner, was listed in the Caldecott Honors for his *Mufaro's Beautiful Daughters* in 1988. Brian Collier gained a Caldecott Honor in 2002 for *Martin's Big Words: the Life of Dr. Martin Luther King, Jr.*, which was also a CSK Honor. Collier had won the CSK illustrator award for 2001. The early winners of this award often showed how young African-Americans could draw inspiration from successful role models in the Black African experience, and to this day the Honor Book list for this award nearly always includes a non-fiction title dealing with some aspect of African-American history. More recently the Coretta Scott King/John Steptoe New Talent (text) Award and the Steptoe New Talent (illustrator) Award have been added as 'occasional extras' to be awarded whenever the judges feel it is appropriate.

The Américas Award is more recent: it was set up in 1993 by the Consortium of Latin American Studies Programs (CLASP) at the University of Wisconsin. The award is given each spring, to a book published in the previous year in English or Spanish, with a commended list of finalists. It is made in recognition of a US work of fiction, poetry, or folklore, from picture books to books for young adults, which authentically and engagingly presents the experience of individuals in Latin America or the Caribbean, or of Latinos in the United States. By linking the Americas, the award seeks to reach beyond geographic borders and cultural boundaries to focus instead upon cultural heritages within the hemisphere. The award winners and other commended books are selected for their quality of story, cultural authenticity, and potential for classroom use. So far this award has not produced any shared titles with the major US awards, although Américas award-winners and Honor list placings such as Tomi dePaola and John Agard, Brian Pinkney, David Diaz and Rachel Isadora are familiar names from their appearance in other award lists. As an encouragement in the early years there were long lists of commendations; as the literature has matured, these have become shorter.

The Pura Belpré Award is given for both fiction and illustration and was instituted in 1996. It is open to 'Latino writers and illustrators whose work best exemplifies authentic cultural experiences in children's works of literature.' It naturally shares many titles with the Américas lists, but is solely for Latino authors and illustrators, and works in Spanish as well as English or dual text are permitted.

The Jane Addams Award has been in existence since 1953, it is given to 'to the children's book of the preceding year that most effectively promotes the cause of peace, social justice and world community.' It is named for Jane Addams, the first American woman to win the Nobel Peace Prize, which she received in 1931. Originally awarded just for writing, it has, since 1993, included a picture book category. It is administered by the Women's International League for Peace and Freedom (WILPF) and the Jane Addams Peace Association (the educational affiliate of WILPF). Eligible titles are: 'books for preschool through age fourteen ... including translations and books published in English in other countries, and subsequently published in the U.S.A. during the preceding year.' Each year an award committee, formed of members of WILPF from across the US who are concerned with children's books, considers submissions from publishers; it can also call in titles for consideration. The award is now made in April on the anniversary of the founding of WILPF, for books published during the preceding year. Several authors and illustrators, Katherine Paterson, Virginia Euwer Wolff, Mitsumaso Anno, are familiar as Newbery or Caldecott Medallists or Honors, but as the Addams judges are looking for a different quality, and are allowed a wider source range than that imposed by the Newbery/Caldecott regulations. Consequently titles will be seen in this list that appear perhaps in the Coretta Scott King, the Américas or the Belpré lists, or perhaps do not qualify in any other listing.

There is another area that has seemed to some people to have been ignored over the years – teenage fiction. For a number of years Librarians were reluctant to set up a purely 'teenage' award as it might be seen to detract from the 'main' award, or to make novels for the 'older reader' (something of a misnomer, as this indicates 11-16-year-olds) ineligible for that award. On both sides of the Atlantic there are now awards which deliberately cover this ground. In the US, the Michael L. Printz Award has been running since 2000 and in the UK the Booktrust Teenage Prize since 2003. In some years the award-winner has been a title that has won another of the major awards, but the award's existence has enabled judges to look specifically at what constitutes a good book for a 'young adult' as opposed to a good children's book. They are not always the same thing.

The Michael L. Printz Award is an award 'for a book that exemplifies literary excellence in young adult literature'. It is named for a school librarian from

Kansas who was a long-time active member of the Young Adult Library Services Association; it is administered by the Young Adult Library Services Association (YALSA), a division of ALA, and sponsored by Booklist magazine. One of its Honor books for 2004 was the Carnegie-winner, Jennifer Donnelly's *A Northern Light* (published in UK as *A Gathering Light*).

The Booktrust Teenage Prize was launched in 2003 with the aim to recognise and celebrate contemporary teenage fiction. It is administered by Booktrust, the current designation of the body that used to be known as the National Book League, and which also oversees the Early Years Award (see below), the W. H Smith Children's Book of the Year and the Smarties Prize (see Chapter 11). The winner for 2003 was Mark Haddon's *Curious Incident of the Dog in the Night-Time*, which won many other awards and plaudits, and would have been difficult for the judges of this new award to overlook. The 2004 winner, Anne Cassidy's *Looking for JJ*, is equally compelling, but has not produced such a publicity furore as the Haddon.

Also administered by Booktrust, the Early Years Award is even newer and is judged in three categories: the best book for babies under one year old, the best book for pre-school children, up to five years of age and an award for the best new illustrator. The first awards were made in 2004. It replaces Sainsbury's Baby Book Award, which ran from 1999 to 2003, the winners of which are included in the Early Years Award list at the end of this chapter. The first winners include Julia Donaldson, whose *The Gruffalo* was a Smarties Prize gold award-winner in 1999.

Finally in this section, the Phoenix Award takes yet another viewpoint. It is awarded to a book that has proved of lasting quality twenty years after its first publication, but which did not win a major award at the time of publication. The list contains authors whose other books are winners and honours in many of the awards listed within these pages, such as Katherine Paterson, William Mayne, Alan Garner, Peter Dickinson, Brian Doyle and E. L. Konigsburg.

The assortment of awards in this chapter is necessarily an eclectic mix. Each takes a different viewpoint from the establishment idea of a national 'best book' award, whilst recognising quality in its various forms. It is a tribute to the strength and variety of children's book publishing in the English-speaking world that there is room in it for such diverse ideas and ideals.

Guardian Award (UK): complete list of winners

1967 Leon GARFIELD. *Devil-in-the-Fog*. Longman.

1968 Alan GARNER. *The Owl Service*. Collins.

1969 Joan AIKEN. *The Whispering Mountain*. Cape.

1970 K. M. PEYTON. *Flambards* (The Trilogy). Oxford U. P.

1971 John CHRISTOPHER. *The Guardians*. Hamish Hamilton.

1972 Gillian AVERY. *A Likely Lad*. Collins.

1973 Richard ADAMS. *Watership Down*. Rex Collings.

1974 Barbara WILLARD. *The Iron Lily*. Longman.

1975 Winifred CAWLEY. *Gran at Coalgate*. Oxford U. P.

1976 Nina BAWDEN. *The Peppermint Pig*. Gollancz.

1977 Peter DICKINSON. *The Blue Hawk*. Gollancz.

1978 Diana Wynne JONES. *A Charmed Life*. Macmillan.

1979 **Joint winners**
Andrew DAVIES. *Conrad's War*. Blackie.

Ann SCHLEE. *The Vandal*. Macmillan.

1980 Peter CARTER. *The Sentinels*. Oxford U. P.

1981 Robert WESTALL. *The Scarecrows*. Chatto & Windus.

1982 Michelle MAGORIAN. *Goodnight Mr Tom*. Kestrel.

1983 Anita DESAI. *The Village by the Sea*. Heinemann.

1984 Dick KING-SMITH. *The Sheep-Pig*. Heinemann.

1985 Ted HUGHES. *What is the Truth?* Faber.

1986 Ann PILLING. *Henry's Leg.* Viking Kestrel.

1987 James ALDRIDGE. *The True Story of Spit MacPhee.* Viking Kestrel.

1988 Ruth THOMAS. *The Runaways.* Century Hutchinson.

1989 Geraldine McCAUGHREAN. *A Pack of Lies.* Oxford U. P.

1990 Anne FINE. *Goggle-Eyes.* Hamish Hamilton.

1991 Robert WESTALL. *The Kingdom by the Sea.* Methuen.

1992 **Joint winners**
Rachel ANDERSON. *Paper Faces.* Oxford U. P.

Hilary McKAY. *The Exiles.* Gollancz.

1993 William MAYNE. *Low Tide.* Cape.

1994 Sylvia WAUGH. *The Mennyms.* Julia MacRae.

1995 Lesley HOWARTH. *Maphead.* Walker Books.

1996 **Joint winners**
Alison PRINCE. *The Sherwood Hero.* Piper.

Philip PULLMAN. *Northern Lights.* Scholastic.

1997 Melvin BURGESS. *Junk.* Andersen Press.

1998 Henrietta BRANFORD. *Fire, Bed and Bone.* Walker Books.

Shortlisted titles
Jamila GAVIN. *The Track of the Wind.* Mammoth.

J. K. ROWLING. *Harry Potter and the Philosopher's Stone.* Bloomsbury.

Jane STEMP. *Secret Songs.* Hodder Children's Books.

1999 Susan PRICE. *The Sterkarm Handshake.* Scholastic.

Shortlisted titles
David ALMOND. *Skellig*. Hodder.

Tanith LEE. *Law of the Wolf Tower*. Hodder.

2000 Jacqueline WILSON. *The Illustrated Mum*. Transworld.

Shortlisted titles
David ALMOND. *Kit's Wilderness*. Hodder.

Bernard ASHLEY. *Little Soldier*. Orchard.

Susan COOPER. *King of Shadows*. Bodley Head.

Jan MARK. *The Eclipse of the Century*. Scholastic.

J. K. ROWLING. *Harry Potter and the Prisoner of Azkaban*. Bloomsbury.

2001 Kevin CROSSLEY-HOLLAND. *Arthur: The Seeing Stone*. Orion.

Shortlisted titles
Allan AHLBERG. *My Brother's Ghost*. Puffin.

Eva IBBOTSON. *Journey to the River Sea*. Macmillan.

Celia REES. *Witch Child*. Bloomsbury.

Karen WALLACE. *Raspberries on the Yangtzee*. Simon and Schuster.

2002 Sonya HARTNETT. *Thursday's Child*. Walker.

Shortlisted titles
Keith GRAY. *Warehouse*. Red Fox.

Elizabeth LAIRD. *Jake's Tower*. Macmillan.

Linda NEWBERY. *The Shell House*. David Fickling.

Terry PRATCHETT. *The Amazing Maurice and his Educated Rodents*. Transworld.

Marcus SEDGWICK. *The Dark Horse*. Orion

2003 Mark HADDON. *The Curious Incident of the Dog in the Night-Time*. Jonathan Cape/David Fickling.

Shortlisted titles
David ALMOND. *The Fire-Eaters*. Hodder.

Kevin BROOKS. *Lucas*. Chicken House.

Alex SHEARER. *The Speed of the Dark.* Macmillan.

2004 Meg ROSOFF. *How I Live Now.* Puffin.

Shortlisted titles
Frank Cottrell BOYCE. *Millions.* Macmillan.

Ann TURNBULL. *No Shame, No Fear.* Walker.

Leslie WILSON. *Last Train from Kummersdorf.* Faber.

The Other Award (UK): complete list of winners

1975 Dorothy EDWARDS. *Joe and Timothy Together.* Methuen.

Jean MacGIBBON. *Hal.* Heinemann.

Susan PRICE. *Twopence a Tub.* Faber.

1976 Bernard ASHLEY. *Trouble with Donovan Croft.* Oxford U. P.

Louise FITZHUGH. *Nobody's Family is Going to Change.* Gollancz.

Shirley HUGHES. *Helpers.* Bodley Head.

1977 Sarah COX & Robert GOLDEN. *Railwayworker; Hospitalworker; Buildingworker; Textileworker.* Kestrel.

Farrukh DHONDY. *East End at your Feet.* Macmillan.

Gene KEMP. *The Turbulent Term of Tyke Tyler.* Faber.

1978 Basil DAVIDSON. *Discovering Africa's Past.* Longman.

Bill NAUGHTON. *Goalkeeper's Revenge.* Puffin.

Rosemary SUTCLIFF. *Song for a Dark Queen.* Pelham.

Mary WATERSON & Lance BROWN. *Gypsy Family.* Black.

1979 Dick COTE. *Old Dog, New Tricks.* Hamilton.

Farrukh DHONDY. *Come to Mecca.* Collins.

Roger MILLS. *A Comprehensive Education.* Centerprise.

Sue WAGSTAFF. *Two Victorian Families.* A. & C. Black.

1980 Allan AHLBERG. *Mrs Plug the Plumber.* Kestrel.

Angela BULL. *The Machine Breakers.* Collins.

Virginia LULING. *Aborigines.* Macdonald.

David REES. *Green Bough of Liberty.* Dobson.

1981 Dorothy EDWARDS. *A Strong and Willing Girl.* Methuen.

Ruth THOMSON. *Have You Started Yet?* Heinemann.

1982 Raymond BRIGGS. *When the Wind Blows.* Gollancz.

Marlene Fanta SHYER. *Welcome Home, Jellybean.* Granada.

1983 KARUSA. *Nowhere to Play.* A. & C. Black.

Gerard MELIA. *Will of Iron.* Longman.

Michael ROSEN. *Everybody's Here.* Bodley Head.

James WATSON. *Talking In Whispers.* Gollancz.

1984 Timothy IRELAND. *Who Lies Inside.* Gay Men's Press.

Chris SEARLE. *Wheel Around the World.* Macdonald.

Robert SWINDELLS. *Brother in the Land.* Oxford U. P.

Vera WILLIAMS. *A Chair for my Mother.* J. MacRae.

1985 Sarah BAYLIS. *Vila.* Longman.

Elyse DODGSON. *Motherland.* Heinemann.

Geraldine KAYE. *Comfort Herself.* André Deutsch.

Beverley NAIDOO. *Journey to Jo'burg.* Longman.

Our Kids. Peckham Publishing Project.

1986 John AGARD. *Say It Again, Granny.* Bodley Head.

Virginia HAMILTON. *The People Could Fly.* Walker Books.

Catherine SEFTON. *Starry Night.* Hamish Hamilton.

1987 Sandra CHICK. *Push Me Pull Me.* Women's Press.

Peter C. HEASLIP. *Grandma's Favourite.* Methuen.

Peter C. HEASLIP. *Which Twin Wins?* Methuen.

1988 Award Discontinued

Red House Children's Book Award (UK): complete list of winners

1980 Quentin BLAKE. *Mr. Magnolia.* Cape.

1981 Leon GARFIELD. *Fair's Fair.* Macdonald.

1982 Roald DAHL. *The BFG.* Cape.

1983 Terry JONES & Michael FOREMAN. *The Saga of Erik the Viking.* Pavilion.

1984 Robert SWINDELLS. *Brother in the Land.* Oxford U. P.

1985 Amanda GRAHAM. *Arthur.* Spindlewood.

1986 No Award

1987 Valerie THOMAS & Korky PAUL. *Winnie the Witch.* Oxford U. P.

1988 Roald DAHL. *Matilda.* Cape.

1989 Robert SWINDELLS. *Room 13.* Doubleday.

1990 Mick INKPEN. *Threadbear.* Hodder.

1991 No Award

1992 Elizabeth LAIRD. *Kiss the Dust.* Heinemann.

1993 Jacqueline WILSON. *The Suitcase Kid.* Doubleday.

1994 **Overall and Longer Novel winner**
Ian STRACHAN. *The Boy in the Bubble.* Methuen.

Picture Book winner
Lorna & Graham PHILPOT. *Amazing Anthony Ant.* Orion. 1994.

Shorter Novel winner
Nigel HINTON. *The Finders.* Viking.

1995 **Overall and Shorter Novel winner**
Dick KING-SMITH. *Harriet's Hare.* Doubleday.

Picture Book winner
Korky PAUL. *The Rascally Cake*, text by Jeanne WILLIS. Andersen.

Longer Novel winner
Sharon CREECH. *Walk Two Moons.* Pan Macmillan.

1996 **Overall and Longer Novel winner**
Jacqueline WILSON. *Double Act.* Doubleday.

Picture Book winner
Paul GERAGHTY. *Solo.* Hutchinson.

Shorter Novel winner
Michael MORPURGO. *The Wreck of the Zanzibar.* Heinemann.

1997 **Overall and Shorter Novel winner**
Jeremy STRONG & Nick SHARRATT. *The Hundred-Mile-An-Hour Dog.* Viking.

Longer Novel winner
Ian STRACHAN. *Which Way is Home?* Methuen.

Picture Book winner
Debi GLIORI. *Mr Bear to the Rescue.* Orchard Books.

1998 **Overall and Longer Novel winner**
J. K. ROWLING. *Harry Potter and the Philosopher's Stone.* Bloomsbury.

Picture Book winner
Giles ANDREAE & David WOJTOWYCZ. *The Lion Who Wanted to Love.* Orchard.

Shorter Novel winner
Robert SWINDELLS. *Nightmare Stairs.* Doubleday.

1999 **Overall and Longer Novel winner**
J. K. ROWLING. *Harry Potter and the Chamber of Secrets.* Bloomsbury.

Picture Book winner
Kate LUM & Adrian JOHNSON. *What!* Bloomsbury.

Shorter Novel winner
Pat MOON. *Little Dad.* Mammoth.

2000 **Overall and Shorter Novel winner**
Michael MORPURGO. *Kensuke's Kingdom.* Mammoth.

Picture Book winner
Nicholas ALLAN. *Demon Teddy.* Hutchinson.

Longer Novel winner
J. K. ROWLING. *Harry Potter and the Prisoner of Azkaban.* Bloomsbury.

2001 **Overall and Picture Book winner**
Kes GRAY & Nick SHARRATT. *Eat Your Peas.* Bodley Head.

Shorter Novel winner
Jacqueline WILSON. *Lizzie Zipmouth.* Doubleday.

Longer Novel winner
J. K. ROWLING. *Harry Potter and the Goblet of Fire.* Bloomsbury.

2002 **Overall and Longer Novel winner**
Malorie BLACKMAN. *Noughts & Crosses.* Doubleday).

Picture Book winner
Allan AHLBERG & Katharine McEWEN. *The Man Who Wore All His Clothes.* Walker.

Shorter Novel winner
Michael MORPURGO. *Out of the Ashes.* Macmillan.

2003 **Overall & Category winner – Books for older readers**
Anthony HOROWITZ. *Skeleton Key.* Walker.

Category Winner – Books for younger children
Giles ANDREAE & Nick SHARRATT. *Pants.* David Fickling.

Category Winner – Books for younger readers
Robert SWINDELLS. *Blitzed.* Doubleday.

2004 **Overall & Category winner – Books for older readers**
Michael MORPURGO. *Private Peaceful.* Collins.

Category Winner – Books for younger children
Kes GRAY & Garry PARSONS. *Billy's Bucket.* Bodley Head.

Category Winner – Books for younger readers
Gwyneth REES. *The Mum Hunt.* Macmillan.

Kathleen Fidler Award: complete list of winners (all published by Blackie/Hodder)

1983 Alan BAILLIE. *Adrift.*

1984 Janet COLLINS. *Barty.*

1985 Elizabeth LUTZEIR. *No Shelter.*

1986 Caroline PITCHER. *Diamond.*

1987 Theresa BRESLIN. *Simon's Challenge.*

1988 Charles MORGAN. *Flight of the Solar Duck.*

1989 Clare BEVAN. *Mightier than the Sword.*

1990 Roger BURT. *Magic With Everything.*

1991 George HENDRY. *Greg's Revenge.*

1992 Susan COON. *Richard's Castle.*

1993 Mij KELLY. *48 Hours with Franklin.*

1994 Catherine MacPHAIL. *Run, Zan, Run.*

1995 Clare DUDMAN. *Edge of Danger.*

1996 John SMITHWAITE. *The Falcon's Quest.*

1997 Mark LEYLAND. *Slate Mountain.*

1998 No Award

1999 Thomas BLOOR. *The Memory Prisoner.*

2000 Gill VICKERY. *The Ivy Crown.*

2001 Patricia ELLIOTT. *The Ice Boy*.

Award Discontinued

Branford Boase Award: complete list of winners

2000 Katherine ROBERTS. *SongQuest.* Chicken House, winning editor: Barry CUNNINGHAM.

2001 Marcus SEDGWICK. *Floodland.* Orion Children's Books, winning editor: Fiona KENNEDY.

2002 Sally PRUE. *Cold Tom.* Oxford University Press, winning editor: Liz CROSS.

2003 Kevin BROOKS. *Martyn Pig.* Chicken House, winning editor: Barry CUNNINGHAM.

2004 Mal PEET. *Keeper.* Walker Books, winning editor: Paul HARRISON.

2005 Meg ROSOFF. *How I Live Now.* Puffin, winning editor: Rebecca McNALLY.

The NASEN Special Educational Needs Award (UK): complete list of winners

1994 David HILL. *See Ya, Simon.* Penguin.

1995 Berlie DOHERTY. *The Golden Bird.* Heinemann.

1996 Anne FINE. *How to Write Really Badly.* Methuen.

1997 Dorothy HORGAN. *Charlie's Eye.* Hamish Hamilton.

1998 Dick KING-SMITH. *The Crowstarver.* Doubleday.

1999 James RIORDAN. *Sweet Clarinet.* Oxford University Press.

2000 Jeanne WILLIS. *Susan Laughs*, ills Tony ROSS. Andersen Press.

2001 Jack GANTOS. *Joey Pigza Swallowed the Key.* Corgi Yearling.

2002 Anna PATERSON. *Running on Empty.* Lucky Duck.

2003 Luke JACKSON. *Freaks, Geeks and Asperger Syndrome.* Jessica Kingsley.

2004 Gennifer CHOLDENKO. *Al Capone Does My Shirts.* Bloomsbury.

The Marsh Award for Children's Literature in Translation: complete list of winners

1997 (eligible books published 1990-1996)
Anthea BELL (translator from the German). *A Dog's Life*, by Christine NOSTLINGER. Andersen Press.

1999 (1997-1998)
Patricia CRAMPTON (translator from the German). *The Final Journey*, by Gudrun PAUSEWANG. Viking.

2001 (1999-2000)
Betsy ROSENBERG (translator from the Hebrew). *Duel*, by David GROSSMAN. Bloomsbury.

2003 (2001-2002)
Anthea BELL (translator from the German). *Where Were You, Robert?* by Hans Magnus ENZENSBERGER. Puffin.

2005 (2003-4)
Sarah ADAMS (translator from the French). *Eye of the Wolf*, by Daniel PENNAC. Walker Books.

Mildred L. Batchelder Award (US): complete list of winners

1968 Erich KÄSTNER, translated from the German by James KIRKUP. *The Little Man.* Knopf.

1969 Babbis FRIIS-BAASTAAD, translated from the Norwegian by Lise Sømme McKINNON. *Don't Take Teddy.* Scribner.

1970 Aliki ZEÏ, translated from the Greek by Edward FENTON. *Wildcat Under Glass.* Holt, Rinehart & Winston.

1971 Hans BAUMANN, translated from the German by Stella HUMPHRIES. *In the Land of Ur: the Discovery of Ancient Mesopotamia.* Pantheon.

1972 Hans Peter RICHTER, translated from the German by Edite KROLL. *Friedrich.* Holt, Rinehart & Winston.

1973 S. R. van ITERSON, translated from the Dutch by Alexander & Alison GODE. *Pulga.* Morrow.

1974 Aliki ZEÏ, translated from the Greek by Edward FENTON. *Petros' War.* Dutton.

1975 Aleksandr LINEVSKI, translated from the Russian by Maria POLUSHKIN. *An Old Tale Carved Out of Stone.* Crown.

1976 Ruth HÜRLIMANN, translated from the German by Anthea BELL. *The Cat and the Mouse Who Shared a House.* Walck.

1977 Cecil BØDKER, translated from the Danish by Gunnar POULSEN. *The Leopard.* Atheneum.

1978 Christine NÖSTLINGER, translated from the German by Anthea BELL. *Konrad.* Watts.

1979 Jörg STEINER, translated from the German by Ann Conrad LAMMERS. *Rabbit Island*, ills Jörg MULLER. Harcourt Brace.

1980 Aliki ZEÏ, translated from the Greek by Edward FENTON. *The Sound of Dragon's Feet.* Dutton.

1981 Els PELGROM, translated from the Dutch by Maryka & Raphael RUDNIK. *The Winter When Time Was Frozen.* Morrow.

1982 Harry KULLMAN, translated from the Swedish by George BLECHER & Lone THYGESEN-BLECHER. *Battle Horse*. Bradbury.

1983 Toshi MARUKI, translated from the Japanese through the Kurita-Bando Literary Agency. *Hiroshima No Pika*. Lothrop.

1984 Astrid LINDGREN, translated from the Swedish by Patricia CRAMPTON. *Ronia, the Robber's Daughter*. Viking.

1985 Uri ORLEV, translated from the Hebrew by Hillel HALKIN. *The Island on Bird Street*. Houghton.

1986 Christophe GALLAZ, translated from the French by Martha COVENTRY & Richard GRAGLIA. *Rose Blanche*, ills Roberto INNOCENTI. Creative Education.

1987 Rudolph FRANK, translated from the German by Patricia CRAMPTON. *No Hero for the Kaiser*. Lothrop.

1988 Ulf NILSSON, translated from the Swedish by George BLECHER & Lone THYGESEN-BLECHER. *If You Didn't Have Me*. Macmillan.

1989 Peter HÄRTLING, translated from the German by Elizabeth D. CRAWFORD. *Crutches*. Lothrop.

1990 Bjarne REUTER, translated from the Danish by Anthea BELL. *Buster's World*. Dutton.

1991 Rafik SCHAMI, translated from the German by Rika LESSER. *A Hand Full of Stars*. Dutton.

Honor Book
Nina Ring AAMUNDSEN. *Two Shorts and One Long*. Houghton Mifflin.

1992 Uri ORLEV, translated from the Hebrew by Hillel HALKIN, *The Man from the Other Side*. Houghton Mifflin.

1993 No Award

1994 Pilar Molina LLORENTE, translated from the Spanish by Robin LONGSHAW. *The Apprentice*. Farrar, Straus & Giroux.

Honor Books
Ruud van der ROL & Rian VERHOEVEN, translated from the Dutch by Tony LANGHAM & Plym PETERS. *Anne Frank: Beyond the Diary*. Viking.

Annemie HEYMANS & Margriet HEYMANS, translated from the Dutch by Johanna H. PRINS & Johanna W. PRINS. *The Princess in the Kitchen Garden.* Farrar, Straus & Giroux.

1995 Bjarne REUTER, translated from the Danish by Anthea BELL. *The Boys from St. Petri.* Dutton.

Honor Book
Vedat DALOKAY, translated from the Turkish by Guener ENER. *Sister Shako and Kolo the Goat.* Lothrop, Lee & Shepherd.

1996 Uri ORLEV, translated from the Hebrew by Hillel HALKIN. *The Lady with the Hat.* Houghton Mifflin.

Honor Books
Jo HOESTLAND, translated from the French by Mark POLIZZOTTI. *Star of Fear, Star of Hope.* Walker.

Lutz van DIJK, translated from the German by Elizabeth D. CRAWFORD. *Damned Strong Love: The True Story of Willi G. and Stephan K.* Henry Holt.

1997 Kazumi YUMOTO, translated from the Japanese by Cathy HIRANO. *The Friends.* Farrar Straus Giroux.

1998 Josef HOLUB, translated from the German by Elizabeth D. CRAWFORD. *The Robber and Me*, edited by Mark ARONSON. Henry Holt.

Honor Books
Tatjana WASSILJEWA, translated from German by Anna TRENTER. *Hostage to War: A True Story.* Scholastic Press.

Elke HEIDENRICH, translated from German by Doris ORGEL. *Nero Corleone: A Cat's Story.* Viking Publishing.

1999 Schoschana RABINOVICI, translated from the German by James SKOFIELD. *Thanks to My Mother.* Dial.

Honor Book
Susie MORGENSTERN, translated from the French by Gill ROSNER. *Secret Letters from 0 to 10.* Viking.

2000 Anton QUINTANA, translated from the Dutch by John NIEUWENHUIZEN. *The Baboon King.* Walker.

Honor Books
Quint BUCHHOLZ, translated from the German by Peter F. NEUMEYER. *Collector of Moments.* Farrar, Straus & Giroux.

Christina BJÖRK, translated from the Swedish by Patricia CRAMPTON. *Vendela in Venice*, illustrated by Inga-Karin ERIKSSON. R&S Books

Ineke HOLTWIJK, translated from the Dutch by Wanda BOEKE. *Asphalt Angels.* Front Street.

2001 Daniella CARMI, translated from the Hebrew by Yael LOTAN. *Samir and Yonatan.* Arthur A. Levine/Scholastic Press.

Honor Book
Christian LEHMANN, translated from the French by William RODARMOR. *Ultimate Game.* David R. Godine.

2002 Karin GÜNDISCH, translated from the German by James SKOFIELD. *How I Became an American.* Cricket Books/Carus Publishing.

Honor Book
Susie MORGENSTERN, translated from the French by Gill ROSNER for the U.S. edition. *A Book of Coupons*, with illustrations by Serge BLOCH. Viking Press.

2003 Cornelia FUNKE, translated from the German by Oliver LATSCH. *The Thief Lord.* The Chicken House/Scholastic Publishing.

Honor Book
Hanna JOHANSEN, translated from the German by John BARRETT. *Henrietta and the Golden Eggs*, illustrated by Käthi BHEND. David R. Godine.

2004 Uri ORLEV, translated from the Hebrew by Hillel HALKIN. *Run, Boy, Run.* Walter Lorraine Books.

Honor Book
Bea Uusma SCHYFFERT, translated from the Swedish by Emi GUNER. *The Man Who Went to the Far Side of the Moon: The Story of Apollo 11 Astronaut Michael Collins.* Chronicle Books.

2005 Joëlle STOLTZ, translated from the French by Catherine TEMERSON. *The Shadows of Ghadames.* Delacorte.

Honor Books
Bodil BREDSDORFF, translated from the Danish by Faith INGWERSEN. *The Crow Girl: The Children of Crow Cove.* Farrar, Straus & Giroux.

David CHOTJEWITZ, translated from the German by Doris ORGEL. *Daniel Half Human and the Good Nazi.* Jackson/Atheneum.

Coretta Scott King Award (US): complete list of winners and honor books – also including winners of the occasionally-awarded Coretta Scott King/John Steptoe New Talent (text) Award and the Steptoe New Talent (illustrator) Award

1970 Lillie PATTERSON. *Martin Luther King, Jr; Man of Peace.* Garrard.

1971 Charlemae ROLLINS. *Black Troubador: Langston Hughes.* Rand McNally.

1972 Elton C. FAX. *17 Black Artists.* Dodd.

1973 Jackie ROBINSON as told to Alfred DUCKETT. *I Never Had it Made: The Autobiography of Jackie Robinson.* Putnam.

1974

Author
Sharon Bell MATHIS. *Ray Charles*, ills George FORD. Crowell.

Illustrator
George FORD. *Ray Charles*, text by Sharon Bell MATHIS. Crowell.

1975

Author
Dorothy ROBINSON. *The Legend of Africana*, ills Herbert TEMPLE. Johnson.

Illustrator
No Award Given

1976

Author
Pearl BAILEY. *Duey's Tale.* Harcourt.

Illustrator
No Award Given

1977

Author
James HASKINS. *The Story of Stevie Wonder.* Lothrop.

Illustrator
No Award Given

1978

Author
Eloise GREENFIELD. *Africa Dream*, ills Carole BYARD. Day/Crowell.

Honor Books
William J. FAULKNER. *The Days When the Animals Talked: Black Folk Tales and How They Came to Be.* Follett.

Frankcina GLASS. *Marvin and Tige*. St. Martin's.

Eloise GREENFIELD. *Mary McCleod Bethune.* Crowell.

James HASKINS. *Barbara Jordan.* Dial.

Lillie PATTERSON. *Coretta Scott King.* Garrard.

Ruth Ann STEWART. *Portia: The Life of Portia Washington Pittman, the Daughter of Booker T. Washington.* Doubleday.

Illustrator
Carole BYARD. *Africa Dream*, text by Eloise GREENFIELD. Crowell.

1979 **Author**
Ossie DAVIS. *Escape to Freedom.* Viking.

Honor Books
Carol FENNER. *Skates of Uncle Richard.* Random.

Virginia HAMILTON. *Justice and Her Brothers.* Greenwillow.

Lillie PATTERSON. *Benjamin Banneker.* Abingdon.

Jeanne W. PETERSON. *I Have a Sister, My Sister is Deaf.* Harper.

Illustrator
Tom FEELINGS. *Something on My Mind*, text by Nikki GRIMES. Dial.

1980 **Author**
Walter Dean MYERS. *The Young Landlords.* Viking.

Honor Books
Berry GORDY. *Movin' Up.* Harper.

Eloise GREENFIELD & Lessie Jones LITTLE. *Childtimes: A Three-Generation Memoir.* Harper.

James HASKINS. *Andrew Young: Young Man With a Mission.* Lothrop.

James HASKINS. *James Van Der Zee: The Picture Takin' Man.* Dodd.

Ellease SOUTHERLAND. *Let the Lion Eat Straw.* Scribner.

Illustrator
Carole BYARD. *Cornrows*, text by Camille YARBROUGH. Coward.

1981 **Author**
Sidney POITIER. *This Life.* Knopf.

Honor Book
Alexis De VEAUX. *Don't Explain: A Song of Billie Holiday*. Harper.

Illustrator
Ashley BRYAN. *Beat the Story-Drum, Pum-Pum*. Atheneum.

Honor Books
Carole BYARD. *Grandmama's Joy*, text by Eloise GREENFIELD. Collins.

Jerry PINKNEY. *Count on Your Fingers African Style*, text by Claudia ZASLAVSKY. Crowell.

1982 **Author**
Mildred D. TAYLOR. *Let the Circle Be Unbroken*. Dial.

Honor Books
Alice CHILDRESS. *Rainbow Jordan*. Coward-McCann.

Kristin HUNTER. *Lou in the Limelight*. Scribner.

Mary E. MEBANE. *Mary: An Autobiography*. Viking.

Illustrator
John STEPTOE. *Mother Crocodile: An Uncle Amadou Tale from Senegal*, text adapted by Rosa GUY. Delacorte.

Honor Book
Tom FEELINGS. *Daydreamers*, text by Eloise GREENFIELD. Dial.

1983 **Author**
Virginia HAMILTON. *Sweet Whispers, Brother Rush*. Philomel.

Honor Books
Julius LESTER. *This Strange New Feeling*. Dial.

Illustrator
Peter MUGABENE. *Black Child*. Knopf.

Honor Books
Ashley BRYAN. *I'm Going to Sing: Black American Spirituals*. Atheneum.

Pat CUMMINGS. *Just Us Women*, text by Jeanette CAINES. Harper.

John STEPTOE. *All the Colors of the Race*, text by Arnold ADOFF. Lothrop.

1984 **Author**
Lucille CLIFTON. *Everett Anderson's Good-Bye*. Holt.

Special Citation
Coretta Scott KING, compiler. *The Words of Martin Luther King, Jr.* Newmarket Press.

Honor Books
Virginia HAMILTON. *The Magical Adventures of Pretty Pearl.* Harper.

James HASKINS. *Lena Horne.* Coward-McCann.

Joyce Carol THOMAS. *Bright Shadow.* Avon.

Mildred Pitts WALTER. *Because We Are.* Lothrop, Lee & Shepard.

Illustrator
Pat CUMMINGS. *My Mama Needs Me*, text by Mildred Pitts WALTER. Lothrop.

1985 **Author**
Walter Dean MYERS. *Motown and Didi.* Viking.

Honor Books
Candy Dawson BOYD. *Circle of Gold.* Apple/Scholastic.

Virginia HAMILTON. *A Little Love.* Philomel.

Illustrator
No Award Given

1986 **Author**
Virginia HAMILTON. *The People Could Fly; American Black Folktales.* Knopf.

Honor Books
Virginia HAMILTON. *Junius Over Far.* Harper.

Mildred Pitts WALTER. *Trouble's Child.* Lothrop.

Illustrator
Jerry PINKNEY. *The Patchwork Quilt*, text by Valerie FLOURNOY. Dial.

Honor Book
Leo & Diane DILLON. *The People Could Fly: American Black Folktales*, text by Virginia HAMILTON. Knopf.

1987 **Author**
Mildred Pitts WALTER. *Justin and the Best Biscuits in the World.* Lothrop.

Honor Books
Ashley BRYAN. *Lion and the Ostrich Chicks and Other African Folk Tales.* Atheneum.

Joyce HANSEN. *Which Way Freedom.* Walker.

Illustrator
Jerry PINKNEY. *Half a Moon and One Whole Star*, text by Crescent DRAGONWAGON. Macmillan.

Honor Books
Ashley BRYAN. *Lion and the Ostrich Chicks and Other African Folk Tales.* Atheneum.

Pat CUMMINGS. *C.L.O.U.D.S.* Lothrop.

1988 **Author**
Mildred D. TAYLOR. *The Friendship.* Dial.

Honor Books
Alexis De VEAUX. *An Enchanted Hair Tale.* Harper.

Julius LESTER. *The Tales of Uncle Remus: The Adventures of Brer Rabbit.* Dial.

Illustrator
John STEPTOE. *Mufaro's Beautiful Daughters; an African Tale.* Lothrop.

Honor Books
Ashley BRYAN. *What a Morning! The Christmas Story in Black Spirituals*, selected by John LANGSTAFF. Macmillan.

Joe SAM. *The Invisible Hunters: A Legend from the Miskito Indians of Nicaragua*, compiled by Harriet ROHMER, *et al.* Children's Press.

1989 **Author**
Walter Dean MYERS. *Fallen Angels.* Scholastic.

Honor Books
James BERRY. *A Thief in the Village and Other Stories.* Orchard.

Virginia HAMILTON. *Anthony Burns: The Defeat and Triumph of a Fugitive Slave.* Knopf.

Illustrator
Jerry PINKNEY. *Mirandy and Brother Wind*, text by Patricia C. McKISSACK. Knopf.

Honor Books
Pat CUMMINGS. *Storm in the Night*, text by Mary STOLTZ. Harper.

Amos FERGUSON. *Under the Sunday Tree*, text by Eloise GREENFIELD. Harper.

1990 **Author**

Patricia C. and Fredrick L. McKISSACK. *A Long Hard Journey: The Story of the Pullman Porter.* Walker.

Honor Books

Eloise GREENFIELD. *Nathaniel Talking*, ills Jan Spivey GILCHRIST. Black Butterfly.

Virginia HAMILTON. *The Bells of Christmas.* Harcourt.

Lillie PATTERSON. *Martin Luther King, Jr., and the Freedom Movement.* Facts on File.

Illustrator

Jan Spivey GILCHRIST. *Nathaniel Talking*, text by Eloise GREENFIELD. Black Butterfly.

Honor Books

Jerry PINKNEY. *The Talking Eggs*, text by Robert San SOUCI. Dial.

1991 **Author**

Mildred D. TAYLOR. *The Road to Memphis.* Dial.

Honor Books

James HASKINS. *Black Dance in America.* Crowell.

Angela JOHNSON. *When I Am Old With You.* Orchard.

Illustrator

Leo and Diane DILLON. *Aïda*, text retold by Leontyne PRICE. Gulliver/HBJ.

1992 **Author**

Walter Dean MYERS. *Now Is Your Time!; The African-American Struggle for Freedom.* HarperCollins.

Honor Book

Eloise GREENFIELD. *Night on Neighborhood Street*, text by Jan Spivey GILCHRIST. Dial.

Illustrator

Faith RINGGOLD. *Tar Beach.* Crown.

Honor Books

Ashley BRYAN. *All Night, All Day: A Child's First Book of African American Spirituals.* Atheneum.

Jan Spivey GILCHRIST. *Night on Neighborhood Street*, text by Eloise GREENFIELD. Dial.

1993 **Author**
Patricia C. McKISSACK. *The Dark-Thirty; Southern Tales of the Supernatural.* Knopf.

Honor Books
Patricia C. & Frederick L. McKISSACK. *Sojourner Truth: Ain't I a Woman?* Scholastic.

Walter Dean MYERS. *Somewhere in the Darkness.* Scholastic.

Mildred Pitts WALTER. *Mississippi Challenge.* Bradbury.

Illustrator
Kathleen Atkins WILSON. *The Origin of Life On Earth; An African Creation Myth*, text by David A. ANDERSON. Sights Productions.

Honor Books
Carole BYARD. *Working Cotton*, text by Sherley Anne WILLIAMS. Harcourt.

Wil CLAY. *Little Eight John*, text by Jan WAHL. Lodestar.

Brian PINKNEY. *Sukey and the Mermaid*, text by Robert San SOUCI. Four Winds.

1994 **Author**
Angela JOHNSON. *Toning the Sweep.* Orchard.

Honor Books
Joyce Carol THOMAS. *Brown Honey in Broom Wheat Tea*, ills Floyd COOPER. HarperCollins.

Walter Dean MYERS. *Malcolm X: By Any Means Necessary*. Scholastic.

Illustrator
Tom FEELINGS. *Soul Looks Back in Wonder.* Dial.

Honor Books
Floyd COOPER. *Brown Honey in Broom Wheat Tea*, text by Joyce Carol THOMAS. HarperCollins.

James RANSOME. *Uncle Jed's Barbershop*, text by Margaree King MITCHELL. Simon & Schuster.

1995 **Author**
Patricia C. and Fredrick L. McKISSACK. *Christmas in the Big House, Christmas in the Quarters.* Scholastic.

Honor Books
Joyce HANSEN. *The Captive.* Scholastic.

Patricia C. & Frederick L. McKISSACK. *Black Diamond: Story of the Negro Baseball League*. Scholastic, Inc.

Jacqueline WOODSON. *I Hadn't Meant to Tell You This*. Delacorte.

Illustrator
James E. RANSOME. *The Creation*, text by James Weldon JOHNSON. Holiday.

Honor Books
Floyd COOPER. *Meet Danitra Brown*, text by Nikki GRIMES. Lothrop, Lee & Shepard.

Terea SHAFFER. *The Singing Man*, text by Angela Shelf MEDEARIS. Holiday House.

1996 **Author**
Virginia HAMILTON. *Her Stories; African American Folktales, Fairy Tales, and True Tales*, ills Leo and Diane DILLON. Blue Sky/Scholastic.

Honor Books
Christopher Paul CURTIS. *The Watsons Go to Birmingham - 1963*. Delacorte.

Rita WILLIAMS-GARCIA. *Like Sisters on the Homefront*. Delacorte.

Jacqueline WOODSON. *From the Notebooks of Melanin Sun*. Scholastic/Blue Sky Press.

Illustrator
Tom FEELINGS. *The Middle Passage: White Ships Black Cargo*. Dial.

Honor Books
Leo & Diane DILLON. *Her Stories*, text by Virginia HAMILTON. Scholastic/Blue Sky Press.

Brian PINKNEY. *The Faithful Friend*, text by Robert San SOUCI. Simon & Schuster.

1997 **Author**
Walter Dean MYERS. *Slam!* Scholastic.

Honor Book
Patricia C. & Frederick L. McKISSACK. *Rebels Against Slavery: American Slave Revolts*. Scholastic.

Illustrator
Jerry PINKNEY. *Minty; A Story of Young Harriet Tubman*, text by Alan SCHROEDER. Dial.

Honor Books
Gregory CHRISTIE. *The Palm of My Heart: Poetry by African American Children*, ed. by Davida ADEDJOUMA. Lee & Low.

Reynold RUFFINS. *Running The Road To ABC*, text by Denize LAUTURE. Simon & Schuster.

Synthia Saint JAMES. *Neeny Coming, Neeny Going*, text by Karen ENGLISH. Bridgewater Books.

1998 **Author**
Sharon M. DRAPER. *Forged by Fire*. Atheneum.

Honor Books
James HASKINS. *Bayard Rustin: Behind the Scenes of the Civil Rights Movement*. Hyperion.

Joyce HANSEN. *I Thought My Soul Would Rise and Fly: The Diary of Patsy, a Freed Girl*. Scholastic.

Illustrator
Javaka STEPTOE. *In Daddy's Arms I am Tall: African Americans Celebrating Fathers*, text by Alan SCHROEDER. Lee & Low.

Honor Books
Ashley BRYAN. *Ashley Bryan's ABC of African American Poetry*. Jean Karl/Atheneum.

Baba Wagué DIAKITÉ. *The Hunterman and the Crocodile*. Scholastic.

Christopher MYERS. *Harlem*, text by Walter Dean MYERS. Scholastic.

1999 **Author**
Angela JOHNSON. *Heaven*. Simon & Schuster.

Honor Books
Nikki GRIMES. *Jazmin's Notebook*. Dial Books.

Joyce HANSEN & Gary McGOWAN. *Breaking Ground, Breaking Silence: The Story of New York's African Burial Ground*. Henry Holt and Company.

Angela JOHNSON. *The Other Side: Shorter Poems*. Orchard Books.

Illustrator
Michele WOOD. *i see the rhythm*, text by Toyomi IGUS. Children's Book Press.

Honor Books
Floyd COOPER. *I Have Heard of a Land*, text by Joyce Carol THOMAS. Joanna Cotler Books/HarperCollins.

E. B. LEWIS. *The Bat Boy and His Violin*, text by Gavin CURTIS. Simon & Schuster.

Brian PINKNEY. *Duke Ellington: The Piano Prince and His Orchestra*, text by Andrea Davis PINKNEY. Hyperion Books for Children.

2000 **Author**

Christopher Paul CURTIS. *Bud, Not Buddy*. Delacorte.

Honor Books

Karen ENGLISH. *Francie*. Farrar, Straus and Giroux.

Patricia C. & Frederick L. McKISSACK. *Black Hands, White Sails: The Story of African-American Whalers*. Scholastic.

Walter Dean MYERS. *Monster*. HarperCollins.

Illustrator

Brian PINKNEY. *In the Time of the Drums*, text by Kim L. SIEGELSON. Jump at the Sun/Hyperion.

Honor Books

E. B. LEWIS. *My Rows and Piles of Coins*, text by Tololwa M. MOLLEL. Clarion.

Christopher MYERS. *The Black Cat*. Scholastic.

2001 **Author**

Jacqueline WOODSON. *Miracle's Boys*. Putnam.

Honor Book

Andrea Davis PINKNEY. *Let It Shine! Stories of Black Women Freedom Fighters*, ills Stephen ALCORN. Harcourt/Gulliver.

Illustrator

Bryan COLLIER. *Uptown*. Henry Holt.

Honor Books

R. Gregory CHRISTIE. *Only Passing Through: The Story of Sojourner Truth*, text by Anne ROCKWELL. Random House.

Bryan COLLIER. *Freedom River*. Jump at the Sun/Hyperion.

E. B. LEWIS. *Virgie Goes to School with Us Boys*, text by Elizabeth Fitzgerald HOWARD. Simon & Schuster.

2002 **Author**

Mildred D. TAYLOR. *The Land*. Phyllis Fogelman Books/Penguin Putnam

Honor Books

Sharon G. FLAKE. *Money-Hungry*. Jump at the Sun/Hyperion.

Marilyn NELSON. *Carver: a Life in Poems.* Front Street.

Illustrator

Jerry PINKNEY. *Goin' Someplace Special*, text by Patricia McKISSACK. Anne Schwartz Book/Atheneum.

Honor Books

Bryan COLLIER. *Martin's Big Words: the Life of Dr. Martin Luther King, Jr.*, text by Doreen RAPPAPORT. Jump at the Sun/Hyperion.

2003 **Author**

Nikki GRIMES. *Bronx Masquerade.* Dial Books.

Honor Books

Nikki GRIMES. *Talkin' About Bessie: The Story of Aviator Elizabeth Coleman*, ills E. B. LEWIS. Orchard Books.

Brenda WOODS. *The Red Rose Box.* Putnam.

Coretta Scott King/John Steptoe New Talent (text) Award

Janet McDONALD. *Chill Wind.* Frances Foster.

Illustrator

E. B. LEWIS. *Talkin' About Bessie: The Story of Aviator Elizabeth Coleman*, text by Nikki GRIMES. Orchard Books.

Honor Books

Bryan COLLIER. *Visiting Langston*, text by Willie PERDOMO. Henry Holt.

Leo & Diane DILLON. *Rap A Tap Tap: Here's Bojangles – Think of That.* Blue Sky Press.

Steptoe New Talent (illustrator) Award

Randy DuBURKE. *The Moon Ring.* Chronicle Books.

2004 **Author**

Angela JOHNSON. *The First Part Last.* Simon & Schuster.

Honor Books

Sharon M. DRAPER. *The Battle of Jericho.* Atheneum.

Patricia C. & Fredrick L. McKISSACK. *Days of Jubilee: The End of Slavery in the United States.* Scholastic.

Jacqueline WOODSON. *Locomotion.* Putnams/Penguin Young Readers.

Illustrator

Ashley BRYAN. *Beautiful Blackbird.* Atheneum.

Honor Books
Colin BOOTMAN. *Almost to Freedom*. Carolrhoda Books/Lerner Publishing Group.

Kadir NELSON. *Thunder Rose*. Silver Whistle/Harcourt.

2005 Author
Toni MORRISON. *Remember: The Journey to School Integration*. Houghton.

Honor Books
Sharon G. FLAKE. *Who Am I Without Him?: Short Stories About Girls and the Boys in Their Lives*. Jump at the Sun/Hyperion.

Sheila P. MOSES. *The Legend of Buddy Bush.* McElderry/Simon

Marilyn NELSON. *Fortune's Bones: The Manumission Requiem*. Front Street.

Illustrator
Kadir NELSON. *Ellington Was Not a Street*, text by Ntozake SHANGE. Simon & Schuster.

Honor Books
Jerry PINKNEY. *God Bless the Child*, text by Billie HOLIDAY & Arthur HERZOG Jr. Amistad/HarperCollins.

Leo & Diane DILLON. *The People Could Fly: The Picture Book*, text by Virginia HAMILTON. Knopf.

Coretta Scott King/John Steptoe New Talent Awards

Author
Barbara HATHAWAY. *Missy Violet and Me*. Houghton.

Illustrator
Frank MORRISON. *Jazzy Miz Mozetta*, text by Brenda C. ROBERTS. Farrar.

Américas Award for Children's and Young Adult Literature. US): complete list of winners

1993 Lulu DELACRE. *Vejigante Masquerader.* Scholastic.

Commended
Lyll Becerra de JENKINS. *Celebrating the Hero.* Lodestar Books.

Merle HODGE. *For the Life of Laetitia.* Farrar, Straus & Giroux.

Commended picture books
Caroline BINCH. *Hue Boy*, text by Rita Phillips MITCHELL. Dial.

Robert CASILLA. *The Little Painter of Sabana Grande*, text by Patricia Maloney MARKUN. Bradbury.

Arthur DORROS. *Radio Man, a Story in English and Spanish.* Spanish translation by Sandra Marulanda DORROS. Harper Collins.

Enrique O. SANCHEZ. *Abuela's Weave*, text by Omar CASTANEDA. Lee and Low.

1994 Lynn JOSEPH. *The Mermaid's Twin Sister: More Stories From Trinidad*, ills Donna PERRONE. Clarion.

Commended
Alma Flor ADA. *Where the Flame Trees Bloom*, ills Antonio MARTORELL. Atheneum.

S. Beth ATKIN. *Voices from the Field: Children of Migrant Farmworkers Tell Their Stories.* Little, Brown.

Carmen T. BERNIER-GRAND. *Juan Bobo: Four Folktales from Puerto Rico*, ills Ernesto Ramos NIEVES. Harper Collins.

Lori CARLSON (ed.). *Cool Salsa: Bilingual Poems on Growing Up Latino in the United States*, with an introduction by Oscar HIJUELOS. Henry Holt.

Omar S. CASTANEDA. *Imagining Isabel.* Lodestar Books.

Mildred Leinweber DAWSON. *Over Here It's Different: Carolina's Story*, photographs by George ANCONA. Macmillan.

Ginger GORDON. *My Two Worlds*, photographs by Martha COOPER. Clarion Books.

Walter JEKYLL (collector). *I Have a News*, rhymes chosen by Neil PHILIP, ills Jacqueline MAIR. William Morrow.

Juan Ramon JIMENEZ. *Platero y Yo/Platero and I*, selected, translated & adapted from the Spanish by Myra Cohn LIVINGSTON & Joseph F. DOMINGUEZ, ills Antonio FRASCONI. Clarion Books.

Sarita KENDALL. *Ransom for a River Dolphin.* Lerner Publications.

Jose Maria MERINO. *Beyond the Ancient Cities*, translated by Helen LANE. Farrar, Straus & Giroux.

Carolyn MEYER. *Rio Grande Stories.* Harcourt Brace.

Laura ROYBAL. *Billy.* Houghton Mifflin.

Victor VILLASENOR. *Walking Stars: Stories of Magic and Power.* Arte Publico Press.

Karen Lynn WILLIAMS. *Tap-Tap*, ills Catherine STOCK. Clarion Books.

Commended picture books

Emery and Durga BERNHARD. *The Tree That Rains: The Flood Myth of the Huichol Indians of Mexico.* Holiday House.

Lulu DELACRE. *The Bossy Gallito: A Traditional Cuban Folktale*, text by Lucia M. GONZALEZ. Scholastic.

Tomie DEPAOLA. *The Legend of the Poinsettia.* Putnam.

Tomie DEPAOLA. *The Tale of Rabbit and Coyote*, text by Tony JOHNSTON. Putnam.

Michael DOOLING. *Lights on the River*, text by Jane Resh THOMAS. Hyperion.

Ismael Espinosa FERRER. *Feliz Nochebuena, Feliz Navidad*, text by Maricel E. PRESILLA. Henry Holt.

Carla GOLEMBE. *How Night Came from the Sea: A Story from Brazil*, text by Mary-Joan GERSON. Little, Brown.

Ronald HIMLER. *A Day's Work*, text by Eve BUNTING. Clarion.

Synthia Saint JAMES. *Tukama Tootles the Flute: A Tale from the Antilles*, text by Phillis GERSHATOR. Orchard Books.

Elisa KLEVEN. *De Colores and Other Latin America Folk Songs for Children*, text by Jose-Luis OROZCO. Dutton.

Cecily LANG. *Pablo's Tree*, text by Pat MORA. Macmillan.

Frane LESSAC. *Caribbean Alphabet.* William Morrow.

Frane LESSAC. *Not a Copper Penny in me House: Poems from the Caribbean*, text by Monica GUNNING. Boyds Mill Press.

Sylvia LONG. *Alejandro's Gift*, text by Richard E. ALBERT. Chronicle Books.

Sally Schofer MATHEWS. *The Sad Night: The Story of an Aztec Victory and a Spanish Loss.* Clarion Books.

Holly MEADE. *Rata, Pata, Scata, Fata: A Caribbean Story*, text by Phillis GERSHATOR. Little, Brown.

Rodolfo MORALES. *Angel's Kite/La Estrella de Angel*, text by Alberto BLANCO. Children's Book Press.

Carol OBER. *How Music Came to the World: An Ancient Mexican Myth*, text by Hal OBER. Houghton Mifflin.

Maria Antonia ORDONEZ. *The Red Comb*, text by Fernando PICO. (Originally published in Spanish. Ediciones Huracan, Puerto Rico & Ediciones Ekare, Venezuela) BridgeWater Books.

Robert ROTH. *When the Monkeys Came Back*, text by Kristine L. FRANKLIN. Atheneum.

Enrique O. SANCHEZ. *Saturday Market*, text by Patricia GROSSMAN. Lothrop, Lee & Shepard Books.

Elivia SAVADIER. *Grandmother's Nursery Rhymes/Las Nanas de Abuelita*, text by Nelly Palacio JARAMILLO. Henry Holt.

Juliana Reyes de SILVA & Juan Hilario SILVA. *The Hummingbird's Gift*, text by Stefan CZERNECKI & Timothy RHODES. Hyperion.

1995 Frances TEMPLE. *Tonight By Sea*. Orchard.

Honorable Mentions
Judith Ortiz COFER. *An Island Like You: Stories of the Barrio*. Orchard Books.

Marc TALBERT. *Heart of a Jaguar*. Simon & Schuster.

Honorable Mentions, Picture Book
Susan GUEVARA. *Chato's Kitchen*, text by Gary SOTO Putnam.

Commended
John AGARD & Grace NICHOLS. *A Caribbean Dozen: Poems From Caribbean Poets*, ills Cathie FELSTEAD. Candlewick Press.

George ANCONA. *Fiesta U.S.A.* (Spanish and English editions). Lodestar.

Diane Gonzales BERTRAND. *Sweet Fifteen*. Arte Publico Press.

Maria Cristina BRUSCA & Tona WILSON. *Pedro Fools the Gringo, and Other Tales of a Latin American Trickster*, ills Maria Cristina BRUSCA. Henry Holt.

Sherry GARLAND. *Indio*. Harcourt Brace.

Kristiana GREGORY. *The Stowaway: A Tale of California Pirates*. Scholastic.

Irene Beltran HERNANDEZ. *The Secret of Two Brothers*. Pinata Books.

Naomi Shihab NYE (ed.). *The Tree Is Older Than You Are: A Bilingual Gathering of Poems and Stories from Mexico*, ills with paintings by Mexican artists. Simon & Schuster.

Gary SOTO (ed.). *Canto Familiar*, ills by Annika NELSON. Harcourt Brace.

Gary SOTO. *Summer On Wheels.* Scholastic.

Marc TALBERT. *A Sunburned Prayer.* Simon and Schuster.

Commended picture books

Maria Cristina BRUSCA. *When Jaguars Ate the Moon and Other Stories About Animals and Plants of the Americas*, text by Maria Cristina BRUSCA & Tona WILSON. Henry Holt.

Donna CLAIR. *Carlos, Light The Farolito*, text by Jean CIAVONNE. Clarion.

Glo COALSON. *Hi*, text by Ann Herbert SCOTT. Philomel.

George CRESPO. *How Iwariwa The Cayman Learned To Share: A Yanomami Myth.* Clarion.

Morella FUENMAYOR. *The Spirit Of Tio Fernando: A Day of the Dead Story*, text by Janice LEVY. Albert Whitman.

Carla GOLEMBE. *People of Corn: A Mayan Story*, text by Mary-Joan GERSON. Little, Brown.

Edward GONZALES. *The Farolitos of Christmas*, text by Rudolfo ANAYA. Hyperion.

Ralfka GONZALEZ & Ana RUIZ. *My First Book of Proverbs/Mi Primer Libro de Dichos.* Children's Book Press.

Kim HOWARD. *Mediopollito/Half-Chicken*, text by Alma Flor ADA. Doubleday.

Douglas KEISTER. *Fernando's Gift/El Regalo de Fernando.* Sierra Club.

Elisa KLEVEN. *Isla/La Isla* (English & Spanish editions), text by Arthur DORROS. Dutton Children's Books.

Philip KUZNICKI. *The Magic Feather: A Jamaican Legend*, text by Lisa ROJANY. Troll Associates.

Nicholasa MOHR & Antonio MARTORELL. *The Song of El Coqui and Other Tales of Puerto Rico.* Viking.

Ruth Wright PAULSEN. *The Tortilla Factory/La Tortilleria* (Spanish and English editions), text by Gary PAULSEN. Harcourt Brace.

Brian PINKNEY. *The Faithful Friend*, text by Robert D. San SOUCI. Simon and Schuster.

Charles REASONER. *Juan Bobo and the Horse of Seven Colors: A Puerto Rican Legend*, retold by Jan MIKE. Troll Associates.

Joyce ROSSI. *The Gullywasher.* Northland Publishing.

Linda SHUTE. *Rabbit Wishes.* Lothrop, Lee and Shepard.

Elly SIMMONS. *Calling the Doves/El Canto De Las Palomas*, text by Juan Felipe HERRERA. Children's Book Press.

Harvey STEVENSON. *The Tangerine Tree*, text by Regina HANSON. Clarion.

Leyla TORRES. *Saturday Sancocho.* Farrar Straus Giroux.

1996 **Fiction**

Lyll Becerra de JENKINS. *So Loud a Silence.* Lodestar.

Victor MARTÍNEZ. *Parrot in the Oven: Mi Vida.* HarperCollins.

Commended

Patricia ALDANA (ed.), translated by Hugh HAZELTON. *Jade and Iron: Latin American Tales from Two Cultures*, ills Luis GARAY. Groundwood/Douglas and McIntyre Ltd.

Elaine Marie ALPHIN. *A Bear for Miguel*, ills Joan SANDIN. HarperCollins.

Pura BELPRÉ. *Firefly Summer.* Arte Público.

Lori Marie CARLSON (ed.). *Barrio Streets Carnival Dreams.* Henry Holt.

Lulu DELACRE. *Golden Tales: Myths, Legends, and Folktales from Latin America/De Oro Y Esmeraldas: Mitos, Leyendas Y Cuentos Populares De Latino America.* Scholastic.

Pat MORA. *Confetti: Poems for Children*, ills Enrique O. SÁNCHEZ. Lee and Low.

Walter Dean MYERS. *Toussaint L'ouverture: The Fight for Haiti's Freedom*, illustrated with paintings by Jacob LAWRENCE. Simon & Schuster.

Ellen SCHECTER. *The Big Idea*, ills Bob DORSEY. Hyperion.

Diane STANLEY. *Elena.* Hyperion.

Erika TAMAR. *Alphabet City Ballet.* HarperCollins.

Picture Book

Carmen Lomas GARZA. *In My Family/En Mi Familia.* Children's Book Press.

Commended picture books

Roberta ARENSON. *A Caribbean Counting Book*, compiled by Faustin CHARLES. Houghton Mifflin.

Andrea ARROYO. *In Rosa's Mexico*, text by Campbell GEESLIN. Alfred A. Knopf.

Andrea ARROYO. *La Boda*, text by Nancy Van LAAN. Little, Brown.

Robert CASILLA. *Jalapeño Bagels*, text by Natasha WING. Atheneum.

Joe CEPEDA. *The Old Man and His Door*, text by Gary SOTO. Putnam.

Martha COOPER & Ginger GORDON. *Anthony Reynoso: Born to Rope.* Clarion.

David DIAZ. *Going Home*, text by Eve BUNTING. HarperCollins.

Karen DUGAN. *Pascual's Magic Pictures*, text by Amy Glaser GAGE. Carolrhoda.

Rosana FARÍA. *Nina Bonita*, text by Ana Maria MACHADO, translated by Elena IRIBARREN. Kane/Miller.

David FRAMPTON. *Miro in the Kingdom of the Sun*, text by Jane KURTZ. Houghton Mifflin.

Christina GONZÁLEZ. *Prietita and the Ghost Woman/Prietita Y La Llorona*, text by Gloria ANZALDÚA. Children's Book Press.

Rudy GUTIÉRREZ. *Old Letivia and the Mountain of Sorrows*, text by Nicholasa MOHR. Viking.

Elisa KLEVEN. *Hooray, A Piñata!* Dutton.

Elisa KLEVEN. *The Magic Maguey*, text by Tony JOHNSTON. Harcourt Brace.

Barbara LAMBASE. *The Garden of Happiness*, text by Erika TAMAR. Harcourt Brace.

Melinda LEVINE. *Good News!* text by Sarita Chávez SILVERMAN. Hampton-Brown.

Edward MARTÍNEZ. *Tonito's Cat*, text by Mary CALHOUN. Morrow.

Leovigildo MARTÍNEZ. *Uncle Snake*, text by Matthew GOLLUB. Tambourine.

Fritz MILLEVOIX. *Sweet, Sweet Fig Banana*, text by Phillis GERSHATOR. Morton Grove, Illinois: Albert Whitman.

Robert ROTH. *Journey of the Nightly Jaguar*, text by Burton ALBERT. Atheneum.

Reynold RUFFINS. *Running the Road to ABC*, text by Denizé LAUTURE. Simon and Schuster.

Enrique O. SÁNCHEZ. *The Golden Flower: A Taino Myth from Puerto Rico*, text by Nina JAFFE. Simon and Schuster.

F. John SIERRA. *My Mexico – Mexico Mio*, text by Tony JOHNSTON. Putnam.

Jenny STOW. *Darkfright*, text by Holly Young HUTH. Atheneum.

Yvonne SYMANK. *Chave's Memories/Los Recuerdos De Chave*, text by María Isabel DELGADO. Arte Público.

Jeanette WINTER. *Josefina*. Harcourt Brace.

1997 **Fiction**

Francisco JIMÉNEZ. *The Circuit*. University of New Mexico Press.

Honorable Mentions

George ANCONA. *Mayeros: A Yucatec Maya Family*. William Morrow.

Commended List

Diana APPELBAUM. *Cocoa Ice*, ills Holly MEADE. Orchard.

Lucía M. GONZÁLEZ. *Señor Cat's Romance and Other Favorite Stories from Latin America*, ills Lulu DELACRE. Scholastic.

Jo Ann Yolanda HERNÁNDEZ. *White Bread Competition*. Piñata Books.

Henry HORENSTEIN. *Baseball in the Barrio*. Gulliver/Harcourt Brace.

Tony JOHNSTON and Jeanette WINTER. *Day of the Dead*. Harcourt Brace.

Floyd MARTÍNEZ. *Spirits of the High Mesa*. Arte Público.

Michèle SOLÁ. *Angela Weaves a Dream*, photographs by Jeffrey Jay FOXX. Hyperion.

Gary SOTO. *Buried Onions*. Harcourt Brace.

Gary SOTO. *Novio Boy*, a play. Harcourt Brace

Joe VIESTI & Diane HALL. *Celebrate in Central America*. Lothrop, Lee & Shepard.

Picture Book

Linda SAPORT. *The Face at the Window*, text by Regina HANSON. Clarion.

Honorable Mention

David AXTELL. *Fruits: A Caribbean Counting Poem*, text by Valerie BLOOM. Henry Holt.

Commended picture books

Jeanne ARNOLD. *Carlos and the Skunk/Carlos Y El Zorrillo*, text by Jan ROMERO. Rising Moon.

Raul COLÓN. *Tomas and the Library Lady*, text by Pat MORA. Knopf.

Felipe DÁVALOS. *The Lizard and the Sun/La Largartija Y El Sol*, text by Alma Flor ADA. Doubleday Dell.

Lois EHLERT. *Cuckoo/Cucu*, translated by Gloria de Aragón ANDÚJAR. Harcourt Brace.

Luis GARAY. *Pedrito's Day*. Orchard.

Christina GONZÁLEZ. *I Am of Two Places/Soy De Dos Lugares*, edited by Mary CARDEN & Mary CAPPELLINI. Rigby.

Maya Christina GONZÁLEZ. *Laughing Tomatoes and Other Spring Poems Jitomates Risuenos Y Otros Poemas De Primavera*, text by Francisco X. ALARCÓN. Children's Book Press.

Margarita GONZÁLEZ-JENSEN. *Mexico's Marvelous Corn/El Maravilloso Maiz De Mexico*. Rigby.

Gershom GRIFFITH. *The Story of Doña Chila/El Cuento De Doña Chila*, text by Mary CAPELLINNI. Rigby.

Elisa KLEVEN. *Diez Deditos/Ten Little Fingers and Other Play Rhymes and Action Songs from Latin America*, selected by Jose-Luis OROZCO. Dutton.

Loretta LÓPEZ. *Birthday Swap/¡Que Sorpresa De Cumpleaños!* Lee & Low.

Marianno de LÓPEZ. *From Father to Son/De Padre a Hijo*, text by Patricia ALMADA. Rigby.

Karen LUSEBRINK. *Grannie Jus' Come*, text by Ana SISNETT. Children's Book Press.

Daniel MORETÓN. *La Cucaracha Martina: A Caribbean Folktale/La Cucaracha Martina: Un Cuento Folklorico Del Caribe*. Turtle.

Mira REISBERG. *Where Fireflies Dance/Ahi, Donde Bailan Las Luciernagas*, text by Lucha CORPI. Children's Book Press.

Enrique O. SÁNCHEZ. *Dear Abuelita/Querida Abuelita*, text by Sofía Meza KEANE. Rigby.

Simón SILVA. *Gathering the Sun: An Alphabet in Spanish and English*, text by Alma Flor ADA. Lothrop.

Sandra SPEIDEL. *A Little Salmon for Witness: A Story from Trinidad*, text by Vashanti RAHAMAN. Lodestar.

Gerardo SUZÁN. *Butterfly Boy*, text by Virginia KROLL. Boyds Mills.

1998 **Fiction**

George ANCONA. *Barrio: José's Neighborhood*. Harcourt Brace.

Honorable Mention
Brian PINKNEY. *Cendrillon: A Caribbean Cinderella*, text by Robert D. San SOUCI. Simon & Schuster.

Commended List
Alma Flor ADA. *Under the Royal Palms: A Childhood in Cuba.* Atheneum.

Francisco X. ALARCÓN. *From the Bellybutton of the Moon and Other Summer Poems/Del Ombligo De La Luna Y Otros Poemas De Verano*, ills Maya Christina GONZÁLEZ. Children's Book Press.

George ANCONA. *Fiesta Fireworks.* Lothrop, Lee & Shepard.

Veronica CHAMBERS. *Marisol and Magdalena: The Sound of Our Sisterhood.* Hyperion.

Gerald HAUSMAN & Ashley WOLFF. *Doctor Bird: Three Lookin' Up Tales from Jamaica.* Philomel.

Olga LOYA. *Momentos Magicos: Tales from Latin America Told in English and Spanish.* August House.

Kirk REEVE. *Lolo and Red-Legs.* Rising Moon.

Gary SOTO. *Petty Crimes.* Harcourt Brace.

Picture Book
Amelia Lau CARLING. *Mama and Papa Have a Store.* Dial.

Commended picture books
Joe CEPEDA. *Big Bushy Mustache*, text by Gary SOTO. Knopf.

Robert CHAPMAN. *A Gift for Abuelita: Celebrating the Day of the Dead/Un Regalo Para Abuelita: En Celebracion Del Dia Do Los Muertos*, text by Nancy LUENN. Rising Moon.

Felipe DÁVALOS. *The Secret Stars*, text by Joseph SLATE. Marshall Cavendish.

Ann GRIFALCONI. *Tio Armando*, text by Florence Parry HEIDE & Roxanne Heide PIERCE. Lothrop, Lee & Shepard.

Rachel ISADORA. *Caribbean Dream.* Putnam.

Synthia Saint JAMES. *Greetings, Sun*, text by Phillis & David GERSHATOR. DK Ink.

Cedric LUCAS. *The Crab Man/El Hombre De Los Cangrejos* (dual editions), text by Patricia E. Van WEST. Turtle Books.

Simón SILVA. *La Mariposa*, text by Francisco JIMÉNEZ. Houghton Mifflin.

Dyanne STRONGBOW. *Big Moon Tortilla*, text by Joy COWLEY. Boyds Mill.

Leyla TORRES. *Liliana's Grandmothers.* Farrar Straus Giroux.

Beatriz VIDAL. *The Magic Bean Tree: A Legend From Argentina*, text by Nancy Van LAAN. Houghton Mifflin.

1999 **Fiction**

Juan Felipe HERRERA. *Crashboomlove: A Novel in Verse.* University of New Mexico Press.

Honorable Mentions

Carmen Lomas GARZA. *Magic Windows/Ventanas Mágicas*, Spanish translation by Francisco X. ALARCÓN. Children's Book Press

Bernard WOLF. *Cuba: After the Revolution.* Dutton.

Commended List

Francisco X. ALARCÓN. *Angels Ride Bikes/Los Angeles Andan En Bicicleta*, ills Maya Christina GONZALEZ. Children's Book Press.

Ineke HOLTWIJK. *Asphalt Angels*, translated from the Dutch by Wanda BOEKE. Front Street Press.

Werner HOLZWARTH. *I'm José and I'm Okay: Three Stories from Bolivia*, translated from the German by Laura McKENNA. Story idea & ills Yatiyawi Studios. Kane/Miller.

Commended picture books

George ANCONA. *Carnaval.* Harcourt, Brace.

Alex AYLIFFE. *Island in the Sun*, text by Harry BELAFONTE & Lord BURGESS. Dial.

Tomie DEPAOLA. *Erandi's Braids*, text by Antonio Hernández MADRIGAL. Putnam.

Daniel GALVEZ. *It Doesn't Have to Be This Way: A Barrio Story/No Tiene Que Ser Así: Una Historia Del Barrio*, text by Luis J. RODRÍGUEZ. Children's Book Press.

Enrique O. SÁNCHEZ. *A is for Americas*, text by Cynthia CHIN-LEE & Terri DE LA PEÑA. Orchard.

Leyla TORRES. *Two Days in May*, text by Harriet Peck TAYLOR. Farrar, Straus & Giroux.

2000 **Fiction**

Lynn JOSEPH. *The Color of My Words.* HarperCollins.

Honorable Mention Fiction

Pam Muñoz RYAN. *Esperanza Rising.* Scholastic Press.

Commended List

George ANCONA. *Cuban Kids.* Marshall Cavendish.

Lulu DELACRE. *Salsa Stories.* Scholastic.

Judd WINICK. *Pedro and Me: Friendship, Loss, and What I Learned.* Henry Holt.

Picture Book

Alfonso RUANO. *The Composition*, text by Antonio SKÁRMETA. Groundwood.

Honorable Mention Picture Book

Maya Christina GONZALEZ. *My Very Own Room/Mi Propio Cuartito*, text by Amada Irma PÉREZ. Children's Book Press.

Commended picture books

Claire B. COTTS. *The Christmas Gift/El Regalo de Navidad*, text by Francisco JIMÉNEZ. Houghton Mifflin.

S. GUEVARA. *Mi Hija, Mi Hijo, El Aguila, La Paloma: Un Canto Azteca/My Daughter, My Son, the Eagle, the Dove: An Aztec Chant*, text by Ana CASTILLO. Dutton.

Pauline Rodriguez HOWARD. *Icy Watermelon/Sandia Fria*, text by Mary Sue GALINDO. Piñata Books/Arte Público.

David DIAZ. *Roadrunner's Dance*, text by Rudolfo ANAYA. Hyperion.

2001

Fiction

Francisco JIMÉNEZ. *Breaking Through.* Houghton Mifflin Company.

Honorable Mention

Russell FREEDMAN. *In the Days of the Vaqueros: America's First True Cowboys.* Clarion Books.

Commended List

George ANCONA. *Harvest.* Marshall Cavendish.

René SALDAÑA, Jr. *The Jumping Tree.* Delacorte Press.

Picture Book

Elizabeth GÓMEZ. *A Movie in My Pillow*, text by Jorge ARGUETA. Children's Book Press.

Commended picture books

Fabricio Vanden BROECK. *Uncle Rain Cloud*, text by Tony JOHNSTON. Charlesbridge.

Maya Christina GONZÁLEZ. *Iguanas in the Snow and Other Winter Poems*, text by Francisco X. ALARCÓN. Children's Book Press.

Edel RODRÍGUEZ. *Mama Does the Mambo*, text by Katherine LEINER. Hyperion.

2002 Award Winner
Julia ALVAREZ. *Before We Were Free.* Knopf.

Honorable Mention Fiction
Edwidge DANTICAT. *Behind the Mountains.* Orchard

Commended List
Ana VECIANA-SUAREZ. *Flight to Freedom.* Orchard

Rafael YOCKTENG. *Messengers of Rain and other Poems from Latin America* (Simultaneous Spanish edition: *Mandaderos de la Lluvia*), compiled by Claudia M. LEE. Groundwood.

Honourable Mention Picture Book
Ana JUAN. *Frida*, text by Jonah WINTER. Scholastic

Commended picture books
Anita DeLUCIO-BROCK. *Grandma and Me at the Flea/Los Meros Meros Remateros*, text by Juan Felipe HERRERA. Children's Book Press.

David DIAZ. *The Pot that Juan Built*, text by Nancy ANDREW-GOEBEL. Lee and Low.

Maya Christina GONZÁLEZ. *My Diary from Here to There/Mi Diario de Aqui Hasta Alla*, text by Amada Irma PÉREZ. Children's Book Press.

Caroline MEROLA. *Me in the Middle*, text by Ana Maria MACHADO, translated by David UNGER. Groundwood.

Elivia SAVADIER. *I Love Saturdays Y Domingos*, text by Alma Flor ADA. Atheneum.

Beatriz VIDAL. *A Library for Juana*, text by Pat MORA. Knopf.

2003 Fiction
Judith Ortiz COFER. *The Meaning of Consuel.* Farrar, Straus & Giroux.

Honorable Mentions
Kathleen KRULL. *Harvesting Hope: The Story of Cesar Chavez*, ills Yuyi MORALES. Harcourt.

Nancy OSA. *Cuba 15.* Delacorte.

Commended
George ANCONA. *Murals: Walls That Sing.* Marshall Cavendish

Sandra COMINO. *Little Blue House.* Groundwood.

Gary SOTO. *The Afterlife.* Harcourt.

Picture Book
Yuyi MORALES. *Just a Minute: A Trickster Tale and Counting Book.* Chronicle Books.

Commended Picture Books

Carl ANGEL. *Xochitl and the Flowers*, text by Jorge ARGUETA. Children's Book Press.

María Hernández DE LA CRUZ & Casimiro DE LA Cruz LÓPEZ. *The Journey of Tunuri and the Blue Deer*, text by James ENDREDY. Bear Cub Books.

Pura Belpré Award: complete list of winners and honor books

1996 **For Narrative**

Medal Winner

Judith Ortiz COFER. *An Island Like You: Stories of the Barrio.* Melanie Kroupa/Orchard Books.

Honor Books

Lucía GONZÁLEZ. *The Bossy Gallito/El Gallo de Bodas: A Traditional Cuban Folktale*, ills Lulu DELACRE. Scholastic.

Gary SOTO. *Baseball in April, and Other Stories.* Harcourt.

For Illustration

Medal Winner

Susan GUEVARA. *Chato's Kitchen*, text by Gary SOTO. Putnam.

Honor Books

George ANCONA. *Pablo Remembers: The Fiesta of the Day of the Dead.* Lothrop. (Also published in a Spanish language edition: *Pablo Recuerda: La Fiesta de Día de los Muertos.* Lothrop).

Lulu DELACRE. *The Bossy Gallito/El Gallo de Bodas: A Traditional Cuban Folktale*, retold by Lucía GONZÁLEZ. Scholastic.

Carmen Lomas GARZA. *Family Pictures/Cuadros de Familia*, Spanish language text by Rosalma ZUBIZARRETA. Children's Book Press.

1998 **For Narrative**

Medal winner

Victor MARTINEZ. *Parrot in the Oven: Mi Vida.* Joanna Cotler/HarperCollins.

Honor Books

Francisco ALARCÓN. *Laughing Tomatoes and Other Spring Poems/Jitomates Risueños y Otros Poemas de Primavera*, ills Maya Christina GONZALEZ. Children's Book Press.

Floyd MARTINEZ. *Spirits of the High Mesa.* Arte Público Press.

For Illustration

Medal Winner

Stephanie GARCIA. *Snapshots from the Wedding*, text by Gary SOTO. Putnam.

Honor Books

Carmen Lomas GARZA. *In My Family/En Mi Familia.* Children's Book Press.

Enrique O. SÁNCHEZ. *The Golden Flower: A Taino Myth from Puerto Rico*, text by Nina JAFFE. Simon & Schuster.

Simón SILVA. *Gathering the Sun: An Alphabet in Spanish and English*, text by Alma Flor ADA, English translation by Rosalma ZUBIZARRETA. Lothrop.

2000 **For Narrative**

Medal Winner

Alma Flor ADA. *Under the Royal Palms: A Childhood in Cuba.* Atheneum Books.

Honor Books

Francisco X. ALARCÓN. *From the Bellybutton of the Moon and Other Summer Poems/Del Ombligo de la Luna y Otro Poemas de Verano*, ills Maya Christina GONZALEZ. Children's Book Press.

Juan Felipe HERRERA. *Laughing out Loud, I Fly: Poems in English and Spanish*, ills Karen BARBOUR. HarperCollins.

For Illustration

Medal Winner

Carmen Lomas GARZA. *Magic Windows.* Children's Book Press.

Honor Books

George ANCONA. *Barrio: José's Neighborhood.* Harcourt Brace.

Felipe DÁVALOS. *The Secret Stars*, text by Joseph Slate. Marshall Cavendish.

Amelia Lau CARLING. *Mama & Papa Have a Store.* Dial Books.

2002 **For Narrative**

Medal Winner

Pam Munoz RYAN. *Esperanza Rising.* Scholastic Press.

Honor Books

Francisco X. ALARCÓN. *Iguanas in the Snow*, ills Maya Christina GONZALEZ. Children's Book Press.

Francisco JIMÉNEZ. *Breaking Through.* Houghton Mifflin.

For Illustration

Medal Winner

Susan GUEVARA. *Chato and the Party Animals*, text by Gary SOTO. Putnam.

Honor Book

Joe CEPEDA. *Juan Bobo Goes to Work*, retold by Marisa MONTES. HarperCollins.

2004 **For Narrative**

Medal Winner

Julia ALVAREZ. *Before We Were Free.* Alfred A. Knopf.

Honor Books
Nancy OSA. *Cuba 15.* Delacorte Press.

Amada Irma PÉREZ. *My Diary from Here to There/Mi Diario de Aquí Hasta Allá*, ills Maya Christina GONZALEZ. Children's Book Press/Editorial Libros Para Niños.

For Illustration

Medal Winner
Yuyi MORALES. *Just a Minute: A Trickster Tale and Counting Book.* Chronicle Books.

Honor Books
Robert CASILLA. *First Day in Grapes*, text by L. King PÉREZ. Lee & Low Books Inc.

David DIAZ. *The Pot That Juan Built*, text by Nancy ANDREWS-GOEBEL Lee & Low.

Yuyi MORALES. *Harvesting Hope: The Story of Cesar Chavez*, text by Kathleen KRULL. Harcourt, Inc.

The Jane Addams Award: complete list of winners and honor books.

1953 Eva Knox EVANS. *People Are Important.* Capital.

1954 Jean KETCHUM. *Stick-in-the-Mud.* Cadmus Books, E.M. Hale.

1955 Elizabeth YATES. *Rainbow Round the World.* Bobbs-Merrill.

1956 Arna BONTEMPS. *Story of the Negro.* Knopf.

1957 Margot BENARY-ISBERT. *Blue Mystery.* Harcourt, Brace.

1958 William O. STEELE. *The Perilous Road.* Harcourt, Brace.

1959 No Award

1960 Edith Patterson MEYER. *Champions of Peace.* Little Brown.

1961 Shirley L. ARORA. *What Then, Raman?* Follett.

1962 Aimee SOMMERFELT. *The Road to Agra.* Criterion.

1963 Ryerson JOHNSON. *The Monkey and the Wild, Wild Wind.* Abelard-Schuman.

1964 John F. KENNEDY. *Profiles in Courage: Young Readers Memorial Edition.* Harper & Row.

1965 Duane BRADLEY. *Meeting with a Stranger.* Lippincott.

1966 Emily Cheney NEVILLE. *Berries Goodman.* Harper & Row.

1967 Robert BURCH. *Queenie Peavy.* Viking.

1968 Erick HAUGAARD. *The Little Fishes.* Houghton Mifflin.

1969 Esther HAUTZIG. *The Endless Steppe: Growing Up in Siberia.* T.Y. Crowell.

1970 Theodore TAYLOR. *The Cay.* Doubleday.

1971 Cornelia MEIGS. *Jane Addams: Pioneer of Social Justice.* Little Brown.

1972 Betty UNDERWOOD. *The Tamarack Tree.* Houghton Mifflin.

1973 S. Carl HIRSCH. *The Riddle of Racism.* Viking.

Honor Book
Johanna REISS. *The Upstairs Room.* Crowell.

1974 Nicholasa MOHR. *Nilda.* Harper & Row.

Honor Books
Alice CHILDRESS. *A Hero Ain't Nothin' but a Sandwich.* Coward, McCann & Geoghegan.

Barbara HABENSTREIT. *Men Against War.* Doubleday.

Marilyn SACHS. *A Pocket Full of Seeds.* Doubleday.

1975 Charlotte POMERANTZ. *The Princess and the Admiral.* Addison-Wesley.

Honor Books
James Lincoln COLLIER & Christopher COLLIER. *My Brother Sam Is Dead.* Four Winds.

Elizabeth Sutherland MARTINEZ & Enriqueta Longeaux y VASQUEZ. *Viva la Raza!* Doubleday.

Milton MELTZER & Bernard COLE. *The Eye of Conscience.* Follett.

1976 Eloise GREENFIELD. *Paul Robeson.* T.Y. Crowell.

Honor Books
Robert C. O'BRIEN. *Z for Zachariah.* Atheneum.

Mildred D. TAYLOR. *Song of the Trees.* Dial.

Laurence YEP. *Dragonwings.* Harper& Row.

1977 Milton MELTZER. *Never to Forget: The Jews of the Holocaust.* Harper & Row.

Honor Book
Mildred D. TAYLOR. *Roll of Thunder, Hear My Cry.* Dial.

1978 Laurence YEP. *Child of the Owl.* Harper & Row.

Honor Books
Ilse KOEHN. *Mischling, Second Degree.* Greenwillow.

Myron LEVOY. *Alan and Naomi.* Harper & Row.

Special Recognition
Lucille CLIFTON. *Amifika.* Dutton.

Ashok DAVAR. *The Wheel of King Asoka.* Follett.

1979 Jamake HIGHWATER. *Many Smokes, Many Moons: A Chronology of American Indian History through Indian Art.* Lippincott,

Honor Books
Ossie DAVIS. *Escape to Freedom.* Viking.

Katherine PATERSON. *The Great Gilly Hopkins.* Crowell.

1980 David KHERDIAN. *The Road from Home: The Story of an Armenian Girl.* Greenwillow.

West Coast Honor Book
Toshio MORI. *Woman from Hiroshima.* Isthmus.

Special Recognition
M. B. GOFFSTEIN. *Natural History.* Farrar Straus Giroux.

1981 Florence Meiman WHITE. *First Woman in Congress: Jeannette Rankin.* Julian Messner.

Honor Books
Phyllis CLARK & Robert LEHRMAN. *Doing Time: A Look at Crime and Prisons.* Hastings House.

Erik HAUGAARD. *Chase Me, Catch Nobody!* Houghton Mifflin.

Hadley IRWIN. *We Are Mesquakie, We Are One.* Feminist Press.

1982 Athena V. LORD. *A Spirit to Ride the Whirlwind.* Macmillan.

Honor Books
Patricia BEATTY. *Lupita Mañana.* Morrow.

Mildred D. TAYLOR. *Let the Circle Be Unbroken.* Dial.

1983 Toshi MARUKI. *Hiroshima No Pika*, translated from the Japanese. First U.S. edition: Lothrop, Lee & Shepard.

Honor Books
Sidney LENZ. *The Bomb.* Lodestar/Dutton.

Charlotte POMERANTZ. *If I Had a Paka: Poems in Eleven Languages.* Greenwillow.

West Coast Honor Book
Betty MORROW. *People at the Edge of the World: The Ohlone of Central California.* Bacon

Special Recognition
Arnold ADOFF. *All the Colors of the Race.* Lothrop, Lee & Shepard.

Children as Teachers of Peace, by Our Children. Celestial Press.

1984 Marion Dane BAUER. *Rain of Fire.* Clarion/Houghton Mifflin.

1985 Hermann VINKE. *The Short Life of Sophie Scholl*, with an interview with Ilse AICHINGER, translated from the German by Hedvig PACHTER. First U.S. edition: Harper & Row.

Honor Books
Uri ORLEV. *The Island on Bird Street*, translated from the Hebrew by Hillel HALKIN. Houghton, Mifflin.

Vera B. WILLIAMS. *Music, Music for Everyone.* Greenwillow.

1986 Milton MELTZER. *Ain't Gonna Study War No More: The Story of America's Peace Seekers.* Harper & Row.

Honor Book
Samantha SMITH. *Journey to the Soviet Union.* Little, Brown.

1987 Judith VIGNA. *Nobody Wants a Nuclear War.* Albert Whitman.

Honor Books
Mitsumasa ANNO. *All in a Day.* Philomel.

Brent ASHABRANNER. *Children of the Maya: A Guatemalan Indian Odyssey*, with photographs by Paul CONKLIN. Dodd, Mead.

1988 Sheila GORDON. *Waiting for the Rain: A Novel of South Africa.* Orchard Books/Franklin Watts.

Honor Books
Leo LIONNI. *Nicolas, Where Have You Been?* Knopf.

Doreen RAPPAPORT. *Trouble at the Mines.* Crowell.

1989 **(Tie)**
Victoria BOUTIS. *Looking Out.* Four Winds Press.

Virginia HAMILTON. *Anthony Burns: The Defeat and Triumph of a Fugitive Slave.* Alfred A. Knopf.

Honor Books
Ann CAMERON. *The Most Beautiful Place in the World.* Alfred A. Knopf.

Mary Downing HAHN. *December Stillness.* Clarion.

Milton MELTZER. *Rescue: The Story of How Gentiles Saved Jews in the Holocaust.* Harper & Row.

1990 Patricia & Fredrick McKISSACK. *A Long Hard Journey: The Story of the Pullman Porter.* Walker.

Honor Books
Eve BUNTING. *The Wednesday Surprise.* Clarion.

Lois LOWRY. *Number the Stars.* Houghton Mifflin.

Carolyn REEDER. *Shades of Gray.* Macmillan.

1991 Ann DURELL & Marilyn SACHS (editors). *The Big Book for Peace.* Dutton.

Honor Books
Sheila GORDON. *The Middle of Somewhere: A Story of South Africa.* Orchard.

Sheila HAMANAKA. *The Journey: Japanese-Americans, Racism and Renewal.* Richard Jackson/Orchard.

1992 Fran Leeper BUSS (with the assistance of Daisy CUBIAS). *Journey of the Sparrows.* Lodestar.

Honor Book
Walter Dean MYERS. *Now Is Your Time! The African-American Struggle for Freedom.* HarperCollins.

1993 **Book for Older Children**
Frances TEMPLE. *A Taste of Salt: A Story of Modern Haiti.* Orchard.

Honor Book
Mary E. LYONS. *Letters from a Slave Girl: The Story of Harriet Jacobs.* Scribners.

Picture Book
Faith RINGGOLD. *Aunt Harriet's Underground Railroad in the Sky.* Crown.

Honor Book
Patricia POLACCO. *Mrs. Katz and Tush.* Bantam.

1994 **Book for Older Children**
Ellen LEVINE. *Freedom's Children: Young Civil Rights Activists Tell Their Stories.* G.P. Putnam's.

Honor Book
Russell FREEDMAN. *Eleanor Roosevelt: A Life of Discovery.* Clarion.

Picture Book
George LITTLECHILD. *This Land Is My Land.* Children's Book Press.

Honor Book
Tom FEELINGS. *Soul Looks Back in Wonder.* Dial.

1995 **Book for Older Children**
Russell FREEDMAN. *Kids at Work: Lewis Hine and the Crusade Against Child Labor.* Clarion.

Honor Books
Mary STOLTZ. *Cezanne Pinto.* Alfred A. Knopf.

Jacqueline WOODSON. *I Hadn't Meant to Tell You This.* Delacorte.

Picture Book
Nancy CARPENTER. *Sitti's Secrets*, text by Naomi Shihab NYE. Four Winds Press.

Honor Book
Michael BRYANT. *Bein' with You This Way*, text by W. NIKOLA-LISA. Lee & Low.

1996 **Book for Older Children**
Mildred D. TAYLOR. *The Well.* Dial.

Honor Books
Christopher Paul CURTIS. *The Watsons Go to Birmingham – 1963.* Delacorte.

On the Wings of Peace: Writers and Illustrators Speak Out for Peace in Memory of Hiroshima and Nagasaki. Clarion.

Jacqueline WOODSON. *From the Notebooks of Melanin Sun.* Blue Sky/Scholastic.

Picture Book
No Award given.

Special Commendation
Tom FEELINGS. *The Middle Passage.* Dial.

1997 **Book for Older Children**
Susan Campbell BARTOLETTI. *Growing Up In Coal County.* Houghton Mifflin.

Honor Books
Mildred Pitts WALTER. *Second Daughter: The Story of a Slave Girl.* Scholastic.

Laura E. WILLIAMS. *Behind the Bedroom Wall.* Milkweed.

Picture Book
David DIAZ. *Wilma Unlimited*, text by Kathleen KRULL. Harcourt Brace.

Honor Book
Sharon WILSON. *The Day Gogo Went to Vote*, text by Elinor Batezat SISULU. Little, Brown.

1998 **Book for Older Children**
Naomi Shihab NYE. *Habibi.* Simon & Schuster.

Honor Books
Paul FLEISCHMAN. *Seedfolks.* HarperCollins.

Francisco JIMENEZ. *The Circuit: Stories from the Life of a Migrant Child.* University of New Mexico Press.

Picture Book
Bethanne ANDERSEN. *Seven Brave Women*, text by Betsy HEARNE. Greenwillow.

Honor Books
Rosmarie HAUSHERR. *Celebrating Families.* Scholastic.

Dom LEE. *Passage to Freedom, the Sugihara Story*, text by Ken MOCHIZUKI. Lee & Low.

1999 **Book for Older Children**
Virginia Euwer WOLFF. *Bat 6.* Scholastic.

Honor Books
Joseph BRUCHAC. *The Heart of a Chief.* Dial.

Tim McKEE. *No More Strangers Now*, photographs by Anne BLACKSHAW. A Melanie Kroupa Book/DK Ink.

Elizabeth PARTRIDGE. *Restless Spirit: The Life and Work of Dorothea Lange.* Viking.

Picture Book
ALIKI. *Painted Words/Spoken Memories: Marianthe's Story.* Greenwillow.

Honor Books
Kathy JAKOBSEN. *This Land Is Your Land*, words & music by Woody GUTHRIE. Little, Brown.

Debbie TILLEY. *Hey, Little Ant*, text by Phillip & Hannah HOOSE. Tricycle Press.

Michele WOOD. *i see the rhythm*, text by Toyomi IGUS. Children's Book Press.

2000 **Book for Older Children**
Ruby BRIDGES. *Through My Eyes*. Scholastic.

Honor Books
Susan Campbell BARTOLETTI. *Kids on Strike!* Houghton Mifflin.

Louise ERDRICH. *The Birchbark House*. Hyperion.

Picture Book
Chris K. SOENTPIET. *Molly Bannaky*, text by Alice McGILL. Houghton Mifflin.

Honor Books
Molly BANG. *When Sophie Gets Angry – Really, Really Angry...* The Blue Sky/Scholastic.

Raúl COLÓN. *A Band of Angels: A Story Inspired by the Jubilee Singers*, text by Deborah HOPKINSON. Anne Schwartz/Atheneum.

2001 **Book for Older Children**
Pam Muñoz RYAN. *Esperanza Rising*. Scholastic Press.

Honor Books
Lynn JOSEPH. *The Color of My Words*. Joanna Cotler/HarperCollins.

Ellen LEVINE. *Darkness over Denmark: The Danish Resistance and the Rescue of the Jews*. Holiday House.

Harriette Gillem ROBINET. *Walking to the Bus-Rider Blues*. Jean Karl/Atheneum/Simon & Schuster.

Picture Book
Alfonso RUANO. *The Composition*, text by Antonio SKÁRMETA. Groundwood.

Honor Book
Henri SORENSEN. *The Yellow Star: The Legend of King Christian X of Denmark*, text by Carmen Agra DEEDY. Peachtree Publishers.

2002 **Book for Older Children**
Beverley NAIDOO. *The Other Side of Truth*. U.S. edition: HarperCollins.

Honor Books
Rachna GILMORE. *A Group of One*. Henry Holt.

Virginia Euwer WOLFF. *True Believer*. Atheneum/Simon & Schuster.

Picture Book
Bryan COLLIER. *Martin's Big Words: The Life of Dr. Martin Luther King, Jr.*, text by Doreen RAPPAPORT. Jump at the Sun/Hyperion.

Honor Book
Vera B. WILLIAMS. *Amber Was Brave, Essie Was Smart.* Greenwillow/HarperCollins.

2003 **Book for Older Children**
Deborah ELLIS. *Parvana's Journey.* Groundwood Books/Douglas & McIntyre.

Honor Books
Linda Sue PARK. *When My Name Was Keoko.* Clarion.

Katherine PATERSON. *The Same Stuff as Stars.* Clarion.

Picture Book
Ann GRIFALCONI. *Patrol: An American Soldier in Vietnam*, text by Walter Dean MYERS. HarperCollins.

Honor Books
Francisco DELGADO. *¡Si, Se Puede! Yes We Can! Janitor Strike In L.A.*, text by Diana COHN. Cinco Puntos Press.

Kadir NELSON. *The Village That Vanished*, text by Ann GRIFALCONI. Dial.

2004 **Book for Older Children**
Beverley NAIDOO. *Out of Bounds: Seven Stories of Conflict and Hope.* U.S. edition: HarperCollins.

Honor Books
Chris CROWE. *Getting Away with Murder: The True Story of the Emmett Till Case.* Phyllis Fogelman Books/Penguin.

Deborah HOPKINSON. *Shutting Out the Sky: Life in the Tenements of New York 1880-1924.* Orchard Books/Scholastic.

Picture Book
Yuyi MORALES. *Harvesting Hope: The Story of Cesar Chavez*, text by Kathleen KRULL. Harcourt.

Honor Books
Ann MARSHALL. *Luba: The Angel of Bergen-Belsen*, text by Michelle R. McCANN. Tricycle Press.

Terry WIDENER. *Girl Wonder: A Baseball Story in Nine Innings*, text by Deborah HOPKINSON. An Anne Schwartz Book/Atheneum.

Special Commendation
Deborah ELLIS. The Breadwinner Trilogy: *The Breadwinner* (2001), *Parvana's Journey* (2002), & *Mud City* (2003). Groundwood Books/Douglas & McIntyre.

2005 **Book for Older Children**
Ann BAUSUM. *With Courage and Cloth: Winning the Fight for a Woman's Right to Vote.* National Geographic Society.

Honor Book
Deborah ELLIS. *The Heaven Shop.* Fitzhenry & Whiteside.

Picture Book
Youme LANDOWNE. *Sélavi, This is Life: A Haitian story of hope.* Cinco Puntos Press.

Honor Books
Karen ENGLISH. *Hot Day on Abbott Avenue.* Clarion Books.

Bruce Edward HALL. *Henry and the Kite Dragon.* Philomel Books/Penguin Young Readers Group.

James RUMFORD. *Sequoyah: The Cherokee Man who Gave His People Writing.* Houghton Mifflin.

Michael L. Printz Award: complete list of winners

2000 Walter Dean MYERS. *Monster.* HarperCollins.

Honor Books
David ALMOND. *Skellig.* Delacorte Press.

Laurie Halse ANDERSON. *Speak*, edited by Elizabeth MIKESELL. Farrar, Straus & Giroux.

Ellen WITTLINGER. *Hard Love*, edited by David GALE. Simon & Schuster.

2001 David ALMOND. *Kit's Wilderness.* Delacorte Press.

Honor Books
Carolyn COMAN. *Many Stones.* Front Street Press.

Carol PLUM-UCCI. *The Body of Christopher Creed.* Harcourt, Inc.

Louise RENNISON. *Angus, Thongs, and Full-Frontal Snogging.* HarperCollins.

Terry TRUEMAN. *Stuck in Neutral.* HarperCollins.

2002 An NA. *Step from Heaven.* Front Street.

Honor Books
Peter DICKINSON. *The Ropemaker.* Delacorte Press.

Jan GREENBERG. *Heart to Heart: New Poems Inspired by Twentieth-Century American Art.* Harry N. Abrams, Inc.

Chris LYNCH. *Freewill.* HarperCollins.

Virginia Euwer WOLFF. *True Believer.* Atheneum.

2003 Aidan CHAMBERS. *Postcards from No Man's Land.* Dutton/Penguin Putnam.

Honor Books
Nancy FARMER. *The House of the Scorpion.* Simon and Schuster/Richard Jackson.

Garret FREYMANN-WEYR. *My Heartbeat.* Houghton Mifflin.

Jack GANTOS. *Hole in My Life.* Farrar, Straus and Giroux.

2004 Angela JOHNSON. *The First Part Last.* Simon & Schuster.

Honor Books
Jennifer DONNELLY. *A Northern Light.* Harcourt.

Helen FROST. *Keesha's House*. Farrar, Straus & Giroux/Frances Foster Books.

K.L. GOING. *Fat Kid Rules the World*. G.P. Putnam's Sons/Penguin Young Readers Group.

Carolyn MACKLER. *The Earth, My Butt and Other Big Round Things*. Candlewick Press.

2005 Meg ROSOFF. *How I Live Now*. Lamb/Random.

Honor Books
Kenneth OPPEL. *Airborn*. EOS/HarperCollins.

Gary D. SCHMIDT. *Lizzie Bright and the Buckminster Boy*. Clarion.

Allan STRATTON. *Chanda's Secrets*. Annick Press.

Booktrust Teenage Prize: complete list of winners and shortlisted titles

2003 Mark HADDON. *Curious Incident of the Dog in the Night-Time.* David Fickling.

Shortlist
Lynne Reid BANKS. *The Dungeon.* Harper Collins.

Kevin BROOKS. *Lucas.* The Chicken House.

Melvin BURGESS. *Doing It.* Andersen Press.

Alan GIBBONS. *Caught in the Crossfire.* Orion.

Alan GIBBONS. *The Edge.* Orion.

Keith GRAY. *Malarkey.* Red Fox.

Nicky SINGER. *Doll.* Harper Collins.

2004 Anne CASSIDY. *Looking for JJ.* Scholastic.

Shortlist
Alison ALLEN-GREY. *Unique.* Oxford University Press.

Julie BERTAGNA. *The Opposite of Chocolate.* Picador.

Berlie DOHERTY. *Deep Secret.* Puffin.

Catherine FORDE. *Fat Boy Swim.* Egmont.

Alan GIBBONS. *The Dark Beneath.* Dolphin.

Bali RAI. *Rani and Sukh.* Corgi.

Matt WHYMAN. *Boy Kills Man.* Hodder.

The Booktrust Early Years Award (until 2003 the Sainsbury's Baby Book Award): complete list of winners

1999 Helen OXENBURY. *Tickle, Tickle.* Walker Books.

2000 Alex AYLIFFE. *Boo Barney.* Orchard Books.

2001 Sandra LOUSADA. *Baby Faces.*

2002 Annie KUBLER. *Head, Shoulders, Knees and Toes.* Child's Play.

2003 Sam LLOYD. *Happy Dog Sad Dog.* Little Tiger Press.

2004 **Baby Book Award**
David ELLWAND & Mike JOLLEY. *I love you!* Templar Publishing.

Pre-School Award
Julia DONALDSON & Axel SCHEFFLER. *The Snail and the Whale.* Macmillan.

Best New Illustrator Award
Polly HORNER. *Polly and the North Star.* Orion.

Phoenix Award: complete list of winners and honor books (original publishers & publication date follows each entry)

1985 Rosemary SUTCLIFF. *The Mark of the Horse Lord.* Oxford, 1965; Walck, 1965.

1986 Robert BURCH. *Queenie Peavy.* Viking, 1966.

1987 Leon GARFIELD. *Smith.* Constable, 1967; Pantheon, 1967.

1988 Erik Christian HAUGAARD. *The Rider and his Horse.* Houghton Mifflin, 1968.

1989 Helen CRESSWELL. *The Nightwatchmen.* Faber, 1969; Macmillan, 1969.

Honor Books
Milton MELTZER. *Brother Can You Spare a Dime?* Knopf 1969.

Adrienne RICHARD. *Pistol.* Little, Brown, 1969.

1990 Sylvia Louise ENGDAHL. *Enchantress from the Stars.* Atheneum, 1970.

Honor Books
William MAYNE. *Ravensgill.* H. Hamilton, 1970; Dutton, 1970.

Scott O'DELL. *Sing Down the Moon.* Houghton Mifflin, 1970.

1991 Jane GARDAM. *A Long Way from Verona.* H. Hamilton, 1971; Macmillan, 1971.

Honor Books
William MAYNE. *A Game of Dark.* H. Hamilton, 1971; Dutton, 1971.

Ursula LeGUIN. *The Tombs of Atuan.* Atheneum, 1971.

1992 Mollie HUNTER. *A Sound of Chariots.* H. Hamilton, 1972; Harper, 1972.

1993 Nina BAWDEN. *Carrie's War.* Gollancz, 1973; Lippincott, 1973.

Honor Book
E. L. KONIGSBURG. *A Proud Taste for Scarlet and Miniver.* Atheneum, 1973

1994 Katherine PATERSON. *Of Nightingales that Weep.* Crowell, 1974.

Honor Books
James Lincoln COLLIER & Christopher COLLIER. *My Brother Sam is Dead.* Four Winds, 1974.

Sharon Bell MATHIS. *Listen for the Fig Tree.* Viking, 1974.

1995 Laurence YEP. *Dragonwings.* HarperCollins, 1975.

Honor Book
Natalie BABBITT. *Tuck Everlasting.* Farrar, 1975; Bantam, 1975.

1996 Alan GARNER. *The Stone Book.* Collins, 1976.

Honor Book
William STEIG. *Abel's Island.* Farrar, 1976.

1997 Robert CORMIER. *I Am the Cheese.* Pantheon, 1977.

1998 Jill Paton WALSH. *A Chance Child.* Macmillan, 1978; Farrar, 1978.

Honor Books
Robin McKINLEY. *Beauty.* Harper, 1978.

Doris ORGEL. *The Devil in Vienna.* Dial, 1978.

1999 E.L. KONIGSBURG. *Throwing Shadows.* Atheneum, 1979.

2000 Monica HUGHES. *The Keeper of the Isis Light.* Atheneum, 1980.

Honor Book
Jane LANGTON. *The Fledgling.* HarperCollins, 1980.

2001 Peter DICKINSON. *The Seventh Raven.* Gollancz, 1981; Dutton, 1981.

Honor Book
Kathryn LASKY. *The Night Journey.* Frederick Warne, 1981.

2002 Zibby ONEAL. *A Formal Feeling.* Viking, 1982.

Honor Book
Clayton BESS. *Story for a Black Night.* Parnassus, 1982; Houghton Mifflin, 1982.

2003 Ivan SOUTHALL. *The Long Night Watch.* Methuen, 1983.

Honor Book
Cynthia VOIGT. *A Solitary Blue.* Atheneum, 1983.

2004 Berlie DOHERTY. *White Peak Farm.* Methuen, 1984; Orchard, 1984.

Honor Book
Brian DOYLE. *Angel Square*. Douglas & McIntyre, 1984.

Chapter 10: The Truth of the Matter – awards for non-fiction and poetry

The Signal Award for Poetry (UK); The CLPE Poetry Award (UK); The Aventis Junior Science Prize (UK); The Orbis Pictus Award for Outstanding Nonfiction for Children (US); The Robert F. Sibert Informational Award (US); The American Institute of Physics Science Writing Award – Children (US); The Eve Pownall Award for Information Books (Australia); The Norma Fleck Award for Canadian Children's Non-Fiction; The Information Book Award (Canada); The Science in Society Children's Book Award (Canada) & The Elsie Locke Medal (*formerly* The Library and Information Association of New Zealand Aotearoa (LIANZA) Young People's Non-Fiction Award).

This chapter deals with awards, some very new, some of rather longer standing, that have been set up to promote quality in non-fiction; to ensure that information books as well as imaginative ones are of a high standard and not just a dry recitation of facts. The Boston-Globe Horn Book Award (Chapter 7) has a section for non-fiction, and has allowed for poetry within its category 'Fiction and Poetry'. Poetry and Non-Fiction are also eligible for the Carnegie and Newbery Medals, but in this chapter awards that are solely for poetry or non-fiction will be discussed. The Giverny Award was covered in Chapter 8, but it could have been included here. I decided that as the illustration – it is for illustration in a children's science book – was the part emphasised in the award criteria, it was best placed with the other illustration awards. The Canadian Red Cedar Awards select one fiction and one non-fiction book each year, so I have treated that with the other Canadian awards within Chapter 12, 'Around the World'.

The Signal Poetry Award (UK) was awarded from 1979 to 2001, and was organised by the magazine *Signal* which had a long history of concern for quality in children's books, and is respected for its in-depth reviews and comment. Each year its May issue was devoted to poetry and poets, with a discussion of the winning poets and titles. The winners were chosen from books published during the previous year. Michael Rosen, Allan Ahlberg, Roger McGough and Charles Causley are names which appear in various listings earlier in this volume; here they are celebrated for their words and the use they make of them – not solely, or even largely for the (often brilliant) illustrations that accompany those words and have taken them into some of those other lists.

Since the Signal Poetry Award has ceased, the CLPE Poetry Award (UK) has been created which will to a large extent fill the gap in awards that was the effect of that demise. This is administered by the Centre for Literacy in Primary Education, and is intended 'to stimulate enthusiasm for poetry in both schools and homes'. There have been two winning announcements so far, for 2003 and 2004. Again, it is awarded to books published during the preceding year. There is news from the US that the Lion & Unicorn, a magazine based at John Hopkins University in Baltimore, MD., and devoted to the serious consideration of children's literature, is shortly to establish a poetry award; its first announcement is due to be made in 2005.

The Aventis Junior Science Prize (UK) is the recently relaunched children's section of the long-standing Aventis Prizes for Science Books, previously called the Science Book Prizes. Dorling Kindersley and Usborne seem to dominate the lists, but this is largely because they are the major UK publishers of children's non-fiction books.

The Orbis Pictus Award for Outstanding Nonfiction for Children (US) was established in 1990 by the National Council of Teachers of English (NCTE) 'to promote and recognize excellence in nonfiction writing'. The award is named for *Orbis Pictus* (*The World in Pictures*) by Johann Comenius, published in 1657 and considered to be the first informational book written specifically for children. It includes many authors, for instance Jean Fritz, Russell Freedman, Walter Dean Myers, Bruce Brooks, Marc Aronson and Jim Murphy, who have appeared in the Newbery or CSK winners and Honor lists.

The Robert F. Sibert Informational Award (US) is also recently established. Several of its winners also appear in recent BGH Nonfiction, and on several Newbery Honor lists. It also shares many titles with recent Orbis Pictus lists.

The American Institute of Physics Science Writing Award – Children (US) was started in 1988. Its list of winners includes books with subject-matter ranging from the child's own bathwater – the first award was for *Splash!* – through the science of microscopes and light, to space exploration, which is the subject-matter of the most recent two winners.

The Eve Pownall Award for Non-Fiction (Australia) was first given in 1988, funded by the family of Eve Pownall. No further awards were made until 1993, when it was brought under the aegis of the Children's Book Council of Australia, and it is now announced along with the other national Children's awards there.

There are now three awards for non-fiction in Canada. The longest-running is the Information Book Award, sponsored by the Children's Literature Roundtables of Canada. It is given to recognise an outstanding information book for children and young people 5 to 15 years of age written in English by a Canadian citizen or landed immigrant. Eligible books will cover issues of culture, concept, life cycle, science, biography, history or geography. The book must have been published in Canada during the previous year.

The Science in Society Children's Book Award was first made in 1994 by the Canadian Science Writers' Association. Its aim is to honour outstanding contributions to science writing. It is open to Canadian citizens or residents of Canada and entries, in either French or English, must have been published in Canada during the current calendar year.

The newest of the three is the Norma Fleck Award for Canadian Children's Non-Fiction, established by the Fleck Family Foundation in 1999 in honour of Norma Fleck (1906-1998), who inspired a deep love of reading in her children and grandchildren. The Award recognises Canada's exceptional non-fiction books for young people, and is administered by the Canadian Children's Book Centre.

The Library and Information Association of New Zealand Aotearoa (LIANZA) established its Young People's Non-Fiction Award in 1987, which was renamed the Elsie Locke Medal in 2001 to commemorate Elsie Locke (1912-2001), who was a well-known children's author and ardent advocate of children's access to the history of Aotearoa New Zealand. It is given for 'the most distinguished contribution to non-fiction for young people'.

Non-fiction is perhaps inevitably more likely to be country-specific than fiction. Most of the non-fiction awards that do not have specific subject constraints deal with the history, natural history or geography of the country in which they are established. It is right and proper that there should be an encouragement for children to learn something of their native land as well as of other countries, and that awards be in place to encourage quality in the production of the books through which they may do so. The awards that have been included in this chapter are concerned to promote both quality and accessibility of books to children whose imaginations are touched by the power of poetry, the magic of science or the romance of history, rather than by story.

Signal Poetry Award UK: complete list of winners

1979/80 Ted HUGHES. *Moon-Bells and Other Poems.* Chatto.

Highly commended
Charles CAUSLEY (ed.). *The Puffin Book of Salt-Sea Verse.* Kestrel/Puffin.

Elizabeth JENNINGS. *After the Ark.* Oxford University Press.

1980/81 No Award

1982 Michael ROSEN, ills Quentin BLAKE (sharing the award). *You Can't Catch Me!* Deutsch.

Highly commended
Roger McGOUGH (ed.). *Strictly Private.* Kestrel.

1983 Seamus HEANEY & Ted HUGHES (editors). *The Rattle Bag.* Faber.

Highly commended
Charles CAUSLEY (ed.). *The Sun Dancing.* Kestrel.

1984 Roger McGOUGH. *Sky in the Pie.* Kestrel.

Highly commended
Allan AHLBERG. *Please Mrs Butler.* Kestrel.

Michael ROSEN, ills Quentin BLAKE. *Quick, Let's Get Out of Here.* Deutsch.

1985 Ted HUGHES. *What is the Truth?* Faber.

1986 Gareth OWEN. *Song of the City.* Fontana.

Highly commended
Naomi LEWIS (ed.). *Messages.* Faber.

Fiona WATERS (ed.). *Golden Apples.* Heinemann.

1987 Charles CAUSLEY. *Early in the Morning.* Viking Kestrel.

Special mention
Christopher LOGUE (ed.). *The Children's Book of Children's Rhymes.* Batsford.

1988 John MOLE. *Boo to a Goose.* Peterloo Poets.

Special mention
Anne HARVEY (ed.). *In Time of War.* Blackie.

Raymond WILSON. *Daft Davy.* Faber.

1989 James BERRY. *When I Dance.* Hamish Hamilton.

Highly commended
Grace NICHOLS. *Come on into My Tropical Garden.* A.& C. Black.

1990 Allan AHLBERG. *Heard it in the Playground.* Viking Kestrel.

Highly commended
Philip GROSS. *Manifold Manor.* Faber.

1991 Gerard BENSON (ed.). *This Poem Doesn't Rhyme.* Viking.

Highly commended
Brian MORSE. *Picnic on the Moon.* Turton & Chambers.

1992 Anne HARVEY (ed.). *Shades of Green.* Julia MacRae.

Special mention
Russell HOBAN. *The Pedalling Man.* Heinemann.

1993 Jackie KAY. *Two's Company.* Blackie.

Highly commended
Gerard BENSON. *The Magnificent Callisto.* Blackie.

Matthew SWEENEY. *The Flying Spring Onion.* Faber.

1994 Philip GROSS. *The All-Nite Café.* Faber.

1995 Helen DUNMORE. *Secrets.* Bodley Head.

1996 Mike HARDING. *Buns for the Elephants.* Viking.

Highly commended
Christian MORGENSTERN. *Lullabies, Lyrics and Gallows Songs.* North-South.

1997 Carol Ann DUFFY (ed.). *Stopping for Death.* Viking.

1998 Roger McGOUGH. *Bad, Bad Cats.* Viking.

1999 Jackie KAY. *The Frog Who Dreamed She Was an Opera Singer.* Bloomsbury.

Highly commended
Roger McGOUGH (ed.). *The Ring of Words*, ills Satoshi KITAMURA. Faber.

2000 Christopher REID. *All Sorts*, ills Sara FANELLI. Ondt & Gracehoper.

2001 Carol Ann DUFFY. *The Oldest Girl in the World.* Faber.

Award discontinued

The CLPE (Centre for Literacy in Primary Education) Poetry Award: complete list of winners

2003 John AGARD & Grace NICHOLS. *Under the Moon and Over the Sea.* Walker Books.

Runner-up
Allan AHLBERG. *Friendly Matches.* Puffin.

2004 Roger McGOUGH. *All the Best - Selected Poems.* Puffin.

Runner-up
Carol Ann DUFFY (ed.). *Overheard on a Saltmarsh.* Macmillan Young Picador.

Aventis Junior Prize for Science Books (formerly The Junior Science Book Prize): complete list of winners

1988 Roger KERROD. *Science Alive – Living Things.* Macdonald.

1989 David MACAULAY & Neil ARDLEY. *The Way Things Work.* Dorling Kindersley.

1990 **Under 14**
Susan MAYES. *What Makes a Flower Grow?; What Makes it Rain?; What's Under the Ground?; Where Does Electricity Come From?* Starting Point Science Series, Usborne.

Under 8
Ian RIDPATH. *The Giant Book of Space.* Hamlyn.

1991 Fran BALKWILL & Mic ROLPH. *Cells Are Us* **and** *Cell Wars.* Collins.

1992 Peter ROWAN. *The Amazing Voyage of the Cucumber Sandwich.* Jonathan Cape.

1993 Thompson YARDLEY. *Mighty Microbes.* Cassell.

1994 Linda GAMLIN. *Eyewitness Guide: Evolution.* Dorling Kindersley.

Rebecca HEDDLE & Paul SHIPTON. *Science with Weather.* Usborne.

David LAMBERT. *The Ultimate Dinosaur Book.* Dorling Kindersley.

1995 Jay YOUNG. *The Most Amazing Pop-Up Science Book.* Watts.

1996 Chris MAYNARD. *The World of Weather.* Kingfisher.

1997 Nick ARNOLD. *Blood, Bones and Body Bits* **and** *Ugly Bugs.* Horrible Science Series, Scholastic.

1998 David LAMBERT. *The Kingfisher Book of Oceans.* Kingfisher.

1999 Kirsteen ROGERS. *The Usborne Complete Book of the Microscope.* Usborne.

2000 Peter BOND. *DK Guide to Space.* Dorling Kindersley.

2001 Michael ALLABY. *DK Guide to Weather.* Dorling Kindersley.

2002 Richard WALKER. *DK Guide to the Human Body: A Photographic Journey Through the Human Body.* Dorling Kindersley.

2003 Frances DIPPER. *DK Guide to the Oceans.* Dorling Kindersley.

2004 Nick ARNOLD & Tony De SAULLES. *Really Rotten Experiments.* Scholastic.

2005 Robert WINSTON. *What Makes Me, Me?* Dorling Kindersley.

Orbis Pictus Award for Outstanding Nonfiction for Children: complete list of winners

1990 Jean FRITZ. *The Great Little Madison*. Putnam.

Honor Books
Rhoda BLUMBERG. *The Great American Gold Rush*. Bradbury Press.

Patricia LAUBER. *The News about Dinosaurs*. Simon & Schuster.

1991 Russell FREEDMAN. *Franklin Delano Roosevelt*. Clarion Books.

Honor Books
Normee EKOOMIAK. *Arctic Memories*. Henry Holt.

Patricia LAUBER. *Seeing Earth from Space*. Orchard Books.

1992 Robert BURLEIGH. *Flight: The Journey of Charles Lindbergh*. Philomel Books.

Honor Books
Pam CONRAD. *Prairie Vision: The Life and Times of Solomon Butcher*. HarperCollins.

Walter Dean MYERS. *Now Is Your Time! The African-American Struggle for Freedom*. HarperCollins.

1993 Jerry STANLEY. *Children of the Dust Bowl: The True Story of the School at Weedpatch Camp*. Crown.

Honor Books
Molly CONE. *Come Back, Salmon*. Sierra.

Pat CUMMINGS. *Talking with Artists*. Bradbury.

1994 Jim MURPHY. *Across America on an Emigrant Train*. Clarion.

Honor Books
Jim BRANDENBURG. *To the Top of the World: Adventures with Arctic Wolves*. Walker.

Bruce BROOKS. *Making Sense: Animal Perception and Communication*. Farrar.

1995 Diane SWANSON. *Safari Beneath the Sea: The Wonder World of the North Pacific Coast*. Sierra.

Honor Books
Jennifer Owings DEWEY. *Wildlife Rescue: The Work of Dr. Kathleen Ramsay*. Boyds Mills.

Russell FREEDMAN. *Kids at Work: Lewis Hine and the Crusade against Child Labor.* Clarion.

Patricia C. & Frederick L. McKISSACK. *Christmas in the Big House, Christmas in the Quarters*. Scholastic.

1996 Jim MURPHY. *The Great Fire*. Scholastic.

Honor Books
Penny COLMAN. *Rosie the Riveter: Women Working on the Home Front in World War II.* Crown.

Laurence PRINGLE. *Dolphin Man: Exploring the World of Dolphins.* Atheneum.

1997 Diane STANLEY. *Leonardo da Vinci.* Morrow.

Honor Books
Rhoda BLUMBERG. *Full Steam Ahead: The Race to Build a Transcontinental Railroad.* National Geographic Society.

Russell FREEDMAN. *The Life and Death of Crazy Horse.* Holiday House.

Mary Pope OSBORNE. *One World, Many Religions: The Ways We Worship.* Knopf.

1998 Laurence PRINGLE. *An Extraordinary Life: The story of a Monarch Butterfly.* Orchard Books.

Honor Books
Arthur DORROS. *A Tree is Growing.* Scholastic.

James Cross GIBLIN. *Charles A. Lindbergh: A Human Hero.* Clarion Books.

Wilborn HAMPTON. *Kennedy Assassinated! The World Mourns: A Reporter's Story.* Candlewick.

Jerry STANLEY. *Digger: The Tragic Fate of the California Indians from the Missions to the Gold Rush.* Crown.

Walter WICK. *A Drop of Water: A Book of Science and Wonder.* Scholastic Press.

1999 Jennifer ARMSTRONG. *Shipwreck at the Bottom of the World: The Extraordinary True Story of Shackleton and the Endurance.* Crown Publishers.

Honor Books
Robert BURLEIGH. *Black Whiteness: Admiral Byrd Alone in the Antarctic.* Atheneum.

Thom HOLMES. *Fossil Feud: The Rivalry of the First American Dinosaur Hunters.* J. Messner.

Steve JENKINS. *Hottest, Coldest, Highest, Deepest.* Houghton Mifflin.

Anita LOBEL. *No Pretty Pictures: A Child of War.* Greenwillow.

2000 Ruby BRIDGES. *Through My Eyes.* Scholastic.

Honor Books
Steve JENKINS. *The Top of the World: Climbing Mount Everest.* Houghton Mifflin.

Sylvia A. JOHNSON. *Mapping the World.* Schuster.

Sy MONTGOMERY. *The Snake Scientist.* Houghton Mifflin.

Walter Dean MYERS. *At Her Majesty's Request: An African Princess in Victorian England.* Scholastic Press.

Susanna REICH. *Clara Schumann: Piano Virtuoso.* Clarion Books.

2001 Jerry STANLEY. *Hurry Freedom: African Americans in Gold Rush California.* Crown.

Honor Books
David A. ADLER. *America's Champion Swimmer: Gertrude Ederle.* Harcourt.

Jim ARNOSKY. *Wild and Swampy.* HarperCollins.

James Cross GIBLIN. *The Amazing Life of Benjamin Franklin.* Scholastic.

Alan B. GOVENAR. *Osceola: Memories of a Sharecropper's Daughter.* Jump at the Sun.

Diane STANLEY. *Michelangelo.* HarperCollins.

2002 Susan Campbell BARTOLETTI. *Black Potatoes: The Story of the Great Irish Famine, 1845-1850.* Houghton Mifflin.

Honor Books
Barbara KERLEY. *The Dinosaurs of Waterhouse Hawkins: An Illuminating History of Mr. Waterhouse Hawkins, Artist and Lecturer.* Scholastic.

Mark KURLANSKY. *The Cod's Tale.* Putnam.

Doreen RAPPAPORT. *Martin's Big Words: The Life of Dr. Martin Luther King, Jr.* Jump at the Sun/Hyperion.

2003 Pam Munoz RYAN. *When Marian Sang: The True Recital of Marian Anderson: The Voice of a Century.* Scholastic.

Honor Books

Raymond BIAL. *Tenement: Immigrant Life on the Lower East Side.* Houghton.

John FLEISCHMAN. *Phineas Gage: A Gruesome but True Story About Brain Science.* Houghton Mifflin.

Russell FREEDMAN. *Confucius: The Golden Rule.* Scholastic.

Jane O'CONNOR. *Emperor's Silent Army: Terracotta Warriors of Ancient China.* Viking Books.

Wendie C. OLD. *To Fly: The Story of the Wright Brothers.* Clarion Books.

2004 Jim MURPHY. *An American Plague: The True and Terrifying Story of the Yellow Fever Epidemic of 1793.* Clarion.

Honor Books

Robert BYRD. *Leonardo: Beautiful Dreamer.* Dutton/Penguin.

Russell FREEDMAN. *In Defense of Liberty: The Story of America's Bill of Rights.* Holiday House.

Deborah HOPKINSON. *Shutting Out the Sky: Life in the Tenements of New York, 1880-1924.* Scholastic/Orchard.

Kathryn LASKY. *The Man Who Made Time Travel.* Farrar Straus & Giroux.

Elizabeth MANN. *Empire State Building: When New York Reached for the Skies.* Mikaya Press.

The Robert F. Sibert Informational Award: complete list of winners

2001 Marc ARONSON. *Sir Walter Ralegh and the Quest for El Dorado.* Clarion.

Honor Books
Joan DASH. *The Longitude Prize.* Frances Foster.

Jim MURPHY. *Blizzard! The Storm That Changed America.* Scholastic.

Sophie WEBB. *My Season with Penguins: An Antarctic Journal.* Houghton, Mifflin.

Judd WINICK. *Pedro and Me: Friendship, Loss, and What I Learned.* Henry Holt.

2002 Susan Campbell BARTOLETTI. *Black Potatoes: The Story of the Great Irish Famine, 1845-1850.* Houghton Mifflin.

Honor Books
Lynn CURLEE. *Brooklyn Bridge.* Atheneum.

Jan GREENBERG & Sandra JORDAN. *Vincent van Gogh: Portrait of an Artist.* Delacorte Press.

Andrea WARREN. *Surviving Hitler: A Boy in the Nazi Death Camps.* HarperCollins.

2003 James Cross GIBLIN. *The Life and Death of Adolf Hitler.* Clarion.

Honor Books
Karen BLUMENTHAL. *Six Days in October: The Stock Market Crash of 1929.* Atheneum.

Jack GANTOS. *Hole in My Life.* Farrar, Straus & Giroux.

Jan GREENBERG & Sandra JORDAN. *Action Jackson*, ills Robert Andrew PARKER. Roaring Brook.

Pam Munoz RYAN. *When Marian Sang*, ills Brian SELZNICK. Scholastic.

2004 Jim MURPHY. *An American Plague: The True and Terrifying Story of the Yellow Fever Epidemic of 1793.* Clarion.

Honor Book
Vicki COBB. *I Face the Wind*, ills Julia GORTON. HarperCollins.

2005 Russell FREEDMAN. *The Voice That Challenged a Nation: Marian Anderson and the Struggle for Equal Rights.* Clarion.

Honor Books
Barbara KERLEY. *Walt Whitman: Words for America*, ills Brian SELZNICK. Scholastic.

Sy MONTGOMERY. *The Tarantula Scientist*, ills Nic BISHOP. Houghton.

James RUMFORD. *Sequoyah: The Cherokee Man Who Gave His People Writing*, translated into Cherokee by Anna Sixkiller HUCKABY. Houghton.

American Institute of Physics Science Writing Award (US): complete list of winners

1988 Susan Kovacs BUXBAUM, Rita Golden GRAHAM, & Maryann COCCA-LEFFLER. *Splash! All About Baths.* Basic Books.

1989 Gail Kay HAINES. *Micromysteries.* Putnam & Grosset.

1990 David MACAULAY. *The Way Things Work.* Houghton Mifflin Company.

1991 Richard MAURER. *Airborne.* Simon & Schuster Inc.

1992 Gloria SKURZYNSKI. *Almost The Real Thing.* Bradbury Press.

1993 Gail GIBBONS. *Stargazers.* Holiday House.

1994 Wendy BAKER, Andrew HASLAM & Alexandra PARSONS. *Make it Work!* Macmillan.

1995 Sally RIDE & Tam O'SHAUGHNESSY. *The Third Planet: Exploring the Earth from Space.* Crown Publishers, Inc.

1996 Steve TOMECEK. *Bouncing & Bending Light.* W.H. Freeman & Co.

1997 Donald SILVER. *Extinction is Forever.* Silver Burdett Press.

1998 Barbara TAYLOR. *Earth Explained.* Henry Holt & Co.

1999 Elaine SCOTT. *Close Encounters.* Hyperion Books for Children.

2000 Jill Frankel HAUSER. *Science Play! Gizmos & Gadgets.* Williamson Publishing.

2001 Cynthia Pratt NICOLSON. *Exploring Space.* Kids Can Press.

2002 Fred BORTZ. *Techno-Matter: The Materials Behind the Marvels.* The Millbrook Press.

2003 Ron MILLER. *Worlds Beyond Series: Extrasolar Planets, The Sun, Jupiter, and Venus.* Twenty-First Century Books, a Division of The Millbrook Press.

2004 Marianne DYSON. *Home on the Moon: Living in the Space Frontier.* National Geographic.

The Eve Pownall Award for Information Books (Australia): complete list of winners

1988 Nadia WHEATLEY. *My Place*, ills Donna RAWLINS. Collins Dove.

[The 1988 award was funded by Eve Pownall's family. No further awards were made until 1993 when funding by CBC of Australia began.]

1993 Gracie GREENE & Joe TRAMACCHI. *Tjarany Roughtail; The Dreaming of the Roughtail Lizard and Other Stories Told by the Kukatja*, ills Lucille GILL. Magabala Books.

1994 Patricia MULLINS. *V for Vanishing: An Alphabet of Endangered Animals.* Margaret Hamilton Books.

Honour books
Kathie ATKINSON. *Life in a Rotten Log.* Allen & Unwin.

Jill MORRIS. *Australian Owls, Frogmouths and Nightjars*, ills Lynne TRACEY. Greater Glider Productions.

1995 Robin E. STEWART. *New Faces: The Complete Book of Alternative Pets.* Agmedia.

Honour Books
Cameron MILLAR & Dominique FALLA. *Woodlore.* Omnibus Books

Alan TUCKER. *Too Many Captain Cooks.* Omnibus Books.

1996 John NICHOLSON. *The First Fleet: A New Beginning in an Old Land.* Allen & Unwin.

Honour Books
Gerald & Guundie KUCHLING. *Yakkinn the Swamp Tortoise: Book 1, the Most Dangerous Year*, ills Guundie KUCHLING. Chelonia Enterprises.

Douglas LITTLE. *Ten Little Known Facts about Hippopotamuses and More Little Known Facts and a Few Fibs about Other Animals*, ills David FRANCIS & Donna RAWLINS. Scholastic.

1997 Gordon CHEERS & Julie SILK. *Killer Plants and How to Grow Them*, ills Marjorie CROSBY-FAIRALL. Puffin, Penguin.

Honour Books
Janeen BRIAN. *Pilawuk: When I Was Young*, ills Sascha HUTCHINSON. Magic Bean In-Fact Era.

Carson CREAGH. *Reptiles*, ills Anne BOWMAN & others. Little Ark Discoveries, Allen & Unwin.

1998 John NICHOLSON. *A Home Among the Gum Trees: The Story of Australian Houses*. Little Ark, Allen & Unwin.

Honour Books
Beth DOLAN. *Cathy Freeman.* Heinemann

Kim Michelle TOFT & Allan SHEATHER. *One Less Fish*, ills Kim Michelle TOFT. Jam Roll, University of Queensland Press.

1999 Yvonne EDWARDS & Brenda DAY. *Going for Kalta: Hunting for Sleepy Lizards at Yalata.* Jukurrpa Books.

2000 John NICHOLSON. *Fishing for Islands: Traditional Boats and Seafarers of the Pacific.* Allen & Unwin.

Honour Books
Jennifer BECK, Dyan BLACKLOCK & Katrina ALLAN. *Crash!: The Search for the Stinson.* Omnibus.

Diana LAWRENSON. *Inside the Australian Ballet.* Allen & Unwin.

2001 David KENNETT & Dyan BLACKLOCK. *Olympia: Warrior Athletes of Ancient Greece.* Omnibus.

Honour Books
John NICHOLSON. *Building the Sydney Harbour Bridge.* Allen & Unwin.

Elaine RUSSELL. *A is for Aunty.* ABC Books.

2002 PAPUNYA School Publishing Committee. *Papunya School Book of Country and History.* Allen & Unwin.

Honour Books
Anthony HILL. *Soldier Boy: The True Story of Jim Martin, the Youngest Anzac.* Penguin Books Australia.

Narelle OLIVER. *Baby Bilby, Where Do You Sleep?* Lothian Books.

2003 Alan TUCKER. *Iron in the Blood: Convicts and Commandants in Colonial Australia.* Omnibus Books, Scholastic Australia.

Honour Books
John NICHOLSON. *The Mighty Murray.* Allen & Unwin.

Carole WILKINSON. *Black Snake: The Daring of Ned Kelly.* Black Dog Books.

2004 John NICHOLSON. *Animal Architects.* Allen & Unwin.

Honour Books
Patrick CARLYON. *The Gallipoli Story.* Penguin Books Australia.

Christine NICHOLLS. *Art, History, Place.* Working Title Press.

The Norma Fleck Award for Canadian Children's Non-Fiction: complete list of winners

1999 Andy TURNBULL & Debora PEARSON. *By Truck to the North: My Arctic Adventure*. Annick Press.

2000 Simon TOOKOOME with Sheldon OBERMAN. *The Shaman's Nephew: A Life in the Far North*. Stoddart Kids.

2001 Gena K. GORRELL. *Heart and Soul: The Story of Florence Nightingale.* Tundra Books.

2002 Jack BATTEN. *The Man Who Ran Faster Than Everyone: The Story Of Tom Longboat.* Tundra Books.

2003 Larry LOYIE with Constance BRISSENDEN. *As Long as the Rivers Flow*, ills Heather D. HOLMLUND. Groundwood Books.

Special recognition
Claire MACKAY. *The Toronto Story*, ills Johnny WALES, originally published in 1990 by Annick Press & reissued in a revised edition in 2002.

2004 Val ROSS. *The Road to There: Mapmakers and Their Stories.* Tundra Books.

Honour Books
Nicolas DEBON. *Four Pictures by Emily Carr.* Groundwood Books.

Anne DUBLIN. *Bobbie Rosenfeld: The Olympian Who Could Do Everything.* Second Story Press.

Reva MARIN. *Oscar: The Life and Music of Oscar Peterson.* Groundwood Books.

John WILSON. *Discovering the Arctic: The Story of John Rae.* Napoleon Publishing.

The Information Book Award (Canada): complete list of winners

1987 David SUZUKI. *Looking at Insects*. Stoddart Publishing.

Honour Book
Dr. Saul LEVINE & Dr. Kathleen WILCOX. *Dear Doctor: Teens Ask About Anorexia, Sibling Rivalry, Hair Loss, and Pregnancy*. Kids Can Press.

1988 Caroline PARRY. *Let's Celebrate*. Kids Can Press.

Honour Books
Terence DICKINSON. *Exploring the Night Sky*, ills John BIANCHI. Camden House.

Joan IRVINE. *How to Make Pop-Ups*, ills Barbara REID. Kids Can Press.

1989 Terence DICKINSON. *Exploring the Sky by Day*. Camden House.

Honour Books
Anne NEWLANDS. *Meet Edgar Degas*. Kids Can Press.

Barbara REID. *Playing With Plasticene*. Kids Can Press.

1990 Celia GODKIN. *Wolf Island*. Fitzhenry & Whiteside.

Honour Books
Paulette BOURGEOIS. *Amazing Paper Book*, ills Linda HENDRY. Kids Can Press.

Katherine GRIER. *Discover Mysteries of the Past and Present*, ills Pat CUPPLES. Kids Can Press.

Robert LIVESEY & A.G. SMITH. *The Fur Traders*. Stoddart.

1991 Camilla GRYSKI. *Hands On, Thumbs Up*, ills Pat CUPPLES. Kids Can Press.

Honour Books
Candace SAVAGE. *Trash Attack*, ills Steve BEINICKE. Douglas and McIntyre.

Valerie WYATT. *Weather Watch*, ills Pat CUPPLES. Kids Can Press.

1992 Jan THORNHILL. *A Tree in a Forest*. Greey de Pencier.

Honour Books
Lesley GRANT. *Discover Bones*, ills Tina HOLDCROFT. Kids Can Press.

Bobbie KALMAN & Janine SCHAUB. *Buried in Garbage*. Crabtree.

1993 Janet LUNN & Christopher MOORE. *The Story of Canada*, ills Alan DANIEL. Key Porter.

Honour Book
Owen BEATTIE, John GEIGER & Shelley TANAKA. *Buried in Ice: The Mystery of a Lost Arctic Expedition.* Random House.

1994 Barbara BONDAR. *On the Shuttle: Eight Days in Space.* Greey de Pencier.

Linda GRANFIELD. *Cowboy: A Kid's Album.* Groundwood Books.

Honour Book
Song Nan ZHANG. *A Little Tiger in the Chinese Night.* Tundra.

1995 Barbara GREENWOOD. *A Pioneer Story: The Daily Life of a Canadian Family in 1840*, ills Heather COLLINS. Kids Can Press.

Honour Book
Sylvia FUNSTON & Jay INGRAM. *A Kid's Guide to the Brain*, ills Gary CLEMENT. Greey de Pencier.

1996 Linda GRANFIELD. *In Flanders Fields: The Story of the Poem by John McCrae*, ills Janet WILSON. Lester Publishing.

Honour Books
Celia GODKIN. *Ladybug Garden.* Fitzhenry and Whiteside.

Camilla GRYSKI. *Let's Play,* ills Dušan PETRIČIĆ. Kids Can Press.

1997 Shelley TANAKA. *On Board the Titanic*, ills Ken MARSCHALL. Scholastic Canada.

Honour book
Shelley TANAKA. *Discovering the Iceman*, ills Laurie McGAW. Scholastic.

1998 Shelley TANAKA. *The Buried City of Pompeii*, ills Greg RUHL. Scholastic Canada.

Honour book
Vivien BOWERS. *Crime Science*, ills Martha NEWBIGGING. Owl Books.

1999 Barbara GREENWOOD. *The Last Safe House: A Story of the Underground Railroad*, ills Heather COLLINS. Kids Can Press.

Honour Book
William KAPLAN with Shelley TANAKA. *One More Border: The True Story Of One Family's Escape From War-Torn Europe*, ills Stephen TAYLOR. Groundwood.

2000 Vivien BOWERS. *Wow Canada! Exploring This Land From Coast to Coast to Coast*, ills Dan HOBBS and Diane EASTMAN. Owl Books/Greey de Pencier.

Honour Book
David WISTOW & Kelly McKINLEY. *Meet the Group of Seven*. Kids Can Press.

2001 Deborah HODGE. *The Kids Book of Canada's Railway and How the CPR was Built*, ills John MANTHA. Kids Can Press.

Honour Book
Linda GRANFIELD. *Pier 21: Gateway of Hope*. Tundra Books.

2002 Linda GRANFIELD. *Where Poppies Grow: A World War One Companion*. Stoddart.

Honour Book
Richard RHODES. *A First Book of Canadian Art*. Owl Books.

2003 Karen LEVINE. *Hana's Suitcase*. Second Story Press.

Honour Book
Annette LeBOX. *Salmon Creek*. Groundwood.

The Science in Society Children's Book Award (Canada): complete list of winners

1994 Jay INGRAM & Sylvia FUNSTON. *A Kid's Guide to the Brain.* Owl Books.

1995 Adrian FORSYTH. *How Monkeys Make Chocolate.* Owl Books.

1996 Catherine Sheldrick ROSS. *Squares: Shapes in Math, Science and Nature.* Kids Can Press.

1997 Vivien BOWERS. *Crime Science: How Investigators Use Science to Track Down the Bad Guys.* Owl Books/Greey de Pencier Books Inc.

1998 Stephen CUMBAA & Susan HUGHES. *Megalodon: The Prehistoric Shark.* Somerville House Publishing.

1999 Shelley TANAKA. *I Was There: Secrets of the Mummies.* Scholastic Canada, Ltd.

2000 Valerie WYATT. *FAQ Weather.* Kids Can Press.

2001 Ron ORENSTEIN. *New Animal Discoveries.* Key Porter Books.

2002 Kathy CONLAN. *Under the Ice, A Canadian Museum of Nature Book.* Kids Can Press.

2003 David SUZUKI & Sarah ELLIS. *Salmon Forest.* David Suzuki Foundation, Greystone Books, Douglas & McIntyre Publishing Group.

The Elsie Locke Medal (*formerly* The Library and Information Association of New Zealand Aotearoa (LIANZA) Young People's Non-Fiction Award): complete list of winners and shortlisted titles

1987 Olive & Ngaio HILL. *Gaijin: Foreign Children in Japan.* Longman Paul.

1988 No Winner

Shortlist
Gordon ELL. *New Zealand's Story in Stamps.* Waiatarua Publishing.

Betty GILDERDALE. *Introducing Margaret Mahy.* Viking Kestrel.

Diane HEBLEY. *The Ballad of Young Nick: How He Sailed with Captain Cook from Plymouth to Botany Bay, 1768-70,* ills Gary HEBLEY. H.A.P. (in association with Longman Paul).

1989 Claire PATTERSON. *It's OK to be You! Feeling Good About Growing Up,* ills Lindsay QUILTER. Century Hutchinson.

Shortlist
Philip TEMPLE. *The Story of the Kakapo, Parrot of the Night,* ills Chris GASKIN. Hodder & Stoughton.

1990 Deborah FURLEY. *The Web: The Triumph of a New Zealand Girl over Anorexia.* Collins.

Shortlist
Ron BACON. *The Green Fish of Ngahue,* ills Mary TAYLOR. Waiatarua Publishing.

Donna BRYANT. *Enjoy It*; *Grow It*; *Save It*; *Watch It*, (a series of 4 books) ills Jan Van der VOO. Hodder & Stoughton (in association with TVNZ Enterprises).

Gwenda TURNER. *New Zealand Colours.* Puffin. (Variant title: *Colours*).

1991 John REID. *Model Boats That Really Go.* Random Century.

Shortlist
Margaret MAHY. *The Seven Chinese Brothers,* ills Jean & Mou-sien TSENG. Scholastic.

John PARKER. *Journey: The Kiwifruit Story.* Ashton Scholastic.

Eddie SUNDERLAND. *Eddie's Home-made Fun,* ills Henry SUNDERLAND. Hamlyn. (Variant title: *Eddie's Homemade Fun*).

Gwenda TURNER. *Once Upon a Time.* Penguin.

1992 Peter GARLAND. *The Damselfly.* Nelson Price Milburn.

Shortlist
Pauline CARTWRIGHT. *Grow a Gift*, ills Jill PARRY. Price Milburn.

Borany KANAL & Adrienne JANSEN. *Borany's Story.* Learning Media, Ministry of Education.

Lorraine TARRANT. *Kahuku.* Te Pou Korero, Te Tahuhu o te Matauranga (Learning Media, Ministry of Education).

1993 Kim WESTERSKOV. *Albatross Adventure*, ills with photos by author. Nelson Price Milburn.

Shortlist
Geoffrey J. COX. *Dinosaurs of New Zealand.* Viking Pacific.

Graham MEADOWS. *Cats, Cats, Cats.* Shortland Publications.

Pat QUINN. *Moving the Earth, from an Interview with Stan Goodman*, ills with photos by Jamie LEAN. Learning Media, Ministry of Education.

1994 Robyn KAHUKIWA. *Paikea.* Viking.

Shortlist
Jenny JONES. *The Hector's Dolphin*, photos by Barbara TODD, Steve DAWSON & Colin MONTEATH courtesy of WWF-NZ; ills by Alan BARNETT; maps by Chris O'BRIEN. Heinemann Education.

Jenny JONES. *The Hoiho*, photos supplied by G. S. COURT (courtesy of WWF), Dean SCHNEIDER and the *Otago Daily Times*; ills by Alan BARNETT; maps by Chris O'BRIEN. Heinemann Education.

Jenny JONES. *The Tuatara*, photos by Alison CREE, Brett ROBERTSON & Marcus SIMONS, courtesy of WWF-NZ; ills Alan BARNETT; maps by Chris O'BRIEN. Heinemann Education.

Mary TAYLOR. *Old Blue: The Rarest Bird in the World.* Ashton Scholastic.

Colin WALKER. *Slugs and Snails*, photos by Paul GAY. Lands End Pub.

Hepora YOUNG, Mange TAUTARI & Waaka VERCOE. *Te Matawai: Tuawha.* Huia Publishers.

1995 Barbara CAIRNS & Helen MARTIN. *Shadows on the Wall: A Study of Seven New Zealand Feature Films.* Longman Paul.

Shortlist
Betty BROWNLIE. *The Life Cycle of the Grasshopper.* Ashton Scholastic.

Lyn RASMUSSEN. *Doing the Washing.* Lands End Pub.

1996 Laura RANGER. *Laura's Poems.* Godwit.

Shortlist
Andrew CROWE. *Which Coastal Plant?: A Simple Guide to the Identification of New Zealand's Common Coastal Plants*, ills Sandra PARKKALI. Viking.

Peter GARLAND. *Nature Speaks.* Shortland Publications.

Trish GRIBBEN. *Aya's Story*, photos by Jenny SCOWN. Ashton Scholastic. (My sea is the Pacific series).

Trish GRIBBEN. *Samantha's Story*, photos by Jenny SCOWN. Ashton Scholastic. (My sea is the Pacific series).

1997 Diana NOONAN. *The Field (I Spy Wildlife)*, photos by Nic BISHOP. Heinemann Education.

Shortlist
Stephen DAWSON & Elisabeth SLOOTEN. *Down-under Dolphins: The Story of Hector's Dolphins.* Canterbury University Press.

Chris GASKIN. *Picture Book Magic*, photos by Denis PAGE. Reed Children's Books.

Diana NOONAN. *The Garden*, photos by Nic BISHOP. Heinemann Education. (I spy wildlife series).

Robert SULLIVAN. *Maui, Legends of the Outcast,* ills Chris SLANE. Godwit Publishing.

1998 Andrew CROWE. *The Life-Size Guide to Native Trees and Other Common Plants of New Zealand's Native Forest.* Penguin.

Shortlist
Wena HARAWIRA. *Te Kawa o te Marae: A Guide for all Marae Visitors.* Reed. (Variant title: *Guide for all Marae Visitors*).

Diana NOONAN & Keith OLSEN. *The Know, Sow & Grow Kids' Book of Plants*, ills Keith OLSEN. Bridge Hill Pub. (Variant title: *Kids' Book of Plants*).

Bronwen WARK. *Seasons of Aotearoa New Zealand.* Heinemann Education.

1999 No Award

2000 No Award

2001 Brian J. PARKINSON. *The Tuatara.* Reed Children's Books.

Shortlist
Chris CAIRNS. *Way to Play.* HarperSports.

Charles COOPER. *Niue.* Reed Children's Books.

Colin HOGG. *The Zoo: Meet the Locals.* Random House New Zealand.

2002 Simon POLLARD. *I am a Spider.* Reed.

Shortlist
John LOCKYER. *The Kea*, photographed by Rod MORRIS. Reed Children's Books.

Brian O'FLAHERTY. *Rocky Shore.* Reed Children's Books.

Glenys STACE & Mike EAGLE. *Yes! We Had Dinosaurs*, paintings by Damon KEEN. Penguin. (Cover subtitle: *Discover New Zealand's Exciting Past*).

2003 Andrew CROWE. *Which New Zealand Insect?: With Over 650 Life-Size Photos of New Zealand Insects.* Penguin.

Shortlist
Alina ARKINS. *The Kauri*, photographed by Len DOEL. Reed.

Ron BACON. *Surf Lifesaving*, photographed by Anthony HEATH. Waiatarua Pub.

Jenny JONES. *Lizards*, photographed by Rod MORRIS. Reed.

Robert SULLIVAN *Weaving Earth and Sky: Myths & Legends of Aotearoa*, ills Gavin BISHOP. Random House New Zealand.

2004 Janet HUNT. *A Bird in the Hand: Keeping New Zealand Wildlife Safe.* Random House New Zealand.

Shortlist
Andrew CROWE. *The Life-Size Guide to New Zealand Wildflowers.* Penguin Books. (Variant title: *The Life-Size Guide to New Zealand Wild Flowers*).

Keith OLSEN. *Pick Up a Pack: A Guide to Tramping and Camping the New Zealand Way.* Reed.

Simon POLLARD. *I Am an Insect.* Reed.

Te Aorere RIDDELL. *Toroa: the Royal Albatross*, photographed by Fifi COULSON. Huia Publishing. (Published in Maori as: *Toroa*).

Chapter 11: Commercial Breaks: awards sponsored by big business

The Nestlé Smarties Prize (UK); The Whitbread Children's Book Award (UK); The W. H. Smith Children's Book of the Year (UK); The Askews Torchlight Award (UK); The Bisto Book Awards (Eire); The Mr Christie's Book Awards (Canada); The New Zealand Post Children's Book Awards (*formerly* The AIM Children's Book Awards, 1990-1996); The M E R Prize for youth literature (South Africa); The M-Net Book Prize (South Africa) & The Sanlam Prize (South Africa).

Within this chapter are included awards which take the name of their sponsors or their commercial originators, regardless of the nature of their administering bodies. Thus the Bisto Awards are considered in this chapter, despite the fact that they are made by Children's Books Ireland (CBI), an amalgam formed in 1996 which replaced the Irish Children's Book Trust (ICBT) and the Children's Literature Association of Ireland. Treated elsewhere, each with a designated chapter, are the Carnegie Medal (Chapter 4) and the Kate Greenaway Medal (Chapter 6), which have received sponsorship from commercial bodies whilst retaining their original title and administration procedures. Also discussed in other chapters are awards sponsored and administered by literary publications: the Boston Globe-Horn Book Award (Chapter 7) and the Guardian Award (within Chapter 9). The Sainsbury's Baby Book Award (UK) has been replaced by the Booktrust Early Years award, so is also covered in Chapter 9.

At first glance, awards which are commercially sponsored can seem easy targets for disdain or to be dismissed as unimportant or irrelevant to questions of quality in children's literature. Indeed one well-known English children's writer is rumoured to have refused a Smarties Prize because s/he did not wish to be associated with a product which ruined children's teeth and there are also concerns about Nestlé's provision of powdered milk to countries in the developing world.

However, publicity is not easy to come by in the children's book world, and in general the arrangement can be as useful for the authors and their books as for the sponsors. It is natural for big commercial names to exploit all the methods at their disposal to keep those names in the public eye. Why else would international companies sponsor sports such as motor racing, baseball, cricket, football, or individual golfers and tennis players? Given that considerable sums of money are available from such sources, it seems reasonable that the world of children's books should share in these benefits. Most of the awards in this category set out pious aims such as 'to encourage high standards and stimulate interest in books for children', 'to reward excellence in the writing and illustrating of . . . children's books'. These are not merely platitudes: the judges are as committed as those of any other award; the winning books are in most cases of equal standard and standing as those of the 'official' award in that country - sometimes even to being the same titles. In the UK, the Library Association itself accepted sponsorship from a library supplier for the Carnegie and Greenaway Medals, and has used other sponsors since that agreement came to an end.

The Nestlé Smarties Prize was established in 1985 to 'encourage high standards and stimulate interest in books for children'. Originally in two age groups, it is now judged in three age-specific categories. Until 1995, an overall winner, the Grand Prix, was chosen from these category winners, but from the 1996 announcements onwards, there are Gold, Silver and Bronze Awards for each age group. The Smarties 0-5 winners are well represented among the Greenaway Commendations, and the Smarties Grand Prix winner in 1988, Martin Waddell's *Can't You Sleep, Little Bear*, illustrated by Barbara Firth, won the Greenaway Medal that year, and the 2001 Greenaway winner, *Pirate Diary*, by Richard Platt and illustrated by Chris Riddell, was the Smarties Silver Award winner for 2002 in the 6-8 years category. There was until recently less correspondence between the Smarties Winners in the 6-8 and 7-11 or 9-11 categories and the Carnegie lists, Jill Paton Walsh and Jacqueline Wilson being honourable exceptions. This was in part because the tendency of Carnegie panels in those years was to give the award to books for older children and teenagers. However, Anne Fine's *Bill's New Frock*, the 1989 Smarties 6-8 category winner was Highly Commended for that year's Carnegie. Since 2000 more titles have appeared in both lists, and Gillian Cross, Robert Westall, Beverley Naidoo, David Almond and Philip Pullman are all Carnegie winners who have also won in one or other Smarties category. There is a high input of children's opinions within the judging processes of the Smarties Prize, showing, as is the case of the Red House Children's Book Award (see Chapter 9) that the so-called 'readers' choice' awards do not necessarily lead to a diminution in the quality of award-winning books. From 2000 onwards the Kids' Club Network award, now renamed the 4Children Special Award, is voted for by the children involved in the judging.

The Whitbread Award has been given since 1972 for 'an outstanding book for children of 7 and up'. This award is administered by the Booksellers Association, and is announced each January for the previous year. There are also Whitbread Awards for novels, poetry, biography and first novel, and until 1994/5 the Whitbread Book of the Year was nominally chosen from all five categories, although the winner of the children's category was never expected to reach those dizzy heights. For a couple of years the Children's Novel Award was renamed the 'Beefeater Children's Novel Award'. 'Beefeater' is the brand name of a series of family restaurants owned by Whitbread Plc, a hospitality company. The announcement of the 1996 award in the Booksellers Association Quarterly, *Bookselling*, Whitbread's marketing department stated that 'The Whitbread Book of the Year was joined for the first time this year by the Whitbread Children's Book of the Year. Formerly the children's novel category of the Whitbread Book of the Year, the new award is now a major prize in its own right, worth £8,000 to the winner'. Thus for the following two years, from 1996 to 1998, although the winner of this category was selected by the final judging panel and received a larger prize than other categories, it was not judged against the winners of the other categories for the Whitbread Book of the Year. Since 1998, the Children's Book Award has once again been judged against the other category winners for the main Whitbread Book of the Year and indeed has taken the top place. One of the effects of the 'Potter Phenomenon' (see Chapter 14) is that children's books have recently been treated with more serious consideration than was once the case – or perhaps have been sufficiently commercially successful to allow their inclusion among the 'grownups', for in 2001 Philip Pullman's *The Amber Spyglass* was both Whitbread Children's Book of the Year and Whitbread Book of the Year. Anne Fine, the 1996 Whitbread winner with *Tulip Touch*, was Highly Commended for the 1996 Carnegie Medal for the same title, and won both the Whitbread Children's Award (1993) and the Carnegie Medal (1992) with *Flour Babies*, also a Boston Globe-Horn Book Award Honor listing in 1994. Many of the titles which appear on the Whitbread list are also included among the Carnegie Medallists and Commendations.

In several cases the Whitbread winners have been by authors whose other works have received at least an honourable mention by the Carnegie judges. A notable exception is the late Roald Dahl, always popular with children, but who never once made even the Carnegie commendations. Dahl is represented among the Smarties winners, in the Children's Book Awards (twice) as well as the Whitbread. This would seem to indicate that his subversiveness has more to appeal to children than to adults, since these are all awards with a high input of children's opinion in their judging. Several of his titles were illustrated by Quentin Blake, whose books have received the Greenaway Medal, the Children's Book Award, the Maschler 'Emil' and the Whitbread itself. Is it the very popularity of authors such as Dahl and Enid Blyton that turns librarians against them? Certainly not all of Dahl's work was of the same standard; yet it is certainly not uniformly bad, and it is no more zany than Dr Seuss. The judging panel since the 1996 Whitbread Children's Book shortlist has included two teenagers among its five members, but the final choice for Children's Book of the Year is made by the same panel who decide the Whitbread Book of the Year. Mark Haddon's *The Curious Incident of the Dog in the Night-Time* won the 2003 Whitbread Book of the Year, having originally been entered for both the Novel and Children's Book categories of the award, and then withdrawn from the Children's Book category by its publishers, as the Whitbread Book Awards rules stipulate that books may only be considered for one category.

The W. H. Smith Children's Book of the Year is now administered as part of the British Book Awards. As it is still known and thought of in association with W. H. Smith, I have felt able to include it in this chapter, although its name has just been changed to 'The Children's Book of the Year – sponsored by W. H. Smith'. All but the first winner – an anthology – are fairly predictable choices – three Harry Potter titles, two of Philip Pullman's 'Dark Materials' trilogy, two from Jacqueline Wilson, and Haddon's *Curious Incident...*, which seems almost to have swept the board in 2003/4.

The Askews Torchlight Award was established in 2003 by the Library Book suppliers, Askew, to highlight the books that are both popular among children and of high quality; books which, as their publicity states 'encourage children to read them by torchlight under the bed covers'. Children are involved in the choice, and the two winning lists so far contain authors such as Cornelia Funke, Philip Ridley and Jenny Nimmo who have also won other awards in the UK.

The Bisto Book Awards are made by the Children's Books Ireland (CBI) and sponsored by RHM Foods (Ireland) Ltd., the makers of Bisto. Books by an author and/or illustrator born or resident in Ireland are eligible. The first award was for a 'Book of the Decade 1980-1990' to cover work published in the ten years leading up to the institution of the award. Since 1991 there has each year been a Book of the Year and three Merit Awards, within which a wide range of children's books have been included. Many are set in the Irish countryside, or have as their themes the experiences of children and young people during periods of Irish history and legend: the time of the Celtic Heroes and Chieftains; the Potato Famine; the Easter Rising. Some tackle the problems faced by the island of Ireland today. A new category was introduced in 1994-95, The Eilís Dillon Memorial Award, for the author of an outstanding first children's book. This is awarded only at the discretion of the judges, so does not invariably appear within a year's award list. Irish writers and artists have contributed to the mainstream of literature in the English language in the past and this continues into the present. P. J. Lynch's *Christmas Miracle of Jonathan Tooley* was the Greenaway Medal-winner for 1995 and the 1995-6 Bisto Book of the Year. Lynch nearly repeated this feat when his *When Jessie Came Across the Sea* won the Greenaway and was a Bisto Merit, and he has appeared several other times in both lists. Eoin Colfer is also gaining a wider audience and popularity, since his *Artemis Fowl* series has been so successful.

The Mr Christie's Book Awards are sponsored by Canadian biscuit manufacturers Christie Brown Nabisco, part of the Kraft Foods conglomerate. These were founded in 1990 'to encourage the development of high quality Canadian children's books, reward excellence in the writing and illustrating of Canadian children's books and to stimulate children's desire to read'. Initially, awards were given in the categories of text and illustration, both for books written in French and in English, for a total of four awards. In 1993, the categories for text were divided into books for ages eight and under and books for ages 9 to 14 to increase the number of awards to six. In 1994, the number of age groups was expanded to three (7 years and under; 8-11 years; and 12-16 years) and it was also decided that books should be judged on their content of text and illustration combined, giving a 'Best Children's Book' for each of the three age groups in each official language, and so maintains a total of six awards. Eligible books are those published in the previous calendar year created by a Canadian author or illustrator. Inevitably there is some overlap with the other Canadian Awards, and in some years the same book has appeared in several lists. However, this is not to denigrate the awards, but commends the extremely high quality of some of the writers, such as Sarah Ellis, Julie Johnston, Jean Little and Tim Wynne-Jones in addition to illustrators like Ron Lightburn and Barbara Reid. The financial rewards brought by the Mr Christie's Awards enable authors and artists to give more time than would otherwise be possible to their writing and book illustration. This situation can only be helpful in the maintenance of high standards in children's book publishing in Canada.

The New Zealand Post Children's Book Awards have been awarded since 1997 in four categories; Children's Fiction, Young Adult Fiction, Picture Book, and Non-Fiction. A Children's Choice is also made, which can be one of the winners or honour books but may be another shortlisted title, and there is a Best First Book, which similarly is sometimes one of the winners in an individual category. In addition the NZ Post Book of the Year is chosen from one of the four category winners. It therefore has many similarities to the Boston-Globe/Horn Book Awards (US) in its range and aims. This award started life in 1982 as The New Zealand Government Publishing Awards, which were awarded at first in Children's Book and Picture Book Categories, and were joined in 1986 by a non-fiction award, but this was not made again before the sponsorship changed, and in the year 1989 no awards were made. It became the AIM Children's Book Award, 1990-1996, when it was sponsored by the toothpaste company AIM, and is now sponsored by *The New Zealand Post*, organised and administrated by Booksellers New Zealand and supported by Creative New Zealand and Book Tokens (NZ).

There are three commercially sponsored awards in South Africa. The M E R Prize for youth literature, open to books in Afrikaans or English, was instituted in 1984. Awarded for the best children's book published by Tafelberg or Human & Rousseau, both subsidiaries of Nasboek, it is named in honour of Maria Elizabeth, also known as Mieme, Rothmann, a journalist and author, one of the first women writers in Afrikaans, who used her initials as a pen name. Now it is sponsored by M-Net. The M-Net Award was established in 1991 and is awarded annually to encourage the writing of quality novels which could also be adapted for the screen. M-Net is the name under which Electronic Media Network, a commercial television station, is widely known. The Award was originally open to adult and children's books, and was three times been awarded to junior novels, in 1991, 1992 and 1995, but children's books are no longer eligible for it. Finally the Sanlam Prize, which was established in 1984 in collaboration with the publishers Tafelberg to promote a strong indigenous literature. Sanlam is the acronym for Suid-Afrikaanse Nasionale Lewensassuransiemaatskappy, a large insurance company which sponsors the award. Originally there were gold, silver and bronze awards for both English and Afrikaans books. The first award was made in 1985, the next in 1988, and since then it has been awarded every second year. It changed format in the mid-1990s and is now open to all the official languages in South Africa, with five equal prizes and a possible two additional 'encouragement' prizes for new authors, but it is still awarded biennially. Each year a theme is given by the organisers, to which the subject of the book must relate. In 2000 Gold and Silver Prizes were awarded in four different categories: Afrikaans, English, Nguni and Sotho languages. These three South African awards are all administered by Nasboek, previously Nasionale Boekhandel, subsidiary companies of which are Tafelberg, Human & Rousseau, Via Afrika, Nasou, J. L. van Schaik and Jonathan Ball Publishers. Whilst it may look as if the number of potential winning books and authors is lessened both by the restrictions imposed in the suggestion of themes and by the fact that books be published by one of Nasboek's subsidiaries, it does reflect the actual situation in South Africa; there are very few publishers of children's books, and the publicity and financial awards given by the sponsorship of Nasboek have in fact allowed a wider range of books to be written and produced in South Africa – allowing for a greater choice for South African children whatever language they speak – and for these books to be sold abroad, allowing their authors to gain outside recognition.

Commercial sponsorship has, on the whole, brought more benefits than disadvantages to the world of children's literature. The awards which are discussed in this chapter have raised the profile of children's books, and any controversy they may have produced has only served to prove the truism that 'all publicity is good publicity'.

The Smarties Prize (UK): complete list of winners

1985 **0-7 years**
Susanna GRETZ. *It's Your Turn, Roger!* Bodley Head.

7-11 years & Grand Prix
Jill Paton WALSH. *Gaffer Samson's Luck.* Viking Kestrel. 1985.

1986 **0-6 years**
Geoffrey PATTERSON. *Goose that Laid the Golden Egg*. Deutsch.

7-11 years & Grand Prix
Jenny NIMMO. *The Snow Spider.* Methuen.

Innovation category (joint winners)
Michael PALIN et al. *The Mirrorstone*. Cape. 1986.

Pat PINNELL. *Village Heritage*. Alan Sutton. 1986.

1987 **0-5 years**
Peter COLLINGTON. *Angel and the Soldier Boy.* Magnet Books.

6-8 years
Benedict BLATHWAYT. *Tangle and the Firesticks*. Julia MacRae.

9-11 years & Grand Prix
James BERRY. *Thief in the Village and Other Stories.* Hamish Hamilton.

1988 **0-5 years & Grand Prix**
Martin WADDELL. *Can't You Sleep, Little Bear?*, ills Barbara FIRTH Walker Books.

6-8 years
Susan HILL. *Can it be True?* Hamish Hamilton.

9-11 years
Theresa WHISTLER & The Brixworth Primary School. *Rushavenn Time.* Hamish Hamilton.

1989 **0-5 years & Grand Prix**
Michael ROSEN. *We're Going on a Bear Hunt*, ills Helen OXENBURY. Walker Books.

6-8 years
Anne FINE. *Bill's New Frock*. Methuen.

9-11 years
Robert WESTALL. *Blitzcat*. Macmillan.

1990 **0-5 years**
Inga MOORE. *Six Dinner Sid*. Simon & Schuster Young Books.

6-8 years
Roald DAHL, *Esio Trot*. Jonathan Cape.

9-11 years & Grand Prix
Pauline FISK. *Midnight Blue*. Lion Publishing.

1991 **0-5 years & Grand Prix**
Martin WADDELL. *Farmer Duck*, ills Helen OXENBURY. Walker Books.

6-8 years
Magdalen NABB. *Josie Smith and Eileen*, ills Pirko VAINIO. Harper-Collins.

9-11 years
Philip RIDLEY. *Krindlekrax*. Cape.

1992 **0-5 years**
Hilda OFFEN. *Nice Work, Little Wolf*. Hamish Hamilton.

6-8 years
Jane RAY. *The Story of the Creation*. Orchard Books.

9-11 years & Grand Prix
Gillian CROSS. *The Great Elephant Chase*. Oxford U. P.

1993 **0-5 years**
Rita Phillips MITCHELL. *Hue Boy*, ills Caroline BINCH. Gollancz.

6-8 years & Grand Prix
Michael FOREMAN. *War Game*. Pavilion.

9-11 years
Maeve HENRY. *Listen to the Dark*. Heinemann.

1994 **0-5 years**
Trish COOKE. *So Much*, ills Helen OXENBURY. Walker Books.

6-8 years
Henrietta BRANFORD. *Dimanche Diller*, ills Lesley HARKER. Young Lions.

9-11 years & Grand Prix
Hilary McKAY. *The Exiles at Home.* Gollancz.

1995 **0-5 years**
Jill MURPHY. *The Last Noo-Noo.* Walker Books.

6-8 years
Jill Paton WALSH. *Thomas and the Tinners.* Macdonald.

9-11 years & Grand Prix
Jacqueline WILSON. *Double Act.* Doubleday.

Joint 9-11
Lesley HOWARTH. *Weather Eye.* Walker Books.

1996 **Gold Awards**

0-5 years
Colin McNAUGHTON. *Oops!* Andersen Press.

6-8 years
Michael MORPURGO. *Butterfly Lion.* Collins.

9-11 years
Philip PULLMAN. *The Firework-Maker's Daughter.* Corgi Yearling.

Silver Awards

0-5 years
Mick MANNING & Brita GRANSTROM. *The World is Full of Babies.* Watts.

6-8 years
Lynne Reid BANKS. *Harry the Poisonous Centipede.* Collins.

9-11 years
Terry PRATCHETT. *Johnny and the Bomb.* Doubleday.

Bronze Awards

0-5 years
Quentin BLAKE. *Clown.* Cape.

6-8 years
Dick KING-SMITH. *All Because of Jackson.* Doubleday.

9-11 years
Geraldine McCAUGHREAN. *Plundering Paradise.* Oxford U. P.

1997 **Gold Awards**

0-5 years
Charlotte VOAKE. *Ginger.* Walker Books.

6-8 years
Jenny NIMMO. *The Owl Tree*, ills Anthony LEWIS. Walker Books.

9-11 years
J. K. ROWLING. *Harry Potter and the Philosopher's Stone.* Bloomsbury.

Silver Awards

0-5 years
Simon JAMES. *Leon and Bob.* Walker Books.

6-8 years
Michael FOREMAN. *The Little Reindeer.* Andersen Press.

9-11 years
Philip PULLMAN. *Clockwork or All Wound Up.* Corgi Yearling.

Bronze Awards

0-5 years
Valerie BLOOM. *Fruits*, ills David AXTELL. Macmillan.

6-8 years
John AGARD. *We Animals Would Like a Word With You*, ills Satoshi KITAMURA. Bodley Head.

9-11 years
Henrietta BRANFORD. *Fire, Bed and Bone.* Walker Books.

1998 **Gold Awards**

0-5 years
Sue HEAP. *Cowboy Baby.* Walker Books.

6-8 years
Harry HORSE. *Last of the Gold Diggers.* Puffin Books.

9-11 years
J. K. ROWLING. *Harry Potter and the Chamber of Secrets.* Bloomsbury.

Silver Awards

0-5 years
Jane SIMMONS. *Come On Daisy.* Orchard Books.

6-8 years
Keith GRAY. *The Runner.* Mammoth Books.

9-11 years
Andrew NORRISS. *Aquila.* Puffin Books.

Bronze Awards
0-5 years
Margaret NASH. *Secret in the Mist.* David & Charles.

6-8 years
Quentin BLAKE. *The Green Ship.* Jonathan Cape.

9-11 years
Dick KING-SMITH. *The Crowstarver.* Doubleday.

1999 **Gold Awards**
0-5 years
Julia DONALDSON. *The Gruffalo*, ills Axel SCHEFFLER. Macmillan.

6-8 years
Laurence ANHOLT. *Snow White and the Seven Aliens*, ills Arthur ROBINS. Orchard Books.

9-11 years
J. K. ROWLING. *Harry Potter and the Prisoner of Azkaban.* Bloomsbury.

Silver Awards
0-5 years
Bob GRAHAM. *Buffy – An Adventure Story.* Walker Books.

6-8 years
Emily SMITH. *Astrid, the Au Pair from Outer Space.* Corgi.

9-11 years
David ALMOND. *Kit's Wilderness.* Hodder.

Bronze Awards
0-5 years
Lydia MONKS. *I Wish I Were a Dog.* Methuen.

6-8 years
Lauren CHILD. *Clarice Bean That's Me.* Orchard Books.

9-11 years
Louise RENNISON. *Angus, Thongs and Full-Frontal Snogging.* Piccadilly Press.

2000 **Gold Awards**
0-5 years
Bob GRAHAM. *Max.* Walker Books.

6-8 years
Jacqueline WILSON. *Lizzie Zipmouth*, ills Nick SHARRATT. Young Corgi – also given the **Kids' Club Network Special Award**.

9-11 years
William NICHOLSON. *The Wind Singer.* Mammoth.

Silver Awards

0-5 years
Satoshi KITAMURA. *Me and My Cat.* Andersen.

6-8 years
Tony MITTON. *The Red and White Spotted Handkerchief*, ills Peter BAILEY. Scholastic.

9-11 years
Beverley NAIDOO. *The Other Side of Truth.* Puffin.

Bronze Awards

0-5 years
John BURNINGHAM. *Husherbye.* Jonathan Cape.

6-8 years
Lauren CHILD. *Beware of the Storybook Wolves.* Hodder.

9-11 years
Kevin CROSSLEY-HOLLAND. *Arthur: The Seeing Stone.* Orion.

2001

Gold Awards

0-5 years
Catherine & Laurence ANHOLT. *Chimp and Zee.* Frances Lincoln.

6-8 years
Emily SMITH. *The Shrimp.* Young Corgi.

9-11 years
Eva IBBOTSON. *Journey to the River Sea.* Macmillan.

Silver Awards

0-5 years
Mick INKPEN. *Kipper's A to Z.* Hodder.

6-8 years
Raymond BRIGGS. *Ug.* Cape.

9-11 years
Chris WOODING. *The Haunting of Alaizabel Cray.* Scholastic.

Bronze Awards

0-5 years
Sarah DYER. *Five Little Friends.* Bloomsbury.

6-8 years
Lauren CHILD. *What Planet Are You From Clarice Bean?* Orchard Books – also given the **Kids' Club Network Special Award.**

9-11 years
Geraldine McCAUGHREAN. *The Kite Rider.* Oxford.

2002 **Gold Awards**

0-5 years
Lucy COUSINS. *Jazzy in the Jungle.* Walker Books.

6-8 years
Lauren CHILD. *That Pesky Rat.* Orchard Books – also given the **Kids' Club Network Special Award.**

9-11 years
Philip REEVE. *Mortal Engines.* Scholastic.

Silver Awards

0-5 years
Charlotte VOAKE. *Pizza Kittens.* Walker.

6-8 years
Richard PLATT. *Pirate Diary – The Journal of Jake Carpenter*, ills Chris RIDDELL. Walker.

9-11 years
Sally PRUE. *Cold Tom.* Oxford.

Bronze Awards

0-5 years
Neal LAYTON. *Oscar and Arabella.* Hodder.

6-8 years
Michael MORPURGO. *The Last Wolf*, ills Michael FOREMAN. Doubleday.

9-11 years
Geraldine McCAUGHREAN. *Stop the Train.* Oxford.

2003 **Gold Awards**

0-5 years
Ursula JONES. *The Witch's Children and the Queen*, ills Russell AYTO. Orchard Books.

6-8 years
S. F. SAID. *Varjak Paw*, ills Dave McKEAN. David Fickling Books.

9-11 years
David ALMOND. *The Fire-Eaters.* Hodder.

Silver Awards

0-5 years
Jeanne WILLIS. *Tadpole's Promise*, ills Tony ROSS. Andersen Press.

6-8 years
Harry HORSE. *The Last Castaways.* Penguin.

9-11 years
Eleanor UPDALE. *Montmorency.* Scholastic.

Bronze Awards

0-5 years
Chris WORMELL. *Two Frogs.* Random House.

6-8 years
Sally GARDNER. *The Countess's Calamity.* Bloomsbury – also given the **Kids' Club Network Special Award.**

9-11 years
Steve AUGARDE. *The Various.* David Fickling Books.

2004

Gold Awards

0-5 years
Mini GREY. *Biscuit Bear.* Jonathan Cape.

6-8 years
Paul STEWART & Chris RIDDELL. *Fergus Crane.* Doubleday – also given the **4Children Special Award**.

9-11 years
Sally GRINDLEY. *Spilled Water.* Bloomsbury.

Silver Awards

0-5 years
Liz PICHON. *My Big Brother Boris.* Scholastic.

6-8 years
Malorie BLACKMAN. *Cloud Busting.* Doubleday.

9-11 years
Eva IBBOTSON. *The Star of Kazan.* Macmillan.

Bronze Awards

0-5 years
Neal LAYTON. *Bartholomew and the Bug.* Hodder.

6-8 years
Geraldine McCAUGHREAN. *Smile!* OUP.

9-11 years
Mal PEET. *Keeper.* Walker.

The Whitbread Children's Book of the Year Award (UK) (Formerly the Children's Novel Category of the Whitbread Book of the Year Award to 1993, then the Beefeater Children's Novel Award 1994-5): complete list of winners.

1972 Rumer GODDEN. *The Diddakoi.* Macmillan.

1973 William PLOMER. *The Butterfly Ball and the Grasshopper's Feast*, ills Alan ALDRIDGE. Cape.

1974 **Joint winners**

Russell HOBAN. *How Tom Beat Captain Najork and his Hired Sportsmen*, ills Quentin BLAKE. Cape.

Jill Paton WALSH. *The Emperor's Winding Sheet.* Macmillan.

1975 No Award

1976 Penelope LIVELY. *A Stitch in Time.* Heinemann.

1977 Shelagh McDONALD. *No End to Yesterday.* Deutsch.

1978 Philippa PEARCE. *The Battle of Bubble and Squeak*, ills Alan BAKER. Deutsch.

1979 Peter DICKINSON. *Tulku.* Gollancz.

1980 Leon GARFIELD. *John Diamond.* Kestrel.

1981 Jane GARDAM. *The Hollow Land.* Julia MacRae.

1982 William CORBETT. *Song of Pentecost.* Methuen.

1983 Roald DAHL. *The Witches.* Cape.

1984 Barbara WILLARD. *The Queen of the Pharisees' Children.* Julia MacRae.

1985 Janni HOWKER. *The Nature of the Beast.* Julia MacRae.

1986 Andrew TAYLOR. *The Coal House.* Collins.

1987 Geraldine McCAUGHREAN. *A Little Lower than the Angels.* Oxford U. P.

1988 Judy ALLEN. *Awaiting Developments.* Julia MacRae.

1989 Hugh SCOTT. *Why Weeps the Brogan?* Walker Books.

1990 Peter DICKINSON. *AK.* Gollancz.

1991 Diana HENDRY. *Harvey Angell.* Julia MacRae.

1992 Gillian CROSS. *The Great Elephant Chase.* Oxford U. P.

1993 Anne FINE. *Flour Babies.* Hamish Hamilton.

1994 Geraldine McCAUGHREAN. *Gold Dust.* Oxford U. P.

1995 Michael MORPURGO. *The Wreck of the Zanzibar.* Methuen.

1996 Anne FINE. *The Tulip Touch.* Hamish Hamilton.

1997 Andrew NORRISS. *Aquila.* Hamish Hamilton.

1998 David ALMOND. *Skellig.* Hodder.

1999 J. K. ROWLING. *Harry Potter and the Prisoner of Azkaban.* Bloomsbury.

2000 Jamila GAVIN. *Coram Boy.* Egmont.

2001 Philip PULLMAN. *The Amber Spyglass.* Scholastic.

2002 Hilary McKAY. *Saffy's Angel.* Hodder.

2003 David ALMOND. *The Fire-Eaters.* Hodder.

*Mark HADDON's *The Curious Incident of the Dog in the Night-Time* (Jonathan Cape/David Fickling) won the Whitbread Book of the Year, having been entered for both the Novel and Children's Book categories of the award, then withdrawn from the Children's Book category by its publishers.

2004 Geraldine McCAUGHREAN. *Not the End of the World.* Oxford U. P.

W. H. Smith Children's Book of the Year Award: complete list of winners

1995 Alison SAGE (ed.) *The Hutchinson Treasury of Children's Literature*. Hutchinson.

1996 Philip PULLMAN. *Northern Lights*. Scholastic.

1997 J. K. ROWLING. *Harry Potter and the Philosopher's Stone*. Bloomsbury.

1998 J. K. ROWLING. *Harry Potter and the Chamber of Secrets*. Bloomsbury.

1999 Jacqueline WILSON. *The Illustrated Mum*. Doubleday.

2000 Philip PULLMAN. *The Amber Spyglass*. Scholastic.

2001 J. K. ROWLING. *Harry Potter and the Goblet of Fire*. Bloomsbury.

2002 Eoin COLFER. *Artemis Fowl*. Viking/Puffin.

2003 Jacqueline WILSON. *Girls in Tears*. Doubleday.

2004 Mark HADDON. *The Curious Incident of the Dog in the Night-Time*. Jonathan Cape/David Fickling.

Askew Torchlight Award (UK): complete list of winners and spotlight titles

2003 Cornelia FUNKE. *The Thief Lord.* Chicken House.

Shortlist
Eve BUNTING. *The Summer of Riley.* Collins Children's Books.

Georgia BYNG. *Molly Moon's Incredible Book of Hypnotism.* Macmillan Children's Books.

Louise COOPER. *Demon's Crossing.* Hodder Children's Books.

Neil GAIMAN. *Coraline.* Bloomsbury Children's Books.

Pete JOHNSON. *Traitor.* Doubleday.

Jackie KAY. *The Straw Girl.* Macmillan Children's Books.

Paul MAY. *Green Fingers.* Corgi.

Daniel PENNAC. *Dog.* Walker.

Philip RIDLEY. *Mighty Fizz Chilla.* Puffin.

2004 Cressida COWELL. *How to Train your Dragon.* Hodder Children's Books.

Spotlight Titles
Jenny NIMMO. *The Time Twister.* Egmont Children's Books.

Holly BLACK & Tony DiTERLIZZI. *The Field Guide.* Simon & Schuster.

Bisto Book Awards (Eire): complete list of winners

1980-90 Bisto Book of the Decade

Fiction Category

Tom MCCAUGHREN. *Run With The Wind*; *Run To Earth*; *Run Swift Run Free*, ills Jeanette DUNNE. Wolfhound Press.

Information Books Category

George Otto SIMMS. *Exploring The Book of Kells*; *Brendan the Navigator*, ills David ROONEY. O'Brien Press.

Winner In The Irish Language Category

Marie-Louise FITZPATRICK *An Chanáil*, translated by Bernadine Nic Ghiolla PHÁDRAIG. An Gúm.

1990-91 Bisto Book of the Year

Eilís DILLON. *The Island of Ghosts.* Faber and Faber.

Best Emerging Children's Author Category

Morgan LLYWELYN. *Brian Boru.* O'Brien Press.

Books For Young Readers Category

Martin WADDELL, *Grandma's Bill.* Simon & Schuster.

Illustration Category

P. J. LYNCH. *Fairy Tales of Ireland*, text by W. B. YEATS. Collins.

Also Shortlisted

Marita CONLON-MCKENNA. *Under The Hawthorn Tree.* O'Brien Press.

Don CONROY. *The Celestial Child.* Kildanore.

Michael MULLINS. *The Long March.* Poolbeg Press.

Eilís Ni DHUIBHNE. *The Uncommon Cormorant.* Poolbeg Press.

Joan O'NEILL. *Daisy Chain War.* Attic Press.

Finola SUMNER. *Double the Boys.* Poolbeg Press.

1991-92 Bisto Book of the Year

John QUINN. *The Summer of Lily and Ernie.* Poolbeg Press.

Historical Fiction Category

Marita CONLON-MCKENNA. *Wildflower Girl.* O'Brien Press.

Picture Book Category

Marie-Louise FITZPATRICK. *The Sleeping Giant.* Brandon Books.

First Children's Novel category
Yvonne MACGRORY. *The Secret of the Ruby Ring.* Children's Press.

1992-93 Bisto Book of the Year
Marita CONLON-MCKENNA. *The Blue Horse.* O'Brien Press.

Information Book Category
Mairin UÍ CHOMAIN. *Tamall Sa Chistin*, ills Bébhinn & Deiri Ó MEADHRA. An Gúm.

Teenage Fiction Category
Sam MCBRATNEY. *Put a Saddle on the Pig.* Methuen.

Historical Fiction Category
Morgan LLYWELYN. *Strongbow.* O'Brien Press.

Also Shortlisted
June CONSIDINE. *View From A Blind Bridge.* Poolbeg Press.

Margrit CRUIKSHANK. *A Monster Called Charlie.* Poolbeg Press.

Maeve FRIEL. *The Deerstone.* Poolbeg Press.

Ní NUADHÁIN. *Cois Trá.* An Gúm.

1993-94 Bisto Book of the Year
Jane MITCHELL. *When Stars Stop Spinning.* Poolbeg Press.

Bisto Merit Awards
[These awards after 1993-94 are all of equal merit, and are not categorised as in previous years.]

Máirín JOHNSTON. *The Pony Express.* Attic Press.

Sam MCBRATNEY. *The Chieftain's Daughter.* O'Brien Press.

Elizabeth O'HARA. *The Hiring Fair.* Poolbeg Press.

Also Shortlisted
Mary ARRIGAN. *Lá Le Mamo.* An Gúm.

Siobhán PARKINSON. *Amelia.* O'Brien Press.

Maria QUIRK-WALSHE. *Searching for a Friend.* Attic Press.

1994-95 Bisto Book of the Year
Elizabeth O'HARA. *Blaeberry Sunday.* Poolbeg Press.

Bisto Merit Awards
Rose DOYLE. *Goodbye Summer, Goodbye.* Attic Press.

P. J. LYNCH. *Catkin*, text by Antonia BARBER. Poolbeg Press.

Ré Ó LAIGHLIS. *Ecstasy agus Scéalta Eile.* Cló Iar-Chonnachta Teo.

The Eilís Dillon Memorial Award
Mark O'SULLIVAN. *Melody for Nora.* Wolfhound Press.

Also shortlisted
Maeve FRIEL. *Distant Voices.* Poolbeg Press.

Tom MCCAUGHREN. *In Search of the Liberty Tree.* The Children's Press.

Kate THOMPSON. *Switchers.* Aran.

1995-96 Bisto Book of the Year
P. J. LYNCH, *The Christmas Miracle of Jonathan Toomey*, text by Susan WOJCIECHOWSKI. Poolbeg Press.

Bisto Merit Awards
Mary BECKETT. *Hannah or Pink Balloons.* Marino Books.

Ré Ó LAIGHLÉIS. *Sceoin Sa Bhoireann.* Cló Iar-Chonnachta.

Frank MURPHY. *Lockie and Dadge.* O'Brien Press.

The Eilís Dillon Memorial Award
Frank MURPHY. *Lockie and Dadge.* O'Brien Press.

Also Shortlisted
Marita CONLON-MCKENNA. *Safe Harbour.* O'Brien Press.

Benedict KIELY. *The Trout In The Turnhole.* Wolfhound Press.

Paul MULDOON. *The Last Thesaurus.* Faber and Faber.

Siobhán PARKINSON. *All Shining in the Spring.* O'Brien Press.

Gabriel ROSENSTOCK. *Naomh Pádraig Agus Crom Dubh*, ills Piet SLUIS. An Gúm.

Martin WADDELL. *John Joe and the Big Hen.* An Gúm.

1996-97 Bisto Book of the Year
Siobhán PARKINSON. *Sisters ... No Way!* O'Brien Press.

The Bisto Merit Awards
Cliodhna CUSSEN & Cormac Ó SNODAIGH. *An Eala Dubh.* Coiscéim.

Maeve FRIEL. *The Lantern Moon.* Poolbeg Press.

Gerard WHELAN. *The Guns of Easter.* O'Brien Press.

Eilís Dillon Award

Gerard WHELAN. *The Guns of Easter.* O'Brien Press.

Also Shortlisted

Dan KISSANE. *The Eagle Tree*, ills Aileen JOHNSTON. O'Brien Press.

P.J. LYNCH. *The King of Ireland's Son.* Poolbeg Press.

Ré Ó LAIGHLÉIS. *Gafa.* Comhar.

Colmán Ó RAGHALLAIGH. *Drochlá Ruairí.* Cló Mhaigh Eo.

Colmán Ó RAGHALLAIGH. *Róisín ar Strae.* An Gúm.

Mark O'SULLIVAN. *More than a Match.* Wolfhound Press.

1997-98 The Bisto Book of the Year

Gerard WHELAN. *Dream Invader.* O'Brien Press.

The Bisto Merit Awards

Soinbhe LALLY. *The Hungry Wind.* Poolbeg Press.

P.J. LYNCH. *When Jessie Came across the Sea.* Poolbeg Press.

Siobhán PARKINSON. *Four Kids, Three Cats, Two Cows, One Witch (maybe).* O'Brien Press.

Eilís Dillon Award

Ed MILIANO. *It's a Jungle Out There.* Wolfhound Press.

Also Shortlisted

Mairéad Ashe FITZGERALD. *The World of Colmcille, also known as Columba*, ills Stephen HALL. O'Brien Press.

Dan KISSANE. *The Eagle Tree*, ills Angela CLARKE. O'Brien Press.

Dan KISSANE. *Jimmy's Leprechaun Trap*, ills Angela CLARKE. O'Brien Press.

Larry O'LOUGHLIN. *The Gobán Saor*, ills John LEONARD. Blackwater Press.

Mark O'SULLIVAN. *Angels Without Wings.* Wolfhound Press.

Mark O'SULLIVAN. *White Lies.* Wolfhound Press.

1998-99 The Bisto Book of the Year

Niamh SHARKEY. *Tales of Wisdom and Wonder.* Barefoot Books.

The Bisto Merit Awards

Marie-Louise FITZPATRICK. *The Long March.* Wolfhound Press.

Siobhán PARKINSON. *The Moon King.* O'Brien Press.

Gabriel ROSENSTOCK. *An Rógaire agus a Scáil*, ills Piet SLUIS. An Gúm.

Eilís Dillon Award
Caitríona HASTINGS. *Dea-Scéala.* Cló Iar-Chonnachta.

Also Shortlisted
Pat BORAN. *All the Way from China*, ills Stewart CURRY. Poolbeg Press.

Sam McBRATNEY. *Bert's Wonderful News.* Walker Books.

Tom McCAUGHREN. *Ride a Pale Horse.* Anvil Press.

Mary MURPHY. *Please Be Quiet.* Methuen.

Niamh SHARKEY (ills) *The Gigantic Turnip.* Barefoot Books.

1999-00 The Bisto Book of the Year
Marilyn TAYLOR. *Faraway Home.* O'Brien Press.

The Bisto Merit Awards
Mary ARRIGAN. *Siúloid Bhreá.* An Gúm.

Marilyn McLAUGHLIN. *Fierce Milly.* Mammoth/Egmont.

Mark O'SULLIVAN. *Silent Stones.* Wolfhound Press.

Eilís Dillon Award
Marilyn McLAUGHLIN. *Fierce Milly.* Mammoth/Egmont.

Also Shortlisted
Eoin COLFER. *Benny and Babe.* O'Brien Press.

Louise LAWRENCE. *The Crowlings.* Collins.

Larry O'LOUGHLIN. *Is Anybody Listening?* Wolfhound Press.

Gabriel ROSENSTOCK. *Paidín Mháire Mhuigín*, ills Piet SLUIS. An Gúm.

Niamh SHARKEY. *Jack and the Beanstalk.* Barefoot Books.

Bill WALL. *The Boy Who Met Hitler.* Mercier Press.

Gerard WHELAN. *Out of Nowhere.* O'Brien Press.

2000-01 The Bisto Book of the Year
Marie-Louise FITZPATRICK. *Izzy and Skunk.* Blackwater Press.

The Bisto Merit Awards
Eoin COLFER. *The Wish List.* O'Brien Press.

Martina MURPHY. *Dirt Tracks.* Poolbeg Press.

Martin WADDELL. *The Orchard Book of Ghostly Stories.* Orchard Press.

Eilís Dillon Award

Patrick DEELEY. *The Lost Orchard.* O'Brien Press.

Also Shortlisted

Malachy DOYLE. *Tales from Old Ireland,* ills Niamh SHARKEY. Barefoot Books.

Jim HALLIGAN & John NEWMAN. *Fowl Deeds.* Wolfhound Press.

Adrienne KENNAWAY (ills). *This is the Tree.* Frances Lincoln.

Michael MULLEN. *An Bóthar Fada.* Coiscéim.

Siobhán PARKINSON. *Call of the Whales.* O'Brien Press.

2001-02 The Bisto Book of the Year

Kate THOMPSON. *The Beguilers.* The Bodley Head.

The Bisto Merit Awards

Eoin COLFER. *Artemis Fowl.* Puffin.

Carlo GÉBLER. *Caught on a Train.* Egmont.

Colmán Ó RAGHALLAIGH. *An Sclábhaí,* ills THE CARTOON SALOON. Cló Mhaigh Eo.

Eilís Dillon Award

Gillian PERDUE. *Adam's Starling.* O'Brien Press.

Also Shortlisted

Trevor J. COLGAN. *The Stretford Enders Away.* Red Fox.

Marie-Louise FITZPATRICK. *I'm A Tiger Too.* Wolfhound Press.

P. J. LYNCH (ills). *Ignis.* Walker Books.

Austin McQUINN. *This Will Take Forever.* Zero to Ten.

Martin WADDELL. *Give it to Joe!* Walker Books.

2002-03 The Bisto Book of the Year – Joint Winners

Marie-Louise FITZPATRICK. *You, Me and the Big Blue Sea.* Gullane.

Kate THOMPSON. *The Alchemist's Apprentice.* The Bodley Head.

The Bisto Merit Awards
Colmán Ó RAGHALLAIGH. *An Tóraíocht*, ills THE CARTOON SALOON. Cló Mhaigh Eo.

Matthew SWEENEY. *Fox*. Bloomsbury.

Gerard WHELAN. *War Children.* O'Brien Press.

Eilís Dillon Award
Grace WELLS. *Gyrfalcon.* O'Brien Press.

Also Shortlisted
Eoin COLFER. *Artemis Fowl, The Arctic Incident.* Puffin Books.

Malachy DOYLE. *Who is Jesse Flood?* Bloomsbury.

Siobhán PARKINSON. *The Love Bean.* O'Brien Press.

2003-04 Bisto Book of the Year
Aubrey FLEGG. *Wings Over Delft.* O'Brien Press.

The Bisto Merit Awards
Anita JERAM. *You Can Do It Sam*. Walker Books.

Niamh SHARKEY. *The Ravenous Beast.* Walker Books.

Kate THOMPSON. *Origins.* Bodley Head.

Eilís Dillon Award
Alan TITLEY. *Amach.* An Gúm.

Also Shortlisted
Carlo GÉBLER. *August '44.* Egmont Books.

P. J. LYNCH. *The Bee Man of Orn,* text by Frank R. STOCKTON. Walker Books.

Mary MURPHY. *I Kissed The Baby.* Walker Books.

Mary MURPHY. *Little Owl and The Star.* Walker Books.

Siobhán PARKINSON. *Kathleen the Celtic Knot.* Pleasant Company Publications.

The Mr Christie's Book Award (Canada): complete list of winners

1989 **English Text**
Kit PEARSON. *The Sky is Falling*. Viking Kestrel.

French Text
Ginette ANFOUSSE. *Rosalie s'en va-t-en Guerre.* La Courte Échelle.

English Illustration
Ian WALLACE. *The Name of the Tree*, text by Celia LOTTRIDGE. Groundwood Books.

French Illustration
Philippe BÉHA. *Mais que Font les Fées Avec Toutes ces Dents?*, text by Michel LUPPENS. Raton Laveur.

1990 **English Text**
Brian DOYLE. *Covered Bridge*. Groundwood Books.

French Text
François GRAVEL. *Le Zamboni.* Boréal.

English Illustration
Kady MacDonald DENTON. *The Story of Little Quack*, text by Betty GIBSON. Kids Can Press.

French Illustration
Pierre PRATT. *Les Fantaisies de l'Oncle Henri*, text by Bénédicte FROISSART. Annick Press.

1991 **English Text**
Dennis LEE. *The Ice Cream Store.* HarperCollins.

French Text
Christiane DUCHESNE. *Bibitsa, ou l'Etrange Voyage de Clara Vic.* Quebec Amérique.

English Illustration
Barbara REID. *Zoe's Rainy Day*; *Zoe's Snowy Day*; *Zoe's Windy Day*; Zoe's *Sunny Day.* (Series of board books). HarperCollins.

French Illustration
Stéphane POULIN. *Un Voyage pour Deux: Contes et Mensonges de Mon Enfance.* Annick Press.

1992 **English Text 8 years & under**
Sheree FITCH. *There Were Monkeys in My Kitchen.* Doubleday Canada.

French Text 8 years & under
Gilles GAUTHIER. *Le Gros Problème du Petite Marcus.* La Courte Échelle.

English Text 9-14 years
Janet LUNN & Christopher MOORE. *The Story of Canada.* Key Porter Books.

French Text 9-14 years
Dominique DEMERS. *Un Hiver de Tourmente.* La Courte Échelle.

English Illustration
Yvette MOORE. *A Prairie Alphabet*, text by Jo BANNATYNE-CUGNET. Tundra Books.

French Illustration
Dominique JOLIN. *C'est pas Juste!* Raton Laveur.

1993 **English 7 years & under**
Berny LUCAS & Russ WILLMS. *Brewster Rooster.* Kids Can Press.

French 7 years & under
Joceline SANSCHAGRIN. *Caillou, la Petite Soeur* **and** *Caillou, le Petit Pot*, ills Hélène DESPUTEAUX. Editions Chouette.

English 8-11 years (Co-Winners)
Song Nan ZHANG. *A Little Tiger in the Chinese Night.* Tundra Books.

Leo YERXA. *Last Leaf First Snowflake to Fall.* Groundwood Books.

French 8-11 years
Christiane DUCHESNE. *La 42e Soeur de Bebert.* Quebec Amérique.

English 12 years & up
Diana WIELER. *RanVan The Defender.* Groundwood Books.

French 12 years & up
Dominique DEMERS. *Les Grands Sapins ne Meurent pas.* Quebec Amérique.

1994 **English 7 years & under**
W. D. VALGARDSON. *Thor*, ills Ange ZHANG. Groundwood Books.

French 7 years & under
Rémy SIMARD. *Mon Chien est un Éléphant*, ills Hélène DESPUTEAUX & Pierre PRATT. Annick Press.

English 8-11 years
Barbara GREENWOOD. *A Pioneer Story*, ills Heather COLLINS. Kids Can Press.

French 7-11 years
Denis COTÉ. *Le Parc aux Sortilèges*. La Courte Échelle.

English 12 years & up
Sarah ELLIS. *Out of the Blue*. Groundwood Books.

French 12 years & up
Raymond PLANTE. *L'Étoile a Pleuré Rouge*. Boréal-Junior.

1995 **English 7 years & under**
Nan GREGORY. *How Smudge Came*, ills Ron LIGHTBURN. Red Deer College Press.

French 7 years & under
Pierette DUBÉ. *Au Lit, Princesse Emilie!* Raton Laveur.

English 8-11 years
Mordecai RICHLER. *Jacob Two-Two's First Spy Case*, ills Norman EYOLFSON. McClelland & Stewart.

French 8-11 years
Christine DUCHESNE. *La Bergère de Chevaux*. Quebec Amérique.

English 12 years & up
Joan CLARK. *The Dream Carvers*. Penguin.

French 12 years & up
Jean LEMIEUX. *Le Trésor de Brion: Roman*. Quebec Amérique.

1996 **English Ages 7 & under**
Don GILLMOR & Marie-Louise GAY. *The Fabulous Song*. Stoddart Publishing.

French Ages 7 & under
Danielle MARCOTTE. *Poil de Serpent Dent d'Araignee*, ills Stéphane POULIN. Les 400 Coups.

English Ages 8-11
Shelly TANAKA & Laurie McGAW. *Discovering the Iceman.* Scholastic Canada/Madison Press.

French Ages 8-11
Francis BACK & Robert DAVIDTS. *Jean-Baptiste, Coureur des Bois.* Boréal.

English Ages 12 & over
Brian DOYLE. *Uncle Ronald.* Groundwood Books.

French Ages 12 & over
Jacques LAZURE. *Le Rêve Couleur d'Orange.* Quebec Amérique.

1997 **English 7 years & under**
Barbara NICHOL. *Biscuits in the Cupboard*, ills Phillipe BÉHA. Stoddart Kids.

French 7 years & under
Lucie PAPINEAU. *Pas de Taches pour un Girafe*, ills Marisol SARRAZIN. Édition Héritage.

English 8-11 years
Kevin MAJOR. *The House of the Wooden Santas*, ills Imelda GEORGE (wood carvings) & Ned PRATT (photography). Red Deer College Press.

French 8-11 years
Dominique DEMERS. *La Mystérieuse Bibliothecaire.* Quebec Amérique.

English 12 years & up
Kenneth OPPEL. *Silverwing.* Harper Collins.

French 12 years & up
Robert SOULIÈRES. *Un Cadavre de Classe.* Soulières.

1998 **English 7 years & younger**
Marilyn HELMER. *Fog Cat*, ills Paul MOMBOURQUETTER. Kids Can Press.

French 7 years & younger
Robert SOULIÈRES. *Une Gardienne pour Étienne*, ills Anne VILLENEUVE. Les 400 Coups.

English 8-11 years
Richard SCRIMGER. *The Nose From Jupiter.* Tundra Books.

French 8-11 years
Gilles TIBO. *Rouge Timide.* Soulières.

English 12 years & up
William BELL. *Zack.* Doubleday Canada.

French 12 years & up
Jean-Michel SCHEMBRÉ. *Les Citadelles du Vertige.* Pierre Tisseyre.

1999 **English 7 years & younger**
Maxine TROTTIER & Rajka KUPESIC. *Claire's Gift.* North Winds Press.

French 7 years & younger
Marie-Louise GAY. *Stella Etoile de la Mer.* Dominique et cie/Heritage.

English 8-11 years
Kenneth OPPEL. *Sunwing.* HarperCollins.

French 8-11 years
Gilles TIBO & Jean BERNECHE. *Les Yeux Noirs.* Soulieres Editeur.

English 12 years & up
Martha BROOKS. *Being with Henry.* Groundwood Books.

French 12 years & up
Stanley PEAN. *Le Temps S'Enfuit.* La Courte Échelle.

2000 **English 7 years & younger**
Stephanie McLELLAN. *The Chicken Cat*, ills Sean CASSIDY. Fitzhenry & Whiteside.

French 7 years & younger
Dominique DEMERS. *Vieux Thomas et la Petite Fée*, ills Stéphane POULIN. Dominique et cie.

English 8-11 years
Jean LITTLE. *Willow & Twig.* Penguin Canada.

French 8-11 years
Francois GRAVEL & Pierre PRATT. *David et le Fantôme.* Dominique et cie.

English 12 years & up
Janet McNAUGHTON. *The Secret Under My Skin.* HarperCollins Canada.

French 12 years & up
Michèle MARINEAU. *Rouge Poison.* Quebec Amérique.

2001

English 7 years & younger
Celia Barker LOTTRIDGE. *The Little Rooster and the Diamond Button*, ills Joanne FITZGERALD. Groundwood Books.

French 7 years & younger
Marie-Francine HEBERT. *Decroche-moi la Lune*, ills Mylene PRATT. Dominique et cie.

English 8-11 years
Polly HORVATH. *Everything on a Waffle.* Groundwood Books.

French 8-11 years
Helene VACHON. *L'Oiseau de Passage*, ills YAYO. Dominique et cie.

English 12 years & up
Arthur SLADE. *Dust.* HarperCollins.

French 12 years & up
Jacques LAZURE. *Llddz.* Soulières Éditeur.

2002

English 7 years & younger
Gold Seal
Anne Laurel CARTER. *Under a Prairie Sky*, ills Alan & Lea DANIEL. Orca Book Publishers.

Silver Seal
Marilynn REYNOLDS. *The Name of the Child*, ills Don KILBY. Orca Book Publishers.

Jane BARCLAY. *Going on a Journey to the Sea*, ills Doris BARRETTE. Lobster Press.

Sean CASSIDY. *Good to Be Small.* Fitzhenry & Whiteside.

French 7 years & younger
Gold Seal
Marie-Francine HÉBERT. *Mon Rayon de Soleil*, ills Steve ADAMS. Dominique et cie.

English 8-11 years
Gold Seal
Alan CUMYN. *The Secret Life of Owen Skye.* Groundwood Books.

Silver Seal
Deborah ELLIS. *A Company of Fools.* Fitzhenry & Whiteside.

Marjorie Blain PARKER. *Jasper's Day*, ills Janet WILSON. Kids Can Press.

French 8-11 years
Gold Seal
Sylvain TRUDEL. *Pourquoi le Monde est Comme Il Est?* ills Suzane LANGLOIS. La Courte Échelle.

English 12 years & up
Gold Seal
Joan CLARK. *The Word for Home.* Penguin/Viking.

French 12 years & up
Gold Seal
Denis CÔTÉ. *L'Empire Couleur Sang*, ills Philippe BÉHA. Hurtubise HMH.

2003

English 7 years and under
Gold Seal
Jean LITTLE. *Pippin the Christmas Pig*, ills Werner ZIMMERMAN. North Winds Press/Scholastic.

Silver Seal
Aubrey DAVIS. *Bagels from Benny*, ills Dušan PETRIČIĆ. Kids Can Press.

Susin NIELSEN-FERNLUND. *Hank and Fergus*, ills Louise-Andrée LALIBERTÉ. Orca Book Publishers.

Chieri UEGAKI. *Suki's Kimono*, ills Stéphane JORISCH. Kids Can Press.

French 7 years & younger
Gold Seal
Dominique DEMERS. *L'Oiseau des Sables*, ills Stéphane POULIN. Dominique et cie.

Silver Seal
Gilles TIBO. *Émilie Pleine de Jouets*, ills Marie LAFRANCE. Dominique et cie.

Marie-Danielle CROTEAU. *L'Autobus Colère*, ills Sophie CASSON. La Courte Échelle.

Gilles TIBO. *Les Chiffres du Petit Bonhomme*, ills Marie-Claude FAVREAU. Québec Amérique Jeunesse.

Dominique DEMERS. *Le Zloukch*, ills FANNY. Les 400 Coups.

English 8-11 years
Gold Seal
Sarah ELLIS. *The Several Lives of Orphan Jack*, ills Bruno ST-AUBIN. Groundwood Books.

Silver Seal
Tim WYNNE-JONES. *Ned Mouse Breaks Away*, ills Dušan PETRIČIĆ. Groundwood Books.

Val ROSS. *The Road to There*. Tundra Books.

French 8-11 years

Gold Seal

Charlotte GINGRAS. *La Boîte à Bonheur*, ills Stéphane JORISCH. La Courte Échelle.

Silver Seal

Camille BOUCHARD. *Des Étoiles sur Notre Maison*, ills Paule THIBAULT. Dominique et cie.

Karoline GEORGES. *L'Itinérante qui Venait du Nord*, ills Catherine CÔTÉ. Leméac.

Élise GRAVEL. *J'Élève Mon Monster*. Les 400 Coups.

Marthe PELLETIER. *Une Lettre pour Nakicha*, ills Rafael SOTTOLICHIO. La Courte Échelle.

English 12 years and up

Gold Seal

Martine LEAVITT. *Tom Finder*. Red Deer Press.

Silver Seal

Janet McNAUGHTON. *An Earthly Knight*. HarperTrophy.

Kevin MAJOR. *Ann and Seamus*, ills David BLACKWOOD. Groundwood Books.

French 12 years & up

Gold Seal

Marie-Francine HÉBERT. *Le Ciel Tombe à Côté*. Québec Amérique Jeunesse.

Silver Seal

Mylène GILBERT-DUMAS. *Mystique*. La Courte Échelle.

Marie-Francine HÉBERT. *Nul Poisson où Aller*, ills Janice NADEAU. Les 400 Coups.

Jacques LAZURE. *Les Chasseurs d'Éternité*, ills Normand COUSINEAU. Soulières Éditeur.

Anique POITRAS. *La Chute du Corbeau*. Québec Amérique Jeunesse.

The New Zealand Post Children's Book Awards (formerly The AIM Children's Book Awards, 1990-1996; previously The New Zealand Government Publishing Awards): complete list of winners and honour books

1982 **(NZGP)**

Children's Book Award
Joy COWLEY. *The Silent One*, ills Sherryl JORDAN. Whitcoulls.

Picture Book Award
Robyn KAHUKIWA. *The Kuia and the Spider*, text by Patricia GRACE. Longman Paul/Kidsarus 2.

1983 **(NZGP)**

Children's Book Award
Maurice GEE. *The Halfmen of O.* Oxford U. P.

Picture Book Award
Gavin BISHOP. *Mr Fox.* Oxford U. P.

1984 **(NZGP)**

Children's Book Award
Anne de ROO. *Jacky Nobody.* Methuen.

Picture Book Award
Lynley DODD. *Hairy Maclary from Donaldson's Dairy.* Mallinson Rendel.

1985 **(NZGP)**

Children's Book Award
Caroline MACDONALD. *Visitors*, ills Garry MELSON. Hodder & Stoughton.

Picture Book Award
Robert H. G. JAHNKE. *The Fish of our Fathers*, text by Ron L. BACON. Waiatarua Publishing.

1986 **(NZGP)**

Children's Book Award
Joanna ORWIN. *Guardian of the Land.* Oxford U. P.

Picture Book Award
Lynley DODD. *Hairy Maclary Scattercat.* Mallinson Rendel.

Non-Fiction Award
Judith BASSETT, Keith SINCLAIR & Marcia STENSEN. *The Story of New Zealand.* Reed Methuen.

1987 **(NZGP)**

Children's Book Award
Barry FAVILLE. *The Keeper.* Oxford U. P.

Picture Book Award
Robyn KAHUKIWA. *Taniwha*. Viking Kestrel.

Non-Fiction Award
No Award

1988 **(NZGP)**
Children's Book Award
Tessa DUDER. *Alex*. Oxford U. P.

Picture Book Award
Lynley DODD. *Hairy Maclary's Caterwaul Caper*. Mallinson Rendel.

Non-Fiction Award
No Award

1989 No Awards

1990 **(AIM)**

Picture Book of the Year
First
Lesley MOYES. *Annie and the Moon*, text by Miriam SMITH. Mallinson Rendel.

Second
Chris GASKIN. *The Story of the Kakapo*, text by Phillip TEMPLE. Hodder & Stoughton.

Third
Lynley DODD. *Hairy Maclary's Rumpus at the Vet*. Mallinson Rendel.

Children's Book of the Year
First
Tessa DUDER. *Alex in Winter*. Oxford U. P.

Second
Maurice GEE. *The Champions*. Puffin.

Third
Caroline MACDONALD. *The Lake at the End of the World*. Hodder & Stoughton.

1991 **(AIM)**

Picture Book of the Year
First
Pamela ALLEN. *My Cat Maisie*. Hodder & Stoughton.

Second
Christine ROSS. *Lily and the Bears*. Methuen.

Third
Lynley DODD. *Slinky Malinky.* Mallinson Rendel.

Storybook of the Year
First
Sherryl JORDAN. *Rocco.* Ashton Scholastic.

Second
Ruth CORRIN. *Secrets.* Oxford U. P.

Third
Caroline MACDONALD. *Speaking to Miranda.* Hodder & Stoughton.

1992 (AIM)

Picture Book of the Year
First
Lynley DODD. *Hairy Maclary's Showbusiness.* Mallinson Rendel.

Second
Trevor PYE. *My Aunt Mary Went Shopping*, text by Roger HALL. Ashton Scholastic.

Third
Penny NEWMAN. *The One That Got Away*, text by John PARKER. Nelson Price Milburn.

Book of the Year
First
Joy COWLEY. *Bow Down, Shadrach.* Hodder & Stoughton.

Second
Sherryl JORDAN. *The Juniper Game.* Ashton Scholastic.

Third
Tessa DUDER. *Alessandra - Alex in Rome.* Oxford U. P.

Special Mention
Margaret MAHY. *Dangerous Spaces.* Hamish Hamilton.

Best First Book
Paula BOOCK. *Out Walked Mel.* John McIndoe.

1993 (AIM)

Picture Book of the Year
Christine ROSS. *Lily and the Present.* Methuen Children's Books.

Honour Award
Trevor PYE. *Grandma McGarvey Paints the Shed*, text by Jenny HESSELL. Ashton Scholastic.

Junior Fiction
Margaret MAHY. *The Underrunners.* Hamish Hamilton.

Honour Award
Bob KERR. *The Optimist.* Mallinson Rendel.

Senior Fiction
Tessa DUDER. *Songs for Alex.* Oxford U. P.

Honour award
Jack LASENBY. *The Conjuror.* Oxford U. P.

Best First Book
Bob KERR. *The Optimist.* Mallinson Rendel.

Non-Fiction
Chris GASKIN. *Picture Magic: Illustrating a Picture Book*, photos Neville PEAT & Visual Art Studio. Ashton Scholastic.

1994 (AIM)

Picture Book
Gavin BISHOP. *Hinepau.* Ashton Scholastic.

Junior Fiction
Diana NOONAN. *A Dolphin in the Bay.* Omnibus Books.

Senior Fiction
Pat QUINN. *The Value of X.* Heinemann Education.

Honour award
Owen MARSHALL. *The Ace of Diamonds Gang.* McIndoe Publishers.

Non-Fiction
Mary TAYLOR. *Old Blue - The Rarest Bird in the World*, ills author. Ashton Scholastic.

Honour award
Brian STOKES. *Stretch, Bend and Boggle*, ills Carolyn SMITH. Waikato Education Centre.

1995 (AIM)

Picture Book
Elizabeth FULLER. *The Best-Loved Bear*, text by Diana NOONAN. Ashton Scholastic.

Junior Fiction & Book of the Year
Maurice GEE. *The Fat Man.* Viking.

Senior Fiction
William TAYLOR. *The Blue Lawn.* HarperCollins Publishers N.Z.

Honour award
James NORCLIFFE. *The Emerald Encyclopedia.* Hazard Press.

Non-Fiction
Andrew CROWE. *Which Native Forest Plant?*, ills Sandra PARKKALI. Viking.

Honour award
Betty BROWNLIE. *The Life Cycle of the Praying Mantis*, ills author. Ashton Scholastic.

1996 (AIM)

Picture Book
Linda McCLELLAND. *The Cheese Trap*, text by Joy COWLEY. Ashton Scholastic.

Honour award
Ruth PAUL. *Tom's Story*, text by Mandy HAGAR. Mallinson Rendel.

Junior Fiction
Jack LASENBY. *The Waterfall.* Longacre Press.

Honour award
David HILL. *Take It Easy.* Mallinson Rendel.

Senior Fiction & Book of the Year
Janice MARRIOTT. *Crossroads.* Reed Children's Books.

Non-Fiction
Trish GRIBBEN. *My Sea is the Pacific-Aya's Story*, photos Jenny SCOWN. Ashton Scholastic.

Honour award
Elsie LOCKE. *Joe's Ruby*, ills Gary HEBLEY. Cape Catley.

Best First Book
Laura RANGER. *Laura's Poems.* Godwit Pub.

1997 (New Zealand Post)

Senior Fiction Winner
Kate De GOLDI. *Sanctuary.* Penguin Books.

Best First Book
Jane WESTAWAY. *Reliable Friendly Girls*. Longacre Press.

Junior Fiction Winner
Jack LASENBY. *The Battle of Pook Island*. Longacre Press.

Overall Winner & Best Picture Book
Robyn BELTON. *The Bantam and the Soldier*, text by Jennifer BECK. Scholastic New Zealand.

Children's Choice
Bob KERR. *Mechanical Harry*. Mallinson Rendel.

Non-Fiction Winner
Chris GASKIN. *Picture Book Magic*, photos Denis PAGE. Reed Children's Books.

1998 (NZ Post)

Senior Fiction Winner & Book of the Year
Paula BOOCK. *Dare Truth or Promise*. Longacre Press.

Honour Award
Jack LASENBY. *Because We Were Travellers*. Longacre Press.

Junior Fiction Winner
Joy COWLEY. *Ticket to the Sky Dance*. Viking.

Honour Award
David CALDER. *The Dragonslayer's Apprentice*. Scholastic.

Best First Book
Judy KNOX. *Trapped*. Scholastic.

Picture Book Winner & Children's Choice
Lesley MOYES. *Alphabet Apartments*. Mallinson Rendel.

Non-Fiction Winner
Diana NOONAN & Keith OLSEN. *The Know, Sow and Grow Kids' Book of Plants*, ills Keith OLSEN. Bridge Hill Pub.

1999 (NZ Post)

Senior Fiction Winner
Jack LASENBY. *Taur*. Longacre Press.

Honour Award
Fleur BEALE. *I Am Not Esther*. Longacre Press.

Junior Fiction Winner
Joy COWLEY. *Starbright and the Dream Eater.* Viking.

Honour Award
Denis EDWARDS. *Killer Moves.* Scholastic.

Best First Book
Hana Hiraina ERLBECK. *Footsteps of the Gods*, ills Manawa-Ote-Rangi WAIPARA. Reed.

Children's Book Award & Picture Book Winner
Selina YOUNG. *A Summery Saturday Morning*, text by Margaret MAHY. Viking.

Honour Award
Lynley DODD. *Slinky Malinki Catflaps.* Mallinson Rendel.

Non-Fiction Winner
Gerard HUTCHING. *The Natural World of New Zealand.* Viking.

Honour Award
Pauline CARTWRIGHT. *All Sorts of Trucks*, photos by Tim HAWKINS, drawings by Allan HOPE. Bridge Hill Pub.

2000 (NZ Post)

Senior Fiction Winner
Tessa DUDER. *The Tiggie Thompson Show.* Penguin.

Honour Award
Kate De GOLDI. *Closed, Stranger.* Penguin.

Junior Fiction Winner & Best First Book
Vince FORD. *2Much4U.* Scholastic.

Honour Award
Margaret MAHY. *A Villain's Night Out*, ills Harry HORSE. Penguin.

Children's Book Award & Picture Book Winner
Gavin BISHOP. *The House That Jack Built: Being the Account of Jack Bull Esq., Who Sailed from These Shores to a Land Far Away to Live There and Trade with the Natives of That Said Land 12th Day of September 1798.* Scholastic.

Honour Award
David ELLIOT. *Sydney and the Sea Monster.* Random House.

Children's Choice
Lynley DODD. *Hairy Maclary and Zachary Quack.* Mallinson Rendel.

Non-Fiction Winner
Hirini MELBOURNE. *Te Wao Nui A Tane*, ills Te Maari GARDINER. Huia.

2001 (NZ Post)

Senior Fiction Winner & Book of the Year
Ken CATRAN. *Voyage with Jason.* Lothian Books.

Honour Award
Margaret MAHY. *Twenty-four hours.* Collins.

Junior Fiction Winner
Joy COWLEY. *Shadrach Girl.* Puffin Books.

Honour Award
Jack LASENBY. *The Lies of Harry Wakatipu.* Longacre Press.

Picture Book Winner & Children's Choice
Sue HITCHCOCK. *Oliver in the Garden*, text by Margaret BEAMES. Scholastic.

Honour Award
Philip WEBB. *Dragor, or, How a Dragon Suffering from Prickly Heat Saved the World from Perpetual Winter and Established a Well-known Weed…* , text by Pat QUINN. Scholastic.

Non-Fiction Winner
Colin HOGG. *The Zoo: Meet the Locals.* Random House New Zealand

2002 (NZ Post)

Senior Fiction Winner
Joanna ORWIN. *Owl: A Novel.* Longacre Press.

Junior Fiction Winner
Sandy McKAY. *Recycled*, ills Jenna PACKER. Longacre Press.

Picture Book Winner & Best First Book Illustrator
Chris MOUSDALE. *Brodie*, text by Joy COWLEY. Scholastic.

Children's Choice
Joy WATSON. *Grandpa' s Shorts*, ills Wendy HODDER. Scholastic.

Non-Fiction Winner & Children's Book of the Year
Lloyd Spencer DAVIS. *The Plight of the Penguin.* Longacre Press.

2003 (NZ Post)

Senior Fiction Winner
Margaret MAHY. *Alchemy*. Collins Flamingo.

Junior Fiction Winner & Best First Book
V. M. JONES. *Buddy*. HarperCollins.

Picture Book Winner
David ELLIOT. *Pigtails the Pirate*. Random House.

Children's Choice
Dawn McMILLAN & Bert SIGNAL. *Why do Dogs Sniff Bottoms?*, ills Ross KINNAIRD. Reed.

Non-Fiction Winner & Children's Book of the Year
Robert SULLIVAN. *Weaving the Earth and Sky: Myths & Legends of Aotearoa*, ills Gavin BISHOP. Random House New Zealand.

2004 (NZ Post)

Senior Fiction Winner & Best First Book
Ted DAWE. *Thunder Road*. Longacre Press.

Junior Fiction Winner
V. M. JONES. *Juggling with Mandarins*. HarperCollins.

Picture Book Winner
Pamela ALLEN. *Cuthbert's Babies*. Viking.

Children's Choice
Ngareta GABEL, translated & adapted from Te Reo Maori by Hannah RAINFORTH. *Oh Hogwash, Sweet Pea!*, ills Ali TEO & Astrid JENSEN. Huia.

Non-Fiction Winner & Children's Book of the Year
Janet HUNT. *A Bird in the Hand: Keeping New Zealand Wildlife Safe*. Random House New Zealand.

The M E R Prize for Youth Literature (S. Africa): complete list of winners

1984 Alba BOUWER. *Vlieg, Swaeltjie, Vlieg Ver.* Tafelberg.

1985 Rona RUPERT. *Al Everest se Voëls.* Human & Rousseau.

1986 Dolf van NIEKERK. *Die Haasvanger.* Tafelberg.

1987 No Award

1988 Jenny SEED. *Place Among Stones.* Tafelberg.

1989 Linda RODE (comp.) and Alida BOTHMA (ills). *Goue Fluit My Storie is Uit.* Tafelberg.

1990 Lawrence BRANSBY. *Down Street.* Tafelberg.

1991 Corlia FOURIE. *Die Meisie Wat Soos 'n Bottervoël Ssing/Tintinyane, the Girl Who Sang Like a Magic Bird.* Human & Rousseau.

1992 Nel SWART. *Elk vir Mekander.* Tafelberg.

1993 Allan JERMIESON. *The Delmonico Two O Five.* Tafelberg.

1994 Elizabeth VAN DER MERWE. *Kaljander van die Karoo.* Tafelberg.

1995 Corlia FOURIE. *Die Towersak en Ander Stories.* Human & Rousseau.

1996 Philip de VOS. *Moenie 'n Miele Kiele Nie.* Tafelberg.

1997 Jenny ROBSON. *One Magic Moment.* Tafelberg.

1998 Leon de VILLIERS. *Die Pro.* Tafelberg.

1999 Barrie HOUGH. *Skilpoppe.* Tafelberg.

2000 Freda LINDE. *Eenders en Anders.* Human & Rousseau.

2001 Jan VERMEULEN. *Geraamtes dra Nie Klere Nie.* Tafelberg.

2002 Dianne HOFMEYER. *The Waterbearer.* Tafelberg.

2003 Youth Literature: Jackie NAGTEGAAL. *Daar is Vis in die Punch.* Tafelberg.

Shortlist Children's Fiction
Marianna BRANDT. *Markus Stermuis.* Human & Rousseau.

Martie PRELLER. *Ek is Simon.* Tafelberg.

George WEIDEMAN. *Die Geel Komplot.* Tafelberg.

Shortlist Juvenile Fiction
Carina DIEDERICKS-HUGO. *Koning Henry.* Tafelberg.

Louise PRINSLOO. *Spookhuis by die See.* Human & Rousseau.

Willem van der WALT. *Ragtime en Rocks.* Tafelberg.

M-Net Book Prize (S. Africa): complete list of children's book winners

1991 Leslie BEAKE. *A Cageful of Butterflies.* Maskew Miller Longman.

1992 Tony SPENCER-SMITH. *The Man who Snarled at Flowers.* Tafelberg.

1995 Dianne HOFMEYR. *Boikie. You Better Believe it.* Tafelberg.

M-Net no longer considers children's books for this award.

The Sanlam Prize (S. Africa): complete list of winners (all titles published by Tafelberg)

1985 Theme: Interpersonal Relations.

Gold

English
Eve MERCHANT. *Ghamka-man-of-men.*

Afrikaans
Maretha MAARTENS. *Die Sakmense.*

Silver

English
Peter SLINGSBY. *The Cave.*

Afrikaans
Louis KRÜGER. *Donkerboskind.*

Bronze

English
Desmond GREIG. *Secret of the Eagles.*

Afrikaans
Chris KARSTEN. *Floris Sapiens.*

1988 Theme: Any Historical Theme – as long as it dealt with something that happened at least fifty years ago.

Gold

English
Allan JERMIESON. *Rebecca's Horse.*

Afrikaans
Pieter PIETERSE. *Die Pad na die See.*

Silver

English
Dianne HOFMEYR. *When Whales Go Free.*

Afrikaans
Maretha MAARTENS. *Oor die Nek van die Draak.*

Bronze

English
Nancy OKES. *The Last of the Huguenots.*

Afrikaans
Franci GREYLING. *Dirkie, Drieka, Frederika.*

1990 Theme: Contemporary Background.

Gold

English

Dianne HOFMEYR. *A Red Kite in a Pale Sky.*

Afrikaans

Maretha MAARTENS. *Plek van Dolfyne.*

Silver

English

Michael WILLIAMS. *Into the Valley.*

Afrikaans

Barrie HOUGH. *Droomwa.*

Bronze

English

Jenny WINTER. *Flash Flood.*

Afrikaans

Kowie ROSSOUW. *Wie se Hart Kan Dit dan Hou.*

1992 Theme: Urban Background.

Gold

English

Michael WILLIAMS. *The Genuine Halfmoon Kid.*

Afrikaans

Barrie HOUGH. *Vlerkdans.*

Silver

English

Gail SMITH. *The Slowacki Snoz.*

Afrikaans

George WEIDEMAN. *Los my Uit, Paloekas.*

Bronze

English

Marie THORPE. *Lucy's Game.*

Afrikaans

Maretha MAARTENS. *Spinnekopsomer.*

1994 Theme: Light Approach.

Gold

English

Dianne HOFMEYR. *Boikie, You Better Believe It.*

Afrikaans

George WEIDEMAN. *Die Optog van die Aftjoppers.*

Silver
English
Jenny ROBSON. *Don't panic, Mechanic.*

Afrikaans
Martie PRELLER. *Anderkantland.*

Bronze
English
Ada-Marie HAUPTFLEISCH. *Rollercoaster.*

Afrikaans
Tertia BOTHA. *Rebel.*

1996 (Five prizes of equal importance) – Theme: Any Theme that deals with Sport or the Outdoors.

Betsie van NIEKERK. *Gamkab.*

Martie PRELLER. *In die Tyd van die Esob.*

Jenny ROBSON. *One Magic Moment.*

Peter SLINGSBY. *The Joining.*

Gail SMITH. *Wheels!*

1998 Theme: Any Theme that dealt with the End of the Century, the Millennium and the Beginning of the New Century.

English
Jenny ROBSON. *The Denials of Kow-Ten.*

Robin SAUNDERS. *Sons of Anubis.*

Beginner
Johnny MASILELA. *Zanemvula the Rain Child.*

Afrikaans
Elsa HAMERSMA. *Die Teken van Crux.*

Barrie HOUGH. *Skilpoppe.*

George WEIDEMAN. *Dana se Jaar Duisend.*

Beginner
Anina SCHULTZ. *Reg, Kommandant!*

2000 **Theme: a Story that dealt with Issues such as "the Community and the Individual", "the Loner and the Group Person", "Herd Animal and Outsider", "Western Individualism and Ubuntu", "Alienation and Belonging", et cetera.**

Gold
English
Jenny ROBSON. *Because Pula Means Rain.*

Afrikaans
Jan VERMEULEN. *Geraamtes dra nie Klere Nie.*

Nguni-languages
No prize awarded

Sotho-languages
No prize awarded

Silver
English
Sarah BRITTEN. *The Worst Year of My Life – So Far.*

Afrikaans
Rena SCHÜLER. *Die Somervakansie Wat te Lank Was.*

Nguni-languages
Zibele SISUSA. *Isahluko Sokugqibela* (*The Last Chapter*). (Xhosa).

Sotho-languages
Kabelo KGATEA. *Njeng Manong Fa ke Sule!* (*Devour Me, Vultures, When I'm Dead!*). (Tswana).

2002 **Theme: a Story with an Upbeat Approach.**

Gold
English
Peter SLINGSBY. *Jedro's bane.*

Afrikaans
Marita van der VYVER. *Die Ongelooflike Avonture van Hanna Hoekom.*

Nguni languages
No prize awarded

Sotho languages
No prize awarded

Silver
English
Sarah BRITTEN. *Welcome to the Martin Tudhope Show.*

Afrikaans
No prize awarded

Nguni languages
Dumisani SIBIYA. *Kungasa Ngifile* (*Over my dead body*).

Sotho languages
Kabelo KGATEA. *Leba Seipone* (*Look in the mirror*).

Chapter 12: Around the World: English-language children's book awards in Australia, Canada, Eire/Republic of Ireland, New Zealand & South Africa.

Four of the five countries dealt with here have more than one official language and so offer prizes in languages other than English. In the case of awards where there are categories in each language, or where the prize may be won by a book in any of the languages of the country, I have listed the non-English language winners along with the English-language ones. If an award is solely for the non-English language, as for instance the Scheepers Prize (South Africa) for Afrikaans literature for adolescents, I have not included it at all. Canada (French) and Eire (Irish Gaelic) both have sections within their major awards for the non-English language, and these are shown in the lists below. In New Zealand there is increasing range of titles available in Te Reo Māori and several picture books are dual language, or have editions simultaneously published in both languages.

Some countries have a large number of awards, aimed at different age groups or set up for purposes of commercial gain as well as the promotion of literary merit. Australia has awards for the different age groups; Canada is particularly rich in the number of awards which are available, though, as will be seen, a number of titles appear in more than one list. In South Africa too there are several awards. Only three South African awards are considered in this chapter, as the others are commercially sponsored, and so will be found in Chapter 11. Ireland has two major awards for children's books, but as one is commercially sponsored, it too has been dealt with in Chapter 11. Some of the awards listed in this chapter are of fairly recent origin, but Australia and New Zealand each have a history of prizes which goes back to the immediate post-war years, as they followed the lead of the UK and US librarians. Awards made in Australia, Canada and New Zealand specifically for non-fiction are treated in Chapter 10, leaving this chapter to list the respective countries' equivalents, in so far as they exist, of the Carnegie and Greenaway Medals.

The countries considered within this chapter include those from the British Commonwealth: parts of the dismembered British Empire. It is interesting to see how far they still look to the UK in terms of their children's books, if that is indeed the case, or whether they turn more to the US. Some authors and illustrators, in particular Margaret Mahy of New Zealand and Patricia Wrightson, Gregory Rogers, Jan Ormerod and Bob Graham of Australia, may also be seen in the Carnegie and Greenaway listings (Chapters 4 and 6), as these awards are open to all-comers as long as the book receives first or simultaneous co-publication in the UK. In the course of this chapter each of the five countries will be taken in turn, in strictly alphabetical order, with some commentary on the award scene in that country, and on the books which have won the awards there, followed by that country's award lists.

There has been considerable discussion of the perceived problem of whether a book judged as 'the best' or 'the most distinguished', or whatever the criteria may state, really is a book for children. Each country brings a different viewpoint, and the split in age-groups which the Children's Book Council of Australia Book of the Year awards have relatively recently decided upon is one way to solve the difficulty. Canada, too, has unashamedly gone for the multiplicity produced by splitting the librarian-judged 'establishment' awards. By contrast, in the US and UK, children's librarians until recently seemed to feel that it would devalue their awards to divide them into age-group sub-sections. This would seem particularly true of the Carnegie Medal administrators (Chapter 4), though the recently established Booktrust Teenage Book Prize (UK) and Michael L. Printz Award (US) go some way towards countering this.

Several of the winning titles from these five countries have been published in the UK and US, perhaps because of their award-winning status. They contribute extra range and depth to the available reading for children brought up in a different set of experiences.

Australia

The Children's Book Council of Australia Book of the Year (Older and Younger Readers); Children's Book Council of Australia Picture Book of the Year; The Children's Book Council of Australia Book of the Year – Early Childhood Award

Established in 1946, the Australian Children's Book Award was administered by a number of Australian state agencies until the formation of the Australian Children's Book Council in 1959 made it possible to establish an all-Australian Book of the Year Award. In 1952 a category for the picture books was created, a Younger Readers category added in 1982 and the Early Childhood Award in 2001, so there are now four awards administered by the Children's Book Council of Australia. The Picture Book of the Year Award was first given in 1956. In 1974, an award for the Best Illustrated Children's Book of the Year was added; this award was also administered by the Australian Children's Book Council, and sponsored and selected by the Visual Art Board of the Australian Council for the Arts, but was discontinued as of 1977. I have listed the Visual Art winners alongside the Picture Book of the year winners for the appropriate years. All these awards are open to books written or, in the case of the Picture Book of the Year illustrated by, Australians or residents of Australia, and published in Australia. The Eve Pownall Award for Non-Fiction is considered in Chapter 10 along with the other non-fiction awards.

Some of the names appearing on the Book of the Year lists are familiar throughout the world as quality writers in English. Peter Carey is probably better-known for his adult novels, and is a Booker Prize winner, but appears in the Honours listing for the 1996 Book of the Year for Younger Readers with *The Big Bazoohley*. Gary Crew, in *Strange Objects* (ACO 1991), shows the reader a collection of seemingly unrelated papers, diary entries – both contemporary and from the seventeenth century, police and medical reports. These are strange objects in themselves, which build a fascinating and rather spooky mystery story. Crew juxtaposes the storyline of a modern teenager's account of his discovery of an Aboriginal sacred relic with the fictionalised story of an actual survivor from the *Batavia*, a real ship which was wrecked off the Western Australian Coast in 1629. The combination of the supernatural, a realistic teenager's experience and the known historical event that two people were punished by being left as castaways from the *Batavia*, make a compelling teenage novel. Yet Crew has also produced texts for winning picture books of the year (ACP 1994 & 1995: ACP Honour 2000). Ruth Park's *Playing Beatie Bow* (ACO 1981) was also a Boston Globe-Horn Book Award-winner (Fiction) in 1982. Judith Clarke's *Wolf on the Fold* (ACO 2001) was very successful in the Northern hemisphere and Sonia Hartnett (ACO 2002 for *Forest* and ACO Honour 1996 for *Sleeping Dogs*) is well-known in UK and US. Garth Nix (ACO Honour 2004) is also achieving worldwide success with his fantasy novels.

Among the illustrators, Ron Brooks (ACP 1974, 1978 & 2001: ACP Commended 1977), Pamela Allen (ACP 1983 & 1984; ACP Commended 1979; ACP Honour 1993; ACE 2004; ACE Honour 2003) and Bob Graham (ACP 1988, 1991 & 1993; ACP Commended 1986; ACP Honour 1990; ACE 2002; ACE Honour 2001; GRE 2002; GRE Highly Commended 1998) are acclaimed in the world of UK children's picture books, and Gregory Rogers, yet to appear in the Australian award lists, was a Greenaway Medallist with *Way Home* in 1994. Libby Hathorn, the author of *Way Home*, has appeared in the Honour lists for both Older and Younger reader categories of the Book of the Year (ACO Honour 1990; ACY Honours 1987 & 1988). In recent years the Picture Book of the Year Award has several times been given to a picture book for older readers. The Early Childhood Book of the Year has perhaps been introduced to compensate for this trend. It is a development that reflects both the worldwide popularity of graphic novels and the increasing ability of children to interpret pictures as fluently as they read text, a facility that comes from the multiplicity of visual stimuli that now surround them.

There is a long-standing tradition of major publishing houses having Australian as well as US and UK branches. This means that Australian authors and illustrators are able to look to the Northern hemisphere as well as their home market for outlets for their work. Thus a lively literary scene is ensured. It is good for children's literature generally that many of the names that appear in the following lists are well-known on a world-wide basis.

Children's Book Council of Australia Book of the Year (since 1987, Book of the Year – Older Readers): complete list of winners and honour books

1946 Leslie REES. *The Story of Karrawingi*, the Emu. John Sands.

1947 No Award

1948 Frank HURLEY. *Shackleton's Argonauts.* Angus & Robertson.

Highly Commended
Veronica BASSER. *Ponny the Penguin*, ills Edwina BELL. Australasian Publishing.

Ada JACKSON. *Beetles Ahoy!*, ills Nina POYNTON. Patersons Press.

J. H. & W. D. MARTIN. *The Australian Book of Trains*, ills with photographs. Angus & Robertson.

Musette MORELL. *Bush Cobbers*, ills Edwina BELL. Australasian Publishing.

Leslie REES. *The Story of Shadow, the Rock Wallaby*, ills Walter CUNNINGHAM. John Sands.

1949 No Competition

1950 Alan VILLIERS. *Whalers of the Midnight Sun.* Angus & Robertson.

Highly Commended
Dora BIRTLES. *Bonza the Bull.* Shakespeare Head.

Dale COLLINS. *Bush Holiday*, ills Sheila HAWKINS. William Heinemann.

Dale COLLINS. *Bush Voyage*, ills Margaret HORDER. William Heinemann.

Jane Ada FLETCHER. *Little Brown Piccaninnies of Tasmania*, ills Margaret SENIOR. John Sands.

Bernard O'REILLY. *Wild River.* Cassell.

Leslie REES. *Bluecap and Bimbi: The Blue Wrens*, ills Walter CUNNINGHAM. Trinity House.

Leslie REES. *The Story of Kurri Kurri the Kookaburra*, ills Margaret SENIOR. John Sands.

Esmée RICE. *The Secret Family*, ills Pixie O'HARRIS. Angus & Robertson.

Special Mention
Dagma DAWSON. *Ladybird Garden.* Australasian Publishing.

1951 Ruth WILLIAMS. *Verity of Sydney Town.* Angus & Robertson.

Highly Commended
William Allan McNAIR. *Starland of the South*, ills William R. TAPLIN. Angus & Robertson.

Commended
Allan ALDOUS. *Kiewa Adventure.* Oxford University Press.

Richard H. GRAVES. *Spear and Stockwhip.* Dymocks.

Nourma HANDFORD. *Carcoola.* Dymocks.

Erle WILSON. *Churinga Tales: Stories of Alchuringa – The Dreamtime of the Australian Aborigines*, ills Sally MEDWORTH. Australasian Publishing.

1952 Eve POWNALL. *The Australia Book.* John Sands.

Highly Commended
Eve POWNALL. *Cousins-Come-Lately: Adventures in Old Sydney Town*, ills Margaret SENIOR. Shakespeare Head.

VARIOUS AUTHORS. Blue Wren Books [Series of 10 titles], ills Margaret HORDER. Angus & Robertson.

Commended
Nourma HANDFORD. *Carcoola Adventure.* Dymocks.

William HATFIELD. *Wild Dog Frontier.* Oxford University Press.

1953 **Joint Winners**
J. H. & W. D. MARTIN. *Aircraft of Today & Tomorrow.* Angus & Robertson.

Joan PHIPSON. *Good Luck to the Rider.* Angus & Robertson.

1954 K. L. PARKER. *Australian Legendary Tales.* Angus & Robertson.

Highly Commended
Fitzmaurice HILL. *Southward Ho with the Hentys.* Whitcombe & Tombs.

Frank NORTON. *Fighting Ships of Australia & New Zealand.* Angus & Robertson.

1955 H. A. LINDSAY & N. B. TINDALE. *The First Walkabout.* Kestrel.

Highly Commended
Mary Elwyn PATCHETT. *Wild Brother*, ills John ROSE. Collins.

Commended
Helen G. PALMER & Jessie MacLEOD. *The First Hundred Years*, ills Harold FREEMAN. Longmans, Green.

1956 Patricia WRIGHTSON. *The Crooked Snake.* Angus & Robertson.

Highly Commended
Doris CHADWICK. *John of the "Sirius"*, ills Margaret SENIOR. Nelson.

Ken DALZIEL. *Penguin Road*, ills Frank NORTON. Angus & Robertson.

Lyla STEVENS. *Birds of Australia*, ills Anne LISSENDEN. Whitcombe & Tombs.

1957 Enid MOODIE-HEDDLE. *The Boomerang Book of Legendary Tales.* Kestrel.

Highly Commended
Mavis Thorpe CLARK. *The Brown Land was Green*, ills Genevieve MELROSE. Heinemann.

Enid MOODIE-HEDDLE (ed.). *The Boomerang Book of Australian Poetry*, ills M. R. DODS. Longmans, Green.

Helen G. PALMER & Jessie MacLEOD. *Makers of the First Hundred Years*, ills Pamela LINDSAY. Longmans, Green.

1958 Nan CHAUNCY. *Tiger in the Bush.* Oxford U. P.

Highly Commended
Lyndsay GARDENER. *Pacific Peoples*, ills Nancy PARKER. Longmans, Green.

Joan PHIPSON. *It Happened One Summer*, ills Margaret HORDER. Angus & Robertson.

1959 **Joint Winners**
Nan CHAUNCY. *Devil's Hill.* Oxford U. P.

John GUNN. *Sea Menace.* Constable.

Highly Commended
Elyne MITCHELL. *The Silver Brumby*, ills Ralph THOMSON. Hutchinson.

Commended
Frank NORTON. *Australia and New Zealand Ships of Today*, ills author. Angus & Robertson.

Eve POWNALL. *Exploring Australia*, ills Noela YOUNG. Methuen.

Patricia WRIGHTSON. *The Bunyip Hole*, ills Margaret HORDER. Angus & Robertson.

1960 Kylie TENNANT. *All the Proud Tribesmen*, ills Clem SEALE. Macmillan.

Commended
Dale COLLINS. *Anzac Adventure: The Story of Gallipoli Told for Young Readers*, ills Frank NORTON. Angus & Robertson.

Eleanor SPENCE. *The Summer in Between*, ills Marcia LANE-FOSTER. Oxford U. P.

Norman B. TINDALE & Harold Arthur LINDSAY. *Rangatira (The High-born)*, ills Douglas F. MAXTED. Rigby.

1961 Nan CHAUNCY. *Tangara*. Oxford U. P.

Commended
Allan ALDOUS. *Doctor with Wings*, ills Roger PAYNE. Brockhampton Press.

Elyne MITCHELL. *Silver Brumby's Daughter*, ills Grace HUXTABLE. Hutchinson of London.

Eleanor SPENCE. *Lillypilly Hill*, ills Susan EINZIG. Oxford U. P.

1962 **Joint Winners**
H. L. EVERS. *The Racketty Street Gang*. Hodder & Stoughton.

Joan WOODBERY. *Rafferty Rides a Winner.* Parrish.

Commended
Ruth PARK. *The Hole in the Hill*, ills Jennifer MURRAY. Ure Smith.

Betty ROLAND. *The Forbidden Bridge*, ills Geraldine SPENCE. Bodley Head.

Colin THIELE. *The Sun on the Stubble*. Rigby.

1963 Joan PHIPSON. *The Family Conspiracy*. Angus & Robertson.

Highly Commended
Robin HILL. *Bushland and Seashore: An Australian Nature Adventure*. Lansdowne Press.

Commended
Raymond Maxwell CRAWFORD. *A Picture History of Australia*, ills Clarke HUTTON. Oxford U. P.

Frank KELLAWAY. *The Quest for Golden Dan*, ills Deborah WHITE. Cheshire.

John WOTHERSPOON. *The Australian Pet Book*, photographs A. F. FLASHMAN. Lansdowne Press.

Patricia WRIGHTSON. *The Feather Star*, ills Noela YOUNG. Hutchinson of London.

1964 Eleanor SPENCE. *The Green Laurel.* Oxford U. P.

Highly Commended
Nan CHAUNCY. *The Roaring 40*, ills Annette MACARTHUR-ONSLOW. Oxford U. P.

Commended
Irene GOUGH. *One Sunday Morning Early*, ills Noela YOUNG. Ure Smith.

Carol ODELL. *Fires and Firemen*, ills photographs. Angus & Robertson.

Joan PHIPSON. *Threat to the Barkers*, ills Margaret HORDER. Constable Young Books.

Betty ROLAND. *Jamie's Discovery*, ills Geraldine SPENCE. Bodley Head.

Colin THIELE. *Storm Boy*, ills John BAILY. Rigby.

1965 Hesba F. BRINSMEAD. *Pastures of the Blue Crane.* Oxford U. P.

Highly Commended
Elyne MITCHELL. *Winged Skis*, ills Annette MACARTHUR-ONSLOW. Hutchinson of London.

Betty ROLAND. *Jamie's Summer Visitor*, ills Prudence SEWARD. Bodley Head.

Commended
Nan CHAUNCY. *High and Haunted Island*, ills Victor G. AMBRUS. Oxford U. P.

Mary DURACK. *The Courteous Savage: Yagan of Swan River*, ills Elizabeth DURACK. Thomas Nelson and Sons.

Nuri MASS. *The Wonderland of Nature.* Writers' Press.

Carol ODELL. *A Day at the Zoo*, ills photographs. Angus & Robertson.

1966 Ivan SOUTHALL. *Ash Road.* Angus & Robertson.

Highly Commended
Reginald OTTLEY. *By the Sandhills of Yamboorah*, ills Clyde PEARSON. André Deutsch.

Commended
Ivan SOUTHALL. *Indonesian Journey*, ills photographs. Lansdowne Press.

Eleanor SPENCE. *The Year of the Currawong*, ills Gareth FLOYD. Oxford U. P.

Colin THIELE. *February Dragon.* Rigby.

1967 Mavis Thorpe CLARK. *The Min Min.* Landsdowne.

Highly Commended
Celia SYRED. *Dick Cocky's Castle*, ills Astra LACIS. Angus & Robertson.

Commended
Jean CHAPMAN. *The Wish Cat*, drawings Noela YOUNG; photographs Dean HAY. Angus & Robertson.

Max FATCHEN. *The River Kings*, ills Clyde PEARSON. Methuen.

Irene GOUGH. *The Golden Lamb*, ills Joy MURRAY. Heinemann.

Reginald OTTLEY. *The Roan Colt of Yamboorah*, ills David PARRY. André Deutsch.

Special Mention
H. F. BRINSMEAD. *Beat of the City*, ills William PAPAS. Oxford U. P.

1968 Ivan SOUTHALL. *To the Wild Sky.* Angus & Robertson.

Highly Commended
Randolph STOW. *Midnite: The Story of a Wild Colonial Boy*, ills Ralph STEADMAN. Cheshire.

Commended
Nan CHAUNCY. *Mathinna's People*, ills Victor G. AMBRUS. Oxford U. P.

Mavis Thorpe CLARK. *Blue Above the Trees*, ills Genevieve MELROSE. Lansdowne Press.

Ivan SOUTHALL. *The Fox Hole*, ills Ian RIBBONS. Hicks Smith/Methuen.

1969 Margaret BALDERSON. *When Jays Fly to Barbmo.* Oxford U. P.

Highly Commended
Patricia WRIGHTSON. *'I Own the Racecourse!'*, ills Margaret HORDER. Hutchinson of London.

Commended
George FINKEL. *The 'Loyall Virginian'.* Angus & Robertson.

John GOODE. *Wood, Wire and Fabric: A Saga of Australian Flying*, ills photographs. Lansdowne Press.

Jack POLLARD. *Cricket the Australian Way*, ills photographs. Lansdowne Press.

Roland ROBINSON. *Wandjina: Children of the Dreamtime: Aboriginal Myths and Legends*, ills Roderick SHAW. Jacaranda.

Ivan SOUTHALL. *Let the Balloon Go*, ills Ian RIBBONS. Methuen.

Phyl & Noel WALLACE. *Children of the Desert*, ills photographs. Nelson Australia.

1970 Annette MACARTHUR-ONSLOW. *Uhu.* Ure Smith.

Highly Commended
Colin THIELE. *Blue Fin*, ills Roger HALDANE. Rigby.

Commended
Deirdre HILL. *Over the Bridge*, ills James HUNT. Hutchinson.

Reginald OTTLEY. *The Bates Family.* Collins.

Marjory Collard O'DEA. *Six Days Between a Second*, ills Jonathon WAUD. Heinemann.

Ivan SOUTHALL. *Finn's Folly.* Angus & Robertson.

Peter WESLEY-SMITH. *The Ombley-Gombley*, ills David FIELDING. Angus & Robertson.

1971 Ivan SOUTHALL. *Bread and Honey.* Angus & Robertson.

Highly Commended
Hui-Min LO. *The Story of China*, ills Elaine HAXTON. Angus & Robertson.

Commended
George FINKEL. *James Cook, Royal Navy*, ills Amnon SADUBIN. Angus & Robertson.

Lilith NORMAN. *Climb a Lonely Hill.* Collins.

1972 Hesba F. BRINSMEAD. *Longtime Passing.* Angus & Robertson.

Highly Commended
Christobel MATTINGLEY. *The Windmill at Magpie Creek*, ills Gavin ROWE. Brockhampton.

Commended
David MARTIN. *Hughie*, ills Ron BROOKS. Nelson Australia.

Favourable Mention
Christobel MATTINGLEY. *Worm Weather*, ills Carolyn DINAN. Hamilton.

Annette MACARTHUR-ONSLOW. *Minnie.* Ure Smith.

1973 Noreen SHELLY. *Family at the Lookout.* Oxford U. P.

Highly Commended
Patricia WRIGHTSON. *An Older Kind of Magic*, ills Noela YOUNG. Hutchinson.

Commended
Meredith HOOPER. *Everyday Inventions.* Angus & Robertson.

1974 Patricia WRIGHTSON. *The Nargun and the Stars.* Hutchinson.

Highly Commended
Max FATCHEN. *The Spirit Wind*, ills Trevor STUBLEY. Hicks Smith.

Commended
Colin THIELE. *The Fire in the Stone.* Rigby.

Special Award
Jenny WAGNER. *The Bunyip of Berkeley's Creek*, ills Ron BROOKS. Longman Young.

1975 No Winner

Highly Commended
Ruth PARK. *Callie's Castle*, ills Kilmeny NILAND. Angus & Robertson.

Commended
Noreen SHELLEY. *Faces in a Looking-Glass*, ills Astra LACIS. Oxford U. P.

Colin THIELE. *Magpie Island*, ills Roger HALDANE. Rigby.

Colin THIELE. *Uncle Gustav's Ghosts.* Rigby.

1976 Ivan SOUTHALL. *Fly West.* Angus & Robertson.

Highly Commended
Margaret BALDERSON. *A Dog called George*, ills Nikki JONES. Oxford U. P.

Worthy of Mention
Nance DONKIN. *Patchwork Grandmother*, ills Mary DINSDALE. Hamilton.

David MARTIN. *Mister P and his Remarkable Flight*, ills Astra LACIS. Hodder & Stoughton.

Special Mention
Simon FRENCH. *Hey Phantom*, ills Alex NICHOLAS. Singlet/Angus & Robertson.

1977 Eleanor SPENCE. *The October Child.* Oxford U. P.

Highly Commended
Joan PHIPSON. *The Cats.* Macmillan.

Commended
Celia SYRED. *Hebe's Daughter.* Hodder & Stoughton.

1978 Patricia WRIGHTSON. *The Ice is Coming.* Hutchinson Australia.

Highly Commended
Eleanor SPENCE. *A Candle for Saint Antony.* Oxford U. P.

Commended
Jack BENNETT. *The Lieutenant: An Epic Tale of Courage and Endurance on the High Seas.* Angus & Robertson.

Thomas Albert ROY. *The Curse of the Turtle*, ills Rex BACKHAUS-SMITH. Bodley Head.

1979 Ruth MANLEY. *The Plum-Rain Scroll*, ills Marianne YAMAGUCHI. Hodder & Stoughton Australia.

Highly Commended
Bill SCOTT. *Boori*, ills A. M. HICKS. Oxford U. P.

Commended
Ted GREENWOOD. *The Pochetto Coat*, ills Ron BROOKS. Hutchinson of Australia.

Ruth PARK. *Come Danger, Come Darkness.* Hodder & Stoughton.

1980 Lee HARDING. *Displaced Person.* Hyland House.

Highly Commended
Hesba F. BRINSMEAD. *Once There was a Swagman*, ills Noela YOUNG. Oxford U. P.

Commended
Don GOODSIR. *The Gould League Book of Australian Birds*, ills Tony OLIVER. Golden Press.

Colin THIELE. *River Murray Mary*, ills Robert INGPEN. Opal Books, Rigby.

1981 Ruth PARK. *Playing Beatie Bow.* Nelson.

Highly Commended
Bill SCOTT. *Darkness Under the Hills*, ills A. M. HICKS. Oxford U. P.

Commended
Barbara BOLTON. *Jandy Malone and the Nine O'Clock Tiger*, ills Alan WHITE. Angus & Robertson.

Eleanor SPENCE. *The Seventh Pebble*, ills Sisca VERWOERT. Oxford U. P.

1982 Colin THIELE. *Valley Between.* Rigby.

Highly Commended
Patricia WRIGHTSON. *Behind the Wind.* Hutchinson.

Commended
Simon FRENCH. *Cannily, Cannily.* Angus & Robertson.

Christobel MATTINGLEY. *Rummage*, ills Patricia MULLINS. Angus & Robertson.

1983 Victor KELLEHER. *Master of the Grove.* Kestrel.

Highly Commended
Eleanor SPENCE. *The Left Overs.* Methuen.

Commended
Morris LURIE. *Toby's Millions*, ills Arthur HORNER. Kestrel.

Nadia WHEATLEY. *Five Times Dizzy*, ills Neil PHILLIPS. Oxford U. P.

1984 Patricia WRIGHTSON. *A Little Fear.* Hutchinson.

Highly Commended
Robin KLEIN. *Penny Pollard's Diary*, ills Ann JAMES. Oxford U. P.

Commended
Helen FRANCES *pseud.* [Helen GRANGER & Frances PEARCE]. *The Devil's Stone*, ills Kerry ARGENT. Omnibus.

Frank WILLMOTT. *Breaking Up.* Collins.

1985 James ALDRIDGE. *True Story of Lilli Stubeck.* Hyland.

Highly Commended
Libby GLEESON. *Eleanor, Elizabeth.* Angus & Robertson.

Commended
Eleanor SPENCE. *Me & Jeshua*, ills Shane CONROY. Dove.

Nadia WHEATLEY. *Dancing in the Anzac Deli*, ills Waldemar BUCZYNSKI, [based on a screenplay by Nadia WHEATLEY & Terry LARSEN]. Oxford U. P.

1986 Thurley FOWLER. *The Green Wind.* Rigby.

Highly commended
Alan BAILLIE, *Little Brother.* Nelson.

Commended
David LAKE. *The Changelings of Chaan.* Hyland House.

Nadia WHEATLEY. *The House that was Eureka.* Viking Kestrel.

1987 Simon FRENCH. *All We Know.* Angus & Robertson.

Honour Books
Victor KELLEHER. *Taronga.* Viking Kestrel.

Gillian RUBINSTEIN. *Space Demons.* Omnibus/Penguin.

1988 John MARSDEN. *So Much to Tell You.* Walter McVitty Books.

Honour Books
Libby GLEESON. *I am Susannah.* Angus & Robertson.

Eleanor SPENCE. *Deezle Boy.* Collins Dove.

1989 Gillian RUBINSTEIN. *Beyond the Labyrinth.* Hyland House.

Honour Books
Caroline MACDONALD. *The Lake at the End of the World.* Viking Kestrel.

Gillian RUBINSTEIN. *Answers to Brut.* Omnibus Puffin.

1990 Robin KLEIN. *Came Back to Show You I Could Fly.* Viking/Kestrel.

Honour Books
Brian CASWELL. *Merryll of the Stones.* University of Queensland Press.

Libby HATHORN. *Thunderwith.* William Heinemann Australia.

1991 Gary CREW. *Strange Objects.* William Heinemann Australia.

Honour Books
Isobelle CARMODY. *The Farseekers.* Penguin Australia.

Victor KELLEHER. *Brother Night.* Penguin Australia.

Eleanor SPENCE. *The Family Book of Mary Claire.* Collins Dove.

1992 Eleanor NILSSON. *The House Guest.* Viking.

Honour Books
Simon FRENCH. *Change the Locks.* Ashton Scholastic.

Kate WALKER. *Peter.* Omnibus Books.

1993 Melina MARCHETTA. *Looking for Alibrandi.* Penguin Australia.

Honour Books
Sue GOUGH. *A Long Way to Tipperary.* University of Queensland Press.

Gillian RUBINSTEIN. *Galax-Arena.* Hyland House.

1994 **Joint Winners**
Isobelle CARMODY. *The Gathering.* Penguin Australia.

Gary CREW. *Angel's Gate.* Heinemann.

Honour Book
James MOLONEY. *Dougy.* University of Queensland Press.

1995 Gillian RUBINSTEIN. *Foxspell.* Hyland House.

Honour books

James MOLONEY. *Gracey.* University of Queensland Press.

Nadia WHEATLEY. *The Night Tolkien Died.* Random House Australia.

1996 Catherine JINKS. *Pagan's Vows.* Omnibus Books.

Honour Books

Ursula DUBOSARSKY. *The First Book of Samuel.* Penguin Australia.

Sonya HARTNETT. *Sleeping Dogs.* Penguin Books Australia.

1997 James MOLONEY. *A Bridge to Wiseman's Cove.* University of Queensland Press.

Honour Books

David METZENTHEN. *Johnny Hart's Heroes.* Penguin Australia.

Wendy ORR. *Peeling the Onion.* Little Ark/Allen & Unwin.

1998 Catherine JINKS. *Eye to Eye.* Penguin Australia.

Honour Books

David METZENTHEN. *Gilbert's Ghost Train.* Scholastic.

Tim WINTON. *Lockie Leonard, Legend.* Pan Macmillan.

1999 Phillip GWYNNE. *Deadly, Unna?* Penguin Australia.

Honour Books
Judith CLARKE. *Night Train.* Penguin Australia.

Sarah WALKER. *Camphor Laurel.* Pan Macmillan.

2000 Nick EARLS. *48 Shades of Brown.* Penguin Australia.

Honour Books
Helen BARNES. *Killing Aurora.* Penguin Australia.

Anna FIENBERG. *Borrowed Light.* Allen & Unwin.

2001 Judith CLARKE. *Wolf on the Fold.* Silverfish, Duffy & Snellgrove.

Honour Books
Bill CONDON. *Dogs.* Hodder Headline.

Markus ZUSAK. *Fighting Ruben Wolfe.* Omnibus Books.

2002 Sonya HARTNETT. *Forest.* Viking, Penguin Books Australia.

Honour Books
Joanne HORNIMAN. *Mahalia.* Allen & Unwin.

Markus ZUSAK. *When Dogs Cry.* Pan Macmillan Australia.

2003 Markus ZUSAK. *The Messenger.* Pan Macmillan Australia.

Honour Books
Catherine BATESON. *Painted Love Letters.* University of Queensland Press.

Alyssa BRUGMAN. *Walking Naked.* Allen & Unwin.

2004 Melina MARCHETTA. *Saving Francesca.* Viking, Penguin Books Australia.

Honour Books
David METZENTHEN. *Boys of Blood & Bone.* Penguin Books Australia.

Garth NIX. *Mister Monday* (Keys to the Kingdom, Bk. 1). Allen & Unwin.

Children's Book Council of Australia Book of the Year – Younger Readers (CBCA JUNIOR Book of the Year 1982-1996): complete list of winners

1982 Christobel MATTINGLEY. *Rummage*, ills Patricia MULLINS.

1983 Robin KLEIN. *Thing*, ills Alison LESTER. Oxford U. P.

1984 Max DANN. *Bernice Knows Best*, ills Ann JAMES. Oxford U. P.

1985 Emily RODDA. *Something Special*, ills Noela YOUNG. Angus & Robertson.

1986 Mary STEELE. *Arkwright.* Hyland House.

1987 Emily RODDA. *Pigs Might Fly*, ills Noela YOUNG. Angus & Robertson.

Honour Books
Libby HATHORN. *All about Anna, Harriet Christopher and me.* Methuen.

Doug MacLEOD. *Sister Madge's Book of Nuns*, ills Craig SMITH. Omnibus .

1988 Nadia WHEATLEY. *My Place*, ills Donna RAWLINS. Collins Dove.

Honour Books
Max FATCHEN. *A Paddock of Poems.* Omnibus Penguin.

Libby HATHORN. *Looking out for Sampson.* Oxford Univ. Press.

1989 Emily RODDA. *The Best Kept Secret.* Angus & Robertson.

Honour Books
Joan GRANT (ed.). *Australopedia: How Australia Works After 200 Years of Other People Living Here*, designed by Keith ROBERTSON. McPhee Gribble-Penguin.

Gillian RUBINSTEIN. *Melanie and the Night Animal.* Omnibus Puffin.

1990 Jeanie ADAMS. *Pigs and Honey.* Omnibus Books.

Honour Books
Ian EDWARDS. *Papa and the Olden Days*, ills Rachel TONKIN. William Heinemann Australia.

Kate WALKER. *The Dragon of Mith*, ills Laurie SHARPE. Allen & Unwin.

1991 Emily RODDA. *Finders Keepers.* Omnibus.

Honour Books
Robin KLEIN. *Boris and Borsch*, ills Cathy WILCOX. Allen & Unwin.

Leone PEGUERO. *Mervyn's Revenge*, ills Shirley PETERS. Margaret Hamilton.

1992 Anna FIENBERG. *The Magnificent Nose, and Other Marvels*, ills Kim GAMBLE. Allen & Unwin.

Honour Book
Morris GLEITZMAN. *Misery Guts.* Pan.

1993 Garry DISHER. *The Bamboo Flute*. Collins/Angus & Robertson.

Honour Books
Morris GLEITZMAN. *Blabber Mouth.* Pan Macmillan.

Nette HILTON. *The Web*, ills Kerry MILLARD. Collins/Angus & Robertson.

1994 Emily RODDA. *Rowan of Rin*. Omnibus.

Honour Books
Elizabeth HONEY. *Honey Sandwich.* Allen & Unwin.

Nadia WHEATLEY. *Lucy in the Leap Year*, ills Ken SEARLE. Omnibus.

1995 Wendy ORR. *Ark in the Park*, ills Kerry MILLARD. HarperCollins/Angus & Robertson.

Honour books
Jackie FRENCH. *Somewhere Around the Corner.* HarperCollins/Angus & Robertson.

Anthony HILL. *The Burnt Stick*, ills Mark SOFILAS. Viking/Penguin Australia.

1996 James MOLONEY. *Swashbuckler.* University of Queensland Press.

Honour Books
Peter CAREY. *The Big Bazoohley.* University of Queensland Press.

Elizabeth HONEY. *45 & 47 Stella St and Everything that Happened.* Allen & Unwin.

1997 Libby GLEESON. *Hannah Plus One*, ills Ann JAMES. Puffin, Penguin.

Honour Books
Elizabeth HONEY. *Don't Pat the Wombat*, ills William CLARKE. Little Ark, Allen & Unwin.

Emily RODDA. *Rowan and the Keeper of the Crystal.* Omnibus.

1998 Elaine FORRESTAL. *Someone Like Me.* Puffin, Penguin.

Honour Books
Odo HIRSCH. *Antonio S and the Mystery of Theodore Guzman*, ills Andrew McLEAN. Little Ark, Allen & Unwin.

Patricia WRIGHTSON. *Rattler's Place*, ills David COX. Puffin Aussie Bites, Penguin.

1999 Meme McDONALD & Boori PRYOR. *My Girragundji*, photos Meme McDONALD. Little Ark, Allen & Unwin.

Honour Books
Nette HILTON. *A Ghost of a Chance*, ills Chantal STEWART. Puffin.

Emily RODDA. *Bob the Builder and the Elves*, ills Craig SMITH. ABC Books.

2000 Jackie FRENCH. *Hitler's Daughter.* A&R, HarperCollins.

Honour Books
Libby GLEESON. *Hannah and the Tomorrow Room*, ills Ann JAMES. Puffin.

James ROY. *Captain Mack.* Storybridge, University of Queensland Press.

2001 Diana KIDD. *Two Hands Together.* Penguin Books.

Honour Books
Errol BROOME. *Away with the Birds.* Fremantle Arts Centre Press.

Ruth STARKE. *Nips XI.* Lothian Books.

2002 John HEFFERNAN. *My Dog*, ills Andrew McLEAN. Margaret Hamilton Books.

Honour Books
Kerry GREENWOOD. *A Different Sort of Real: The Diary of Charlotte McKenzie, Melbourne 1918-1919.* Scholastic Press, Scholastic Australia.

Odo HIRSCH. *Have Courage, Hazel Green!* Allen & Unwin.

2003 Catherine BATESON. *Rain May and Captain Daniel.* University of Queensland Press.

Honour Books
Anna FIENBERG. *Horrendo's Curse*, ills Kim GAMBLE. Allen & Unwin.

Leonie NORRINGTON. *The Barrumbi Kids.* Omnibus Books, Scholastic Australia.

2004 Carole WILKINSON. *Dragonkeeper.* Black Dog Books.

Honour Books
Steven HERRICK. *Do-Wrong Ron*, ills Caroline MAGERL. Allen & Unwin.

Glenda MILLARD. *The Naming of Tishkin Silk*, ills Caroline MAGERL. ABC Books

Children's Book Council of Australia Picture Book of the Year: complete list of winners and honour books

1955 No Winner

Highly Commended
Peter CLARK. *Things My Family Makes*, text by Sue LIGHTFOOT (aged 11 years). John Sands.

Commended
Elisabeth MacINTYRE. *Mr Koala Bear.* Scribner.

Margaret PAICE. *Mirram.* Angus & Robertson.

1956 Sheila HAWKINS. *Wish and the Magic Nut*, text by Peggy BARNARD. John Sands.

1957 No Award

1958 Axe POIGNANT. *Piccaninny Walkabout.* Angus & Robertson.

1959-63 No Awards

1964 No Winner

Commended
Noela YOUNG. *Flip the Flying Possum.* Methuen.

1965 Elisabeth MacINTYRE. *Hugo's Zoo.* Angus & Robertson.

1966 No Award

1967 No Winner

Honourable Mention
Margaret LEES. *Naughty Agapanthus*, text by Barbara MACFARLANE. Thos. Nelson Australia.

1968 No Winner

Commended
Elaine HAXTON. *Moggie and Her Circus Pony*, text by Katharine Susannah PRICHARD. Cheshire.

John MASON. *Puffing Billy: A Story for Children*, text by Esta de FOSSARD. Lansdowne Press.

Virginia SMITH. *Sharpur the Carpet Snake*, text by Lydia PENDER. Abelard-Schuman.

1969 Ted GREENWOOD. *Sly Old Wardrobe*, text by Ivan SOUTHALL. Cheshire.

1970 No Winner

Commended
Ted GREENWOOD. *Obstreperous*. Angus and Robertson.

Penelope JANIC. *Donovan and the Lost Birthday*, text by Marion ORD. Heinemann.

Noela YOUNG. *John, the Mouse who Learned to Read*, text by Beverley RANDELL. Collins.

1971 Desmond DIGBY. *Waltzing Matilda*, text by A. B. PATERSON. Collins Australia.

1972 No Award

1973 No Winner

Highly Commended
Ted GREENWOOD. *Joseph and Lulu and the Prindiville House Pigeons*. Angus & Robertson.

Commended
Judith COWELL. *Barnaby and the Rocket*, text by Lydia PENDER. Collins.

Special Mention
Paul MILTON. *Art Folios; Volume One: 12 Australian Paintings in the Art Gallery of New South Wales*. Heinemann.

1974 **Picture Book**
Ron BROOKS. *The Bunyip of Berkeley's Creek*, text by Jenny WAGNER. Kestrel.

Commended
Dick ROUGHSEY. *The Giant Devil Dingo*. Collins.

Visual Arts
Kilmeny & Deborah NILAND. *Mulga Bill's Bicycle*, text by A. B. PATERSON. Collins Australia.

1975 **Picture Book**
Quentin HOLE. *The Man from Ironbark*, text by A. B. PATERSON. Collins Australia.

Commended
Francia FORBES (Collages). *The Wind Comes*, text by Ron FORBES. Hicks Smith.

Recorded and illustrated by students of KORMILDA College in the Northern Territory. *Djugurba: Tales from the Spirit Time.* ANU Press.

Visual Arts
Robert INGPEN. *Storm Boy*, text by Colin THIELE. Rigby.

Commended
Roger HALDANE. *The Magpie Island*, text by Colin THIELE. Rigby.

1976

Picture Book
Dick ROUGHSEY. *The Rainbow Serpent.* Collins Australia.

Highly Commended
Ron BROOKS. *Annie's Rainbow.* Collins.

Commended
Ron BROOKS. *Aranea: A Story about a Spider*, text by Jenny WAGNER. Kestrel.

Ted GREENWOOD. *Terry's Brrrmmm GT.* Angus & Robertson.

Visual Arts
Ted GREENWOOD. *Terry's Brrrmmm GT.* Angus & Robertson.

1977

No Winner

Highly commended
Deborah NILAND. *ABC of Monsters.* Hodder & Stoughton Australia.

Commended
Deborah & Kilmeny NILAND. *Tell Me Another Tale: Stories, Verses, Songs and Things to Do*, text by Jean CHAPMAN; song settings by Margaret MOORE. Hodder & Stoughton.

1978

Ron BROOKS. *John Brown, Rose and the Midnight Cat*, text by Jenny WAGNER. Kestrel.

Highly Commended
Ronda & David ARMITAGE. *The Lighthouse Keeper's Lunch.* Deutsch.

Commended
Deborah NILAND. *The Sugar-Plum Christmas Book: A Book for Christmas and all the Days of the Year*, text by Jean CHAPMAN; song settings by Margaret MOORE. Hodder & Stoughton.

Written and illustrated by AUSTRALIA'S ABORIGINAL CHILDREN. *The Aboriginal Children's History of Australia.* Rigby.

1979 Percy TREZISE & Dick ROUGHSEY. *The Quinkins.* Collins Australia.

Highly Commended
Ronda & David ARMITAGE. *The Trouble with Mr Harris.* Deutsch.

Commended
Stephen AXELSEN. *The Oath of Bad Brown Bill.* Nelson.

Andrew & Janet McLEAN. *The Riverboat Crew.* Oxford U. P.

1980 Peter PAVEY. *One Dragon's Dream.* Nelson Australia.

Commended
Jennifer ALLEN. *Sinabouda Lily: A Folk Tale from Papua New Guinea*, text by Robin ANDERSON. Oxford U. P.

Judith COWELL. *The Useless Donkeys*, text by Lydia PENDER. Methuen.

1981 No Winner

Highly Commended
Bruce TRELOAR. *Marty Moves to the Country*, text by Kate WALKER. Methuen.

Commended
Pamela ALLEN. *Mr Archimedes' Bath.* Collins.

1982 Jan ORMEROD. *Sunshine.* Viking Kestrel.

Highly Commended
Julie VIVAS. *The Tram to Bondi Beach*, text by Libby HATHORN. Methuen.

Commended
Craig SMITH. *Whistle up the Chimney*, text by Nan HUNT. Collins.

Bruce TRELOAR. *Bumble's Dream.* Bodley Head.

1983 Pamela ALLEN. *Who Sank the Boat?* Nelson Australia.

Highly Commended
Witold GENEROWICZ. *The Train.* Kestrel.

Commended
David COX. *Tin Lizzie and Little Nell.* Aurora.

Dick ROUGHSEY. *Turramulli the Giant Quinkin*, text by Percy TREZISE. Collins.

1984 Pamela ALLEN. *Bertie and the Bear.* Nelson Australia.

Highly Commended
Julie VIVAS. *Possum Magic*, text by Mem FOX. Omnibus.

Commended
Roland HARVEY. *The Friends of Emily Culpepper*, text by Ann COLERIDGE. Five Mile Press.

Junko MORIMOTO. *The White Crane.* Collins.

1985 No Winner

Highly Commended
Junko MORIMOTO. *The Inch Boy.* Collins.

Commended
Jeannie BAKER. *Home in the Sky.* Julia MacRae.

David COX. *Ayu and the Perfect Moon.* Bodley Head.

1986 Terry DENTON. *Felix & Alexander.* Oxford U. P.

Highly Commended
Junko MORIMOTO. *A Piece of Straw.* Collins.

Commended
Bob GRAHAM. *First there was Frances.* Lothian.

Alison LESTER. *Clive Eats Alligators.* Oxford U. P.

1987 Junko MORIMOTO. *Kojuro and the Bears.* Collins.

Honour Books
Graeme BASE. *Animalia.* Viking Kestrel.

Judy ZAVOS. *Murgatroyd's Garden*, ills Drahus ZAK. Heinemann.

1988 Bob GRAHAM. *Crusher is Coming.* Lothian.

Honour Books
Jeannie BAKER. *Where the Forest Meets the Sea.* Julia MacRae.

Margaret POWER. *The Long Red Scarf.* Omnibus.

1989 **Joint Winners**
Jane TANNER. *Drac and the Gremlin*, text by Alan BAILLIE. Viking Kestrel

Graeme BASE. *The Eleventh Hour.* Viking Kestrel.

Honour Books
Roland HARVEY & Joe LEVINE. *My Place in Space*, text by Robin & Sally HIRST. The Five Mile Press.

1990 Julie VIVAS. *The Very Best of Friends*, text by Margaret WILD. Hamilton Books.

Honour Books
Bob GRAHAM. *Grandad's Magic.* Viking Kestrel.

Alison LESTER. *The Journey Home.* Oxford U. P.

1991 Bob GRAHAM. *Greetings from Sandy Beach.* Lothian.

Honour Books
Rod CLEMENT. *Counting on Frank.* Collins Ingram.

Andrew & Janet McLEAN. *Hector and Maggie.* Allen & Unwin.

1992 Jeannie BAKER. *Window.* Julia MacRae Books.

Honour Books
Margaret EARLY. *William Tell.* Walter McVitty Books.

P. J. GOULDTHORPE & C. J. DENNIS. *Hist!* Walter McVitty Books.

1993 Bob GRAHAM. *Rose Meets Mr. Wintergarten.* Viking/Penguin.

Honour Books
Pamela ALLEN. *Belinda.* Viking/Penguin.

Craig SMITH. *Where's Mum?*, text by Libby GLEESON. Omnibus.

1994 Peter GOULDTHORPE. *First Light*, text by Gary CREW. Lothian.

Honour Books
Terry DENTON. *The Paw*, text by Natalie Jane PRIOR. Allen & Unwin.

Andrew McLEAN. *Dog Tales*, ills Janet McLEAN. Allen & Unwin.

1995 Steven WOOLMAN. *The Watertower*, text by Gary CREW. Era Publications.

Honour Books
David LEGGE. *Bamboozled.* Ashton Scholastic.

Elizabeth STANLEY. *The Deliverance of Dancing Bears.* University of Western Australia/Cygnet Books.

1996 Narelle OLIVER. *The Hunt.* Lothian Books.

Honour Books
Jeannie BAKER. *The Story of Rosy Dock.* Random House.

Anne SPUDVILAS. *The Race*, text by Christobel MATTINGLEY. Scholastic.

1997 Elizabeth HONEY. *Not a Nibble!* Little Ark, Allen & Unwin.

Honour Books
Ann JAMES. *The Midnight Gang*, text by Margaret WILD. Omnibus.

Julie VIVAS. *Let's Eat!*, text by Ana ZAMORANO. Omnibus.

1998 Junko MORIMOTO. *The Two Bullies*, translated by Isao MORIMOTO. Mark Macleod, Random House.

Honour Books
Andrew McLEAN. *Josh*, text by Janet McLEAN. Little Ark, Allen & Unwin.

Bruce WHATLEY & Rosie SMITH. *Detective Donut and the Wild Goose Chase*. HarperCollins.

1999 Shaun TAN. *The Rabbits*, text by John MARSDEN. Lothian.

Honour Books
Andrew McLEAN. *Highway*, text by Nadia WHEATLEY. Omnibus.

Noela YOUNG. *Grandpa*, text by Lilith NORMAN. Margaret Hamilton.

2000 Anne SPUDVILAS. *Jenny Angel*, text by Margaret WILD. Viking, Penguin.

Honour Books
Matt OTTLEY. *Luke's Way of Looking*, text by Nadia WHEATLEY. Hodder Children's.

Shaun TAN. *Memorial*, text by Gary CREW. Lothian.

2001 Ron BROOKS. *Fox*, text by Margaret WILD. Allen & Unwin.

Honour Books
Tohby RIDDLE. *The Singing Hat*. Penguin Books.

Shaun TAN. *The Lost Thing*. Lothian Books.

2002 Armin GREDER. *An Ordinary Day*, text by Libby GLEESON. Scholastic Press Australia.

Honour Books
Andrew McLEAN. *My Dog*, text by John HEFFERNAN. Margaret Hamilton.

Shaun TAN. *The Red Tree*. Lothian Books.

2003 Brian HARRISON-LEVER. *In Flanders Fields*, text by Norman JORGENSEN. Sandcastle Books.

Honour Books
Andrew McLEAN. *A Year on Our Farm*, text by Penny MATTHEWS. Omnibus Books.

Bruce WHATLEY. *Diary of a Wombat*, text by Jackie FRENCH. Angus & Robertson.

2004 Neil CURTIS. *Cat and Fish*, text by Joan GRANT. Lothian Books.

Honour Books
Ann JAMES. *Shutting the Chooks In*, text by Libby GLEESON. Scholastic Press Australia.

Colin THOMPSON. *The Violin Man*. Hodder Headline Australia.

Children's Book Council of Australia Book of the Year – Early Childhood: complete list of winners

2001 Catherine JINKS. *You'll Wake the Baby!*, ills Andrew McLEAN. Penguin Books.

Honour Books
Bob GRAHAM. *Max.* Walker Books.

Lyn LEE. *Pog*, ills Kim GAMBLE Omnibus Books.

2002 Bob GRAHAM. *'Let's Get a Pup!'* Walker Books Australia.

Honour Books
Janeen BRIAN. *Where does Thursday go?*, ills Stephen Michael KING. Margaret Hamilton Books, Scholastic Australia.

Narelle OLIVER. *Baby Bilby, Where Do You Sleep?* Lothian Books.

2003 Penny MATTHEWS. *A Year on Our Farm*, ills Andrew McLEAN. Omnibus Books, Scholastic Australia.

Honour Books
Pamela ALLEN. *The Potato People.* Viking, Penguin Books Australia.

Sofie LAGUNA. *Too Loud Lily*, ills Kerry ARGENT. Omnibus Books, Scholastic Australia.

2004 Pamela ALLEN. *Grandpa and Thomas.* Viking, Penguin Books Australia.

Honour Books
Margaret BARBALET. *Reggie, Queen of the Street*, ills Andrew McLEAN. Viking, Penguin Books Australia.

Margaret WILD. *Little Humpty*, ills Ann JAMES. Little Hare.

Canada

Canadian Library Association Book of the Year Award for Children; Canadian Library Association Young Adult Book Award; The Governor General's Literary Awards/The Canada Council Children's Literature Prizes; The IODE Violet Downey Book Award; The Ruth Schwartz Children's Book Award; The Amelia Frances Howard-Gibbon Illustrator's Award; The Elizabeth Mrazik-Cleaver Canadian Picture Book Award; The Geoffrey Bilson Award for Historical Fiction For Young People; The Arthur Ellis Award for Best Juvenile Mystery; The Red Cedar Book Awards

Canada has many prizes for authors and illustrators of children's books, including several which are limited to a single province, which I have not listed here, since I am dealing only with national awards. As Canada is a dual-language country there are also national awards for French texts. I have listed these within the awards where they are relevant, for completeness sake, but have not otherwise referred to them in the descriptive text. Many of the titles have won several awards, which confirms their merit. It raises some concern as to the reasoning behind setting up an award, however, if the same book is likely to win them all. Those awards which have monetary value, naturally allow writers, especially those who would otherwise have to fit their writing round a full-time wage-paying job, to concentrate more exclusively on the writing side of their lives, at least for a time. This must be of general benefit to the literature of a country, and if there are benefactors whose generosity or bequest have made this possible, one can only be thankful. Details of the Mr Christie's Awards will be found in Chapter 11, with other awards made by commercial enterprises.

Canada has a long and rich history of children's librarianship. In addition, it has influenced its southern neighbour at least as much as it has itself been influenced by the US. The Osborne Collection of Early Children's Books at Toronto Public Library is a resource of which any country, young or old, may justly be proud.

The Canadian Library Association (CLA) Book of the Year Award for Children is the Canadian equivalent of the Newbery and CILIP Carnegie Medals. It is presented annually to the author of the best book in English published in Canada for that year by a Canadian author or a permanent resident of Canada. The selection is made by a panel of judges from the Canadian Association for Children's Librarians (CACL), who also, since 1989, administer the CLA Young Adult Book Award. It was always the intention of the Young Adult Caucus of the Saskatchewan Library Association, who established the award, that it would one day be taken over by the CLA. This has now occurred, and the award is in the hands of the Young Adult Services Interest Group of the CLA, but one Saskatchewan member will continue to sit on the selection committee, and the Book Award seal, designed by a young adult from Regina, will continue to appear on the winning title each year. The winning book must be published in Canada and must be a work of creative literature (novel, play or poetry) for young adults and written by a Canadian citizen or landed immigrant.

The Governor General's Literary Awards were first established in 1936 by the Canadian Author's Association in permanent recognition of literary merit. A bronze medal was presented for the best books of poetry, fiction, non-fiction and juvenile literature. Later the Canada Council financed the awards, offering a cash prize and a deluxe binding of the award books. The prize was in abeyance from 1960 to 1974. Then, in 1975, the Children's Literature Prizes were established by the Canada Council and presented annually, and awards for illustration were first made in 1977. In 1987 they were once again named The Governor General's Literary Awards. Currently, up to four awards can be given each year, one each to an English-language writer, a French-language writer, an illustrator of an English-language book, and an illustrator of a French-language book. The two panels of judges, one for the English-language books, one for the French-language books, are appointed by The Canada Council and prizes are presented each year along with the other Governor General's Literary Awards. All books for young people, written or illustrated by a Canadian citizen in the previous year, are eligible, whether published in Canada or abroad.

In 1985, the National Chapter of the Canadian Imperial Order of the Daughters of the Empire (IODE) established an annual award, the IODE/Violet Downey Award for the best English language book, which contains at least 300 words of text, suitable for children aged 13 and under. The book must be written by a Canadian citizen and must be published in Canada. The award-winner is chosen by a five member panel of judges, which includes the National President, the National Education Secretary, a third IODE member appointed annually by the National Executive Committee, and two non-members who are recognised specialists in the field of children's literature. The award may be divided between two people.

The Ruth Schwartz Children's Book Award is awarded annually to the writer or creative source of an outstanding work of Canadian children's literature. The award is presented by the Canadian Booksellers' Association, usually at their annual convention, or by any other group appointed by the Ontario Arts Council, who administers the award fund. The winning book must be published in Canada during the previous year and the author must be a Canadian citizen. This award, too, may be divided between two people. In 1994, as a result of an increase from the Ruth Schwartz Foundation, the award was divided into two categories: picture books and young adult fiction and non-fiction.

The Amelia Frances Howard-Gibbon Illustrator's Award is given by the Canadian Association of Children's Librarians, and goes to the best illustrated Canadian book published for children. A committee of librarians from the CACL makes the selection and the presentation takes place at the annual meeting of the CLA in June. The illustrator must be a Canadian citizen, the books must be published in Canada, and in addition, have as their subject Canada or some aspect of Canadian life.

Amelia Frances Howard-Gibbon was the granddaughter of Charles Howard, the eleventh Duke of Norfolk. In 1798, although his second legal wife was still alive in a lunatic asylum, Charles Howard was secretly married in his Cumberland castle of Greystoke to Miss Amelia Gibbon, a cousin of Edward Gibbon who wrote *The Decline and Fall of the Roman Empire*. Their son, Edward Howard Gibbon, married Miss Amelia Dendy in 1824 and two years later (on 25 July 1826) their first daughter, Amelia Frances, was born. She emigrated to Canada, and was joined by her widowed mother by the end of the 1850s. Amelia Frances taught in an art school in New York for a while, before she returned to England in 1873 to claim an inheritance from her uncle Matthew. She died in 1874. Amelia Howard-Gibbon drew the pictures of her 'Tom Thumb's Alphabet' in 1859, well before the era of coloured picture books began in the UK, and some twenty years before the first picture-books of Kate Greenaway and Caldecott would be published. This 'Alphabet' was never published in Amelia Howard-Gibbon's lifetime, and was rediscovered only in 1959, when the hundred-year-old manuscript was donated to the Osborne Collection. Eventually it was published as a picture book by Oxford U. P. in 1967.

More recently the Elizabeth Mrazik-Cleaver Canadian Picture Book Award was established according to the will of the late author/illustrator Elizabeth Cleaver (1939-1985), who left a fund to endow the award in her name. It is administered by a committee of three members of the Canadian section of the International Board on

Books for Young People (IBBY), and is open to Canadian illustrators of picture books published in Canada, in English or in French, during the previous calendar year. Books must be first editions and contain original illustrations. All genres are considered: fiction, non-fiction, poetry, folk and fairy tales. The award is presented annually by IBBY Canada unless no book is judged to be deserving of the award, as occurred in 2002.

The Geoffrey Bilson Award for Historical Fiction For Young People is presented annually to an outstanding work of historical fiction for young people. The author must be Canadian, and the book must have been published in the previous calendar year. The winner is chosen by a jury appointed by The Canadian Children's Book Centre and was established in 1988 in memory of Geoffrey Bilson, a historian and children's author who died in 1987. Names such as Kit Pearson and Brian Doyle will be familiar from other Canadian award lists, as their books, though 'historical' in the terms of the Bilson Award are also strong stories with relevance to today's world and are highly thought of among critics of children's literature generally.

The Arthur Ellis Award for Best Juvenile Mystery was established in 1993, though there has been an adult mystery award of this name since 1984. It is named after Canada's last official hangman and are awarded annually by the Crime Writers of Canada. The award is open either to Canadian residents, regardless of nationality, or to Canadian writers living abroad, and books must have been published within the preceding year.

The Red Cedar Book Awards were set up in 1998 to encourage children to read books by Canadian children's authors. Each year, a Red Cedar Book Award is presented to one fiction and one non-fiction author whose books receive the most votes from readers in the programme. To be eligible a book must have been written by a Canadian citizen or landed immigrant who has lived in Canada for at least two years, and published by a recognised publisher two calendar years before the nomination date. It must be recognised by other reviewers of Canadian children's literature and of general interest to students aged 9 to 12.

One of my Canadian contacts remarked that although Canada has two official languages, it should not be regarded as a dual language country, rather as a country – and in particular a literary scene – *divided* by language. Even to discover the French-language prizewinners is not particularly easy in the English-speaking provinces, and the converse may also be true.

Canadian authors produce a wealth of high-quality titles for all ages, not so often published in the UK, but in many cases easily available in the US. Monica Hughes's and Jean Little's books have been well regarded on both sides of the Atlantic for many years, but the writing of Julie Johnston, Tim Wynne-Jones, Sarah Ellis and Polly Horvath deserve a wider UK audience. Sarah Ellis in particular has a knack of getting under the skin of teenage perceptions. Canadian illustrators seem to be even less well-known in the UK. With the plethora of titles flooding into the UK from the US, perhaps the time is ripe, or even overdue, for UK publishers to look a little further north for their trans-Atlantic imports.

Canadian Library Association Book of the Year Award for Children: complete list of winners

1947 Roderick HAIG-BROWN. *Starbuck Winter Valley.* William Morrow.

1948 No Award

1949 Mabel DUNHAM. *Kristli's Trees.* McClelland & Stewart.

1950 Richard S. LAMBERT. *Franklin of the Arctic; a life of adventure.* McClelland & Stewart.

1951 No Award

1952 Catherine Anthony CLARK. *The Sun Horse.* Macmillan of Canada.

1953 No Award

1954 No Award

1955 No Award

1956 Louise RILEY. *Train for Tiger Lily.* Macmillan of Canada.

1957 Cyrus MACMILLAN. *Glooscap's Country.* Oxford U. P.

1958 Farley MOWAT. *Lost in the Barrens.* Little, Brown & Co.

1959 John F. HAYES. *The Dangerous Cove.* Copp Clark.

1960 Charles Marius BARBEAU & Michael HORNYANSKY. *The Golden Phoenix and Other French Canadian Fairy Tales.* Oxford U. P.

1961 William TOYE. *The St. Lawrence.* Oxford U. P.

1962 No Award

1963 Sheila BURNFORD. *The Incredible Journey: A Tale of Three Animals.* Little, Brown & Co.

1964 Roderick HAIG-BROWN. *The Whale People.* Collins.

1965 Dorothy M. REID. *Tales of Nanabozho.* Oxford U. P.

1966 James HOUSTON. *Tikta'liktak: An Eskimo Legend.* Longmans.

James McNEILL. *The Double Knights.* Oxford U. P.

1967 Christie HARRIS. *Raven's Cry.* McClelland & Stewart.

1968 James HOUSTON. *The White Archer: An Eskimo Legend.* Academic Press.

1969 Kay HILL. *And Tomorrow the Stars: The Story of John Cabot.* Dodd Mead.

1970 Edith FOWKE. *Sally Go Round the Sun.* McClelland & Stewart.

1971 William TOYE. *Cartier Discovers the St. Lawrence.* Oxford U. P.

1972 Ann BLADES. *Mary of Mile 18.* Tundra Books.

1973 Ruth NICHOLS. *The Marrow of the World.* Macmillan of Canada.

1974 Elizabeth CLEAVER. *The Miraculous Hind.* Holt, Rinehart & Winston.

1975 Dennis LEE. *Alligator Pie.* Macmillan of Canada.

1976 Mordecai RICHLER. *Jacob Two-Two Meets the Hooded Fang.* McClelland & Stewart.

1977 Christie HARRIS. *Mouse Woman and the Vanished Princesses.* McClelland & Stewart.

1978 Dennis LEE. *Garbage Delight.* Macmillan of Canada.

1979 Kevin MAJOR. *Hold Fast.* Clarke, Irwin.

1980 James HOUSTON. *River Runners.* McClelland & Stewart.

1981 Donn KUSHNER. *The Violin Maker's Gift*, ills Doug PANTON. Macmillan of Canada.

1982 Janet LUNN. *The Root Cellar.* Lester & Orpen Dennys.

1983 Brian DOYLE. *Up to Low.* Groundwood Books.

1984 Jan HUDSON. *Sweetgrass.* Tree Frog Press.

1985 Jean LITTLE. *Mama's Going to Buy You a Mockingbird.* Penguin/Viking.

1986 Cora TAYLOR. *Julie.* Western Producer Prairie Books.

1987 Janet LUNN. *Shadow in Hawthorn Bay.* Lester & Orpen Dennys.

1988 Kit PEARSON. *A Handful of Time.* Viking Kestrel.

1989 Brian DOYLE. *Easy Avenue.* Groundwood Books.

1990 Kit PEARSON. *The Sky is Falling.* Viking Kestrel.

1991 Michael BEDARD. *Redwork.* Lester & Orpen Dennys.

1992 Kevin MAJOR. *Eating Between the Lines.* Doubleday.

1993 Celia Barker LOTTRIDGE. *Ticket to Curlew.* Groundwood Books.

1994 Tim WYNNE-JONES. *Some of the Kinder Planets.* Groundwood Books.

1995 Cora TAYLOR. *Summer of the Mad Monk.* Douglas & McIntyre.

1996 Maxine TROTTIER. *The Tiny Kite of Eddie Wing.* Stoddart.

1997 Brian DOYLE. *Uncle Ronald.* Groundwood/Douglas & McIntyre.

1998 Kenneth OPPEL. *Silverwing.* HarperCollins.

1999 Tim WYNNE-JONES. *Stephen Fair.* Groundwood/Douglas & McIntyre.

2000 Kenneth OPPEL. *Sunwing.* HarperCollins.

2001 Nan GREGORY. *Wild Girl & Gran.* Red Deer Press.

2002 Jean LITTLE. *Orphan at My Door: The Home Child Diary of Victoria Cope.* Scholastic Canada.

2003 Karen LEVINE. *Hana's Suitcase*. Second Story Press.

2004 Brian DOYLE. *Boy O'Boy*. Groundwood/Douglas & McIntyre.

Canadian Library Association Young Adult Book Award: complete list of winners

1981 Kevin MAJOR. *Far From Shore.* Clark Irwin.

1982 Jamie BROWN. *Superbike!* Clarke Irwin.

1983 Monica HUGHES. *Hunter in the Dark.* Clarke, Irwin.

1984 O. R. MELLING. *The Druid's Tune.* Penguin Books.

1985 Mary Ellen LANG-COLLURA. *Winners.* Western Producer Prairie Books.

1986 Marianne BRANDIS. *The Quarter Pie Window.* Porcupine's Quill.

1987 Janet LUNN. *Shadow in Hawthorn Bay.* Lester & Orpen Dennys.

1988 Margaret BUFFIE. *Who is Frances Rain?* Kids Can Press.

1989 Helen Fogwell PORTER. *January, February, June or July.* Breakwater Books.

1990 Diana WIELER. *Bad Boy.* Groundwood Books. 1989.

1991 Budge WILSON. *The Leaving.* House of Anansi Press.

1992 Susan Lynn REYNOLDS. *Strandia.* HarperCollins.

1993 Karleen BRADFORD. *There Will Be Wolves.* HarperCollins.

1994 Seán STEWART. *Nobody's Son.* Maxwell Macmillan Canada.

1995 Julie JOHNSTON. *Adam and Eve and Pinch-Me.* Lester Publishing.

1996 Tim WYNNE-JONES. *The Maestro.* Groundwood Books.

1997 R. P. MacINTYRE. *Takes: Stories for Young Adults.* Thistledown.

1998 Martha BROOKS. *Bone Dance.* Groundwood Books/Douglas & McIntyre.

Winning Books

1999 Gayle FRIESEN. *Janey's Girl.* Kids Can Press Ltd.

2000 Katherine HOLUBITSKY. *Alone at Ninety Foot.* Orca Book Publishers.

2001 Beth GOOBIE. *Before Wings.* Orca Book Publishers.

2002 William BELL. *Stones.* Doubleday Canada.

2003 Martha BROOKES. *True Confessions of a Heartless Girl.* Groundwood Books/Douglas & McIntyre.

2004 Polly HORVATH. *The Canning Season.* Groundwood Books/Douglas & McIntyre.

The Governor General's Literary Awards/The Canada Council Children's Literature Prizes: complete list of winners

1950 Richard LAMBERT. *Franklin of the Arctic.* McClelland & Stewart.

1951 Donalda DICKIE. *The Great Adventure.* Dent.

1952 John F. HAYES. *A Land Divided.* Copp, Clark.

1953 Marie McPHEDRAN. *Cargoes on the Great Lakes.* Macmillan of Canada.

1954 John F. HAYES. *Rebels Ride at Night.* Copp, Clark.

1955 Marjorie CAMPBELL. *The Nor'Westers.* Macmillan of Canada. 1954.

1958 Kerry WOOD. *The Great Chief.* Macmillan of Canada.

1959 Edith SHARPE. *Nkwala.* Little, Brown and Co.

1960-74 No record of awards

1975

English text
Bill FREEMAN. *Shantyman of Cache Lake.* James Lorimer.

French text
Louise AYLWIN. *Ramingradu.* Éditions du Jour.

1976

English text
Myrna PAPERNY. *The Wooden People*, ills Ken STRAMPNICK. Little, Brown and Co.

French text
Bernadette RENAUD. *Emilie, la Baignoire a Pattes*, ills France BÉDARD. Éditions Heritage.

1977

English text
Jean LITTLE. *Listen for the Singing.* Clarke, Irwin.

French text
Denise HOULE. *Lane de Neige.* Guy Maheux.

French Illustration
Claude LAFORTUNE. *L'Evangile en Papier*, text by Henriette MAJOR. Éditions Fides.

1978 **English text**
Kevin MAJOR. *Hold Fast.* Clarke, Irwin.

English Illustration
Ann BLADES. *A Salmon for Simon*, text by Betty WATERTON. Douglas & McIntyre.

French Illustration
Ginette ANFOUSSE. *La Varicelle and La Chicane.* La Courte Échelle.

1979 **English text**
Barbara SMUCKER. *Days of Terror.* Clarke, Irwin.

English Illustration
Laszlo GAL. *The Twelve Dancing Princesses*, text by Janet LUNN. Methuen.

French text
Gabrielle ROY. *Courte-Queue.* Éditions Alain Stanké.

French Illustration
Roger PARE. *Une Fenêtre dans Ma Tête.* La Courte Échelle.

1980 **English Text**
Christie HARRIS. *The Trouble With Princesses.* McClelland & Stewart.

English Illustration
Elizabeth CLEAVER. *Petrouchka.* Macmillan of Canada.

French Text
Bertrand GAUTHIER. *Hébert Luée.* La Courte Échelle.

French Illustration
Miyuki TANOBE. *Les Gens de Mon Pays.* La Courte Échelle.

1981 **English Text**
Monica HUGHES. *The Guardian of Isis.* Hamish Hamilton.

English Illustration
Heather WOODALL. *Ytek and the Arctic Orchid.* Douglas & McIntyre.

French Text
Suzanne MARTEL. *Nos Amis Robots.* Héritage.

French Illustration
Joanne OUELLET. *Les Papinachois.* Hurtubise HMH.

1982 **English Text**
Monica HUGHES. *Hunter in the Dark.* Clarke, Irwin.

English Illustration
Vlasta van KAMPEN. *ABC, 123 The Canadian Alphabet and Counting Book.* Hurtig.

French Text
Ginette ANFOUSSE. *Fabien 1 & Fabien 2.* Lemeac.

French Illustration
Darcia LABROSSE. *Agnes et le Singulier Bestiaire.* Pierre Tisseyre.

1983 **English Text**
Sean O. HUIGIN. *The Ghost Horse of the Mounties.* Black Moss Press.

English Illustration
Laszlo GAL. *The Little Mermaid*, text by Margaret MALONEY. Methuen.

French Text
Denis COTE. *Hockeyeurs Cybernetiques.* Paulines.

French Illustration
Philippe BÉHA. *Petit Ours*, text by Sylvie ASSATHIANY & Louise PELLETIER. Ovale.

1984 **English Text**
Jan HUDSON. *Sweetgrass.* Tree Frog Press.

English Illustration
Marie-Louise GAY. *Lizzy's Lion*, text by Dennis LEE. Stoddart Publishing Co.

French Text
Daniel SERNINE. *Le Cercle Violet.* Pierre Tisseyre.

French Illustration
Marie-Louise GAY. *Drôle d'École.* Ovale.

1985 **English Text**
Cora TAYLOR. *Julie.* Western Producer Prairie Books.

English Illustration
Terry GALLAGHER. *Murdo's Story*, text by Murdo SCRIBE. Pemmican Publications.

French Text
Robert SOULIERES. *Casse-tete Chinois.* Cercle du livre de France/Pierre Tisseyre.

French Illustration
Roger PARE. *L'Alphabet.* La Courte Échelle.

1986 **English Text**
Janet LUNN. *Shadow in Hawthorn Bay.* Lester & Orpen Dennys.

English Illustration
Barbara REID. *Have You Seen Birds?* text by Joanne OPPENHEIM. North Winds Press.

French Text
Raymond PLANTE. *Le Dernier des Raisins.* Quebec/Amérique.

French Illustration
Stéphane POULIN. *Album de Famille.* Michel Quintin.

Stéphane POULIN. *As-tu Vu Josephine?* Livres Tundra.

1987 **English Text**
Morgan NYBERG. *Galahad Schwartz and the Cockroach Army.* Groundwood Books.

English Illustration
Marie-Louise GAY. *Rainy Day Magic.* Stoddart.

French Text
David SCHINKEL & Yves BEAUCHESNE. *Le Don.* Cercle du Livre de France.

French Illustration
Darcia LABROSSE. *Venir au Monde*, text by Marie-Francine HÉBERT. La Courte Échelle.

1988 **English Text**
Welwyn Wilton KATZ. *The Third Magic.* Groundwood Books.

English Illustration
Kim LaFAVE. *Amos's Sweater*, text by Janet LUNN. Groundwood Books.

French Text
Michele MARINEAU. *Cassiopée ou l'Ete.* Quebec/Amérique.

French Illustration
Philippe BÉHA. *Les Jeux de Pic-Mots.* Publications Graficor.

1989 **English Text**
Diana WIELER. *Bad Boy.* Groundwood Books.

English Illustration
Robin MULLER. *The Magic Paintbrush.* Doubleday.

French Text
Charles MONPETIT. *Temps Mort.* Éditions Paulines.

French Illustration
Stéphane POULIN. *Benjamin et la Saga des Oreillers.* Annick Press.

1990 **English Text**
Michael BEDARD. *Redwork.* Lester & Orpen Dennys.

English Illustration
Paul MORIN. *The Orphan Boy*, text by Tololwa MOLLEL. Oxford U. P.

French Text
Christiane DUCHESNE. *La Vraie Histoire du Chien de Clara Vic.* Quebec/Amérique.

French Illustration
Pierre PRATT. *Les Fantaisies de l'Oncle Henri*, text by Bénédicte FROISSART. Annick Press.

1991 **English Text**
Sarah ELLIS. *Pick-Up Sticks.* Groundwood Books.

English Illustration
Joanne FITZGERALD. *Dr. Kiss Says Yes*, text by Teddy JAM. Groundwood Books.

French Text
Francois GRAVEL. *Deux Heures et Demie Avant Jasmine.* Boréal.

French Illustration
Sheldon COHEN. *Un Champion*, text by Roch CARRIER. Tundra Books.

1992 **English text**
Julie JOHNSTON. *Hero Of Lesser Causes.* Lester Publishing.

English Illustration
Ron LIGHTBURN. *Waiting For The Whales*, text by Sheryl McFARLANE. Orca Book Publishers.

French Text
Christiane DUCHESNE. *Victor.* Quebec/Amérique.

French Illustration
Gilles TIBO. *Simon et la Ville de Carton.* Tundra Books.

1993 **English Text**
Tim WYNNE-JONES. *Some of the Kinder Planets.* Groundwood.

English Illustration
Mireille LEVERT. *Sleep Tight Mrs. Ming*, text by Sharon JENNINGS. Annick Press.

French Text
Michele MARINEAU. *La Route de Chlifa.* Quebec/Amérique.

French Illustration
Stéphane JORISCH. *Le Monde Selon Jean de...*, text by André VANDAL. Doutre et Vandal, Editeurs.

1994 **English Text**
Julie JOHNSTON. *Adam and Eve and Pinch-Me.* Lester Publishing.

English Illustration
Murray KIMBER. *Josepha A Prairie Boy's Story*, text by Jim McGUGAN. Red Deer College Press.

French Text
Suzanne MARTEL. *Une Belle Journee pour Mourir.* Éditions Fides.

French Illustration
Pierre PRATT. *Mon Chien Est un Éléphant*, text by Rémy SIMARD. Annick Press.

1995 **English Text**
Tim WYNNE-JONES. *The Maestro.* Groundwood.

English Illustration
Ludmila ZEMAN. *The Last Quest of Gilgamesh.* Tundra.

French Text
Sonia SARFATI. *Comme une Peau de Chagrin.* La Courte Échelle.

French Illustration
Annouchka Gravel GALOUCHKO. *Sho et les Dragons d'Eau.* Annick Press.

1996 **English Text**
Paul YEE. *Ghost Train*, ills Harvey CHAN. Groundwood.

English Illustration
Eric BEDDOWS. *The Rooster's Gift*, text by Pam CONRAD. Groundwood.

French Text
Giles TIBO. *Noémie – Le Secret de Madame Lumbago.* Québec/Amérique.

French Illustration
No Award

1997 **English Text**
Kit PEARSON. *Awake and Dreaming.* Viking Books.

English Illustration
Barbara REID. *The Party.* North Winds Press/Scholastic Canada.

French Text
Michel NOËL. *Pien.* Michel Quintin.

French Illustration
Stéphane POULIN. *Poil de Serpent, Dent d'Araignée*, text by Danielle MARCOTTE. Les 400 Coups.

1998 **English Text**
Janet LUNN. *The Hollow Tree.* Alfred A. Knopf Canada.

English Illustration
Kady MacDonald DENTON. *A Child's Treasury of Nursery Rhymes.* Kids Can Press.

French Text
Angèle DELAUNOIS. *Variations sur un Même «T'Aime».* Héritage.

French Illustration
Pierre PRATT. *Monsieur Ilétaitunefois*, text by Rémy SIMARD. Annick Press.

1999 **English Text**
Rachna GILMORE. *A Screaming Kind of Day.* Fitzhenry & Whiteside.

English Illustration
Gary CLEMENT. *The Great Poochini.* Groundwood Books/Douglas & McIntyre.

French Text
Charlotte GINGRAS. *La Liberté? Connais pas...* La Courte Échelle.

French Illustration
Stéphane JORISCH. *Charlotte et l'Île du Destin.* Les 400 Coups.

2000 **English Text**
Deborah ELLIS. *Looking for X.* Groundwood Books.

English Illustration
Marie-Louise GAY. *Yuck, a Love Story.* Stoddart Kids.

French Text
Charlotte GINGRAS. *Un Été de Jade.* La Courte Échelle.

French Illustration
Anne VILLENEUVE. *L'Écharpe Rouge.* Les 400 Coups.

2001 **English Text**
Arthur SLADE. *Dust.* HarperCollins Canada.

English Illustration
Mireille LEVERT. *An Island in the Soup.* Groundwood Books/Douglas & McIntyre

French Text
Christiane DUCHESNE. *Jomusch et le Troll des Cuisines.* Dominique et cie.

French Illustration
Bruce ROBERTS. *Fidèles Élèphants.* Les 400 Coups.

2002 **English Text**
Martha BROOKS. *True Confessions of a Heartless Girl.* Groundwood Books/Douglas & McIntyre.

English Illustration
Wallace EDWARDS. *Alphabeasts.* Kids Can Press.

French Text
Hélène VACHON. *L'Oiseau de Passage.* Dominique et cie/Héritage.

French Illustration
Luc MELANSON. *Le Grand Voyage de Monsieur.* Dominique et cie/Héritage.

2003 **English Text**
Glen HUSER. *Stitches.* Groundwood Books/Douglas & McIntyre.

English Illustration
Allen SAPP. *The Song Within My Heart.* Raincoast Books.

French Text
Danielle SIMARD. *J'ai Vendu Ma Soeur.* Soulières Éditeur.

French Illustration
Virginie EGGER. *Recette d'Éléphant à la Sauce Vieux Pneu.* Les 400 Coups.

2004

English Text
Kenneth OPPEL. *Airborn.* HarperCollins Canada.

English Illustration
Stéphane JORISCH. *Jabberwocky*, text by Lewis CARROLL. Kids Can Press.

French Text
Nicole LEROUX. *L'Hiver de Léo Polatouche.* Boréal.

French Illustration
Janice NADEAU. *Nul Poisson où Aller*, text by Marie-Francine HÉBERT. Les 400 Coups.

The IODE Violet Downey Book Award: complete list of winners

1985 Mary Ellen LANG-COLLURA. *Winners.* Western Producer Prairie Books.

1986 Marianne BRANDIS. *The Quarter Pie Window.* Porcupine's Quill.

1987 Janet LUNN. *Shadow in Hawthorn Bay.* Lester & Orpen Dennys.

1988 Donn KUSHNER. *A Book Dragon.* Macmillan of Canada.

1989 No Award

1990 Paul YEE. *Tales From Gold Mountain.* Groundwood Books.

1991 Michael BEDARD. *Redwork.* Lester & Orpen Dennys.

Barbara SMUCKER. *Incredible Jumbo.* Penguin Books Canada.

1992 Sheryl McFARLANE. *Waiting for the Whales,* ills Ron LIGHTBURN. Orca Book Publishers.

1993 Julie JOHNSTON. *Hero of Lesser Causes.* Lester Publishing.

1994 Kit PEARSON. *The Lights Go On Again.* Viking Kestrel.

1995 Sarah ELLIS. *Out of the Blue.* Groundwood Books.

1996 Jean LITTLE. *His Banner Over Me.* Viking.

1997 Janet McNAUGHTON. *To Dance at the Palais Royale.* Tuckamore Books.

1998 Celia Barker LOTTRIDGE. *Wings to Fly.* Groundwood Books.

1999 Gayle FRIESEN. *Janey's Girl.* Kids Can Press.

2000 Katherine HOLUBITSKY. *Alone at Ninety Foot.* Orca Book Publishers.

2001 Sharon McKAY. *Charlie Wilcox.* Stoddart Kids.

2002 Brian DOYLE. *Mary Ann Alice.* Groundwood Books.

2003 Karen LEVINE. *Hana's Suitcase*. Second Story Press.

The Ruth Schwartz Children's Book Award: complete list of winners

1976 Mordecai RICHLER. *Jacob Two-Two Meets the Hooded Fang.* McClelland & Stewart.

1977 Robert Thomas ALLEN. *The Violin.* McGraw-Hill Ryerson.

1978 Dennis LEE. *Garbage Delight.* Macmillan of Canada.

1979 Kevin MAJOR. *Hold Fast.* Clarke, Irwin.

1980 Barbara SMUCKER. *Days of Terror.* Clarke, Irwin.

1981 Suzanne MARTEL. *The King's Daughter.* Groundwood Books.

1982 Marsha HEWITT & Claire MACKAY. *One Proud Summer.* Women's Press.

1983 Jan TRUSS. *Jasmin.* Groundwood Books.

1984 Tim WYNNE-JONES. *Zoom at Sea.* Groundwood Books.

1985 Jean LITTLE. *Mama's Going to Buy You a Mockingbird.* Penguin Books.

1986 Robert MUNSCH. *Thomas' Snowsuit.* Annick Press.

1987 Barbara REID. *Have You Seen Birds?* North Winds Press.

1988 Cora TAYLOR. *The Doll.* Western Producer Prairie Books.

1989 Janet LUNN. *Amos's Sweater*, ills Kim LaFAVE. Groundwood Books.

1990 Diana WIELER. *Bad Boy.* Groundwood Books.

1991 William BELL. *Forbidden City.* Doubleday Canada.

1992 Paul YEE. *Roses Sing on New Snow*, ills Harvey CHAN. Groundwood Books.

1993 Phoebe GILMAN. *Something from Nothing.* Scholastic Canada Ltd.

1994 **Picture Book**
Vladyana KRYKORKA. *Northern Lights: The Soccer Trails*, text by Michael KUSUGAK. Annick Press.

Young Adult
O. R. MELLING. *The Hunter's Moon.* HarperCollins.

1995 **Picture Book**
Heather COLLINS. *A Pioneer Story*, text by Barbara GREENWOOD. Kids Can Press.

Young Adult
Julie JOHNSTON. *Adam and Eve and Pinch-Me.* Lester Publishing.

1996 **Picture Book**
Geoff BUTLER. *The Killick.* Tundra Books.

Young Adult
Welwyn Wilton KATZ. *Out of the Dark.* Groundwood Books.

1997 **Picture Book**
Harvey CHAN. *Ghost Train*, text by Paul YEE. Groundwood Books.

Young Adult/Middle Reader
Kit PEARSON. *Awake and Dreaming.* Viking.

1998 **Picture Book**
Laura FERNANDEZ & Rick JACOBSON. *Jeremiah Learns to Read*, text by Jo Ellen BOGART. North Winds Press.

Young Adult/Middle Reader
Martha BROOKS. *Bone Dance.* Groundwood Books.

1999 **Picture Book**
Harvey CHAN. *Music for the Tsar of the Sea*, text by Celia Barker LOTTRIDGE. Groundwood Books.

Young Adult/Middle Reader
Eric WALTERS. *War of the Eagles.* Orca Book Publishers.

2000 **Picture Book**
Marie-Louise GAY. *Stella Star of the Sea.* Groundwood Books.

Young Adult/Middle Reader
Kenneth OPPEL. *Sunwing.* HarperCollins Publishers.

2001 **Picture Book**
Sean CASSIDY. *The Chicken Cat*, text by Stephanie McLELLAN. Fitzhenry & Whiteside.

Young Adult/Middle Reader
Janet McNAUGHTON. *The Secret Under My Skin.* HarperCollins Canada.

2002 **Picture Book**
Stephane JORISCH. *Oma's Quilt*, text by Paulette BOURGEOIS. Kids Can Press.

Young Adult/Middle Reader
Mary C. SHEPPARD. *Seven for a Secret.* Groundwood Books.

2003 **Picture Book**
Martin SPRINGETT. *The Night Walker*, text by Richard THOMPSON. Fitzhenry & Whiteside.

Young Adult/Middle Reader
Deborah ELLIS. *Parvana's Journey.* Groundwood Books.

2004 **Picture Book**
Barbara REID. *The Subway Mouse.* North Winds Press/Scholastic Canada.

Young Adult/Middle Reader
Brian DOYLE. *Boy O'Boy.* Groundwood/Douglas & McIntyre.

The Amelia Frances Howard-Gibbon Illustrator's Award: complete list of winners

1971 Elizabeth CLEAVER. *The Wind Has Wings*, compiled by Mary Alice DOWNIE & Barbara ROBERTSON. Oxford U. P.

1972 Shizuye TAKASHIMA. *A Child in a Prison Camp.* Tundra Books.

1973 Jacques de ROUSSAN. *Au Dela du Soleil/Beyond the Sun.* Tundra Books.

1974 William KURELEK. *A Prairie Boy's Winter.* Tundra Books.

1975 Carlo ITALIANO. *The Sleighs of My Childhood/Les Traineaux de Mon Enfance.* Tundra Books.

1976 William KURELEK. *A Prairie Boy's Summer.* Tundra Books.

1977 Pam HALL. *Down By Jim Long's Stage*, text by Al PITTMAN. Breakwater Books.

1978 Elizabeth CLEAVER. *The Loon's Necklace*, text by William TOYE. Oxford U. P.

1979 Ann BLADES. *Salmon for Simon*, text by Betty WATERTON. Douglas & McIntyre.

1980 Laszlo GAL. *The Twelve Dancing Princesses*, text by Janet LUNN. Methuen.

1981 Douglas TAIT. *The Trouble With Princesses*, text by Christie HARRIS. McClelland & Stewart.

1982 Heather WOODALL. *Ytek and the Arctic Orchid*, text by Garnet HEWITT. Douglas & McIntyre.

1983 Lindee CLIMO. *Chester's Barn.* Tundra Books.

1984 Ken NUTT. *Zoom at Sea*, text by Tim WYNNE-JONES. Groundwood Books.

1985 Ian WALLACE. *Chin Chiang and the Dragon's Dance.* Groundwood Books.

1986 Ken NUTT. *Zoom Away*, text by Tim WYNNE-JONES. Groundwood Books.

1987 Marie-Louise GAY. *Moonbeam on a Cat's Ear.* Stoddart Publishing.

1988 Marie-Louise GAY. *Rainy Day Magic.* Stoddart Publishing.

1989 Kim LaFAVE. *Amos's Sweater*, text by Janet LUNN. Groundwood Books.

1990 Kady MacDonald DENTON. *Till All The Stars Have Fallen*, edited by David BOOTH. Kids Can Press.

1991 Paul MORIN. *The Orphan Boy*, text by Tololwa MOLLEL. Oxford U. P.

1992 Ron LIGHTBURN. *Waiting for the Whales*, text by Sheryl McFARLANE. Orca Book Pub.

1993 Paul MORIN. *The Dragon's Pearl*, text by Julie LAWSON. Oxford U. P.

1994 Leo YERXA. *Last Leaf First Snowflake To Fall.* Groundwood Books.

1995 Barbara REID. *Gifts*, text by Jo Ellen BOGART. Scholastic Canada Ltd.

1996 Karen RECZUCH. *Just Like New*, text by Ainslie MASON. Groundwood Books.

1997 Harvey CHAN. *Ghost Train*, text by Paul YEE. Groundwood/Douglas & McIntyre.

1998 Barbara REID. *The Party.* Scholastic Canada.

1999 Kady MacDonald DENTON. *A Child's Treasury of Nursery Rhymes.* Kids Can Press.

2000 Zhong-Yang HUANG. *The Dragon New Year: A Chinese Legend.* Raincoast Books.

2001 Laura FERNANDEZ & Rick JACOBSON. *The Magnificent Piano Recital.* Orca Book Publishers.

2002 Frances WOLFE. *Where I Live.* Tundra Books.

2003 Pascal MILELLI. *The Art Room*, text by Susan Vande GRIEK. Groundwood Books/Douglas & McIntyre.

2004 Bill SLAVIN. *Stanley's Party*, text by Linda BAILEY. Kids Can Press.

Honours
Barbara REID. *The Subway Mouse*. Scholastic.

Stéphane JORISCH. *Suki's Kimono*, text by Chieri UEGAKI. Kids Can Press.

The Elizabeth Mrazik-Cleaver Canadian Picture Book Award: complete list of winners

1986 Ann BLADES. *By the Sea*. Kids Can Press.

1987 Barbara REID. *Have You Seen Birds?*, text by Joanne OPPENHEIM. North Winds Press.

1988 Stéphane POULIN. *Can You Catch Josephine?* Tundra Books.

1989 Ken NUTT. *Night Cars*, text by Teddy JAM. Groundwood Books.

1990 Ian WALLACE. *The Name of the Tree*, text by Celia LOTTRIDGE. Groundwood Books.

1991 Paul MORIN. *The Orphan Boy*, text by Tololwa MOLLEL. Oxford U. P.

1992 Ron LIGHTBURN. *Waiting for the Whales*, text by Sheryl McFARLANE. Orca.

1993 Barbara REID. *Two by Two*. North Winds Press.

1994 Leo YERXA. *Last Leaf First Snowflake to Fall*. Groundwood Books.

1995 Murray KIMBER. *Josepha: A Prairie Boy's Story*, text by Jim McGUGAN. Red Deer College Press.

1996 Janet WILSON. *Selina and the Bear Paw Quilt*, text by Barbara SMUCKER. Lester Publishing.

1997 Harvey CHAN. *Ghost Train*, text by Paul YEE. Groundwood Books.

1998 Pascal MILELLI. *Rainbow Bay*, text by Stephen Eaton HUME. Raincoast Books.

1999 Kady MacDonald DENTON. *A Child's Treasury of Nursery Rhymes*. Kids Can Press.

2000 Michele LEMIEUX. *Stormy Night*. Kids Can Press.

2001 Marie Louise GAY. *Stella, Queen of the Snow*. Groundwood Books.

2002 Award deferred to 2003

The Geoffrey Bilson Award For Historical Fiction For Young People (Canada): complete list of winners

1988 Carol MATAS. *Lisa.* Lester & Orpen Dennys.

1989 Martyn GODFREY. *Mystery in the Frozen Lands.* James Lorimer & Co.

Dorothy PERKYNS. *Rachel's Revolution.* Lancelot Press, 1988.

1990 Kit PEARSON. *The Sky is Falling.* Viking Kestrel.

1991 Marianne BRANDIS. *The Sign of the Scales.* The Porcupine's Quill.

1992 No Award

1993 Celia Barker LOTTRIDGE. *Ticket to Curlew.* Groundwood Books.

1994 Kit PEARSON. *The Lights Go On Again.* Viking.

1995 Joan CLARK. *The Dream Carvers.* Viking.

1996 Marianne BRANDIS. *Rebellion: A Novel of Upper Canada.* The Porcupine's Quill.

1997 Janet McNAUGHTON. *To Dance at the Palais Royale.* Tuckamore Books.

1998 Irene N. WATTS. *Good-bye Marianne.* Tundra Books.

1999 Iain LAWRENCE. *The Wreckers.* Delacorte Press/Random House of Canada.

2000 Award moved to Canada Book Day on April 23 of following year.

2001 Sharon McKAY. *Charlie Wilcox.* Stoddart Kids.

2002 Virginia Frances SCHWARTZ. *If I Just Had Two Wings.* Stoddart Kids.

2003 Joan CLARK. *The Word for Home.* Penguin/Viking.

2004 Brian DOYLE. *Boy O'Boy.* Groundwood Books.

The Arthur Ellis Awards (Canada): complete list of winners

1994 John DOWD. *Abalone Summer.* Raincoast Books.

1995 James HENEGHAN. *Torn Away.* Viking.

1996 Norah McCLINTOCK. *Mistaken Identity.* Scholastic Canada.

1997 Linda BAILEY. *How Can a Frozen Detective Stay Hot on the Trail?* Kids Can Press.

1998 Norah McCLINTOCK. *The Body in the Basement.* Scholastic Canada.

1999 Norah McCLINTOCK. *Sins of the Father.* Scholastic Canada.

2000 Linda BAILEY. *How Can a Brilliant Detective Shine in the Dark?* Kids Can Press.

2001 Tim WYNNE-JONES. *The Boy in the Burning House.* Groundwood/Douglas & McIntyre.

2002 Norah McCLINTOCK. *Scared to Death.* Scholastic Canada.

2003 Norah McCLINTOCK. *Break and Enter.* Scholastic Canada.

2004 Graham McNAMEE. *Acceleration.* Wendy Lamb Books.

The Red Cedar Book Awards (Canada) : complete list of winners

1998 **Fiction**

Bernice Thurman HUNTER. *Amy's Promise*. Scholastic.

Non-Fiction

Linda GRANFIELD. *In Flanders Fields: The Story of the Poem by John McCrae*, ills Janet WILSON. Stoddart Kids.

1999 **Fiction**

Kit PEARSON. *Awake and Dreaming*. Penguin.

Non-Fiction

Hugh BREWSTER. *Anastasia's Album*. Madison Press.

2000 **Fiction**

Kenneth OPPEL. *Silverwing*. HarperCollins.

Non-Fiction

Dave BOUCHARD. *The Great Race*. Raincoast Books.

2001 **Fiction**

Gayle FRIESEN. *Janey's Girl*. Kids Can Press.

Non-Fiction

Marg MEIKLE. *Funny You Should Ask*. Scholastic.

2002 **Fiction**

Kenneth OPPEL. *Sunwing*. HarperCollins.

Non-Fiction

Vivien BOWERS. *Wow Canada!* Owl Books/Greey de Pencier.

Eire/Republic of Ireland: Reading Association of Ireland Awards

There are two main administrators of awards in Ireland, the Reading Association of Ireland and Children's Books Ireland. Since the award made by CBI is sponsored by RHM Foods (Ireland) Ltd. and called the Bisto Books of the year, of the decade, or Bisto Merit Awards, these have been described and listed with other commercial awards in Chapter 11.

The Reading Association of Ireland is affiliated to The International Reading Association whose aim is to encourage reading and reading education world wide. In order to encourage the writing, publication and appreciation of children's literature in Ireland, the RAI instituted the first award for children's literature in Ireland in 1985. Since 1989, it presents two awards bi-annually, 'The RAI Children's Book Award' and 'The RAI Special Merit Award'. All books submitted are read and discussed by a panel of experts. This panel comprises specialists in children's literature, teachers, librarians, parents, and general publishers. The winning books carry the prestigious RAI Book Award Stamp. After the Awards Ceremony at the end of the year, all books are donated to the Library at Dublin's National Children's Hospital. Publishers may enter any book which complies with the conditions for the awards, and all books are judged according to these criteria. Both fiction and non-fiction are considered for the awards, but school text books are not eligible. All elements that make the book suitable and attractive for the intended readership are considered – subject matter, language level, design, illustration, production, etc. The RAI Special Merit Award is presented for the book which the judges consider to have made a significant contribution to a particular aspect of publishing for children in Ireland. The Special Merit Award has in recent years been given to publishers instead of to individual titles, and I have shown the publisher at the appropriate place in the list when this has occurred. The awards are non-monetary, and presentations are made to the authors and the publishers of the winning books. Either or both of the awards may be withheld if the judges consider that nothing suitable has been submitted. The RAI awards are only made in alternate years.

The first winner of the award, Tom McCaughren's *Run With The Wind*, was one of three titles in the series designated Bisto Books of the Decade 1980-90 in the Fiction category. One of the 1989 winners, too, George Otto Simms's *Discovering The Book of Kells*, won the Bisto Book of the Decade 1980-90 Information Books category. *The Christmas Miracle of Jonathan Toomey* by Susan Wojciechowski and illustrated by P. J. Lynch has been an international success; indeed several books illustrated by P. J. Lynch have won awards all around the world. The RAI awards also celebrate books in the Irish language, and the Special Merit award in particular has been used to recognise the contribution publishers have made towards providing books for children in the Gaeilge.

As the publishing scene in Ireland is relatively small, it is understandable that there should be some overlap with the Bisto winners. This takes nothing from the prestige of either the award or the winning author; quality needs to be acknowledged, whether seeking the best of thirty or of three thousand. Regardless of the size of the operation, the vitality of the children's book world in Ireland, whether in terms of authors, publishers, or librarians is apparent.

Reading Association of Ireland Awards: complete list of winners and special merit awards

1985 **Children's Book Award**
Tom McCAUGHREN. *Run With The Wind.* Wolfhound Press.

1987 **Children's Book Award**
Eugene McCABE. *Cyril: The Quest of an Orphan Squirrel.* O'Brien Press.

1989 **Children's Book Award**
Marie Louise FITZGERALD. *An Chanail.* An Gúm.

Special Merit Award
George Otto SIMMS. *Discovering The Book of Kells.* O'Brien Press.

1991 **Children's Book Award**
Marita Conlon McKENNA. *Under The Hawthorn Tree.* The O'Brien Press.

Special Merit Award
Joan O'NEILL. *The Daisy Chain War.* Bright Sparks/Attic Press.

1993 **Children's Book Award**
Morgan LLYWELYN. *Strongbow, The Story of Richard and Aoife.* O'Brien Press.

Special Merit Award
Margrit CRUIKSHANK. *Circling The Triangle.* Poolbeg Press.

1995 No records available

1997 **Children's Book Award**
Susan WOJCIECHOWSKI. *The Christmas Miracle of Jonathan Toomey*, ills P. J. LYNCH. O'Brien Press.

Special Merit Award
Publishers The O'Brien Press for exceptional care, skill and professionalism in publishing, resulting in a consistently high standard in all of the children's books published by them.

1999 **Children's Book Award**
Mark O'SULLIVAN. *Angels Without Wings.*

2001 **Children's Book Award**
Mark O'SULLIVAN. *Silent Stones.* Wolfhound.

Special Merit Award
Publishers An Gúm for all-round excellence in the publication of children's books in the Irish Language.

2003 **Children's Book Award**
Gerard WHELAN. *War Children.* O'Brien Press.

Special Merit Award
Colmán O RAGHALLAIGH of Cló Mhaigh Eo, for his graphic novels *An Sclábhaí* and *An Tóraíocht* (both published by Cló Mhaigh Eo) and for his contribution to the publishing of children's books in the Irish Language.

New Zealand

The Esther Glen Award; the Russell Clark Award; the Tom Fitzgibbon Award & the Gaelyn Gordon Award for a Much-Loved Book

New Zealand is becoming richer in awards; the Esther Glen Award & the Russell Clark Award have now been joined by two others considered in this section. In addition there is a Non-Fiction award, the Elsie Locke Medal, discussed in Chapter 10, and the New Zealand Post Awards, which are covered in Chapter 11. I have not included the Te Kura Pounamu Medal as it is solely for books in the Maori language. The Esther Glen Award is the equivalent of the Newbery Medal or the CILIP Carnegie Medal, and the Russell Clark Award is for illustration, and so corresponds to the Caldecott Medal or the CILIP Kate Greenaway Medal. Both are administered by the Library and Information Association of New Zealand Aotearoa (LIANZA). New Zealand also has its own equivalents to the Kathleen Fidler Award (UK) and the Phoenix Award (US) in the Tom Fitzgibbon Award and the Gaelyn Gordon Award for a Much-Loved Book.

Esther Glen was born in 1881, and is remembered as a journalist and pioneer writer of children's books in New Zealand. The Esther Glen Award was established in 1944 by the New Zealand Library Association. It is awarded to the author considered to have made the most distinguished contribution to literature to children during the year. This award is longer-established than the Australian equivalent, and as an award for children's fiction is younger only than the Newbery and Carnegie Medals. Authors from New Zealand are becoming better-known in the UK and US. Probably the most well-known New Zealand author is Margaret Mahy. She has won the Esther Glen Award on six occasions, been shortlisted for it seven times, and won the Carnegie Medal twice – for *The Haunting* and *The Changeover* – both also Esther Glen winning titles, and is internationally acclaimed.

The Russell Clark Award is more recent, being established in 1976, and first awarded in 1978. It is named in honour of New Zealand illustrator Russell Clark, and is presented to 'a New Zealand illustrator responsible for the most distinguished illustrations for a children's book'. Pamela Allen and Gavin Bishop are also popular in the UK, and Allen has also won the Australian Picture Book of the Year Award, but by and large the illustrators on this list are less well-known outside New Zealand than the Esther Glen-winning authors.

The Tom Fitzgibbon Award was first made in 1996. It has some similarities to the now defunct Kathleen Fidler Award (see Chapter 9) as it is for a previously unpublished writer for 7-13 year-olds, and the winning manuscript is then published; in this case by Scholastic New Zealand Ltd. who sponsor the award. Tom Fitzgibbon was a lecturer at North Shore Teachers' College and later Auckland College of Education, a founding member of Children's Literature Association and the first chairman of New Zealand Children's Book Foundation. The award is administered by the Children's Literature Foundation of New Zealand, a body formed in 2000 by the amalgamation of the New Zealand Children's Book Foundation and the Children's Literature Association of New Zealand. Two Tom Fitzgibbon-winning titles, Vince Ford's *2much4U* (NZP 2000) and Alison Robertson's *Knocked for six* (EGA 2002) have gone on to win other New Zealand Awards, which speaks well for the quality of its selections.

The Gaelyn Gordon Award has been given annually since 1999 for a children's book that has 'stood the test of time' and is generally recognised as successful and enduring. It is named in honour of Gaelyn Gordon, a New Zealand author whose books appear in the New Zealand Post Awards listings (see Chapter 11), but not in the LIANZA awards. The winning book must be by a living author and it must still be in print and have been in print for at least five years at the time of the judging. The book must not have won a major New Zealand award but it may have been shortlisted, and it may have won an award overseas. Maurice Gee and Pamela Allen are predictably in this list, and its first winner was Elsie Locke, for whom the New Zealand Non-Fiction Award is now named (see Chapter 10).

That New Zealand has a fairly small literary scene is noticeable in the relatively frequent repeat of authors' and illustrators' names in the winning lists. This lower quantity does not reflect on the quality of output; what seems to be occurring is that the best people's work is being published, and any limitation of funding means that authors and illustrators who do not reach the required high standards are simply not accepted for publication.

Esther Glen Award: complete list of winners & shortlisted titles

1945 Stella MORICE. *Book of Wiremu*, ills Nancy BOLTON. Progressive Publication Society.

1946 Award Withheld

1947 Alexander REED. *Myths and Legends of Maoriland*, ills George WOODS & W. DITTMER. Reed.

1948-49 Award Withheld

1950 Joan SMITH. *The Adventures of Nimble, Rumble and Tumble.* Paul's Book Arcade.

1951-58 Award Withheld

1959 Maurice DUGGAN. *Falter Tom and the Water Boy*, ills Kenneth ROWELL. Paul's Book Arcade.

1960-63 Award Withheld

1964 Lesley POWELL. *Turi: The Story of a Little Boy*, photos by Pius BLANK. Paul's Book Arcade.

1965-69 Award Withheld

1970 Margaret May MAHY. *A Lion in the Meadow*, ills Jenny WILLIAMS. Watts.

1971-72 Award Withheld

1973 Margaret MAHY. *The First Margaret Mahy Story Book*, ills Shirley HUGHES. Dent.

1974 Award Withheld

1975 Eve SUTTON. *My Cat Likes to Hide in Boxes*, ills Lynley DODD. Hamilton.

1976-77 Award Withheld

1978 Ronda ARMITAGE. *The Lighthouse Keeper's Lunch*, ills David ARMITAGE. Deutsch.

1979 Joan de HAMEL. *Take the Long Path*, ills Gareth FLOYD. Lutterworth Press.

1980-81 Award Withheld

1982 Katherine O'BRIEN. *The Year of the Yelvertons*, ills Gavin BISHOP. Oxford U. P.

1983 Margaret MAHY. *The Haunting*. Dent.

1984 Caroline MACDONALD. *Elephant Rock*. Hodder & Stoughton.

1985 Margaret MAHY. *The Changeover: A Supernatural Romance*. Waiatarua.

1986 Maurice GEE. *Motherstone*. Oxford U. P.

1987 Award Withheld

1988 Tessa DUDER. *Alex*. Oxford U. P.

Shortlist
Steve DICKINSON. *City Night*. Waiatarua Publishing.

Margaret MAHY. *Memory*. Dent.

RENEE. *Finding Ruth*, ills Vanya LOWRY. Heinemann.

William TAYLOR. *Possum Perkins*. Ashton Scholastic.

1989 Jack LAZENBY. *The Mangrove Summer*. Oxford U. P.

Shortlist
Judy CORBALIS. *Oskar and the Ice-Pick*, ills David PARKINS. Deutsch.

Beverley DUNLOP. *Spirits of the Lake*. Hodder & Stoughton.

Caroline MACDONALD. *The Lake at the End of the World*. Hodder & Stoughton.

Margaret MAHY. *The Door in the Air and Other Stories*, ills Diana CATCHPOLE. Dent.

1990 Tessa DUDER. *Alex in Winter*. Oxford U. P.

Shortlist
Lynley DODD. *Hairy Maclary's Rumpus at the Vet*. Mallinson Rendel.

Barry FAVILLE. *Stanley's Aquarium*. Oxford U. P.

Maurice GEE. *The Champion.* Puffin.

Margaret MAHY. *The Blood-and-Thunder Adventure on Hurricane Peak.* Dent.

1991 William TAYLOR. *Agnes the Sheep.* Ashton Scholastic.

Shortlist
Ruth CORRIN. *Secrets.* Oxford U. P.

Diana NOONAN. *The Silent People.* John McIndoe.

Mere WHAANGA-SCHOLLUM (translated by Ngawini KERERU). *Tangaroa's Gift* (*Te koha a Tangaroa*). Ashton Scholastic.

1992 Tessa DUDER. *Alessandra: Alex in Rome.* Oxford U. P.

Shortlist
Paula BOOCK. *Out Walked Mel.* John McIndoe.

Sherryl JORDAN. *The Juniper Game.* Ashton Scholastic.

Sherryl JORDAN. *The Wednesday Wizard.* Ashton Scholastic.

1993 Margaret MAHY. *Underrunners.* Hamish Hamilton.

Shortlist
Tessa DUDER. *Songs for Alex.* Oxford U. P.

David HILL. *See Ya, Simon.* Mallinson Rendel.

William TAYLOR. *Knitwits.* Ashton Scholastic.

1994 Paula BOOCK. *Sasscat to Win.* John McIndoe.

Shortlist
Pauline CARTWRIGHT. *What! No TV?* Ashton Scholastic.

Janice MARRIOTT. *Brain Drain.* Ashton Scholastic.

Heather MARSHALL. *Picking Up the Pieces.* Cape Catley.

Diana NOONAN. *A Dolphin in the Bay.* Omnibus Books.

1995 Maurice GEE. *The Fat Man.* Penguin.

Shortlist
Joy COWLEY. *Gladly, Here I Come.* Viking.

Sherryl JORDAN. *Tanith.* Omnibus Books.

Margaret MAHY. *The Greatest Show Off Earth*, ills Wendy SMITH. Hamish Hamilton.

William TAYLOR. *The Blue Lawn.* HarperCollins Publishers N.Z.

1996 Janice MARRIOTT. *Crossroads.* Reed.

Shortlist
David HILL. *Take it Easy.* Mallinson Rendel.

Margaret MAHY. *Tingleberries, Tuckertubs and Telephones: A Tale of Love and Ice-Cream*, ills Robert STAERMOSE. Hamish Hamilton.

William TAYLOR. *Annie & Co. and Marilyn Monroe.* Penguin.

William TAYLOR. *Numbskulls.* Ashton Scholastic.

1997 Kate De GOLDI. *Sanctuary.* Penguin Books.

Shortlist
Ken CATRAN. *The Onager.* HarperCollins Publishers N.Z.

Jack LASENBY. *The Battle of Pook Island.* Longacre Press.

Margaret MAHY. *The Other Side of Silence.* Hamish Hamilton.

Jane WESTAWAY. *Reliable Friendly Girls: Stories.* Longacre Press.

1998 David HILL. *Fat, Four-Eyed and Useless.* Scholastic.

Shortlist
Paula BOOCK. *Dare Truth or Promise.* Longacre Press.

Joy COWLEY. *Ticket to the Sky Dance.* Viking.

Kate De GOLDI. *Love, Charlie Mike.* Penguin.

Jack LASENBY. *Because We Were the Travellers.* Longacre Press.

1999 No Award

2000 No Award

2001 Margaret MAHY. *Twenty-Four Hours.* Collins.

Shortlist
Ken CATRAN. *Voyage with Jason.* Lothian Books.

Joy COWLEY. *Shadrach Girl.* Puffin Books.

Bob KERR. *After the War*, ills author. Mallinson Rendel.

2002 Alison ROBERTSON. *Knocked for Six*. Scholastic.

Shortlist
Fleur BEALE. *Ambushed*, ills Martin BAILEY. Scholastic.

David HILL. *The Sleeper Wakes*. Puffin.

Tim TIPENE. *Taming the Taniwha*, ills Henry CAMPBELL. Huia.

2003 David HILL. *Right Where It Hurts*. Mallinson Rendel.

Shortlist
Ken CATRAN. *Letters from the Coffin-Trenches.* Random House.

Sarah ELL. *When the War Came Home.* Scholastic New Zealand.

V. M. JONES. *Buddy.* HarperCollins.

Margaret MAHY. *Alchemy.* Collins Flamingo.

2004 Ken CATRAN. *Jacko Moran: Sniper.* Lothian Books.

Shortlist
Ted DAWE. *Thunder Road.* Longacre Books.

Brian FALKNER. *Henry and the Flea.* Mallison Rendel.

V. M. JONES. *Juggling with Mandarins.* HarperCollins.

V. M. JONES. *The Serpents of Arakesh.* HarperCollins.

Russell Clark Award: complete list of winners & shortlisted titles

1978 Robert H. G. JAHNKE. *The House of the People*, text by Ron L. BACON. Waiatorua.

1979 Bruce TRELOAR. *Kim*. Collins.

1980-81 Award Withheld

1982 Gavin BISHOP. *Mrs. McGinty and the Bizarre Plant*. Oxford U. P.

Highly Commended
Robyn KAHUKIWA. *The Kuia and the Spider*, text by Patricia GRACE. Longman Paul/Kidsarus 2.

1983 Award Withheld

1984 Gwenda TURNER. *The Tree Witches*. Penguin.

Commended
Lynley DODD. *Hairy Maclary from Donaldson's Dairy*. Mallinson Rendel.

1985 Robyn BELTON. *The Duck in the Gun*, text by Joy COWLEY. Shortland.

1986 Pamela ALLEN. *A Lion in the Night*. Hodder.

1987 Robyn KAHUKIWA. *Taniwha*. Penguin.

1988 Dick FRIZZELL. *The Magpies*, text by Denis GLOVER. Century Hutchinson.

Shortlist
Pamela ALLEN. *Mr McGee*. Hodder & Stoughton.

Gavin BISHOP. *A, Apple Pie*. Oxford U. P.

Clare BOWES. *Captain Clancy the Flying Clothesline*, text Tui SIMPSON. Mallinson Rendel.

Lynley DODD. *Hairy Maclary's Caterwaul Caper*. Mallinson Rendel.

Kelvin HAWLEY. *The Taniwha's Afternoon Snooze*, text Allan TRUSSELL-CULLEN. Century Hutchinson.

Mandy NELSON. *What's Wrong with Bottoms?*, text Jenny HESSELL. Century Hutchinson.

1989 Chris GASKIN. *Joseph's Boat*, text by Caroline MacDONALD. Hodder.

Shortlist
Pamela ALLEN. *Fancy That.* Hodder & Stoughton.

Lesley MOYES. *Annie & the Moon*, text by Miriam SMITH. Mallinson Rendel.

Mere WHAANGA-SCHOLLUM. *The Legend of the Seven Whales of Ngai Tahu Matawhaiti.* Mahia Publishers.

1990 Chris GASKIN. *A Walk to the Beach.* Heinemann-Reed.

Shortlist
Pamela ALLEN. *I Wish I Had a Pirate Suit.* Hodder & Stoughton.

Clare BOWES. *Dragons 'n' Things: Stories and Poems*, text by Louis JOHNSON. Mallinson Rendel.

1991 David ELLIOT. *Arthur and the Dragon*, text by Pauline CARTWRIGHT. Nelson Price Milburn.

Shortlist
Robyn BELTON. *David's Dad*, text by Jennifer BECK. Random Century.

Gavin BISHOP. *Katarina.* Black Cat Books.

Caroline CAMPBELL. *Escape from Zarcay*, text by Pauline CARTWRIGHT. Nelson Price Milburn.

Mere WHAANGA-SCHOLLUM. *Tangaroa's gift*, translated by Ngawini KERERU. Ashton Scholastic.

1992 Sandra MORRIS. *One Lonely Kakapo.* Hodder.

Shortlist
Martin BAYNTON. *Baby Floats.* Ashton Scholastic.

Lynley DODD. *Hairy Maclary's Showbusiness.* Mallinson Rendel.

Elspeth WILLIAMSON. *Parera, Parera*, text by Peti NOHOTIMA. New Zealand Natural Heritage Foundation.

1993 Christine ROSS. *Lily and the Present.* Methuen.

Shortlist
Pamela ALLEN. *Mr McGee Goes to Sea.* Hodder & Stoughton.

Elspeth WILLIAMSON. *Sione's Talo*, text by Lino NELISI. Ashton Scholastic.

1994 Kerry GEMMILL. *The Trolley*, text by Patricia GRACE. Viking.

Shortlist
Pamela ALLEN. *Alexander's Outing*. Hodder & Stoughton.

Lynley DODD. *Slinky Malinki, Open the Door.* Mallinson Rendel.

Robyn KAHUKIWA. *Paikea*, retold from the traditional story. Viking.

Lesley MOYES. *Two Tigers*, text by Helen BEAGLEHOLE. Shearwater.

1995 Chris GASKIN. *Kotuku: the Flight of the White Heron*, text by Philip TEMPLE. Hodder Moa Beckett.

Shortlist
David ELLIOT. *Dragon Tangle.* Ashton Scholastic.

Te Maari GARDINER. *Kahukura and the Sea Fairies*, retold by Pauline CARTWRIGHT. Ashton Scholastic.

Sandra MORRIS. *Discovering New Zealand Birds.* Hodder & Stoughton.

1996 Linda McCLELLAND. *The Cheese Trap*, text by Joy COWLEY. Scholastic.

Shortlist
Murray BALL. *Mrs Windyflax and the Pungapeople*, text by Barry CRUMP. Hodder Moa Beckett.

Manu SMITH. *Tulevai and the Sea*, text by Joy COWLEY. Ashton Scholastic.

Nicki WISE. *Little Duck Checks It Out*, text by Grey ARMSTRONG. Ashton Scholastic.

1997 Murray GRIMSDALE. *George's Monster*, text by Amanda JACKSON. Learning Media.

Shortlist
Robyn BELTON. *The Bantam and the Soldier*, text by Jennifer BECK. Scholastic New Zealand.

Tracey MORONEY. *Nicketty-nacketty, Noo-noo-noo*, text by Joy COWLEY. Scholastic New Zealand.

Karen OPPATT. *Far Away Moon*, text by Jane BUXTON. Learning Media.

Chris SLANE. *Maui: Legends of the Outcast*, text by Robert SULLIVAN. Godwit Publishing.

1998 Sue HITCHCOCK-PRATT. *Emily's Wonderful Pie*, text by Jane CORNISH. Scholastic.

Shortlist
Gavin BISHOP. *Little Rabbit and the Sea.* North-South Books.

Kerry GEMMILL. *The Sandman*, text by Esther TAMEHANA. Huia Publishers.

Lesley MOYES. *Alphabet Apartments.* Mallinson Rendel.

Ruth PAUL. *The Penguin's Day Out*, text by Vivienne JOSEPH. Mallinson Rendel.

Pamela WOLFE. *Midnight at the Museum*, text by Richard WOLFE. Scholastic.

1999 No Award

2000 No Award

2001 Bob KERR. *After the War.* Mallinson Rendel.

Shortlist
Pamela ALLEN. *Can You Keep a Secret?* Viking.

Gavin BISHOP. *Stay Awake, Bear!*. Orchard Books.

Pamela ALLEN. *Inside Mary Elizabeth's House.* Viking.

Sue HITCHCOCK. *Oliver in the Garden*, text by Margaret BEAMES. Scholastic.

2002 Anton PETROV. *A Book of Pacific Lullabies*, edited by Tessa DUDER. HarperCollins.

Shortlist
Theo BAYNTON. *Looking for Larry.* Scholastic.

Jennifer COOPER. *The Pipi and the Mussels*, text by Dot MEHARRY. Reed Children's Books.

Anton PETROV. *The Last Whale*, text by Renee Hapimarika van de WEERT. Reed Children's Books.

2003 Sarah WILKINS. *The Immigrants*, text by Alan BAGNALL. Mallinson Rendel.

Shortlist
Pamela ALLEN. *The Potato People.* Viking.

David ELLIOT. *Pigtails the pirate.* Random House.

Elizabeth FULLER. *The Best-Dressed Bear*, text by Diana NOONAN. Scholastic.

Christine ROSS. *Auntie Rosie and the Rabbit*, text by Diana NOONAN. Scholastic New Zealand.

2004 Graeme GASH. *Napoleon and the Chicken Farmer*, text by Lloyd JONES. Mallison Rendel.

Shortlist
Pamela ALLEN. *Grandpa and Thomas.* Viking.

Gavin BISHOP. *The Three Billy-Goats Gruff.* Scholastic New Zealand.

Ali TEO and Astrid JENSEN. *Oh Hogwash, Sweet Pea!*, text by Ngareta GABEL, translated & adapted from Te Reo Maori by Hannah RAINFORTH. Huia.

Pamela WOLFE. *Mouse on the Moon*, text by Richard WOLFE. Scholastic.

The Tom Fitzgibbon Award: complete list of winners (all published by Scholastic New Zealand)

1996 Iona McNAUGHTON. *Summer of shadows.*

1997 Heather CATO. *Dark Horses.*

1998 Vince FORD. *2Much4U.*

1999 Shirley CORLETT. *The Stolen.*

2000 Alison ROBERTSON. *Knocked for Six.*

2001 No Award

2002 Janet PATES. *Mystery at Tui Bay.*

2003 Jillian SULLIVAN. *Shreve's Promise.*

2004 Brigid FEEHAN. *Stella Star.*

The Gaelyn Gordon Award for a Much-Loved Book: complete list of winners

1999 Elsie LOCKE *The Runaway Settlers*, ills Gary HEBLEY. Hazard Press. (First pub. 1965).

2000 Joy WATSON. *Grandpa's Slippers*, ills Wendy HODDER. Ashton Scholastic. (First pub. 1989).

2001 Pamela ALLEN. *Who Sank the Boat?* Puffin. (First pub. 1982).

2002 David HILL. *See Ya, Simon*. Mallinson Rendel. (First pub. 1992).

2003 Betty GILDERDALE. *The Little Yellow Digger*, ill. Alan GILDERDALE. Ashton Scholastic. (First pub. 1992).

2004 Maurice GEE. *Under the Mountain*. Puffin Books. (First pub. 1979).

South Africa: The Percy Fitzpatrick Prize, The Katrine Harries Award & The VIVI Award

South Africa is a country which has now marked more than ten years since its emergence from isolation from the rest of the literary world, due to its previous political situation. It has taken time for the results of the South African government's policies towards children's literature to develop, and the award situation is still uncertain. In the mean time, it is right that South Africa, so long excluded from such listings, should have a place here. The Children's Book Award scene has been in a state of flux for a number of years, as the South African Institute for Library and Information Science (SAILIS), which administered the three most prestigious prizes until the summer of 1997, was replaced by a new body, the Library and Information Association of South Africa (LIASA). This body did not feel able to continue with the prizes, and it took some years for them to find other homes and sponsors.

There are now some thirty publishers who produce children's books – more than twice the number of than was the case in 1997. In that year only five of them had put out ten or more English Language titles. The largest, Nasboek, still has a significant part to play in the commercial award scene, as noted in Chapter 11. Apparently five of the new provinces of South Africa still 'lack the infrastructure to provide not only public libraries but also school media centre services'. This naturally has an impact on purchasing levels, and consequently publishing policy, since the purchasing patterns of the four former (larger) provinces 'sustained children's publishing, especially of books in the Black languages.' There have recently been calls for the removal of VAT on books, but this is not seen as a universal remedy, as it is felt that 'the real issue is that all South Africans should have free and easy access to books through a wide network of well-stocked public libraries'. One can hope things will continue to improve on the children's publishing scene, though some strategies might be seen as counter-productive. For instance, in order to increase the range of books from which award-winners can be chosen, it is now possible for a book published outside South Africa to be eligible for the Katrine Harries award, as noted below.

Naturally there are also several awards purely for books in the Afrikaans language, and as such they have no real place here. However, for the sake of completeness, and to minimise confusion, these are their titles: the Tienie Holloway Medal (Afrikaans pre-school literature), the Alba Bouwer Prize (Afrikaans literature), the Scheepers Prize (Afrikaans literature for 10 years and older) and the C. P. Hoogenhout Prize (Afrikaans children's literature). Awards which are open to English-language titles, to both English and Afrikaans, or to any South African language, are listed fully here. The M-Net, M E R Prize and the Sanlam Prize, however, are included in Chapter 11 with other commercially sponsored awards. I have not included the Noma Award for Publishing in Africa which now has a children's book section, and is open to African writers and scholars whose work is published anywhere in Africa. Books in all African languages as well as English are eligible, but – most importantly in terms of the criteria for this book – a large number of titles are cited, rather than a single winner selected, so I have felt able to leave it out.

The Percy Fitzpatrick Award (English) was instituted in 1971, but no award was made until 1979. It was then made in odd-numbered years, for books published during the preceding two years. It commemorates the author of *Jock of the Bushveldt*, a book set in South Africa, and one of the best-known throughout the rest of the world of that country's books. It is awarded for a children's book in English, and until 1997 was administered by the Committee for Children's Books, SAILIS. The English Academy of South Africa has become the new custodians for the Percy Fitzpatrick Prize but there was a hiatus in the awards from 1996 to 2000.

Until its demise in 1998, the Committee for Children's Books, SAILIS was also responsible for awarding the Katrine Harries Award, for picture book illustrations, which was awarded in even-numbered years and open to books in any South African language published during the preceding two years. Katrine Harries was herself an illustrator, and her books won on the first two instances the picture book award was made, after which it bore her name. The majority of winners until 1990 were titles in Afrikaans. The Katrine Harries Award also 'disappeared' for a number of years and regrets at this situation expressed by publishers and illustrators motivated the Children's Literature Research Unit (CLRU) of The University of South Africa (Unisa) to take over the responsibility of the award. As the Award had last been awarded in 1997, it was decided that the 2003 award would cover books published during 1997 and 1998. In 2004, books published in 2000 and 2001 would be considered for the award, and so on, until the backlog has been recovered. Thereafter the award will be awarded biennially. Because there had been such a long gap there were several 'Honourable Mentions' listed for 2003.

The CLRU has also decided that all South African illustrators will be considered for the award irrespective of whether their books are published abroad. Sadly this seems to do nothing to help the publishing scene in South Africa itself. But by accepting nominations for works published elsewhere, the CLRU feels it is both acknowledging local artists and also making the South African public more aware of books published abroad. Perhaps this will motivate local publishers to make these works available in South Africa.

There is also a relatively new illustration award, The 'VIVI', more formally the Vivian Wilkes Award. This is given to 'the illustrator of a children's book which has made a special contribution to South African children's literature' and has been established by the South African Children's Book Forum (SACBF). SACBF is the South African link with IBBY, and is also rumoured to be considering establishing another award, presumably for children's fiction, but if so the details are not yet available. The judging panel includes children as well as adult librarians and publishing professionals. It is open to fiction and non-fiction, and the text may be in any of the official South African languages. The first winner, Ian Lusted's illustrations to a retelling of a Nigerian folk tale, was commended for its 'stunning use of colour and dramatic style, in which the people of Africa stand with striking dignity. Pictures to intrigue and attract children, while impressing more mature eyes as well.' The organisers of this award seem more optimistic about the home publishing capability, and stipulate that the book must have had a South African edition published in the particular year of the prize, and that the illustrator is normally resident within South Africa.

It has been difficult to discover some of the information as to the current status of awards in South Africa, and I am told that even people who are supposedly on the judging panels are not sure when the next round of announcements will be. The lists which follow are, therefore, as up to date as I have been able to make them, but may be less current than those for other countries. It seemed to me more important to include what *is* known than to leave South Africa out altogether, when so many people are working so hard to bring good books to all their children.

Percy Fitzpatrick Prize: complete list of winners

1971-78 No award

1979 Marguerite POLAND. *Mantis and the Moon.* Ravan.

1980-81 No award

1982-83 Marguerite POLAND. *Wood-ash Stars.* David Philip.

1984-85 No award

1986-87 Lesley BEAKE. *The Strollers.* M. M. Longman.

1988-89 Lesley BEAKE. *Cageful of Butterflies.* Maskew Miller.

1990-91 Dianne CASE. *92 Queens Road.* M. M. Longman.

1992-93 Christel & Hans BODENSTEIN & Linda RODE, (comp). *Stories South of the Sun: 28 South African Read-aloud Stories.* Tafelberg.

1994-95 Lawrence BRANSBY. *The Boy Who Counted to a Million.* Human & Rousseau.

1996-7 No award

1998-9 No award

2000 Elana BREGIN. *The Slayer of the Shadows.* Gecko.

2002 Patricia SCHONSTEIN. *Skyline.* David Philip Publishers.

Katrine Harries Award: complete list of winners

1974 Katrine HARRIES. *Rympies vir Kleuters,* text by L. ROUSSEAU. Human & Rousseau.

1975 No award

1976 Katrine HARRIES. *Herelandgoed,* text by L. ROUSSEAU. Human & Rousseau.

1977 No award

1978 No award

1979 Cora COETZEE. *Oupa Kyken,* text by M. POLAND. Institut vir Navorsing in Kinder-en-Jeugletuur.

Cora COETZEE. *Muis Sonder Snorbaard,* text by M. POLAND. Tafelberg.

1980 Ann WALTON. *Sy Wat die Soen op Haar Voorkop Dra,* text by H. M. HEESE. Qualitas.

1981/82 Adriaan Van ZYL. *Kobus Het 'n Blom,* text by H. M. HEESE. Qualitas.

1983/84 Alida BOTHMA. *Al Everest se Voëls* , text by R. RUPERT. Tafelberg.

Alida BOTHMA. *Die Aarde Moet vry Wees*, text by P. W. GROBBELAAR. Daan Retief.

1985/86 Niki DALY. *Not So Fast Songolo.* Human & Rousseau.

1987/88 Jeremy GRIMSDELL. *Lank Lewe Leeuhart/ Long Live Lionheart,* text by P. W. GROBBELAAR. Daan Retief.

Jeremy GRIMSDELL. *Moesan Muis,* text by P. W. GROBBELAAR. Daan Retief.

1989/90 Joan RANKIN. *Dancing Elephant.* Human & Rousseau.

Joan RANKIN. *Vra vir Frederika.* Human & Rousseau.

Joan RANKIN. *Twelve Days of Christmas.* Daan Retief.

1991/92 Catherine STOCK. *Armien's Fishing Trip.* Songololo Books/David Philip.

1993/94 Jeremy GRIMSDELL. *Kalinzu and the Oxpeckers.* Songololo Books/David Philip.

1995/96 Jude DALY. *Gift of the Sun,* text by D. STEWARD. Tafelberg. (co-production with UK publishers Frances Lincoln of London).

2003 Jude DALY. *The Stone.* Francis Lincoln.

Honourably Mentioned
Niki DALY. *Boy on the Beach.* Human & Rousseau.

Niki DALY. *Bravo! Zan Angelo.* Farrar Strauss & Giroux.

Piet GROBLER. *Carnaval of the Animals.* Human & Rousseau.

Elizabeth PULLES. *Lulama's Magic Blanket.* Tafelberg.

Joan RANKIN. *Wow! Its Great to Be a Duck.* Bodley Head (UK); McElderry (USA)

Annelise VOIGT. *The Red Dress.* Garamond.

Vivian Wilkes Award (VIVI): complete list of winners

1996 Ian LUSTED. *The King's Magic Drum.* Garamond.

1997 Annelise VOIGT. *The Red Dress.* Garamond.

1998 Elizabeth PULLES. *Lulama's Magic Blanket.* Tafelberg.

1999 Niki DALY. *Jamela's Dress.* Tafelberg.

2000 Niki DALY. *Fly, Eagle, Fly!* Tafelberg.

2001 Vian OELOFSEN (ills) & Sue KRAMER (photos). *Ah-Bekutheni?* Early Learning Resource Unit [ELRU] & Project for Alternative Education in South Africa [PRAESA].

Chapter 13: Did the Right Book Always Win?

The first question, perhaps, is what is the 'right book'? On occasion there have been remarks, often published, that such-and-such a winning book was not its author's best. This is not normally what is being judged, however. A winning book may be less than that author's or illustrator's best work by comparison with his or her other output, but it is being compared with the whole publishing output in that country in a particular year. Even if it is not that author's best ever, it may well be head-and-shoulders above anything else that met the submission criteria that year. The book must be judged against its contemporaries, bearing in mind the publishing situation at the time. Some books, despite the constraints of the printing techniques, or the paper shortages, or whatever made things difficult at the time of publication, shine like beacons on our path through the forest of reading. They are books for all time, and many of them are, as we would hope, among the prize-winners, or at the very least included on the shortlisted, commended, or Honor book lists. E. B. White's *Charlotte's Web* springs immediately to mind as one of these; it was a Newbery Honor Book in 1953. Further back, however, there is the strange omission of Tolkien's *The Hobbit*, published in 1937, which did not get so much as an honourable mention in that second year of the Carnegie's existence.

Something that also merits consideration is the occasion when a book was awarded a medal, or honor place, for the sake of the author's or illustrator's previous work. The awards under discussion were not set up for this purpose, but can we really castigate the panels who decided that there would be no other chance for C. S. Lewis to win the Carnegie Medal if it was not awarded to *The Last Battle* – very obviously the final title in its series – or who realised with dismay that the ageing Bill Peet had never won the Caldecott Medal, so gave an Honor place to his illustrated autobiography? These are occasions, which are particularly noticeable in the early years of both the Newbery and the Carnegie Medals, as may be seen in Chapters 3 and 4, when a book seems to have won because it was perceived as the author's 'last chance' to be given the award. It is possible that the introduction of the awards for a body of work, such as the Eleanor Farjeon and the IBBY's Hans Andersen have freed the judges of the awards under discussion in this book to make the right decision once more.

The choice of a first winner will always be difficult. What standard should the judges set? If it is too high, nothing will meet the criteria; if too low, there is no point having the award. The Carnegie judges decided on three occasions to withhold the award. In the 1950s the Greenaway judges decided that no book had met their expected standards in that award's first and fourth years. It may perhaps have been easier to make such a decision in the days when less publicity surrounded awards, though it is doubtful whether the decision to withhold an award is ever taken lightly, but one cannot imagine it being done in these days of greater interest in, and publicity about, all awards.

In contrast to the position of the Carnegie and Greenaway administrators, Frederic Melcher was adamant from the beginning of the Newbery and Caldecott Medals that there should always be a medallist. His insistence is set out within the original principles of the award, and he held that there will always be an outstanding book in a particular year. It may not be as good as the previous or succeeding winners, but it will be the best representative for its own year of publication. Hence the standard is to be new-minted each year, depending on the publication output of the year. There is no 'pass mark', no independently determined level a title must reach; it is comparative, and subjective. This does not, however, mean that the judging is anything less than rigorous and systematic.

The constitution of judging panels, and the capacity of their members to make 'the right decision', was been called into question in the 1990s. Nicholas Tucker expressed concern in the July 1996 issue of *Books for Keeps* that the decision (for the Carnegie Medal) is made by an all-female group of librarians who 'share very similar outlooks.' Certainly librarians, especially children's librarians, are a predominantly female group, as are teachers in the UK, particularly those of younger children. In certain years it will happen that no YLG branch sends a male representative to the Carnegie/Greenaway judging panel. Equally there will be some years when no non-whites will be on the panel. This is not exclusion; it reflects the way elections have gone in that particular year among YLG members. Regardless of the 'outlooks' of the librarians themselves, the children they work with come from all backgrounds. Additionally, to say that women are incapable of judging what boys may like, or of judging the literary – or any other – value of a book is as ridiculous as claiming that men cannot write about female characters. Some indeed cannot, but others can. It is a major part of the training for all librarians, all over the world, to evaluate books of every kind for their suitability and quality for whatever readership.

Librarians judge the Carnegie Medal, as well as the Greenaway, the Newbery, the Caldecott and many others world-wide, because it was within that profession that some of the first concerns about the quality of children's publishing were expressed. Frederic Melcher believed that children's librarians 'were the most competent judges of merit' since they worked with all kinds of children. Other awards are judged by publishers, journalists or media personalities, some by children themselves, as we have seen. All have a part to play in the children's book scene. If an award is true to the criteria and principles under which it was established, there should be no carping as long as it fulfils its stated aims. Anyone who disagrees with the principles, as has occurred several times over the last three-quarters of a century, is free to set up an award with different aims and criteria.

A perusal of the Honor Books, or Commended and Highly Commended titles is often illuminating. Why, we say, did Philip Turner's *The Grange at High Force*, on the face of it a run-of-the-mill adventure story (though better than many) win the Carnegie Medal at the expense of Alan Garner's *Elidor*? Why did *Charlotte's Web* give place to *The Secret of the Andes*, a coming-of-age novel? These were books of timeless appeal: perhaps their authors' best works. Certainly *Elidor* is more accessible than some of Garner's later titles. Then we see that, far from being ignored, *Charlotte's Web* was a Newbery Honor Book in 1953, and *Elidor* was one of six titles commended by the Carnegie panel in 1965. Admittedly they have lasted in appeal and availability, not to mention collectability, for far longer than their companions on those lists, but at least they were recognised at the time as being among the contenders. The judges may have plumped for the choices which seemed best at the time, outstanding examples of genres which were at least read by children. *Elidor* was recognised in the commendation for its excellence and special quality. With hindsight it is easy to say that it has 'lasted' better than *Grange*, and would today be considered the 'outstanding' one, but it was not ignored, as a list which gives winners alone would suggest. The very qualities which today make these books seem special may have made them appear almost outlandish, rather than outstanding, at the time of their publication. I have been told that Charles Keeping's illustrations counted against *Elidor* during the judging; they are highly collectable today. Fantasy, especially that arising from everyday life, was not then as fashionable as it has become. It was seen as a mere genre, and rather mistrusted. Other accusations in the 1960s were that the books chosen by the Carnegie judges were never read by children – the people for whose benefit they were intended! Some might say that the panel were on to a loser whatever they had decided.

Another factor – which did not apply in the case of *Elidor* – was that in the early days of the Carnegie, it was 'understood' that an author could not win a second time. Hence William Mayne, who is on record as saying that he would refuse a second Carnegie Medal, were it offered, seemed to appear in the Commended list constantly during the 1950s. Indeed, in 1957, the year his *A Grass Rope* was awarded the medal, another of his titles, *The Blue Boat*, was commended, and he had also been commended in 1955 and, for two titles, in 1956. Similarly K. M. Peyton, whose *The Edge of the Cloud* won the 1969 medal, was commended in 1962, 1964, 1965, 1966, 1967, and for a further title in her winning year. For authors of such consistent quality, whilst it is right to commend them, it seems wrong for them to monopolise the medal itself while at the peak of their career. Lucy Boston, as we have seen, was slightly suspicious of the value of her award if it meant that she would not have been considered until after the books by others who had already won the medal were 'knocked out'. The Carnegie rules have been altered since then to allow subsequent wins, in line with the Newbery Medal and most other awards now in existence. The Newbery amended its regulations in 1958 to allow previous winners to win again without the need for a unanimous vote, which had been the position since 1932. The logic is inescapable: how can an award be made for 'the best book' or 'the outstanding book' if any title by a previous winner is ineligible?

So what is the right decision? No one can be entirely objective and unbiased about judging decisions. The judges themselves certainly should not be, since a dispassionate judging panel can end up making a 'safe' choice. This has too often been an accusation in the past. The winning title should have fervent advocates on the panel, even if, as must frequently be the case, the decision is not unanimous. Equally, the winner, when announced if not before, will have critics as fierce as its advocates. In many if not most cases, the reasoning behind the awarding of a prize to a particular title is evident. We may not ourselves have chosen that book, but we can see why that particular panel, at that specific time, did.

In 1991 Robert Dunbar was one of the judges for the Bisto Awards in Eire, then administered by the ICBT. More recently he served for several years as chairman of that judging panel. In an article announcing the winners, he put together some of the tenets by which the panel had gone about their 'exciting, if challenging, task'. Here are his comments, which have particular relevance to the question of adults judging children's books:

> Literary awards are for literary excellence. That, at least, was accepted by all of us engaged in the exciting, if challenging, task of deciding on the winners of the 1991 Irish Children's Book Trust awards.
>
> The problem, however, was in reaching some measure of agreement as to what constitutes excellence, particularly when the books under discussion were published for children and therefore intended by their writers, illustrators and publishers for a readership different in a number of respects from those adults on the judging panel. We were conscious therefore in the making of our decisions of the need to ask ourselves whether our own evolving criteria were likely to match with those of children who might eventually find their way to the books; and we were likewise conscious throughout the process of the need to allow for the possibility that such matching might not necessarily occur. In this effort to combine our adult perceptions with what we hoped would be a fair guess about children's responses, we started with a number of assumptions.
>
> Since virtually all of the books submitted for consideration were works of fiction, it seemed right to demand a narrative which, from page one onwards, had the power to gain and maintain a reader's attention. We looked for variety of pace and incident; for characterisation and setting which showed some colour and originality and did not indulge in simplified stereotyping, for a style which, while accessible to a young reader, would make some gesture towards encouraging an awareness of the riches of language. We rejected the didactic or the patronising and anything which savoured of the sexist or racist. These were our basic requirements, therefore, but we hoped that in the best of the books we could move beyond them into stories which, without being pompous or solemn, had something worthwhile and stimulating to convey to readers about the world in which they are growing up. This, we felt, would be one indication of a book's permanent, perhaps classic qualities.
>
> Additionally, we paid considerable attention to what, as adults, we might call a book's aesthetic dimension. We argued about standards of presentation, about cover design, about illustration, about size of print, about quality of paper, about details of spelling and punctuation, and about value for money. In our reading and frequent re-reading of the books submitted we encountered several titles which met many of our criteria, though predictably perhaps fewer which met all of them.

> As a generalisation we feel confident in saying that care is being taken to ensure that quality is not being sacrificed in the current increase in the number of Irish books for children. The standards of production continue to rise and the range of subject matter is being impressively extended: there are many new and exciting authors now at work . . . Eventually, though, final decisions had to be made and we reached these decisions with a genuine belief that the books chosen for the awards will match in every respect those written and published anywhere.
> [from *The Irish Guide to Children's Books*, ed. Covonan, Dunbar & others, ICBT, Dublin 1991]

These are not pedestrian guidelines, nor are they rigid rules. They do not shy away from the problems of 'what constitutes excellence' or of deciding on behalf of a group of people different from themselves, but set out clear strategies for dealing with them. If the ideals set down in these remarks are followed, then the intrinsic qualities of a book – the excitement, the magic – will shine through. It is interesting to compare the Guidelines for Book Discussion which are used by the judging panels for several of the US awards. This set of guidelines was produced in 1989, in order to facilitate discussions about books for selection purposes, by Ginny Moore Kruse and Kathleen T. Horning, who hold the copyright. Both are children's librarians by training, based at the Cooperative Children's Book Center (CCBC) at the University of Wisconsin, Madison:

> ALL PERSPECTIVES AND VOCABULARIES ARE CORRECT. THERE IS NO 'RIGHT' ANSWER OR SINGLE CORRECT RESPONSE.
>
> 1) Listen openly to **what** is said, rather than **who** says it.
> 2) Respond to the comments of **others**, rather than merely waiting for an opportunity to share **your** comments.
> 3) Talk with **each other**, rather than to the discussion facilitator.
> 4) Comment to the group **as a whole**, rather than to someone seated near you.
>
> LOOK AT EACH BOOK FOR WHAT IT *IS*, RATHER THAN WHAT IT IS NOT.
>
> 1) Make positive comments first. Try to express what you liked about the book and why. (e.g. 'I like the illustrations because...')
> 2) After everyone has had the opportunity to say what they liked about the book, you may talk about difficulties you had with a particular aspect of the book. Try to express difficulties as questions, rather than declarative judgements on the book as a whole. (e.g. 'Would Max's dinner really still have been warm?' rather than 'That would never happen.')
> 3) Avoid recapping the story or booktalking the book. There is not time for a summary.
> 4) Refrain from relating personal anecdotes. The discussion must focus on the book at hand.
> 5) Try to compare the book with others on the discussion list, rather than other books by the same author or other books in your experience.

The 'positive comments first' approach has since taken on a life of its own, and is widely used in book discussion situations throughout the US. The guidelines are a worthy attempt to ensure that all books are treated with a similar degree of seriousness by the judging panel concerned. They, too, strive to come to terms with some of the problems that are identified by Robert Dunbar. If these guidelines are used with discretion – in other words if everyone on the panel is aware of the ideas and ideals behind them and has read all the books under discussion – they will not only speed up the discussion process, but focus the minds of the panel on the particular books in question. Similar guidelines have been produced for the judging panels of the Carnegie and Greenaway Medals, and the rules and criteria set out for awards in Australia, Canada and New Zealand imply that a broadly similar range of assumptions are in use throughout the English-speaking world.

A few words should be said here of the adult collector of children's books. At one time it was fashionable to collect early children's books, chapbooks, eighteenth- and early nineteenth-century school readers and improving texts. Marjorie Moon and Iona and Peter Opie are perhaps the most famous examples of such collecting in the UK; the Opie Collection is housed at the Bodleian Library in Oxford, and indeed covers a longer time span of publications including items from the twentieth century. The Osborne Collection at the Children's Book House in Toronto is a North American example of this trend. Later, decorative bindings became popular with collectors, and more recently turn of the nineteenth to the twentieth century stories, often set in schools.

Some so-called 'school story' authors still command prices of hundreds of pounds for their rarer titles. Collecting books goes by fad and fashion; some authors who were once in great demand are no longer collected, and their prices have plummeted. The usual reason for this is that the relatively small number of people who were looking for the author in question have either completed their collection, or cannot justify paying the prices which were latterly being asked. A number of the award-winning authors have become collectable during recent years – Arthur Ransome, William Mayne, Alan Garner, Rosemary Sutcliff and Peter Dickinson are especially desirable, in the US and Japan as well as the UK. Eagerly sought, too, are several illustrators – in particular Edward Ardizzone, Charles Keeping, Maurice Sendak and Pauline Baynes. Collectors of such books are looking for pristine first editions: no names or inscriptions, unless by the author or artist; complete with perfect dustwrappers, preferably not even price-clipped. Because so many of the first hardback editions of children's books were bought by libraries, and those that were not may not have been treated with as much care as a collector would lavish on them – we are, after all, talking about books for children here – these perfect first editions are rare, even chimerical. First editions with dustjacket of some of Alan Garner's early titles fetch nearly a hundred pounds sterling; most firsts of titles by Rosemary Sutcliff, if in fine condition, command over thirty pounds.

By contrast, a hardback first edition of J. R. R. Tolkien's *The Hobbit*, not an award-winner, is well up into the thousands, and some Enid Blyton titles are into the hundreds. Indeed, many of the most seriously collected authors, several of whom have societies dedicated to their works, are not award-winners at all. For some, this is in part a question of chronology: for instance, G. A. Henty died well before the establishment of the first award, the Newbery Medal, though he was until recently keenly collected on both sides of the Atlantic. L. M. Montgomery, too, produced the bulk of her work before any awards were in being. In all probability these authors would have been discounted under other considerations: the Carnegie Medal, at least, was deliberately intended to appeal to both sexes. A specifically boys' book, such as those written by Henty, Percy Westerman, R. M. Ballantyne, F. S. Brereton, W. E. Johns, George Manville Fenn – all of whom are collected in the UK – would not therefore have had the slightest chance of being considered. They provided escapism and strong male heroes, who came to life in the imagination of the boys who read them. They were also avidly read, sometimes clandestinely, by such girls as could get hold of them.

Similarly, L. M. Montgomery, Elinor Brent-Dyer, Elsie J. Oxenham, Dorita Fairlie Bruce, Angela Brazil and other specifically girls' authors, are reaching high prices because of the enthusiasm of the collectors and members of the various societies dedicated to them. As their work was in the main aimed solely at girls and young women, they just would not have been looked at by Carnegie panels. In addition, they were considered 'genre' writers, and their work often dismissed simply as 'school stories' – especially by those who had seen only the many reprinted titles by, for instance, Elsie Oxenham, which are not at all representative of her best work. Violet Needham, too, has a flourishing society which includes men and women, but her work was never considered for the Carnegie. One of that society's members suggests that it was her very popularity with children that counted against her: "she was also an author who could not be slotted into a pigeon-hole. She created a unique and distinctive imaginative world and her most important and popular books can't really be categorised in the way that librarians then preferred ... none of the conventional descriptions apply." Another of my respondents suggested that "giving the Carnegie Medal to [an Elsie Oxenham book] would, in those days, have been a bit like giving it to a 'Point Horror' novel now."

The appeal of these authors nowadays is largely to the adults who remember them from their own childhoods, although some of the societies have enthusiastic junior sections. At the time of their first publication, however, they had a great deal to say to the children of their time, and this is why they are remembered with such affection. They created strong female role models, as Rosemary Auchmuty has shown in her book, *A World of Girls* (London, Women's Press 1992). A book which is chosen and read by a child, and which speaks to that child, stays in the child's mind and will be remembered into adulthood. This contributes to its desirability when that adult comes to collect books – it is not simply a matter of nostalgia.

Collecting books cannot be done, as it were, by numbers. If you want to collect children's books, the advice is the same as collecting any art form: buy what you like, what you want to live with, or what you feel you cannot live without, and buy the best edition, in the best condition, that you can afford. You will then enjoy the benefit of both the contents and the appearance of your collection. Just possibly, your heirs may have the benefit of any increased value, but there are no guarantees. Books are not an investment comparable with property, wine, or stocks and shares. They are an intellectual resource, with all the implications of that terminology.

Perhaps the right decisions on awards have not always been made in the past. There will always be arguments about the particular choices, and some winners will be inevitably be queried. Taken together, the winning titles do show an amazing variety and a wealth of quality reading for any child to select from. If judging panels combine the virtues of the Kruse/Horning guidelines with the imagination of Robert Dunbar's inspirational guiding principles, then in future years a 'right decision' cannot help but be made.

Chapter 14: Magical Changes – the effect of Harry Potter and the Crossover Phenomenon.

In 1998, when the last edition of this book was published, a book with a very ordinary sounding title was beginning to be talked about as a potential contender for the Carnegie Medal. Apparently this was a book which not only was liked and 'approved' by librarians and teachers, but was a runaway bookselling success in terms of that harshest of critics, word of mouth. *Harry Potter & the Philosopher's Stone* (*Harry Potter & the Sorcerer's Stone* in US) changed the world of children's publishing. At the same time, Philip Pullman's *The Subtle Knife* – the sequel to his 1995 Carnegie Winner, *Northern Lights* (*Golden Compass* in US) – was also intriguing young, and not so young, readers. These two were in the vanguard of the phenomenon sometimes known as the 'Harry Potter Effect' but more properly, if inelegantly, termed 'crossover books' – books which are enjoyed by adults though originally published for children. J. K. Rowling's publishers encouraged – some might say pandered to – this extended readership by producing an 'adult' edition of each of the Harry Potter titles; identical words within, but a more sophisticated design for the dustwrapper, so that the adults reading HP on the tube would not be ashamed to be seen with 'a kids' book'. This trend for two separate editions has been followed for several titles since.

Suddenly, children's books were fashionable, they were money-spinners. The love of story, inherent in both the HP and Dark Materials series somehow broke down the barriers between 'readers' and 'non-readers'. Children who had not been interested in books before – even teenaged boys, to the amazement of teachers and librarians – were reading, and what was more, reading long books. As each series progressed, it became clear that the idea that teenagers would neither want to be seen with, nor be able to cope with, large hardback books was no longer valid. In the year 2000, the third Dark Materials volume, *Amber Spyglass*, ran to 548 pages, and the fourth Harry Potter – *HP & the Goblet of Fire* – contained 636; in 2003 HP5 – *Harry Potter and the Order of the Phoenix* – was 766 pages long.

It was not just the length of these books, but the upsurge in fantasy as a genre that has made a big difference, too. Gone is the dictum that books should be realistic or children – especially those much-maligned boys! – will not read them. Of course the phenomenon has spawned a large number of imitators – some of which are very much a result of other publishers trying to cash in on the success of Bloomsbury (HP) and David Fickling (Dark Materials). Many of these will fall by the wayside, but it will allow a few – such as the translated *Inkheart*, by German author Cornelia Funke – to be given a chance in both the UK and US which might not have been accorded it had it been published ten years ago.

What have come to be known as 'crossover books' are now a popular, money-making and, in the main, approved sector of children's publishing. They take an increasing share of the market, and the May/June 2004 issue of *The Horn Book* is devoted entirely to the theme. In it Perry Nodelman, a

Canadian academic and children's book critic, has several pertinent points to make, including that as adults we *have* to bring our own experiences to the reading of children's books. His article, 'Reading Across the Border' contends that the very 'same-old same-old' that an adult feels when reading a children's book actually constitutes a 'children's literature habitus'. As adults we cannot help but make references to other books we have read, other knowledge we have – we cannot un-know something – but children see these things as fresh. He goes on to say 'Realizing that children's literature is and always has been a literature of the same-old is important for it suggests an excellent use for adult expertise in it. That expertise is a matter of knowing what works – what has always worked in the past and what continues to work now. And, yes, it works in good part because it's safe ... children get so much of the same-old same-old that they too find it most recognizable and feel most comfortable with it. But it may also [work] because it's what is indeed most likely to give inexperienced readers pleasure.' Nodelman is right, but only considers part of the literature. Some of the success of the crossover phenomenon is the fact that adults are seeing freshness in children's literature. And to some extent that must be because some children's literature like *Tom's Midnight Garden*, like *Inkheart*, like *Elidor*, like – yes, even *Harry Potter* – have escaped from the expected 'same-old' paths, even when they draw on some of the archetypes. In addition, as Nodelman notes elsewhere in the piece, books that at first seem fresh gain extra layers of meaning when you know more, and therefore bring more both from other, 'same-old' stories, and from one's own experience, to them. Harry Potter is much more fun if you already know the Latin words used for the spells!

Crossover, too, needs to acknowledge the books that were intended – insofar as an author ever *intends* an audience – for adults, but which have been appropriated by children. This too is not new – as mentioned in Chapter 2 it has a long history – but because of the instantaneous world of the twenty-first century, when anything more than ten years old is 'history', it is seen as a new and odd phenomenon. Books like J. D. Salinger's *Catcher in the Rye* have long been seen as chronicling teenage self-discovery; Emily Brontë's *Wuthering Heights* has been wept over by countless fifteen-year-old girls. More recently Yann Martel's *Life of Pi* has introduced magic realism to books that are 'on the border', and Mark Haddon's *The Curious Incident of the Dog in the Night Time*, in trying to circumvent the difficulty of where a volume should be placed in the bookshops, was brought out in two editions – by different publishers – though the text was identical.

In 2001 Philip Pullman's *The Amber Spyglass* was the first children's book to be the outright winner of the overall Whitbread Award. Also in 2001 Terry Pratchett won the Carnegie Medal with a book aimed at children, but which shared the same setting, the 'Discworld' as a long series of adult books he has been writing for over twenty years. Mark Haddon's *The Curious Incident of the Dog in the Night Time*, having, as mentioned above, two different editions, was originally entered into both the adult novel and the children's section of the Whitbread for 2003 by its two publishers. As the criteria for this award allow for books to be entered only into one category, the children's section entry was withdrawn. It, too, won the overall prize, and we shall never know whether it would have done so as a children's section winner.

There have been many discussions, and many 'academic' books on the 'HP Phenomenon'. Some have put the whole thing down to the appeal of magic, but J. K. Rowling is not the first author to use such themes, nor yet the first to have parallel worlds and 'ordinary' children involved with the magic world. The fact that most of Diana Wynne Jones' output is currently being brought back into print shows that somehow the time must be right for this particular form of escapism. I do not use the term pejoratively, for in the current world there is much from which both adults and children need to escape. Whatever is going on in the 'real' world, we all need some way of switching off. It could be conjectured that in times of war, or 'troubles' in the world, books of fantasy and magic are more popular, and in times of peace, books of war and adventure come to the fore. The right book at the right time to the right child – which all publishers, librarians and teachers aim to provide – is dependent on the needs of the child at the time. And if a book answers that need for a large number of children and adults at once, it was probably published at the 'right' time, too.

'Fiction can reveal profound truths and facts can be spun into vivid gripping stories, in the best of children's literature', says Judy O'Malley – in her editorial for the May 1999 issue of *Book Links* ALA (US). Fiction and fact – is this where those boys have been all along? It seems to me that the myth of boys not reading was to a large extent a question of boys not reading the sort of book – usually fiction – that teachers and librarians thought they *ought* to read. They read what interested them; motor cycle manuals and magazines, football programmes – dense material but not borrowed from libraries! When a fiction book came along that grabbed their interest, they devoured it. Some will just have been sucked into the popularity stream and only read the *Harry Potter* series. Others have lapped up that, the Pullmans, *Inkheart* – and asked for more. There is more – much more to offer them, from the magic realism of *Life of Pi* to fantasy yet to come from Rowling, Diana Wynne Jones, Pullman, Pratchett and Funke.

A survey for Powergen in 2002 showed that 90% of parents read to their children compared with 25% of parents when a similar survey had been done two years previously. One might question whether more parents were actually doing it or more prepared to admit to doing it in a climate where reading books, and in particular children's books, has become more acceptable as an adult pastime. But even if the increase is not for that reason quite as startling, there is certainly more common ground between children's and adults' reading now than for much of the twentieth century. The 'kidult lit'; Tolkien, Pullman, Haddon and Potter can be shared and enjoyed by the child and the adult reading to her/him at the same time. The films of Tolkien's *Lord of the Rings* trilogy, as well as the Harry Potter films, the staging of part of Pullman's *Dark Materials* all combine to reinforce and confirm the trend.

Philip Pullman, in an article in *Youth Library Review* No. 28, Spring 2000, after listing some of the things about the book scene in general 'for the new millennium' that worried him, sounds a note of cautious optimism with his 'wish list' of things that he couldn't 'quite see yet with [his] eyes open, but ... applying the spyglass of hope to the minds eye' he hoped for more informed attention and consideration of children's' literature in the broadsheet papers and serious magazines ... and for the formation of 'a body that includes us all, and that acts as a powerful and influential voice for children's books in a way that none of us can do separately'. Pullman had other wishes, but with the imminent opening of the Newcastle Centre for the Children's Book, and the increased page area given regularly to children's book reviews, including regular profiles of children's writers, within UK newspapers such as *The Independent*, *The Guardian*, *The Times* and *The Daily Telegraph*, not to mention their Sunday stable mates, perhaps his vision is beginning to come true.

Children's books are certainly being taken more seriously now. Since 2000 there has been a children's laureateship. Quentin Blake was the first incumbent, followed by Anne Fine, Michael Morpurgo (whose idea it had been in the first place) and currently Jacqueline Wilson. Jacqueline Wilson has toppled Catherine Cookson from the head of the list of most-borrowed books from public libraries. Children are reading – perhaps they never stopped! But it is more overt now, and everyone is on the bandwagon. Reading groups and book clubs, on television, radio, via the net, or in people's houses, proliferate. Despite the blandishments of television, computers and X-boxes, the book is flourishing. Long live the magic of the book!

Chapter 15: Reactions

I What the Authors and Artists say

So what about the people who produce the raw material for the publishers to publish; the critics to discuss; the judges to acclaim? During the research for the first edition of this book I contacted a number of writers and illustrators, and sent a brief questionnaire to several award-winners. Many of them responded, either by letter or telephone, or both, and whilst some of them were willing to be quoted, giving me *carte blanche* in the use of what they had said, others were concerned that they might be misquoted, or wanted their replies disguised, or were reluctant even to be acknowledged. I have therefore synthesised and on occasion paraphrased the replies I received, and put with them some of the remarks made to me in the intervening years by authors I have met at Children's Literature New England Summer Institutes and other conferences. In my acknowledgements I include all the authors whose comments, whether in conversation or by direct response to my questionnaire, have contributed to this section, but I do not directly attribute anything to any one of them. This seems to be the fairest method, which protects the anonymity of those who were uneasy at the thought of being taken out of context without giving overemphasis to those who said 'quote away!'. I hope I have not distorted anything anyone said: I have made a conscious effort not to. The effect of putting like statements together may have had an effect of strengthening what were intended as asides, or supplementary remarks, though the very fact of having more than one remark in the same vein tends to add weight to the opinion behind it.

Of course I should have known better than to try to constrain authors into the set formula of a questionnaire. Many honestly tried to answer my questions, but found them irrelevant either to them or their situation. In essence I was trying to see whether the authors' perception of their work, status or career was in any way altered by winning or being shortlisted for an award, and whether, from an 'insider' point of view, any one award was more desirable than any other. The questions I asked, and the various responses to them, I shall therefore use as my framework for the remainder of the first section of this chapter.

What was your reaction to winning/being shortlisted?

There was quite a wide range of reactions across the authors and artists who responded. For several authors it depended on the award that had been won, some of which left their recipients relatively unmoved, while others brought them to tears. A number of authors and illustrators believed that awards were on the whole of more benefit to publishers than to authors. One author who naturally did not wish to be identified had been told by 'kindly friends' that a book was 'rumored to be a hot contender' for the Newbery Medal. When in the end it was not even shortlisted, that particular author's reaction was, predictably, 'nearer to disbelief than disappointment'. Typical comments at the positive end of the spectrum were:

> My reaction to winning/being shortlisted for awards, is, of course, delight ... I was tickled to bits by winning and being shortlisted ... I was delighted. I was thrilled to bits ... I felt overwhelmed by it all – still do! ... Pleasure – nothing more – it is always nice ... Like everyone else, I am always delighted to win a prize. It is like being given a bunch of flowers – who could object? ... Of course my reaction was great delight, particularly since [the book] was rejected by almost every publisher ... It made me feel honoured and validated in what I do and a bit famous.

Another positive comment was made by two authors, at opposite ends of their writing careers. The new author's first book had won a prize; the second-quoted has been writing for a considerable number of years:

> I'll tell you what – it gave me confidence! ... Writing is a lonely profession, awards are great confidence builders.

There were also some rather mixed reactions:

> The reaction depends on the prize – it is always nice ... I didn't think [my book] was likely to win; it seemed more probable that it would get an honourable mention ... My reaction to winning was a mixture of joy and fear ... My initial reaction was one of disbelief ... Receiving the Carnegie is somewhat like dying. Newspapers publish articles about you ... Of course I was thrilled to win, but I was also afraid that my life would change and I rather liked it as it was ... My reaction to all this was mainly surprise.

Also noted was the importance of being judged and recognised by one's peers:

> Any writer will be gratified by the recognition of the critical readership/media/peer group/ – and most of all, the readership he/she is writing for ... However despairing I might have felt about the work, it must have struck a chord with someone somewhere! ... How we all need to be recognised from time to time by our peers!

The make-up of the jury came in for comment, too:

> Naturally, awards are given according to the bias of the jury. You can tell by the make-up of the jury the kind of work which will probably be successful ... The chief consequence of winning the award was that I was co-opted on to the selection committee [for subsequent years]. This, though it was extremely interesting, both for the books I read and the people I met, has given me a slightly cynical opinion of the whole Awards business, or at least very mixed feelings ... Often the dominant voice is one of a small number of ubiquitous pundits who have constructed careers out of reviewing ... I've been on too many awards juries myself to think that the 'best' book means anything other than the book that happened to appeal most to that particular group of people at that time ... I perceive a huge element of luck in any book being chosen out of a tableful of similarly competent books, by a group of assorted judges on one particular day of the year ... Committees always choose the least controversial book. This of course reflects back on my own award ... The final choice for an award can be rather random, often a compromise.

However a major exception was noted by some authors:

> [The Carnegie/Greenaway] panel would seem to be an exception in that the shortlist stems from the national network of Libraries (God Bless them) ... The [Carnegie/Greenaway] selection process is lengthy, careful and sensitive, and it is democratic – layer on layer. So by the time the writers see their titles on the shortlist, they know the process has involved hundreds of professional children's librarians all over the country ... Of course the final small judging panel of Librarians [for the Carnegie and Greenaway Medals] is open to agendas and horse-trading but to get a book on to this shortlist is probably the soundest honour around ... Behind the final choice was what's so important to us all: honouring not just the book that will walk off the shelves, but honouring the book that will make *readers.*

Reactions to getting on to a shortlist were also interesting:

> Being shortlisted was brilliant! but I never expected to get any further ... I think now when I'm on a shortlist that I look at what else is in competition with my book and make some sort of judgement about whether I deserve to win – or not ... I had felt a great sense of achievement and wonder at being on the shortlist ... Particularly nice to be shortlisted because you know you are being taken seriously, after that it becomes too subjective ... Being shortlisted was really very exciting ... I asked who else was on the shortlist. When I heard the names, I said, 'Well, I won't win then.' And I forgot about it. When I got the phone call to say I'd won, I was very surprised indeed.

Equally fascinating are the remarks made by authors which show another side to the picture; the reaction of others, or the lack of emotion felt by authors themselves – some of whom were nonetheless extremely pleased or gratified at winning or being shortlisted:

> Everyone else seemed more impressed ... My reaction in each case was one of mild pleasure but not of great excitement ... It's my impression that the book awards, like the Oscars, are mainly for people in the business ... They are both high profile awards but it was really the reaction of my publishers that showed me how important this might be ... Any reply would potentially be churlish towards the good friends I have in my editor and publisher. The publisher needs the prize; not the writer, not the book ... My publishers seem disappointed by my failure to leap over rooftops in my joy ... I wouldn't be so downright ungracious as to spit in anyone's eye who was ready to put up a great deal of money and go to trouble to promote books, especially books for children ... Outside the book world, who cares much?

Finally, the 'old hands' who have won, or been shortlisted for, several awards:

> It is always nice to win awards. You know *somebody* has liked your book quite a lot – on the other hand, speaking as one who has been shortlisted for [several awards], I prefer not to know at that stage. If you don't win the award then you feel: *Someone has disliked my book rather a lot.* Not a nice feeling ... My reaction to being shortlisted for an award has, I suppose, changed over the years – I'm still just as delighted but I used to feel that maybe there had been some mistake and that I would be 'found out' ... I was absolutely overwhelmed by each one of my awards, and not just for my own sake but for my editor, too

> ... The pleasure did not diminish with each award which came after [the first] ... The second time [I won] was much easier. My life had changed. My family and I had all survived. We just had lots of fun the second time around ... If, as in my case, the first award comes after many years working in the business it makes less impact. (Possibly because you have become rather jaundiced by the award system and think 'Why, if they got it wrong so many times before, should I believe they have got it right this time?') ... Winning a prize is undeniably a huge encouragement. A reassuring pat on the back for people in a profession full of uncertainty and depression and even despair ... I was interested to discover that when the book won a third award several months later, I felt merely pleased. How quickly we become blasé!

Do you think that winning your first award made any difference to sales of the winning title?

Much hardback children's fiction is sold to the library market. Libraries are not as able to experiment with new authors as in the heady days of the 1970s, but are concerned to make up in quality what they may lack in quantity. Awards judged by librarians are no help in boosting an author's sales of course, as the librarians will need to have bought and evaluated titles in order even to nominate them, but reputation is naturally taken into consideration. Many libraries have a policy of close evaluation before anything is bought, so a less-good book by a well-known author will not necessarily get into the system, except perhaps as a single copy, even if s/he has won an award in the past.

The question of sales and print runs caused some difficulty. Some authors referred me to their publishers – they are not told too much (or, sometimes, do not concern themselves) about the commercial side of things. Some authors found their first award had made a considerable difference to sales:

> Sales. Dramatic difference ... Sales – so I'm told – of [the winning title] tripled and earned me dozens of pounds ... Like all prizes, sometimes they seem to make a huge difference, often none ... I have a bit of a control group since one of my books did *not* win any prizes. And while it is true that that book has had slightly lower sales [at home] it has had the highest sales of all my books in the US ... I suppose [the award] helped with library sales at a time when library buying power was stronger than it is now ... It *must* make a difference to sales – propels interest – especially if in the age-group that parents buy for.

But in some cases there was little or no effect noted:

> I have noticed no increase in sales as the result of winning an award ... I have a feeling that awards that result in a little seal or medal on the book itself may have some effect on the great public. But I haven't noticed any great leaps or anything on award-winning books ... Not sure – selling well anyway. As it puts the title in the limelight, it gives a boost but not a major one, and certainly doesn't do as well for a title as being a Waterstones choice for 'Book of the Month' does in terms of [UK] sales.

Foreign rights and translations were mentioned as a positive contribution towards sales which might not have been taken up if the book had not won an award:

> Yes, I do think the award made a difference to the sales of [the winning book] It has barely been out of print since. The most notable effect was that it was almost instantly translated into several languages ... It may affect my publisher's ability to secure foreign publishers ... The only book of mine to be translated into Welsh ... The Japanese publisher produced a ravishing edition, with Ardizzone-like illustrations ... Yes, and not only to UK and Commonwealth sales, but also to the sale of foreign rights.

Do you think that winning your first award made any difference to sales of future titles?

Some authors mentioned that being able to have 'award-winning author' on a book was a help for sales, but others mentioned the danger of this going under the author's name when the book itself had not won anything, and might indeed not be the author's best work. Such publicity can be counter-productive, and is often misleading, since it conveys the message to the parent or other adult who is choosing the book that a title is more prestigious than is actually the case. Foreign translations were mentioned again here. It also seems that award stickers on books do perhaps increase sales to adults. Whether they affect the readership of children in libraries and schools is more problematic. There is a tendency for teachers and librarians to use shortlisted titles as ready-made reading lists; perhaps no bad thing if it keeps them abreast of what is current in writing for children rather than recommending solely from their own childhood favourites:

> Sales of future titles. Yes ... My publisher's London book rep assures me that prizes and awards *do* sell books – the booksellers look out for them ... They do shift units – to adults; I don't know if prizes influence children's buying patterns ... Since children's older fiction hardly sells at all in any numbers, *only* the prize-winners break even or make a profit for the publisher ... My income has certainly increased since I won [the first award], but there are other factors involved ... It's always difficult for me to know what makes any of my books sell ... How much it helped *sales* I can't judge, but it made certain that from then on my books would at least be *reviewed* ... Of course a list of awards improves the appearance of your biographical details on the jacket ... This meant that later books of mine, not only those which were sort of sequels to [the winning title], were regularly translated into an ever-widening number of languages ... For instance about ten years later a French publisher did a series based on those books which had won [the award]. So yes, it has affected sales of future titles, at least in other countries ... If winning [the first award] did increase sales of later books I hate to think what they'd have been like without it!

Do you think that winning your first award made any difference to print runs of future titles?

Print runs, and in particular reprints, are not these days so much of a problem as they once were, and hence are not so important a feature in prospective success. A publisher who has underestimated demand can easily make up the quantity in a very short time. The days are long gone of hot type and having to gauge demand to a precise figure. It does seem that the hardback initial run – which is to some extent a measure of the confidence that publishers have in whether a book will be successful – is greater when an author is a proven success, as attested by an award, than otherwise.

> Print runs of future titles. Yes, certainly of novels, not such a great difference on other kinds of books ... A long track record influences print runs more than honours ... I think my publisher learned from the initial sales of [the winning title] that they could gamble on a larger hardcover print run with the next book ... Now there is talk of a large-format gift edition. So the difference was both immediate and long-lasting ... I think it may have helped with print runs, but only a publisher would really know (or an author with an agent, perhaps – anyway a different kind of author) ... A little! ... Some effect on print runs – my latest novel has been given a print run of 2,000 – which is more than my titles had when I was starting out ... Print runs are getting smaller and smaller anyway, though, since several printings no longer cost more than one big one ... Print runs are always mysterious. They are less important now that reprinting has become easier and cheaper ... I'm not well informed about sales figures or print runs, so I can't be of much help there ... I have no information about print runs, I'm afraid ... Print runs I know nothing about. Nobody tells you nothing in the publication business!

Do you think that winning your first award made any difference to your status or standing as an author?

Again, a variety of opinions was expressed. Some authors felt it had helped, or would have helped, to win an award at the beginning of their career:

> To win a major award when just starting out would probably give your career a kick-start and encourage publishers to be nice to you ... From being an unknown, I became recognised as an established writer, almost instantly ... In those days I think yes, it did make a great difference to my status as a writer.

The converse is therefore also true, both in terms of being a runner-up (i.e. *not* winning) and in winning a prize later in one's career:

> I don't think any of these awards individually made much difference – The cluster of awards around [the book] helped to put it and me on the map, though not nearly so much as its serialisation on TV. I do think, however that *not* winning the Carnegie for [that book] made an adverse difference to my standing; if it had won it might have put me on the all-important plateau of success and esteem ... If, as in my case, the first award comes after many years working in the business it makes less impact.

Perhaps in America, because there is more publicity, or simply due to the larger constituency of people within the children's book world, there was a greater feeling that winning had made a difference to one's status:

> Status: Yes. I will now go to my grave as Newbery medallist X. Worse things could happen to a person ... But there is no doubt winning of awards helps your standing as an author.

There was also comment about the limiting effect of being stuck in a 'ghetto' of children's writing, by writers on both sides of the Atlantic:

> As for my status as an author, I think it has been somewhat limiting, as some people only think of me as a children's writer .... After the award I found it impossible for publishers or booksellers to regard me as anything but child-minded (I use that expression deliberately: there was a lot of contempt in it), to the extent that a friend once remarked that I was 'trapped in the children's book ghetto'. I would not put it so strongly myself, but I knew what he meant.

As so often, the opposite point was also made:

> Until I won [the award] with a children's book, I had never even managed to get an adult book published at all. The week after I won it – lo and behold – somebody liked my unpublished, much-circulated, oft-rejected first adult novel. Strange, that, eh?

Do you think that winning your first award made any difference to the direction of your writing career – that is, either in confirming you in the type of books you write, or in giving you the 'permission' to experiment?
The thought that anything might change the type of books written caused quite a flurry of denial in some quarters. I had of course already heard several times that 'the next book that wants to be written is the next book that is written' or some comparable statement. Similarly that in the white heat of creation, or the slow drip-feed by which the story arrives, or the fuzzy reception on an old radio with a low battery – all of these being ways used by authors to describe how inspiration reaches them – the author has no choice as to what is coming through:

> The pattern was set before I won the medal ... I have a feeling that one writes the type of book that needs being written next, and sometimes a pot-boiler racy moneyspinner would be quite welcome, but it's not the hottest idea in your brain ... I don't think awards have affected the direction of my writing. I hope not ... Winning doesn't change what I write: I always write what I feel like writing – about characters and situations I enjoy. Any other attitude denies the author the chance to speak in his or her unique voice ... Winning awards does not affect the direction of my work neither does it give me 'permission' to experiment. Ideas direct my work, and trying to illustrate those ideas causes me to experiment. Hopefully when the work is seen it does not look like an experiment, but a solution ... Permission to experiment?: that's true and important ... Writing is not the hundred-meter dash ... You sit and scribble on the basis of the strongest signal you can get at the time – no matter who or what is asking you for something else (including yourself) ... Prizes, for me, have nothing to do with writing ... I couldn't write something I didn't enjoy ... All awards are delightful. However they are not why we write ... Awards have nothing to do with the creative process, as far as I'm concerned; I simply write to entertain & hope for the best!

Do you think some awards are more likely to affect future status, sales, etc. than others?
This question produced a fair measure of agreement:

> I don't see how this could help but be true...The Guardian was the most help career-wise ... The Newbery is the Big People's Clubhouse. Financially, as well as, usually, aesthetically ... In this country, the Newbery has a dramatic effect on sales. The National Book Award has, in literary circles, more status, but it doesn't do for sales nearly what the Newbery does ... An article I read in the *Washington Post* said that only three prizes in the US guarantee sales: The Nobel, the Newbery, and the Caldecott ... When I won the Newbery my publisher informed me that traditionally it had a more positive effect on US sales than a Pulitzer Prize, a National Book Award or even the Nobel Prize for Literature!

Publicity and prestige were acknowledged as part of the winning process:

> Probably the extent to which an award affects future status is due to the amount of publicity it gets. An award given by a national newspaper is bound to be noticed ... [The Carnegie] brings with it more prestige than any other prize in the [UK] field of writing. Invitations pour in. You could spend a year just answering letters, giving talks and writing articles ... In Canada I think the Governor-General's award is the most influential ... The Ruth Schwartz Award and the Mr Christie's Award are both high profile [in Canada].

There was a definite feeling that in terms of status, publishers were the people who took the most notice of prizes, and that there was hardly any effect at all on the general public:

> It's my opinion that the book awards, like the Oscars, are mainly for people in the business. Publishers and agents get tremendously excited by them: a writer's standing goes up in their eyes if they win an award ... Publishers like the phrase 'award-winning author' ... When a writer wins an award, suddenly other publishers hear about them and begin trying to poach them ... I think winning did make a difference to my status – certainly amongst librarians and publishers ... You can tell how important prizes are to status as an author just by seeing what publishers print on the flap! Accumulated honours are very important ... I'm not convinced it made much impact in the bookshops ... Awards for children's books, even when accompanied by a fair chunk of cash, just aren't news here [in Canada].

And of course there were the slightly cynical, though nonetheless valid, points about the reactions that winning prizes produces – in other people as well as in the winners themselves:

> I rather suspect that some awards are not as helpful as their reputation ... Two or three prizes and they start to look at you rather oddly, as if you have found out the secret of rigging the judges ... I would love once to win an award which had some real filthy lucre attached to it ... Awards that come with a cash component really can be very useful, not only in terms of ready funds but in the amount of publicity and status they garner, the world being what it is ... Cynically, I think awards impress people because they are *facts*; it is not a fact but a matter of difficult judgement whether *X* is a good book or Y is a good writer, but it is a matter of fact that they won the 'Z' award ... If readers don't like my books then all the [awards] in the galaxy won't do me much good; winning doesn't improve your writing! (Look around).

Were you better pleased by receiving/being shortlisted for any one award over another?

This was another area where it was generally agreed that awards do not all have the same effect:

> In the US the Newbery is so head-and-shoulders above any others the question is moot. (Newbery and Caldecott, I mean) ... I guess I'd have to say the Newbery, since I'd been looking at that gold seal since I was a child ... I think the Kate Greenaway Medal pleased me more than other British prizes, but it's always flattering to get one from abroad ... The Carnegie is the highest accolade of the Library Association, long standing, with previous winners now classics ... I was always delighted to win anything, but particularly the Carnegie, partly because I have a high regard for children's librarians and their opinions ... The Smarties Prize is pleasantly lucrative; the Guardian as it used to be run the most gratifying because it was bestowed by other writers ... The Smarties Prize meant so much because it was chosen from a short-list by the *children themselves* ... The Whitbread and Smarties – because of the extra promotion – but the Carnegie has at least as much prestige ... The Whitbread because it has connections with the adult book world which helps the prestige ... I was equally pleased by each award as they all have slightly different criteria and 'tone'.

Generally, as I suppose I might have suspected would be the case, the remarks made 'outside' of the responses to particular questions were more revealing and often more interesting than the 'straight' answers, where these were forthcoming.

> In general prizes are a necessary way of attracting attention to good books ... Fortunately, for publishers, writers and illustrators, awards not only recognise talent and hard work, but encourage readers and buyers to a long hard work ... Anything which raises the profile of children's books is great ... Prizes are influential, in the field of children's books perhaps more than any other, because those prize lists and little gold stickers are found so helpful by parents and teachers bemused by the annual array of new titles ... I don't really approve of them; choice is so subjective, and for every prize-winner there are probably several other books as good, if not better ... [Awards and shortlists] are great signposts for the development of children's literature ... I'm sure you'll be bearing in mind that children's books are not a self-contained phenomenon but are part of the whole complex process by which books are generated, distributed and mediated; and this process itself has changed as the world has changed ... In France there are more prizes of less significance, with juries all over the country. The Dutch system is good, too ... A prize always involves choosing between apples and oranges, because books are each one so individual in their impact on readers that the whole idea of 'best book' is rather silly ... I can't really see the point in comparing unlike with unlike (as in the Whitbread, for the overall prize). It is like Crufts Dog of Dogs ... The regrettable aspect of prizes is the artificial competition into which it forces writers whose instinct is usually to support and promote each other ... I'm keeping my fingers crossed that I may yet win another before I unplug my word-processor for the last time ... Luck, of course, has little to do with the recognition of excellence in children's book illustration. Juries of librarians and people deeply committed to children's books, look for the best in original art ... I write seriously for children and give them the best that I can produce, but I put my faith in adult criticism ...

> In the light of eternity the only praise worth having is that of people whose judgement one respects ... I'm not greatly convinced by children's juries ... We need more children-judged awards ... Children do not make the best judges ... Authors are usually delighted to win awards but there is an especially delicious feeling when their books have been honoured by a jury of readers. In a traditional children's author award competition, a task force chooses the books and a jury of the writers' peers or professionals in the field of children's literature reads each of the submissions and makes a choice by consensus ... Judges usually feel they are conferring honour on the winners, and yet long term the value of the prize depends on its being given to fine books – i.e. the winners bestow value on a prize. Stupid awards soon render a prize worthless ... What one really longs for, and what hardly exists in the children's field, is serious and searching criticism. I would rather have that than threadbare expressions of praise. Setting aside the matter of making a living, one wants circulation, in the hope of pleasing readers and perhaps opening windows for a few of them, and next to that one wants to be respected as a writer by those whose respect is worth having, especially I think one's peers. Awards are somewhat tangential to that.

Nearly every opinion expressed was balanced by a contradictory remark by somebody else. Whilst this is probably inevitable it was also interesting to find that authors, though strong, as one of them said, on mutual support, do not inhabit a cosy world where everyone thinks alike. This is a comforting thought – for one thing there is less chance of indoctrination! It also emphasises that children's authors can come from all walks of life, all parts of society, and are not an elite 'literary set'. In the same way that books show a wide range of subjects and views, so too do their authors.

II What the Critics & Librarians say

Having considered the authors' views, we now turn to other people who may have valid opinions to express about children's books. This is an area in which many people feel they are as able as anyone else to have a voice, since we were all children once. Sadly this does not make us all experts in the field. We all lose – during the turmoil of puberty, or the pressure of adult working life – the feeling of being a child. Some people do not want even to think about a time when they were smaller, less powerful, less capable, than the grown-up world they could not wait to join. In attempting to make value judgements on children's books, a balance must be struck between the one extreme of pretending to know or remember *exactly* what it was like to be a child, and the other of deliberate aloofness from 'childish things'.

Librarians and teachers, who work with children for all or part of their time, have some of the best opportunities to observe what children actually read. They can see not only what children like to read or what they select unprompted, but also what riches are gained when, whether by recommendation or serendipity, 'the right book' gets into the hands of 'the right [child] at the right time'.

I have written to and spoken with librarians and critics who have been working in the field of children's books over a number of years. Some of them are writers as well as librarians or critics, others have many years experience in evaluating children's books in libraries or colleges. All have something valid to contribute. Those who were also authors often added extra relevant comments with their replies to the list of questions which formed the framework of Section 1 of this chapter. In addition, I showed these questions to some of the librarians and critics with whom I am in touch, and asked for comments from their side of the equation. Here too I include paragraphs of unattributed quotations and once again the names of those consulted – though not necessarily quoted – appear within the list of acknowledgements.

Children's Librarians promote children's literature as a matter of their daily round. Awards are both aids to promotion – 'Have you tried this, it won the Such-and-Such Prize?' – and arise from the feedback to librarians of the children's own opinions of the books they have read. There are opportunities afforded for librarian's or children's participation in the process of at least one of the awards in most of the countries under discussion in this book. Here are some of the more general comments from librarians, teachers and critics:

> Every day children's librarians are involved in selecting picture books, sometimes marvelling at their originality, sometimes wondering how they ever got published! ... One of the major library promotions each year centres around the awarding of the Carnegie and Greenaway Medals. The unique feature of the Medals is the way in which librarians (throughout the UK) are involved ... Many YLG branches hold their own Carnegie/Greenaway selection meetings as do many library authorities ... Promoting the Carnegie and Kate Greenaway Medals provides a good opportunity to engage colleagues in the critical reviewing process ... We each have our own perspective on the world of children's books; depending upon where we work in it, those perspectives may be slightly different, but they are not mutually exclusive ... Being the oldest and most prestigious of the [UK] children's book prizes, the [Carnegie/Greenaway] award ceremony is seen by many as the highlight of the children's book year ... How can you tell which are the best books for children? Fortunately professional and commercial interest maintains a high profile for the pursuit of excellence in children's literature and book awards provide the perfect focus for this attention ... Lists of award winners do not solve all book selection problems but they do represent a range of judging panels, suggesting at least a consensus of bias and at best wisdom and expertise ... Award winners provide a useful starting point for our inexperienced students ... When you read a story you do something that no animal can, however well trained; only man can do it; you are stepping out of your own mind into someone else's ... Who decides which children's books win awards? In most cases not children ... Many adults have reviewed children's books, pontificated upon book selection, made awards and conducted surveys, but seldom have the children been asked for their opinion of modern publications ... The politically correct will cringe at the fact that Enid Blyton tops the list of parents' favourite authors and is clearly much enjoyed by children ... The children preferred voting to proposing titles; they may have been introduced to other authors as these books were recommended by their peers, who are the critics children really trust. From the nine hundred and twenty suggestions only one medallist was list-worthy [from a 1971 survey of 2,000 Yorkshire children] ... Once upon a time it was the children who had all the adventures – now it's just as likely to be the adults ... the winners of recent years do seem to reflect more accurately the actual reading tastes of children rather than the reading preferences of children's

librarians ... Stories are a vital part of the way we understand and order the world. They are the stuff of our daily emotional communication ... Controversy is an essential part of the formula [of book award announcements] ... Of course, some writers who sell millions are great storytellers, and not much else. They don't open our eyes to anything much – and don't really claim to ... The danger of 'literary' élitism is that we allow ourselves to be persuaded that a book with a story can't be quite the best. When we were children we knew better. We walked hand in hand with Roald Dahl, Frances Hodgson Burnett, Enid Blyton, Noel Streatfeild. We trusted them and those stories stayed with us for ever. We grew up and lost the key to that magic world. And so books changed their function. Instead of passports to another world they became status symbols of this one ... Literature can help children explore life's dark side. They can do this in the safe sensitive hands of such excellent authors.... The area of awards is almost a microcosm of the history of children's publishing since [the 1930s]

Some reviews and opinions written by children themselves about award-winning books show their enthusiasm and the value of reading to them:

All the characters are believable, I even thought I had met some of them. This story could have taken place in any school or college at any time ... This book is a real book! Its plot is both interesting and believable, as are its characters. It made me laugh, it made me cry, it made me sad and it made me angry. I loved it and I think all teenagers should read it! ... the best book we've ever read in our lives ... [the author] has successfully described the feelings, realisations, dreams and expectations of all involved.

Adult judges, too have strong opinions, both in terms of the way they see the judging process, and the quality of the books that they are given to consider:

Using a combination of discussion, debate and voting we settled on the final shortlist. Every title earned its place, some brilliant books fell at the final hurdle ... I kept putting off reading the books I did not fancy, but when I got to reading them I was often surprised how good many of them were. In some cases, however, the books were difficult to get into. You needed to persist. Adults will do this, but I wonder if children would bother ... judging a hundred books in two months [was] very demanding ... illustrations and words are beautifully blended to make a near perfect picture book ... Kate Greenaway was an illustrator for her times. The people on this year's shortlist reflect their own times, but there are links – the most fundamental of which is the enduring power of picture books to stimulate children ... Not all illustrators appeal to the two different categories of adult and child that share so many children's books ... it was not a question of how beautifully illustrated a book was but how it appealed to children and how well it illustrated the story ... winners, as well as the shortlisted books, reflect the robust good health of children's publishing in Britain, with a pleasing mix of established writers and illustrators, and some very welcome newcomers ... Children's publishing has changed and some of the public attitudes are outdated ... There are always going to be critics of awards made. I am sad that people like Geoffrey Trease and Helen Cresswell never won [the Carnegie Medal], but I don't think it matters too much *who* wins as long as their work meets the basic criteria ... Children are so often blasted with the zany, the zappy and the 30-second sound bite. But they also need and appreciate the quietness and depth of emotion which this medal winner

> has...the quality of the story was always going to be more important than the issues involved ... In a way it's a pity there has to be a winner because every contender is brilliant in its own right ... having to chose the final winner from the shortlist was the really difficult stage, but as long as the key question being asked is 'what will the children like?', they should be able to find the answer.

And who judges the judges? Some criticism not just of the winners, but of the way in which the decision has been made, is inevitable:

> Book prizes always involve disagreements, with no guarantee that history will necessarily agree with the final decision ... Judges need to be able to compare like with like ... I was impressed by the high level of discussion about books in the selection meetings – this is something you could achieve only with a committee made up of 'experts' ... the literary criteria are sensible enough, but not always consistently applied ... A male judge may not necessarily be better [than an all-female panel] at looking after boys' reading interests but he might more easily remember his own former tastes ... room must still be left for those flawed writers who still possess giant merits ... [The Carnegie Medal] now routinely passes over the most important and perhaps most difficult of all writing for children; the kind that creates readers in the first place ... recent years have seen the Carnegie and Kate Greenaway shortlists being read by groups of children who have provided an alternative winner or sometimes even the same winner ... The medal is not awarded as the result of a plebiscite; it is awarded by a small body of experts who bring to the assessment of the eligible books high standards of criticism.

And how are the awards and their winners perceived from the point of view both of critics in the press and of the publicity machines for the awards?

> Controversial winners work best – negative stories are more likely to be taken up ... I would not like to think that YLG selected *Dear Nobody* and *Stone Cold* because they thought these would attract comment from the press ... If I didn't read the children's books and bookselling press, I would never know that the Carnegie Medal existed! ... reaching the shortlist gets the book seen by the television adapters ... old book prizes such as [the Carnegie and Greenaway] produce a feeling of joining a 'club' – the impact of this on authors is amazing ... one tries to get mainstream coverage – not to wait for the next children's page – getting out of the ghetto is gradually becoming easier

There have been some strong comments expressed within this chapter, but the fact that somebody cares about the results of these award judgements, rather than being disinterested, is a positive sign. Children's books need a measure of emotional investment, not apathy. If awards are perceived as attempting to raise or maintain high standards in children's publishing, then someone should ensure that they continue to try and achieve this objective. However defensive the judging panel may be at the concerns expressed by the critics, there needs to be a system of checks and balances. Awards should not be made in a vacuum, nor should children's literature be seen as a cosy backwater where nothing important happens, and children are shielded from the real world – that would be like refusing to teach someone self-defence in case it made them afraid they might get attacked. Children's reading *is* important, for the sake of the child as well as for the sake of society. By reading, children discover who they are and where they come from; how they fit into the world in which they live.

Chapter 16: Some Conclusions

What have we learnt in our consideration of the world of children's book awards? The trite answer is that they are in the main good, or that they are fighting to maintain the standards of children's books against the tide of electronic media, comics and the modern equivalent of 'penny dreadfuls'. Naturally, it is not quite as straightforward as this – indeed few things are as simple as they at first appear. The child of the twenty-first century lives in a very different world from his counterpart in the 1920s, when the first Newbery Medal was awarded. Communications have changed beyond recognition; the whole world is immediately accessible to today's child at the touch of a television switch, or computer mouse, and inevitably this has produced concerns that 'children have stopped reading'. There have always been some children who prefer other activities to reading. Indeed there are many adults who do not read many books for pleasure; it is only one of the many recreations available to us all. Information, too, can be gained through many channels, reading is only one of these, and the time-lag which is inevitable in the physical production of books make them less useful than electronic media for up-to-date fact-finding. The cry has been less frequent since the success of Harry Potter *et al* but the question 'is the book about to disappear?' still gets asked.

In the UK, the number of titles published for children has increased fivefold since as recently as the 1970s. Up until that time it was mainly adults who were targeted by such marketing and publicity as the children's publishers gave out. First the (adult) buyers for the bookshops, then the (adult) teacher, librarian or parent was needed, to buy or borrow the book. Finally the child him/herself would get it, either to read or be read to. A high proportion of those titles produced in the 1970s were picture books, and children's paperbacks were mainly reprints of classics, both old and new, many published by Puffin. Backlists of both classic and newer authors were maintained in print. During the 1980s the marketing of products for children changed. Toys, clothes, food and finally books were packaged and advertised directly to the children themselves, rather than to any intermediary adult. Also in the 1980s books in series, usually paperback, were produced specifically for the pre-teen market and became immensely popular. The 'Point' series – Point Horror, Point Romance, Point Crime – have covers which deliberately mimic those of adult books of similar genres. The theory was that the child would choose, and would have the cash, or sufficient influence on how it was spent, to do this choosing and buying for themselves: children were being treated as adult consumers. This market-centred approach tends to bring the quantity of books sold into higher prominence than the quality of the titles published. Another major disadvantage is that for the very reason that children go for runs of books, whether of a single author's work or a genre series, their loyalty to a 'brand' name means that it will take quite a time for a new author's work to become familiar to children. It is still necessary for the teacher, librarian, or parent to have read a review, to read the new book, then to read it, or recommended it, to the child. Author visits to schools, too, are more common than they once were, giving children the chance to read over a wider range. But often by the time children are recommending that title to each other – which is when the book can be said to have taken off – it may be out of print in the modern accountant-led world of publishing, where back stocks of titles are almost unknown. As mentioned in Chapter 14, the popularity of a few, J. K. Rowling, Philip Pullman, may encourage some titles perceived as similar to be brought back into print, but many more will go, or stay, out of print very quickly.

Winning prizes seems suddenly to alert press reporters to the existence of authors that those of us in the children's literature world have known about for a long time. The 1995 Carnegie medallist, Philip Pullman, was treated by the news media at the time as a 'new' writer, yet his first book for children was written in the 1970s. Michael Morpurgo too was hailed as a new discovery in the late 1990s; he had been writing children's books for some twenty years prior to that, and has appeared many times on the Carnegie commended lists, though is not yet a medallist. However, he did win the 1996 Children's Book Award in the shorter novel category, an award determined by the vote of children themselves, as well as the Whitbread in 1995 and a 1996 Gold Smarties Prize, both of the latter being awards where children have some input into the judging. He was the third Children's Laureate.

A considerable number of the books in these award lists may no longer be available. Books by some of the major US authors are not available in the UK, except as second-hand copies and through libraries. Not one Cynthia Voigt title is in print in the UK; the only title of hers shown on the Amazon UK website is a US edition of a book published in 2002. Maurice Sendak is now more accessible for UK children than when the first edition of this book was published, at which time he was represented in the UK by just two titles: the ubiquitous *Where the Wild Things Are*, now forty years old, and *In the Night Kitchen*, from 1971. Nowadays the availability of many US titles through the UK portal of Amazon has made it easier to buy his and other non-English author's titles. Not every country has the resources to keep in print the whole list of winners for its national award. Not every award-winner, and certainly not all the Honor Books and Commended titles, will be available in every other English-speaking country, though as we have seen, an award helps towards selling editions in countries other than that of original publication.

Reviews of children's books are beginning to reappear in the national daily and Sunday newspapers. Whilst many so-called reviews in these outlets still do little more than a round-up of the autumn lists at a conveniently 'pre-Christmas' date, with the occasional children's 'special' at another time in the year when they are low on copy, often called 'Holiday reading', some 'quality' papers are beginning to treat children's literature with a measure of seriousness, as noted in Chapter 14. As part of the change wrought by the success of the Harry Potter series and other books in its wake, there are now many more column inches given to children's books. Even so, for real reviewing and in-depth criticism it is necessary to turn to specialist children's book magazines, in particular *The Horn Book*, *School Librarian*, and a few other library- (and school library-) oriented periodicals which contain reviews and evaluations. These are not normally seen by the general public, though in most cases there is nothing to prevent anyone reading them. Since the last edition of this book, both *Signal* and *Junior Bookshelf* have ceased publication, making access to printed reviews even more difficult. Sadly, too, budget cuts have meant that many library authorities in England, including some of the larger ones, do not have even a single subscription to the US magazine *The Horn Book* within their system, so that their children's librarians, who would benefit, do not get an opportunity to see it. In these cases there is certainly no possibility that anyone else will get the chance to keep up with the field. But new ways of finding out about children's books are now available. In the same way that it is now possible to get books from overseas through internet booksellers, there are internet reviewing and children's literature news sites. In the UK Achuka is one of the most active, and more serious discussions of children's literature can be found in the on-line pages of net magazines such as Looking Glass, or academic mail-lists such as Jisc-mail.

With over ten thousand children's titles published last year in the UK alone, slightly fewer in the US, some choices have to be made. It would be impossible even for a single adult to read every one. Any attempt by a child to do so would require the omission of older or 'classic' titles from that child's reading experience. Because we are no longer in an era when one person can know all there is to know, if indeed we ever were – though some authorities would suggest that it was theoretically possible until the Renaissance – we naturally seek some means of selecting from this vast range. The existence of awards, choices which have already been made by knowledgeable and concerned adults or well-read children, gives those of us who are not directly involved in children's literature the chance to make our selections in an informed manner, since, at least while our children are young, we need to choose on their behalf. As they grow older, awards lists may help them to make informed choices and develop their own tastes, and we shall be able to stand back in the hope that by then they will have learned discernment.

I hope that the journey through the world of children's books will prove as enjoyable and rewarding for you, and for the children in your life, as it has been for me. I trust that this book has been useful as a navigational aid, and that any by-ways it has led you to follow have been at least as interesting as the main road. Good reading!

Award Index

Including originators/sponsors of Awards, organisations and professional bodies, and periodicals.

Title Index

Including series titles. Leading definite and indefinite articles in all languages have been omitted for sequencing purposes. Titles mentioned in Award lists are followed by three-letter code[s] in brackets () to indicate those award[s] – see Award Index for codes.

Author Index

Including illustrators, translators, publishers (if they have actually won an award or are mentioned in the text) publisher's editors and people quoted. [If a 'double' surname is hyphenated it will be listed under the first element of the name, if not, it will be under the last element; equally de, de la; van and vande are ignored for sequencing purposes if they are separate parts of the surname. If no gap, then sorted as single word. All Mac and Mc names are shown together in one sequence at the start of the M section.]